CONTEMP CASE STUDIES IN HEALTH COMMUNICATION

Theoretical & Applied Approaches

Maria Brann

West Virginia University

EDITOR

Kendall Hunt
publishing company

Book Team

Chairman and Chief Executive Officer   Mark C. Falb
President and Chief Operating Officer   Chad M. Chandlee
Vice President, Higher Education   David L. Tart
Director of Publishing Partnerships   Paul B. Carty
Editorial Manager   Georgia Botsford
Senior Editor   Angela Willenbring
Vice President, Operations   Timothy J. Beitzel
Assistant Vice President, Production Services   Christine E. O'Brien
Senior Production Editor   Charmayne McMurray
Senior Permissions Editor   Colleen Zelinsky
Senior Cover Designer   Suzanne Millius

Cover image © Shutterstock, Inc.

Kendall Hunt
publishing company

www.kendallhunt.com
Send all inquiries to:
4050 Westmark Drive
Dubuque, IA 52004-1840

Printed in the United States of America
10 9 8 7 6 5 4 3 2 1

For my always supportive husband, Matt, whose constant encouragement and practical advice never cease. And for ALL of my children, whom I love dearly and think of daily.

—M.B.

CONTENTS

FOREWORD

I am very happy to see the timely publication of *Contemporary Case Studies in Health Communication: Theoretical & Applied Approaches*. This exciting new volume clearly illustrates the breadth, depth, and complexity of health communication in actual practice! Health communication is an inherently applied area of social science inquiry that examines the central role of human and mediated communication in the delivery of care and the promotion of health. It is also a very complex area of study that involves a broad range of participants (doctors, nurses, therapists, pharmacists, patients, family caregivers, patient advocates, health care administrators, technologists, government regulators, scientists, and many more), working conjointly in many different contexts (for example, within hospitals, clinics, doctors' offices, workplaces, homes, and schools), using an amazingly diverse number of communication channels and media (such as face-to-face interaction, telephone conversations, computer-mediated searching and interaction, video games, television shows, radio programs, books, magazines, newspapers, pamphlets, posters, and even more). Even more importantly, it is often very challenging for patients and providers to use communication effectively to achieve their desired health goals. This is due to the complexities of the many difficult and uncertain health challenges that consumers confront, the growing bureaucracy and technological sophistication of the modern health care system, the growth of competing (and sometimes confusing) sources and channels for health information, and the demand to elicit close cooperation and coordination between many different participants in the health system. Health care/ promotion is most demanding. Accurate and timely information is needed to guide coordinated actions and important decisions.

This book captures the demanding applications of human and mediated communication in responding effectively to these issues in the delivery of care and promotion of health by contextualizing health communication practices. The chapters illustrate a broad sampling of many intricate and demanding communication situations that confront diverse participants in the modern health care system. The cases vividly show the communication challenges that health care/promotion participants encounter and suggest strategies they can use to overcome these challenges. The cases are an ideal vehicle for illustrating sophisticated applications of key communication principles, theories, and models for solving health problems. They also provide models for students of health communication to follow in addressing real health communication issues they are likely to confront in their lives, their research, and their professions.

I like the way the chapters embed and enliven health communication practices and challenge readers to develop creative solutions to vexing health communication problems. This is a book that will be fun to read and interesting to discuss within classes and within professional in-service training programs for health care providers and consumers. Solutions to the many problems outlined in the cases are only limited by the creativity demonstrated by case analysts. There are many different ways to use communication creatively to enhance health outcomes. It is my hope that this book will encourage careful reflection, analysis, and the development of innovative practices and policies for strategic health communication to promote health and wellness.

Gary L. Kreps, Ph.D.
University Distinguished Professor and Chair
Department of Communication
Director of the Center for Health and Risk Communication
George Mason University

ACKNOWLEDGMENTS

First, I would like to thank all of the scholars who submitted their work to this book. I appreciate the response from individuals recognizing the importance of case study pedagogy in health communication. I am particularly thankful for the authors' willingness to undertake revisions to produce theoretically grounded and pedagogically useful cases.

I would like to acknowledge the insightful work of the 53 editorial board members who reviewed précis and chapters for the edited book (see the list that follows for a complete directory of the reviewers). I appreciate their commitment to this project and mentoring approach used to advance the chapters of the authors.

I would also like to thank the editorial assistants: Piotr Bobkowski (University of North Carolina at Chapel Hill), Amanda Martinez (Texas A&M University), and Kyle Rudick (Southern Illinois University-Carbondale). They have worked tirelessly throughout this process, assisting from the project's inception until its final fruition. They have fully participated in the editorial process by assisting with the following responsibilities: communicating with prospective authors and reviewers during all review phases, managing précis and chapter submissions and reviews, copyediting final chapter submissions, contributing to the writing and development of the introductory chapter, and senior editorial assistant (Piotr Bobkowski) also assisted with making decisions with conflict of interest submissions.

I would also like to thank Angela Willenbring (Senior Editor), Paul Carty (Director of Publishing Partnerships), Charmayne McMurray (Senior Production Editor), Suzanne Millius (Graphic Design Coordinator), and Colleen Zelinsky (Senior Permissions Editor) at Kendall Hunt for their tremendous support, assistance, and mentoring spirit.

I would also like to thank my husband, Matt Brann, for his assistance with this project. From listening to ideas to providing editorial direction, he has always championed my work, particularly this important project.

Finally, I would like to thank special colleagues who supported me during this process. From believing in me and my abilities to being a sounding board for ideas and concerns, each of you knows who you are and how you helped me. Thank you.

—M.B.

EDITORIAL BOARD

ABOUT THE EDITOR

Maria Brann (Ph.D., University of Kentucky, 2003) is an Associate Professor in the Department of Communication Studies, Affiliate Faculty with the Injury Control Research Center, and Associate Member of the Mary Babb Randolph Cancer Center at West Virginia University. Dr. Brann's research focuses on ethical communication in health care contexts and the promotion of healthy and safe behaviors. She has published articles and book chapters regarding health care providers' confidentiality disclosures; promotion of physical activity, vehicle safety, and tobacco communication; tensions and support for stroke survivor spouses and AIDS volunteers; and maintenance of healthy sibling relationships. Her work has been published in refereed journals including *Health Communication, Communication Studies, Journal of Physical Activity and Health, Health Care Analysis, AIDS Care, Qualitative Research Reports in Communication*, and *Communication Research Reports*, and in the scholarly book *Gender in Applied Communication Contexts*.

About the Editorial Assistants

Piotr (Peter) Bobkowski (Ph.D., University of North Carolina at Chapel Hill, 2010) is a postdoctoral fellow in the School of Journalism and Mass Communication at the University of North Carolina at Chapel Hill, and a research assistant at the Carolina Population Center. His research focuses on adolescents' and emerging adults' media uses and effects. His dissertation work investigated emerging adults' self-disclosures in MySpace, particularly with regard to their religious identities, sexual risk behavior, and substance use. His work has been published in the *Journal for Research on Adolescence, Journal for the Scientific Study of Religion, Journal of Media and Religion*, and *Religion & Education*. He is a former high school teacher and student media adviser.

Amanda R. Martinez (M.A., University of Houston, 2007) is a doctoral student and diversity fellow in the Department of Communication at Texas A&M University. She earned her B.A. in Multinational Organization Studies with a minor in Communication, and a concentration in Spanish from St. Mary's University, and an M.A. from the University of Houston in Mass Communication with a Women's Studies Graduate Certificate. Her dissertation work focuses on Latino in-group racial/ethnic humor in the mass media. Other research areas center on health communication and mass media, with particular emphasis on stereotypes, body image, race/ethnicity, culture, and identity. She has taught a variety of courses, including Intercultural and Gender Communication, at the University of Houston (Main Campus and Downtown), Texas A&M University, and Blinn College. Forthcoming publications appear in *The Handbook of Health Communication* (2nd ed.), *Food, Culture and Society*, and *Food as Communication/Communication as Food*.

C. Kyle Rudick (M.A. West Virginia University, 2010) is a doctoral student and research fellow in the Department of Speech Communication at Southern Illinois University Carbondale. He earned his B.A.Ed in Communication Education at Northeastern State University in Oklahoma and his M.A. in Communication Studies from the Department of Communication Studies at West Virginia University. His thesis work examined students' use of politeness strategies based on their perceptions of classroom justice. His interests include the intersection of communication and education, especially in regard to critical communication pedagogy.

About the Contributing Authors

Ashley E. Anker (Ph.D., University at Buffalo, 2009) is a research instructor and postdoctoral research associate in Department of Communication at University at Buffalo. Her research is focused on evaluation and design of social influence messages to promote health behavior in adults. She has published in several health communication journals including *Health Communication* and *Journal of Health Communication* and has worked on federally funded grant projects in organ and tissue donation for the past three years.

Meagan J. Araujo (M.A., DePaul University, 2008) is a doctoral student in the Department of Communication at the University of South Florida. Ms. Araujo's research looks at the intersection of health and organizational communication through an intercultural lens. She speaks Spanish and Portuguese and volunteers as a medical interpreter at a local clinic.

Lucinda Austin (M.A., University of Maryland, 2008) is a Ph.D. student and instructor of public relations in the Department of Communication at the University of Maryland, College Park, where she is affiliated with the University's Center for Risk Communication Research. Her research focuses on the intersections of public relations with health and risk communication for campaigns and organization-public relationship building. Ms. Austin concurrently works as a communication analyst in the Strategic Communications and Marketing Division at ICF Macro in Rockville, Maryland, a firm offering communication research and support to government and non-profit organizations. In her role at ICF Macro, she has provided research, writing, analysis, and program development services to several Federal Government agencies including the Centers for Disease Control and Prevention (CDC), the Department of Health and Human Services, the Federal Emergency Management Agency, the U.S. Department of Agriculture, the Department of Education, and the American Red Cross. Ms. Austin's work has been featured in publications such as *Social Marketing Quarterly*, *Public Relations Review*, and the *Handbook of Health Communication*, and has been presented at numerous national and international communication and public relations conferences.

Judy Berkowitz (Ph.D., Michigan State University, 1998) With 20 years experience in research and evaluation, Dr. Berkowitz is currently a senior research scientist at Battelle Memorial Institute. She is conducts program evaluation projects that focus on dissemination research and communication outcomes. Her areas of expertise include program evaluation methodology and research design, strategic planning, and health communication and social marketing. She has developed and evaluated health information materials and websites on topics including sexually transmitted disease, physical activity, reproductive health, and laboratory medicine. In addition, she has designed and implemented usability tests to improve health information products. Dr. Berkowitz designed, implemented, analyzed, and reported on campaign components as part of formative, process, and outcome evaluations using qualitative and quantitative research techniques.

Cynthia M. Bulik (Ph.D., University of California at Berkeley, 1988) is the William R. and Jeanne H. Jordan Distinguished Professor of Eating Disorders in the Department of Psychiatry in the School of Medicine at the University of North Carolina at Chapel Hill where she is also Professor of Nutrition in the Gillings School of Global Public Health and the Director of the UNC Eating Disorders Program. Dr. Bulik's research focuses on treatment, laboratory, animal, epidemiological, twin, and molecular genetic studies of eating disorders and body weight regulation. She explores innovative means of integrating technology into treatment for eating disorders and obesity in order to broaden the public health reach of evidence-based interventions. Her work has been published in refereed journals including *Psychological Medicine, International Journal of Eating Disorders, American Journal of Psychiatry, and American Journal of Human Genetics*. She is also author of the books *Eating Disorders: Detection and Treatment* (Dunmore), *Runaway Eating: The 8 Point Plan to Conquer Adult Food and Weight Obsessions* (Rodale), *Crave: Why You Binge Eat and How To Stop* (Walker, 2009), and *Abnormal Psychology* (Beidel, Bulik & Stanley (Pearson)).

Jennifer J. Bute (Ph.D., University of Illinois at Urbana-Champaign, 2007) is an Assistant Professor in the School of Communication Studies at Ohio University. Dr. Bute studies communication about health in interpersonal relationships and public discourse about women's health. She is particularly interested in issues related to privacy, social support, and gender. She teaches graduate and undergraduate courses in health, interpersonal, and gender communication. Her work has appeared in numerous edited books and journals including *Health Communication, Human Communication Research, Communication Studies, Review of Communication, Qualitative Health Research*, and *Social Science and Medicine*.

Kerry Byrnes (Ph.D., West Virginia University, 2010) is a professor in the Communication Studies Department at Collin County Community College, Spring Creek Campus. Dr. Byrnes' research focuses on the effects of addiction on family relationships and teacher-student interactions. She has coauthored articles regarding teaching communication concepts to undergraduate students, using groups to improve student learning, and assessing student participation. Her co-authored work has been published in refereed journals including *Communication Research Reports* and *Communication Teacher*.

Suwichit (Sean) Chaidaroon (Ph.D., University of Memphis, 2005) is an Assistant Professor in the Division of Public and Promotional Communication, Wee Kim Wee School of Communication and Information, Nanyang Technological University, Singapore. Dr. Chaidaroon's research focuses on corporate and organizational communication from an intercultural perspective. Recently, he studies cancer survivors and their lives in workplaces with the ultimate aim to promote justice and fairness in organizations through corporate communication. He has published a scholarly book on business communication with Thai people as well as refereed articles in *Media Asia: An Asian Communication Quarterly, The Humanistic Psychologist, Global Media Journal*, and *Intercultural Communication Studies*.

Heather R. Clark (M.S.P.H., Texas A & M Health Science Center School of Rural Public Health, 2005) is Evaluation Manager of the Center for Community Health Development (Texas A&M School of Rural Public Health) where after 10 years working in the private sector with roles as a health educator, clinic assistant, and prevention services coordinator, she now applies her practical knowledge of working in the public sector to research efforts at the Center. Joining the Center in 2005, Ms. Clark currently manages evaluation projects which include Center-level evaluation and data collection, as well as external evaluation of local community health development efforts and community partnership building. Her scope of work includes program evaluation, project management, grant writing, and training. She has served as co-investigator for a variety of supplemental grants and contracts in the Center. Ms. Clark is currently pursuing her Doctorate in Public Health.

George N. Dionisopoulos (Ph.D., Purdue University, 1984) is a Professor in the School of Communication at San Diego State University. Dr. Dionisopoulos' research interests include public argument, political communication, and media rhetoric. His work has been published in refereed journals including *Quarterly Journal of Speech*, *Communication Monographs*, *Western Journal of Communication*, *Popular Communication*, *Communication Quarterly*, *Communication Studies*, and *Journal of Film and Television*, and in scholarly books *The 2008 Presidential Campaign: A Communication Perspective* and *New Approaches to Rhetoric*.

Thomas Hugh Feeley (PhD, University at Buffalo, 1996) is an Associate Professor and Chair in the Department of Communication at University at Buffalo. Dr. Feeley is an expert in health persuasion and has been principal investigator on eight previous federally funded projects in the area of health promotion and public education. He has published more than 50 refereed journal articles in communication and social psychology.

Carol Freeman (B.A., Georgetown University, 1981) is a vice president in ICF International's Strategic Communications and Marketing Division. Ms. Freeman has led communication and social marketing projects addressing health issues and communication challenges with many government agencies and nonprofit organizations, including the Federal Emergency Management Agency, CDC's National Center for Injury Prevention and Control, the National Center for Environmental Health, the U.S. Department of Agriculture, the Small Business Administration, and the American Red Cross. She provides clients with a broad array of audience research, strategic planning, communication and partnership campaign development, and program development services. She helps government and private sector clients develop marketing, social marketing, framing, and risk communication strategies that support specific organizational objectives. She is currently project director for NCIPC, where she is working to develop a coordinated communication platform to reframe how the public perceives injury prevention.

Brandi N. Frisby (Ph.D., West Virginia University, 2010) is an Assistant Professor in the Department of Communication at the University of Kentucky. Dr. Frisby's research focuses on instructor-student relationships in the college classroom and on both prosocial and antisocial communicative processes in romantic relationships and marriages. She has published articles regarding student participation, rapport in the classroom, mediated romantic relationship conflict, flirting within the marriage, forgiveness of transgressions, and post-divorce relationship maintenance. Her work has been published in refereed journals including *Communication Studies, Communication Education, Qualitative Research Reports in Communication*, and *Communication Research Reports*, with upcoming work in *Journal of Social and Personal Relationships, Communication Quarterly*, and *Sex Roles*.

Traci K. Gillig (B.A., Purdue University, 2009) is a graduate student in the Department of Communication at Purdue University. Her studies focus on health communication and marketing, and she has volunteered with the Motorcycle Safety at Purdue campaign since her time as an undergraduate student at Purdue University. Ms. Gillig has served as an intern for the National Center for Health Marketing, a branch of the U.S. Centers for Disease Control and Prevention. Additionally, she has worked as a Brand Corporate Affairs intern for AstraZeneca Pharmaceuticals.

Tamar Ginossar (Ph.D., University of New Mexico, 2002) is a Research Assistant Professor at the University of New Mexico School of Medicine, and an Adjunct Research Assistant Professor at the Department of Communication and Journalism. Dr. Ginossar's research examines health information behavior and health disparities, including the use of new communication technologies for information seeking and exchange as well as for advocacy and social change. Using mixed methods and community-based participatory research approaches, she has worked and lived in diverse settings nationally and internationally. Her work has been published in refereed journals including *Health Communication, Journal of Applied Communication, Communication Education, Journal of Computer Mediated Communication, Health Care for Women International, Journal of Intergroup Relation*, and in different scholarly books.

Mindi Ann Golden (Ph.D., University of Utah, 2005) is an Assistant Professor in the Communication Studies Department at San Francisco State University. Dr. Golden's research focuses on dementia caregiving and the end of life. She has published articles and book chapters regarding communication in a caregiver support group, placement in the context of dementia caregiving, dementia in bi-ethnic families, grandchildren as caregivers, and dialectical tensions experienced by a family member when a loved one is dying in a hospital setting. Her work has been published in refereed journals including *Iowa Journal of Communication, Journal of Gerontological Social Work, International Journal of Self Help & Self Care, Communication Research Reports*, and in scholarly books: *Applied Health Communication and Handbook of Communication and People with Disabilities: Research and Application.*

Emily Joy Haas (M.A., University of Dayton, 2008) is a doctoral student in Health Communication at Purdue University. Ms. Haas' research focuses on health campaign design, implementation, and evaluation utilizing the social marketing process. Specifically, her research has addressed health campaigns pertaining to motorcycle safety and sexual violence prevention targeting college students. In addition, a focus of Ms. Haas' campaign research is re-conceptualizing the use of harm reduction theory for positive use in the development and evaluation of health campaigns.

Wendy Holmes (M.S., Tufts University, 1990) serves as the Associate Director of Communications Science for CDC's National Center for Injury Prevention and Control. Through her more than 19 years of marketing and management experience at CDC, Ms. Holmes has designed and led major initiatives addressing a wide range of issues including adolescent health, diabetes, flu vaccination, nutrition, and physical activity. In various leadership positions, she has advised staff on media strategies, partnership outreach, audience selection and segmentation, audience research, distribution channels, message testing, and materials development. Prior to joining NCIPC, Ms. Holmes was Deputy Branch Chief and Deputy Director for CDC's Emergency Communication System where she assisted in strategic planning for CDC's emergency communication response and served as Joint Information Center lead during Director's Emergency Operations Center activations and exercises. Ms. Holmes also worked in the Division of Partnerships and Strategic Alliances of CDC's National Center for Health Marketing where she led staff in developing and providing resources to help partners prepare for pandemic influenza.

Julie Parrish St. John (M.P.H. in Epidemiology) is working on a doctorate of public health in health promotion and health behavior. Ms. St. John is currently the South Texas Regional Director for the Center for Community Health Development (Texas A&M School of Rural Public Health). Julie's scope of work includes: grant-writing, health status assessments, strategic and operational planning, continuums of care, program evaluation, facilitating community partnerships, managing and participating in research projects, promotora (community health worker) certified trainings and program development.

Michelle Dixon Johns (M.A., M.P.H., New Mexico State University, 1999) is in her twelfth year as a Public Health Educator in the Health Communications Branch of the Center for Disease Control and Prevention's (CDC) Office on Smoking and Health. She is the coordinator for CDC's Media Campaign Resource Center—a collection of more than 1,800 tobacco counter-advertisements. She has published many articles and presented on various aspects of health communication campaigns, especially in multicultural contexts, such as work with tobacco-related health disparities in American Indian/Alaskan Native and Hispanic/Latino populations. Some of her other foci are communication planning, technical assistance, formative research, product development, and evaluation.

Elizabeth Karras (Ph.D., The State University of New York at Buffalo, 2010) is a health communication post-doctoral fellow in the Department of Communication at the University of Illinois at Urbana-Champaign. Her research interests focus on Deaf people's health information management and subsequent decision-making, problematic provider-patient interactions, and patient self-advocacy. Her research is designed to inform the clinical care and health education of the Deaf.

Carin L. Kosmoski (Ph.D., Purdue University, 2009) is a Research Scientist at the National Institute for Occupational Safety and Health (NIOSH) Office of Mine Safety and Health Research in Pittsburgh, PA. Dr. Kosmoski's research focuses on developing interventions to improve the health and safety of miners in the United States. She has published articles regarding online health information seeking, media presentation of tanning and skin cancer, and a case study of the development of the Motorcycle Safety at Purdue campaign. Her work has been published in refereed journals including *Journal of Computer Mediated Communication, Health Communication*, and *Cases in Public Health Communication and Marketing*.

Betty A. Levine (M.S., University of Massachusetts at Amherst, 1983) is the Division Head of the eHealth and Telemedicine group at the Imaging and Information Systems Center, Georgetown University Medical Center, and a Senior Scientist at the U.S. Army Telemedicine and Advanced Technology Research Center (TATRC). She completed her M.S. degree in Industrial engineering and Operations Research and her B.S. degree (1981) in Applied Math and Statistics from the State University of New York (SUNY) at Stony Brook. Ms Levine has published work related to the use of technology in clinical care in several journals including *Health Communication, Journal of Diabetes Science and Technology, Journal of Communication, Diabetes Care, Diabetes Technology and Therapeutics, Healthcare Management Review, Telemedicine Journal, IEEE Transactions on Information Technology and Biomedicine, Diagnostic Imaging* among others.

Corey Jay Liberman (Ph.D., Rutgers University, 2008) is an Assistant Professor of Communication Arts at Marymount Manhattan College. His research interests include the effects of organizational identification on work processes and job satisfaction, organizational and societal communication networks, social influence in interpersonal relationships and during the small group process, and persuasion in the context of health communication. Some of his most recent work differentiates cognitive social networks from behavioral social networks, examining both the theoretical and practical implications of both. He routinely teaches courses in interpersonal communication, small group communication, and organizational communication, focusing primarily on the role of social influence and communication networks in these three areas.

Angela Ka Ying Mak (Ph.D., University of Oregon, 2004) is an Assistant Professor in the Division of Public and Promotional Communication, Wee Kim Wee School of Communication and Information, Nanyang Technological University, Singapore. Dr. Mak's research focuses on organizational-stakeholder relationships, identification, and reputation, as well as the economic impact of cancer from a communication perspective. Currently, she's been supervising the first-ever cancer cookbook with an Asian approach and a collective effort from the cancer community for National Cancer Center Singapore. She has won several top paper awards at major international communication conferences and published refereed articles in *Public Relations Review, Journal of Public Relations Research, Journal of Brand Management, Journal of Nonprofit and Public Sector Management*, and *Visual Communication Quarterly*.

Jennifer A. Malkowski (M.A., San Diego State University, 2008) is pursuing doctoral work in communication studies at the University of Colorado at Boulder. Her research focuses on the rhetoric of health and medicine and pays particular attention to how issues of identity, gender, and inequality influence the healthcare process. The work presented in this book stems from her master's thesis research completed while she was a student in the graduate program in the School of Communication at San Diego State University. Valerie R. Renegar and George N. Dionisopoulos served as members of her thesis committee.

Marifran Mattson (Ph.D., Arizona State University, 1995) is an Associate Professor in the Department of Communication at Purdue University. Dr. Mattson's research and teaching program explores the intersection of health, interpersonal, organizational, and public communication. She is particularly interested in questions regarding the relationship between communication processes and problems related to human health and safety. She seeks to identify critical interactive features to improve communication and reduce harm in a diversity of contexts including a public health campaign for motorcycle safety (www.ItInvolvesYou.com), HIV testing, and patient/health care provider confidentiality. Her advocacy experience includes working with the Indiana Amputee Insurance Protection Coalition to pass legislation in Indiana that provides parity across health insurance plans for coverage of prosthetic devices. She also is a member of the Amputee Coalition of America's Government Relations Advisory Committee. Dr. Mattson's research has been published in journals including *Communication Monographs, Journal of Health Communication, Health Communication, Health Promotion Practice, Health Marketing Quarterly*, and *Journal of Applied Communication Research*.

Jane Mitchko (M.Ed., University of Georgia, 2000) serves as the Deputy Associate Director of the Health Communication Science Office at CDC's National Center for Injury Prevention and Control. She has led several important health communication initiatives, including development, implementation, and evaluation of an Injury Framing approach to reframe injury and violence as a prevalent and preventable public health problem. Prior to her current role, Ms. Mitchko served as the Lead Health Communications Specialist in the Division of Injury Response at the Injury Center for more than seven years where she developed and evaluated several national education and communication initiatives on traumatic brain injury prevention and management. She also led several key acute care and terrorism-related communication projects. Prior to joining the CDC, she worked as an Exercise Physiologist at a community hospital in East Atlanta where she led a cardiac and pulmonary rehabilitation program as well as an employee wellness program.

Samantha A. Nazione (M.A., Michigan State University, 2009) is a doctoral student in the Communication Department at Michigan State University where she has worked on research with the Breast Cancer and Environment Research Centers. Her research focuses on breast cancer messages, health website accessibility, and health inequalities. Her work has been published in refereed journals including *Journal of Health Communication, Health Communication*, and *Journal of Computer Mediated Communication*.

Lindsay B. Neuberger (M.A., Wake Forest University, 2007) is a doctoral candidate in the Department of Communication at Michigan State University. Her research focuses on persuasion in the contexts of health and political campaigns and has covered diverse topics ranging from breast cancer risk reduction and blood donation patterns to political issue framing and environmental policy research. She has worked on research with the Breast Cancer and Environment Research Centers and her current research seeks to reveal patterns in uncertainty and information seeking regarding health care policy reform. Her research has been published in refereed journals including *Journal of Health Communication* and *Communication Research Reports*.

Jennifer E. Ohs (Ph.D., The Pennsylvania State University, 2008) is an Assistant Professor in the Department of Communication at Saint Louis University. Dr. Ohs' research interests lie at the intersection of interpersonal and health communication across the life span with an emphasis on older adulthood. Her research has focused on the personal social networks involved in health-care decisions at the latter end of the life span, ageism, and family communication about health-related decisions. Her work has appeared in *The Journal of Social Issues, The Journal of Divorce and Remarriage*, and the *Routledge Handbook of Applied Communication Research*.

Janet Osuch (M.D., 1979, Michigan State University (MSU); M.S., 2000, MSU) is a Professor of Surgery and Epidemiology at MSU. After completing a surgical residency and fellowship in surgical oncology at Northwestern University, she devoted her clinical practice to breast surgery for 12 years until 1998. She then pursued a degree in Epidemiology. She currently practices breast cancer risk counseling and conducts epidemiologic research, in addition to serving as Assistant Dean of Preclinical Curriculum in the College of Human Medicine at MSU. She is the author of several journal articles and book chapters on breast cancer, and has also published on topics in medical education and the patient-physician relationship. Her current epidemiologic research focuses on environmental toxicology. Her work has been published in refereed journals including *Breast Disease: An International Journal, Occupational and Environmental Medicine, Academic Medicine, Annals of Human Biology, Annals of Surgery, Cancer, Environmental Health Perspectives, Journal of Clinical Endocrinology and Metabolism, Journal of Clinical Epidemiology, Journal of Mammary Gland Biology and Neoplasia, Medical Education, Obesity*, and *Surgical Neurology*.

Sheetal J. Patel (M.A., University of Texas at Austin, 2006) is a Roy H. Park Doctoral Fellow in the School of Journalism and Mass Communication at the University of North Carolina at Chapel Hill. Ms. Patel's research focuses on health and nonprofit communication. She has conducted research regarding health and nonprofit communication online, health campaign interventions, and compassion in health and nonprofit communication strategy. Her work has been presented at the International Communication Association, the Centers for Disease Control and Prevention, and the Association for Education in Journalism and Mass Communication.

David M. Peek (M.D., St. George's University, 2010) is a practicing physician with research interests in provider-patient communication and cultural competency surrounding Deaf and HIV-positive patient care. Previously, he worked for the San Bernardino County Department of Public Health, HIV/STD Control Programs doing community health outreach to people at high risk for HIV transmission, as well as giving clinical support to patients and providers in both HIV and STD clinics.

Valerie R. Renegar (Ph.D., University of Kansas, 2000) is an Associate Professor in the School of Communication at San Diego State University. Dr. Renegar studies the rhetoric of emerging feminist movements and other rhetorical avenues of social change. Her research interests tend to be grounded in popular culture and include issues of agency and empowerment. Her work has been published in refereed journals including *Philosophy and Rhetoric*, *Hypatia*, *Southern Communication Journal*, *The Journal of Environmental Communication*, *The Howard Journal of Communications*, and *Communication Studies*.

Lance S. Rintamaki (Ph.D., University of Illinois at Urbana-Champaign, 2003), is an Assistant Professor in the Departments of Communication and Health Behavior at the State University of New York, University at Buffalo. His research interests focus on provider-patient interaction, medical education, social support, and social stigma. His research is designed to facilitate coping and adjustment among people newly diagnosed with chronic illnesses, as well as equip caregivers with skills that enhance care provision and health outcomes among those for whom they provide care. His work has been published in refereed journals including *AIDS and Behavior*, *AIDS Patient Care and STDs*, *Health Communication*, *Journal of the American Geriatrics Society*, *Journal of General Internal Medicine*, and *Journal of Social and Personal Relationships*.

James D. Robinson (Ph.D., Purdue University, 1982) is a Professor of Communication and the Director of Graduate Studies at the University of Dayton. He also completed degrees at West Virginia University (M.A., 1979), University of the Pacific (B.A., 1978) and West Valley Community College (A.A., 1976). He has published work in a number of journals including *Health Communication, Journal of Diabetes Science and Technology, Health Care Management Review, Journal of Broadcasting & Electronic Media, Sex Roles, Women in Health, Journal of Social and Personal Relationships, Communication Reports, Sociology of Religion, Review of Religious Research, Geriatrics and Gerontological Education, Journalism Quarterly, Communication Research Report, Mass Comm. Review*, and *Progress in Transplantation*.

Lori A. Roscoe (Ph.D., University of South Florida, 2000) is an Assistant Professor in the Department of Communication at the University of South Florida. Dr. Roscoe's research interests include end-of-life decision making, physician-patient communication, health literacy, and quality of life and serious illness. She has published articles and book chapters regarding what defines a good death, physician-assisted suicide and euthanasia, barriers to hospice admission, and social support and caregiving for patients with late-stage Huntington's disease and serious mental illness, as well as on geriatrics in medical education. Her work has been published in refereed journals including *The*

New England Journal of Medicine, Health Communication, The Gerontologist, Journal of Medical Humanities, Journal of Pain and Symptom Management, and *Journal of Palliative Medicine*, and in scholarly books including the *Handbook of Disease Burdens and Quality of Life Measures, Encyclopedia of Death and the Human Experience,* and *Ethical Dilemmas for Geriatric Teams: A Casebook.*

Autumn Shafer (M.A., Washington State University, 2003) is a Roy H. Park Fellow and doctoral student in the School of Journalism and Mass Communication at the University of North Carolina at Chapel Hill. Her research interests focus on health communication and how individuals process or resist persuasive messages. She has studied the effects of media, narratives, and framing on psychological and behavioral outcomes in numerous health contexts. Her research has been published in *Health Communication, Journal of Adolescent Health, Sexually Transmitted Diseases,* and the *Howard Journal of Communication.*

Kami J. Silk (Ph.D., University of Georgia, 2002) is an Associate Professor jointly appointed to the Department of Communication and the Michigan Agricultural Experiment Station at Michigan State University where she is also the Graduate Director of the Health and Risk Communication Masters Program. Her recent research has focused on breast cancer risk reduction with the Breast Cancer and Environment Research Centers, promoting positive nutrition outcomes, and blood donation social norms. Her research has been published in refereed journals including *Journal of Health Communication, Human Communication Research, Health Communication, Social Science & Medicine, Communication Research Reports, Preventive Medicine, Journal of Nutrition Education & Behavior,* and *Health Promotion & Practice.*

Jennifer S. Somerville (M.A., University of Akron, 2008) is a Ph.D. candidate in the School of Communication Studies at Ohio University. Jennifer's main area of study is Health Communication with special emphasis on online support groups and environmental health communication. She teaches undergraduate courses in public speaking, persuasion, communication theory, and interpersonal communication.

Michael T. Stephenson (Ph.D., University of Kentucky, 1999) is a Professor of Communication and Associate Dean in the College of Liberal Arts at Texas A&M University. His most recent research focuses on the effective design and implementation of anti-drug ads directed at parents and youth. Additionally, he conducted CDC-funded research to prevent second-hand smoke exposure among children living in colonias along the Texas-Mexico border. He has served as a co-investigator on a Division of Transplantation grant to investigate the promotion of organ donation as well as a co-investigator on a National Institute on Drug Abuse grant aimed at preventing marijuana use among adolescent sensation seekers. Some of his publications appear in *Human Communication Research, Communication Research, Communication Studies, Communication Monographs, Journal of Communication, American Journal of Public Health, Journal of Applied Communication Research, Health Communication,* and *Journal of American College Health.*

Yan Tian (Ph.D., Temple University, 2004) is an Associate Professor of Communication at the University of Missouri–St. Louis. Her research interests focus on health communication, research methods, mass communication, political communication and new technologies—particularly as they apply to health. She has published work in a number of journals including *Health Communication,*

Patient Education and Counseling, New Media and Society, Communication Quarterly, Communication Research Reports, and *Asian Journal of Communication*.

Jeanine Warisse Turner (Ph.D., The Ohio State University, 1996) is an Associate Professor in the Communication, Culture, and Technology program at Georgetown University. She also completed degrees at University of Dayton (M.A., 1993; B.A., 1987). She has published work in a number of journals including *Academy of Management Review, Health Communication, Social Marketing Quarterly, Journal of Diabetes Science and Technology, Journal of Communication, International Journal of Medical Marketing, Journal of Telemedicine and Telecare, Annual Review of Biomedical Engineering, Administrative Radiology Journal*, and *Teleconference* among others.

Elizabeth A. Baiocchi-Wagner (M.A., Abilene Christian University, 2006) is a doctoral student in the Department of Communication at the University of Missouri. Her research explores the intersections of family and health communication, with particular attention to issues of gender and aging. She serves as the assistant director for the university's basic communication course, and also teaches classes in public speaking and interpersonal communication.

Nancy L. Zucker (Ph.D., Duke University, 2000) is the Director of the Duke Center for Eating Disorders and an Assistant Professor of Psychiatry and Behavioral Sciences in the Duke School of Medicine. Her research interests include the development of novel treatments for individuals with eating disorders and children who struggle with weight management and the integration of family members into effective treatment strategies. She focuses on strategies that improve interpersonal functioning and self-awareness. The basic research she pursues in this area involves understanding the neurocognitive correlates of social information processing and somatic sensitivity so deficits in these domains can be characterized and addressed in novel interventions. Her work has been published in *Lancet, Psychological Bulletin, Eating and Weight Disorders, International Journal of Eating Disorders, Eating Disorders: The Journal of Treatment and Prevention*, and *Child and Adolescent Mental Health*. She is also author of the book, *A Parent Skills Manual for Eating Disorder Treatment* (New Harbinger).

INTRODUCTION

Have you ever watched a young child try to put together a puzzle for the first time? The child will push and turn and slap each piece trying to make it fit. It can be very frustrating for the child *and* the person watching the child. But then, when the piece finally fits into place, there is often a feeling of excitement *and* relief. Our experiences with health communication can be a lot like those of the child, or spectator, grappling with, and then fitting the pieces into, the puzzle. Sometimes the pieces fit; sometimes they don't. And sometimes, there are pieces missing and just no way to "fix" the puzzle. Whether you are communicating with a friend who needs you to listen as s/he shares physical and emotional challenges, seeking advice from a physician for a new health concern, evaluating a health campaign advertisement you recently read, or wondering if the government has become too involved in your health care, you have probably experienced initial frustration when things did not fit the way you wanted them to but were later relieved, and maybe excited, to help find a resolution to the health issue.

It is likely that you participate in health communication nearly every day. Whether you are healthy or ill, communicatively adept or apprehensive, a caregiver or care recipient, persuasive or persuaded, you have been influenced by, and have influenced others through, health communication. Our everyday lives are affected by our health and our communication. This occurs when we talk with a friend, visit a physician, view an advertisement, or choose political representatives based on health care perspectives. We are surrounded by health and communication. We cannot escape it. This is evident in the cases represented in this book. Each case presented will provide you with a glimpse into someone's experience with health communication. Through your reading, thinking, and discussing, you too may experience the frustration and subsequent joy of trying to put together the pieces of the puzzle.

Project Goals and Vision

As editor, I had six primary goals for this project: (1) showcase an array of health communication scholarship encompassing and intersecting multiple levels (e.g., interpersonal, group, organizational, mass, multicultural) employing a case study format; (2) help readers better understand and appreciate the central role of health communication across a rich contextual landscape; (3) foster and/or sharpen the development of critical thinking skills; (4) encourage readers to become more informed health care consumers and advocates; (5) motivate students to develop additional research skills so they might aspire to become health communication researchers; and (6) mentor prospective authors to help them craft engaging, compelling, theoretically sound, and pragmatically appealing chapters.

The vision for the book evolved during the process (described in the next section) and ultimately emphasized the following features: blending lay (or popular) and academic writing styles; providing a theoretical foundation to explain and contextualize health communication concepts and processes; and explicating key research design terminology and practices spanning qualitative, quantitative, and mixed-method designs across the chapters (e.g., statistical tests, interrater or intercoder procedures, formative research, social science standards for hypothesis testing and scale reliability levels). Chapter authors were challenged, through the revision process (with each chapter averaging four revisions), to appeal to a wide-ranging audience with varying levels of expertise and interest in the chapter context, research methods, and featured chapter populations or characters. Because of these varying levels, chapter authors were also instructed to elaborate on what might be unfamiliar or complex terms and procedures in detailed chapter endnotes, which I recommend readers peruse for additional clarification and elaboration.

Selecting Chapters

As I began working on this project, I was excited, anxious, overwhelmed, and inspired. I experienced all of these emotions for many reasons, but most notably because so many scholars supported this project with their submissions and willingness to review submissions. Of the 59 original précis submitted, 19 full chapters were published in this case study book. Except for Chapter 1 (i.e., the introductory chapter providing background into health communication and case study pedagogy), all other chapters were peer-reviewed through a masked process (i.e., the 53-member editorial board reviewed submissions without knowing the identities of respective authors) at the précis and initial chapter submission stages. Through this masked peer-review process, usually three editorial board members (i.e., assistant professor, associate professor, and full professor) reviewed each précis (and later full chapters) on 8 (or 10 if data driven) criteria (i.e., topic saliency/relevancy, theoretical rationale, pragmatic rationale, data-driven [if so, research design quality], case relevance, case engagement level, supporting literature, blending lay and academic writing, and overall cogency). They also gave an overall score and rated their likelihood of using the case in their own classes. Authors of 26 of the 59 original précis submissions were invited to develop full chapters for further review. All authors agreed and once chapters were submitted, when possible, the same review team reviewed full-length chapters. Based on both quantitative and qualitative recommendations from the review teams, 19 chapters were ultimately selected for inclusion. To avoid any conflicts of interest, any submissions with West Virginia University affiliations were shepherded by Dr. Piotr Bobkowski, senior editorial assistant. As editor, I was not privy to the identities of any of the reviewers for those submissions, and Dr. Bobkowski ultimately made acceptance and rejection decisions for those submissions (which were scored very clearly above or below the quantitative cut-off points).

Book's Organization

Following the opening chapter, there are seven sections. These emerged after the reviews had been completed and the chapters were selected. For some chapters, it was evident how they should be categorized; for other chapters, it is possible that they could fit into multiple sections. After careful review of each chapter, I also contacted the chapter authors to let them know in which section I planned to place their chapter to verify the accuracy of that choice. Everyone agreed.

Sections of This Book

Seven sections ranging from interpersonal to societal communicative behaviors are featured in the book. The sections focus on provider-patient interactions, social support, multiple influences affecting decision-making, formative research, campaign design, innovative strategies and partnerships, and public health initiatives.

Section I, *Experiencing Challenging Provider-Patient Communication Interactions*, focuses on problematic interpersonal interactions between patients and health care providers (and sometimes third parties). In Chapter 2, I share a personal transformation as I present the case of how I lost my first child during a very physician-centered communication encounter and how I tried to make sense, and regain some control, of the situation by using active patient participation behaviors. In Chapter 3, by using research from a variety of sources, Rintamaki et al. present the composite perspectives of a Deaf patient and medical student as they must interact with each other and a hurried physician. Araujo and Roscoe present Araujo's experience serving as a medical interpreter with a non-English speaking patient and the implications for the patient, family, provider, and herself with the changing interpreter roles in Chapter 4.

Section II, *Communicating Social Support During Daunting Life Events*, focuses on various types of, and contexts for, social support. In Chapter 5, as a participant observer, Golden explores different types of social support that a support group offers when a caregiver makes a choice to place her spouse in residential care. In Chapter 6, based on in-depth interviews, Bute and Somerville share how communicating social support is part of everyday talk with important health outcomes and the challenges that can be experienced when trying to give, and receive, social support from a friend. Revealed during an interview, Mak and Chaidaroon in Chapter 7 address the cultural challenges and support a Malay-Muslim Singaporean woman faces after her diagnosis with second-stage breast cancer.

Section III, *Identifying Multiple Influences Affecting Health and Decision-Making*, addresses how health behaviors are affected by multiple entities ranging from intrapersonal to societal influences. In Chapter 8, Baiocchi-Wagner uses media coverage and personal communication to present a timely case of a woman charged with felony neglect of her son, simply because he is obese, and offers a socio-ecological perspective into the issue of obesity. Ohs also addresses the multiple perspectives presented in an ecological model in Chapter 9 to help understand the decision-making process of an older adult woman who must decide whether to consent to surgery. Liberman looks more closely at multiple intrapersonal influences that affect a person's decision to manage diabetes by using insulin pump therapy in Chapter 10.

Section IV, *Recognizing and Addressing Campaign Challenges Through Formative Research*, focuses on the necessary research that needs to be completed before designing and implementing a health campaign. In Chapter 11, Patel et al. share the extensive formative research process they underwent before developing messages to help parents of children with eating disorders. Clark et al. provide strategies in their case regarding how to overcome challenges related to adapting campaign materials so that they are culturally appropriate, use the desired channel, and are effective, particularly for reducing secondhand smoke, in Chapter 12.

Section V, *Designing, Implementing, and Evaluating Effective Health Campaigns*, focuses on the steps necessary to create, disseminate, and assess health campaigns. In Chapter 13, Mattson et al. provide a theoretical model and highlight the benefits of health campaign pedagogy in their case describing the Motorcycle Safety at Purdue campaign. Frisby et al. also advocate for health campaign pedagogy and share the steps they used to not only implement an effective grassroots campaign but also provide experiential learning to students in their case about ATV safety in Chapter 14. Anker and Feeley focus on the use of formative and summative evaluation when designing health campaigns by offering a case of two campaigns that encourage people to become organ donors in Chapter 15.

Section VI, *Utilizing Innovative Strategies and Partnerships for Meeting Health Needs*, focuses on the use of newer approaches and collaborations for improving people's health and lives. In Chapter 16,

Ginossar used multiple methods to gather data to share how the use of a community-based approach can meet the needs of an underserved community. In Chapter 17, Robinson et al. content analyzed nearly 1,000 messages to provide support for the use of a telecommunication tool to help Native Americans monitor their diabetes regimen. Silk et al. present the case of a unique collaboration of breast cancer centers that utilizes a transdisciplinary team approach in Chapter 18.

Section VII, *Framing Public Health Initiatives*, focuses on framing, or reframing, important health topics for the public. In Chapter 19, Malkowski et al. present the political implications of framing public health messages for policy actions by analyzing the messages communicated by the Texas governor, and his opponents, regarding HPV vaccinations. Austin et al. provide the need, process, and solution for reframing and coordinating messages related to injury and violence prevention after communicating with partner organizations and community members in Chapter 20.

As is evident by the breadth of these topics, the cases in this book provide experiences from the intrapersonal, interpersonal, group, family, organizational, mediated, multicultural, and public perspectives. Each chapter presents a unique case but also provides commonly used theoretical underpinnings and health communication concepts to help analyze the case.

Features of This Book

To help you preview each chapter, there is an **abstract** with **keywords** or **key concepts**. Within each chapter, as previously mentioned, there may be some **explanatory endnotes**. In addition, there are **discussion questions** preceding the **references**. *What has been purposively excluded, however, is the authors' case conclusion.* Those are available online for adopting instructors from the publisher, Kendall Hunt Publishing Company, along with 10 multiple choice and two essay questions for each chapter. In close consultation with Paul Carty and Angela Willenbring of Kendall Hunt, it was decided that to best encourage classroom discussions and multiple case resolutions, the authors' conclusions should be available only to instructors. Ideally then, students would be less likely to focus exclusively on only one resolution to the case or a "right" or "wrong" response.

In this book, you will find powerful cases that communicate the complexity, frustration, and relief experienced by engaging in different types of health communication. Much like a child fitting the pieces of the puzzle together, you now have the opportunity to start turning and placing the pieces of the cases together to determine possible resolutions. As you think about and discuss each case, consider what fits, what doesn't, and what is missing.

CHAPTER 1

Exploring Health Communication and Case Study Pedagogy

Maria Brann, Piotr Bobkowski, Amanda R. Martinez, and C. Kyle Rudick

KEY TERMS

Health communication

Case study pedagogy

Abstract

Merging health communication with case study pedagogy affords scholars an opportunity to apply theoretical concepts to real-life scenarios. The purpose of this chapter is to introduce readers to health communication and case study pedagogy. Specifically, we begin the chapter by defining health communication and providing an overview of the history of health communication as an area of study. Next, we move into discussing case study pedagogy. We briefly trace the historical roots of case study pedagogy and provide readers with descriptions of this methodology. Then, we present characteristics of effective case studies, provide instruction on how to use case study pedagogy, and finally, offer several advantages and some disadvantages of using case study pedagogy in the classroom.

Health communication has developed into a vibrant and necessary area of study within the communication studies discipline. Even with it's fairly young history—less than half a century—health communication has evolved from communication, social science, and medical disciplines into a growing field of study that continues to impact individuals, organizations, and society. Even younger is the use of case study pedagogy within health communication, although case study pedagogy has flourished as an effective teaching tool in other disciplines for more than a century. To better understand the history of health communication, and case study pedagogy, and how health communication students can benefit from the use of case studies, we first begin this chapter with a definition and brief historical view of health communication, followed by a more detailed exploration of case study pedagogy and its benefits.

Health Communication

For some, describing what health communication entails, how scholars "do" health communication, and what makes it distinct from other disciplines is an elusive task. Although health communication can include several different facets of health and communication and scholars study these areas using a variety of methods, we still attempt to provide an encompassing view of health communication. At the very minimum, we hope to offer an understanding of what we mean when we discuss health communication. Then, we provide a brief overview of the history of health communication to help situate this area of study within academia.

Defining Health Communication

Similar to other types of communication (e.g., interpersonal, organizational, family, mass, intercultural), there is not one universally accepted definition of health communication.[1] Still, it is important to be aware of common themes among definitions to better understand what health communication is, and is not. Egbert, Query, Quinlan, Savery, and Martinez (in press) offer the following definition: "health communication is the systematic study of message behavior, across a rich array of contexts, with the overarching goals of facilitating positive health outcomes, as well as reducing the prevalence and likelihood of a myriad of health threats." The preceding definition is based on several underlying premises including: (a) although "health" and "communication" are combined, it is paramount to develop a strong knowledge base of both areas (see Ratzan's 1993, 1996 POISE model; Parrott, 2004; Thompson, Robinson, Anderson, & Federowicz, 2008); (b) message behaviors should be conceptualized as symbolic with the potential to shape interactions and meanings of illness/disease (see Barnlund, 1976), thereby distinguishing health communication from other related areas such as health psychology; (c) health communication occurs in many different contexts other than traditional health care encounters (Cline, 2003); and (d) although health communication processes and practices have the potential to influence health outcomes along a continuum ranging from positive to negative, there is not only one way to achieve favorable results.

Historical Overview of Health Communication

Disciplines other than communication helped forge health communication as its own area of study. The area was shaped by literature drawn from anthropology, psychology, sociology, instructional design, nursing, social marketing, government, politics, and medicine among others[2] (see Clift & Freimuth, 1995; Kreps, Query, & Bonaguro, 2008; Ratzan, 1996). At least three additional events also prompted the field's development:

1. In 1962, the U.S. Surgeon General held a conference on health communication, which played an instrumental role in the 1963 Surgeon General's report on the hazards of smoking (U.S. Department of Health, Education, and Welfare, 1963; see also Rogers, 1996).

2. Also in 1962, Neal conducted a limited, but arguably, first content analysis of extant literature related to health and communication.

3. In 1971, the Stanford Heart Disease Prevention Program (SHDPP) was launched, which was led by a cardiologist and communication specialist research team. Rogers (1994,

1996) considers the SHDPP to be the single most important catalyst in the beginning of health communication.

These interdisciplinary contributions helped shape what would eventually become the field of health communication. In 1972, at an annual conference of the International Communication Association (ICA; attended by communication faculty, practitioners, and students), the "therapeutic communication" interest group[3] was formed (see Kreps, Bonaguro, & Query, 1998; Kreps et al., 2008; Sharf, 1993). Three years later at another ICA conference, the name was changed to "health communication," and the interest group earned division status, indicative of a sustained membership of at least 200–300 individuals (M. L. Haley, personal communication, December 6, 2010). In 1986, a commission (i.e., somewhat similar to an interest group in size) on health communication was formed by the then-named Speech Communication Association (SCA; now named National Communication Association [NCA]; Donohew & Ray, 1990; Kreps et al., 1998, 2008; Ratzan, Payne, & Bishop, 1996; Sharf, 1993), and it would also quickly achieve division status. As of 2010, there are also health communication interest groups in three of the four regional communication associations: Central States (CSCA), Eastern (ECA), and Western States (WSCA). Southern States Communication Association (SSCA) does not have a health communication division or interest group; however, a large amount of health communication scholarship is presented through the applied communication division to "showcase [that] health communication research often exemplifies how our research and discipline can be applied to the benefit of many beyond academic walls" (J. M. Smith, personal communication, October 11, 2010).

The communication associations are not the only groups to offer meetings where health communication scholars can showcase their research. The longest series of conferences centering on health communication has been coordinated and sponsored by the University of Kentucky's Department of Communication. As N. G. Harrington (personal communication, October 8, 2010) reports, the first University of Kentucky Health Communication Conference (KCHC), *Persuasive Communication and Drug Abuse Prevention*, occurred in 1989 with funding from a National Institute on Drug Abuse grant, spearheaded by Dr. Lewis Donohew, University of Kentucky, as the Principal Investigator. This inaugural conference was a small, invitation-only event centered exclusively on research in substance abuse prevention. Since its initiation, KCHC has occurred on a biennial basis and expanded into a nationally recognized forum for researchers, practitioners, and students from health communication and a variety of related disciplines. Attendees share cutting-edge research on a variety of health-related topics, converse about current health communication issues, and develop strong professional relationships further promoting a health communication research and practice agenda.

Associations and conferences have afforded health communication scholars opportunities to engage in dialogue about relevant issues, but they are not the only outlets to share scholarship. Scholarly journals have provided health communication researchers an avenue for sharing as well. Since the early 1960s, a growing number of scholarly journals have published special issues (SI) centering on health communication.[4] The earliest SI occurred in 1963 in the *Journal of Communication*. Guest Editors Joost and Meerloom published refereed articles focusing on the central theme: "Communication and Mental Health." A quarter century later, in the *Journal of Applied Communication Research*, Guest Editor Smith published several competitively selected articles examining "Values in Health Communication." In 1994, Guest Editor Ratzan published "Health Communication: Challenges for the 21st Century" appearing in the *American Behavioral Scientist*, and in 1996, Guest Editor Kreps published "Messages and Meanings: Health Communication and Health Psychology" in the *Journal of Health Psychology*. In 2002 and 2003,[5] Editor Query published "Health Communication and Public Health: Pedagogical and Research Insights" in *Communication Studies*. More recently, Guest Editors Noar and Palmgreen (2009) published "Evaluating Health Communication Campaigns: Key Issues and Alternative Approaches" in *Communication Methods and Measures*, and in 2010, Guest Editors Kreps, Sparks, and Villagran published "Communication Education and Health Promotion" in *Communication Education*.

In addition to the preceding SIs, *Health Communication* was launched under the auspices of Lawrence Erlbaum and Associates. Teresa L. Thompson, a highly regarded Ph.D. in the communication discipline, is its founding editor and continues to serve in that capacity. The first issue was published in 1989, and it continues to flourish (see Thompson, 2010) with four senior editors. In 1996, a second scholarly journal, *Journal of Health Communication: International Perspectives*, was founded by Scott C. Ratzan, an M.D. with a Master's of Public Health who continues to be a global champion of health care advocacy and efficacy as well as health communication. This journal's growth and development mirrors the success of *Health Communication* in many ways (see Freimuth, Massett, & Meltzer, 2006).

Having outlined some of the milestones achieved within the field of health communication, it seems clear that the growth has been expansive, the interest is unfaltering, and the field is a "vibrant and important interdisciplinary area of study" (Kreps et al., 2008, p. 3).

Case Study Pedagogy

Now that we have a better understanding of what health communication is and its origin, it is important to address what case studies are and how they can be used as an effective pedagogical tool within health communication. First, though, we begin with a brief précis of the history of case study pedagogy.

Historical Overview of Case Study Pedagogy

Using case studies to learn about different content areas within various disciplines has a long and distinguished history (Kimball, 1995). Case studies were originally used in religious education (Braithwaite & Wood, 2000); however, secular schools have also used the case study approach. Harvard Law School, for example, was one of the earliest establishments to employ this type of pedagogy, dating back to 1870 (Lynn, 1999). By 1908, law schools were the leading institutions to recognize and use this valuable teaching tool for reflective thinking (Hartman, 1992). In the 1920s, business schools recognized the value of case study pedagogy focusing in particular on organizational processes and practices not traditionally available in classrooms (Keyton & Shockley-Zalabak, 2006). The case study approach became so popular within business schools that this method is often associated with Harvard Business School, which published the first book of cases in 1921 (Scott, 2007; Weil, Oyelere, Yeoh, & Firer, 2001). Soon other disciplines (e.g., public administration medicine, management, education, finance, communication studies [see McAdoo & Nelson, 1975]) began to incorporate case study pedagogy within their teaching practices.

Particularly relevant to the field of communication was the formal published recognition by organizational communication scholars of the merits associated with case study pedagogy beginning in 1990 when Beverly D. Sypher published the first edition of a case study book to teach students communication concepts that could be applied in organizations. Shortly thereafter, health communication scholars recognized the importance of this approach and began to use case studies as well, particularly with the publication of Eileen Berlin Ray's first health communication case study book in 1993, followed by additional case study books in 1996 and 2005. Other health communication case study books, as well as other communication case study book exemplars, are reported in **TABLE 1.1**.

TABLE 1.1 Communication Case Study Book Examples and Reviews

CONTENT AREA	SELECTED CITATION(S)
Gender Communication	Kirby & McBride (2009)
Group Communication	Schnell (2003)
Health Communication	Pagano (2010); Ray (1993, 1996, 2005); Wright & Moore (2008)*
Interpersonal Communication	Braithwaite & Wood (2000, 2011)
Mass Communication Ethics	Christians, Fackler, McKee, Kreshel & Woods (2009); Day (2006)
Organizational Communication	Keyton & Shockley-Zalabak (2006); May (2006); Sypher (1990, 1997); Taylor & Van Every (2010)
Public Health Communication & Marketing	Colburn, Sowola & Williams-Bader (2007); Fairbanks & Candelaria (1998); Fortenberry (2011); Gwayi-Chore (2010); Hallett, Padmanabhan, Pitorak & Roberson (2009); Mottern, Sogor & Zarbalian (2008)
Sport Communication	Brown & O'Rourke (2003)
Health Communication Case Study Book Reviews	
du Pré (2008); Harter & Quick (2006); Robinson (1993, 1998)	

* This edited volume does not feature case studies exclusively.

Defining Case Studies

With the acceptance of case studies as a rigorous pedagogical method during the last century (Kimball, 1995), the number of scholarly definitions for case studies has increased. Although some definitions may seem better, much like the definition of health communication, we do not attempt to create a "perfect" definition. Instead, we examine distinct, and sometimes competing, views of case studies gleaned from several teacher-scholars'[6] interpretations concerning this type of pedagogy. Harrington (1995) supported such an approach noting that case studies are designed to promote multiple interpretations of situations (see also Dreher & Kreps, 1990).

Dreher and Kreps (1990) observed that case studies in education are used to pose complex problems that stimulate student learning through concerted attempts to solve, or lessen the intensity of, particular case issues. Although case studies are used in places other than educational settings, Dreher and Kreps contended that case studies can be used as powerful pedagogical tools. Sypher (1997) stated that case studies reflect the co-construction of knowledge through communication between individuals. In particular, she stated that "each case study is a view—a view of what we see, a view of how we choose to report what we see, a view of others' views" (p. 1). In this way, Sypher acknowledged that case studies are subjective, reflecting in part the authors' and the readers' prior frames of reference or biases.

Another key point is the recognition that case studies may be real or fictional. McAdoo and Nelson (1975) concurred, defining a case study as the "use of actual or hypothetical communication situations which demonstrate how communication concepts function in human discourse and human relationships" (p. 29). The preceding definition is useful because it recognized that case studies are intended to instill more than rote learning, and it clearly championed a communication perspective (i.e., message behavior is the primary focus of this pedagogical approach).

Characterizing Effective Case Studies

In examining what makes a good or effective case study for classroom use, it is important to consider the characteristics the case study exhibits. As Lawrence (1953) argued, sound case studies are "the vehicle by which a chunk of reality is brought into the classroom" (p. 215). That is, case studies are meant to promote a sense of realism in the classroom by providing life-like scenarios that students can relate to and learn from. Sypher (1990) further stated that case studies provide a useful tool for teacher-scholars as they are a means to apply theory to everyday situations. Deetz (1990) explained that all too often there is a tendency to perceive that practice and theory are divorced. Proceeding from Deetz's position, a sound case study is one that is simple enough that the reader does not become bogged down by the abstractions of theory. Simultaneously, it is also complex enough that without the underlying theory, the case study cannot be effectively analyzed or explained.

Keyton and Shockley-Zalabak (2006) also argued that case studies are powerful tools, as their use in classrooms promotes students' ability to take the perspective of the person(s) in the case study, apply their knowledge to everyday scenarios, and immerse themselves in the process of communication. Harrington (1995) argued that case study pedagogy provides instructors with a powerful alternative to the behaviorist-driven approach to handling teaching situations by emphasizing the importance of contextual and cultural factors that are a part of classroom dilemmas. Recognizing that knowledge is multi-faceted promotes the idea that learning is personal and demands that readers reflect upon their own life experiences and knowledge to find their own personal truths. As case studies are usually open to multiple interpretations and resolutions,[7] these pedagogical tools promote a critical mindset and emphasize that knowledge is dynamic. It seems reasonable to conclude, then, that good case studies demand readers' attention and reflection.

Specific characteristics of effective case studies. Although some teacher-scholars, such as those previously mentioned, have described broader characteristics of sound case studies, others have been very specific. For example, Dunne and Brooks (2004) proposed 10 characteristics of a good case study including that the case study must have pedagogic utility, represent a general issue beyond the case itself, tell an engaging story, focus on an interest-arousing issue, pose a problem with no obvious answer, create empathy for the characters, require the reader to use information from the case to create a solution for the problem(s) posed, require the reader to think critically about the problem, exemplify economical writing providing sufficient information for effective analysis, and be relevant to students.

Other teacher-scholars have noted the functions that sound case studies serve in academic literature. Sypher (1997) stated that there are four functions of case studies: epistemic, rhetorical, skill-enhancement, and narrative. The epistemic function describes how case studies can serve to promote particular ways of knowing. In particular, case studies provide a snapshot of individuals' lives or stories, which in turn lets you see the world through others' eyes. The social constructionist perspective, for example, suggests that social reality and meaning are constructed through dialogue with individual communication partners and with broader cultural discourses. For instance, a dialogue between a patient and her/his doctor concerning a diagnosis may generate meaning and new self-identity for the patient (e.g., "I am diabetic") and be interpreted within broader cultural discourses concerning chronic conditions and their management, lifestyle choices, medical costs, etc. Because many case studies feature extensive passages of dialogue, case studies may be used effectively to demonstrate the subjectivity of constructed meanings. Instructors may thus rely on case studies to help their students hone critical discourse assessment skills (Kirby & McBride, 2009).

The rhetorical function is based on the belief that each case study constitutes an argument. The argumentative nature of the case study should be apparent since each case study provides a competing, subjective account for the story that occurred. As case studies are also designed to impart experience in a situation, they can serve a skills-enhancement function.

The underlying premise is that one's communication-based abilities can be enhanced by examining and critiquing various levels of communication effectiveness posed by the cases.

The final function of case studies is the narrative function. Because case studies generally take the form of a story, this function also encompasses the case plot, characters, and settings. Narrative theory underlies case studies as it accentuates the critical role that "detailed accounts of people, situations, and events" (Braithwaite & Wood, 2000, p. 9) play in human learning. Instructors who endorse the efficacy of the narratives in instructional settings may use case studies for the vivid and engaging characters, descriptions, and plotlines that many case studies recount.

While differences exist, so do commonalities between the different interpretations of case studies. To enhance case study efficacy, it is helpful to consider case study types based on perceived educational outcomes relevant to the specific subject matter. At the very least, effective cases should be grounded in practicality and underlying theory, provoke self-reflection, as well as be engaging.

Using Case Studies in the Classroom

Instructors can practice a range of teaching techniques when employing case studies in their classrooms. One way to distinguish between various teachings styles is to focus on the degree of students' participation in how a case study is communicated and resolved. At one extreme of the continuum, instructors present case studies within their lectures. These "demonstrator" (Dooley & Skinner, 1977, p. 285) teachers treat case studies as useful illustrations of the concepts and frameworks being covered in the class; however, they reserve the exposition and resolution of the cases to themselves. Students are not encouraged to actively participate, although this approach is antithetical to many of the active learning objectives of case studies (discussed later). In some circumstances, however, it may be useful for some instructors.

At the opposite end of the continuum is a teaching approach in which students do most of the work in the exposition and resolution, as well as the very construction of the case study. Argyris (1980) identified several central features of applying the case study method, chief among them being students' "maximal possible involvement" (p. 291) in the scenarios and dilemmas presented. Argyris (1980) emphasized the expansive and open-ended discussion that case studies should stimulate, with students articulating and evaluating diverse reactions and points of view in response to the featured information. In this situation, an instructor prompts students with a specific problem or topic to research and resolve, leaving students with the responsibility to articulate the parameters of the case, reason their way to the most appropriate channels of inquiry, gather the necessary information, and generate evaluations of, or resolutions to, the problem (Barrows, 1986). In this format, the instructor acts only as a "facilitator" (Dooley & Skinner, 1977, p. 285) of the students' self-directed learning. Hence, instructors who value open-ended discussions as a learning tool may employ case studies as the basis of conversation and debate in their classrooms.

Many instructors who teach with case studies, however, reside somewhere between these two extremes. In a common iteration, the case study teaching method involves instructors assigning students a complete case—such as the ones presented in this book—to study and prepare for discussion in a subsequent class meeting (Barrows, 1986). Instructors then serve in the role of a "coach" (Dooley & Skinner, 1977, p. 285) during the class period, providing a general structure and direction for the students' exploration and discussion of the case particulars. Having a set of concepts and objectives in mind, instructors may steer the discussion toward specific points, pose probing questions for students to consider, help students make connections between the observations or conclusions at which they arrive, or connect the discussion toward broader topics or goals of the course.

Regardless of instruction technique, Bloom (1956) proposed that the effective learning process includes students' exposure to facts and theories, and more importantly, the application, analysis, synthesis, and evaluation of these "building blocks" within novel scenarios. Many instructors employ case studies to assist their students in developing higher-order learning skills identified by Bloom. Additional support was found in a recent nationwide survey of 77 health communication faculty where the results indicated that critical thinking skills were viewed as the most important learning goal ($M = 6.13/7.0$, $SD = .81$) and teaching strategies including case studies and PSA analysis yielded a mean of $5.0/7.0$ $SD = 1.24$ (Query, Wright, Bylund, & Mattson, 2007). Critical thinking skills can be integrated when students examine cases thoughtfully and systematically to unveil the patterned behaviors that underlie a given situation. As noted by Mier (1982) in her discussion of using the case method in organizational communication, case studies should help students by "formulat[ing] key concepts," "reinforc[ing] learning through application of key concepts," and "pinpoint[ing] the communication issue as it relates to organizational contingencies" (p. 151). Ideally then, case studies prompt students to assess, apply, and extend basic concepts and frameworks presented in textbooks or lectures to realistic and innovative real-world situations (Dunne & Brooks, 2004).

Most instructors will shift their case study teaching approach toward one end of the student participation continuum or the other, depending on the topic being covered, the nature of the case study, and individual class dynamics. Because of the more open-ended nature of the case study teaching method, a wider variety of variables may influence the successful implementation of a case study as a teaching tool rather than, for instance, a teacher-centered lecture. Presenting and modifying the case study approach to a new group of students may also require some patience on the part of both students and instructors, but both parties can benefit because case studies offer opportunities for greater student learning and growth than more static teaching methods.

Case Study Advantages and Disadvantages

Although case studies are widely used in teaching environments and not necessarily limited to the university classroom setting, there are some advantages and disadvantages that some teacher-scholars have identified across the disciplines. Notwithstanding their long tradition, case studies may still be viewed as works in progress as their implementation into learning environments continues to evolve.

Advantages. The depth of content presented through many case studies cannot be understated. Well-crafted case studies have the potential to shed light on murky complexities clouding pragmatic situations while also encouraging critical skill development in students. Perhaps addressing the empirical shortcomings of strictly quantitative work is one advantage of the case studies. In particular, story depth—a common hallmark of case studies—can contribute to other layers of understanding valuable to grasping the holistic and interrelated nature of real-world issues. While Newey (1987) demarcated case studies according to their respective objectives (i.e., descriptive/analytical, problem identification, problem solving/synthetical, and goal/solution), Sypher (1990) noted that "they do not have to focus exclusively on problematic, nationally important, or unusual events" (p. 7) to have educational value. Incorporating common knowledge or the familiar (for example, what is viewed in the media) in case study development can be an effective approach. Cullen, Richardson, and O'Brien (2004) concurred, suggesting "case studies should be chosen that students find interesting and motivating, using household names because these are familiar, and topical issues where plenty of media coverage is available to fill in the gaps" (p. 254). Similarly, allowing instructors to have the choice among a variety of case studies to fit particular audience interests and contexts is another important consideration.

Case studies may also be implemented into a course alongside conventional methods of teaching and learning to add a rich depth of understanding and promote practical skill development and application. Barrows (1986) identified four educational objectives that case studies may be used to achieve. First, case study-based learning is future-oriented, in that case studies often allow students to practice working through the types of practical challenges they will be facing. Second, by practicing solving real-world scenarios, students hone their reasoning skills concerning a broad range of problems with which they may grapple. Third, because the instructor generally plays a lesser role when the case study method is being implemented, case studies facilitate students' development of independent learning skills. Finally, due in part to the self-directed learning that many case studies promote, case studies may be more motivating to students than passive teaching methods. Subsequently, instructors may use case studies to encourage any of these goals, or their combination, in their classrooms.

As Cullen et al. (2004) found, "students may need greater engagement with the context, seeking information to inform thinking on issues such as conflict, rationality, [and] behavioural responses" (p. 261). Braithwaite and Wood (2000) cogently observed:

> Traditional methods of education introduce students to concepts individually—one
> at a time. This approach makes it difficult to appreciate how multiple concepts

work together to shape what happens in human interaction. Because case studies present communication situations in detail, they can give us insight into multiple processes and issues that are simultaneously present and interactive. (p. 7)

Again, the depth of case studies as detailed stories frequently provides a strong pedagogical tool because "they are carefully constructed accounts, or explanations, of human action. They give us insight into why certain things happened and not others, and why characters did some things and not others" (Braithwaite & Wood, 2000, p. 9).

Many scholars readily acknowledge the applied nature of case studies that tends to bridge the gap between the theoretical and pragmatic (Argyris, 1980; Berger, 1983; Braithwaite & Wood, 2000). As Cullen et al. (2004) stated, "teaching abstract theories, concepts and techniques is not enough" (p. 251), which has garnered interest in using empirically researched case studies as a way to bring these two approaches together. There is a great need for students to learn how to take abstract ideas and conceptualize them as a first step in forming judgments. Deetz (1990) echoed this sentiment by criticizing universities and organizations for moving too slowly to recognize the theory-practice connection inherent in many sound case studies. Within interpersonal communication, and health communication in particular, case studies promote active learning in practical situations, which in turn can help students expand their repertoires of communication choices that can lead to more effective adaptation across diverse contexts (Braithwaite & Wood, 2000).

Although a significant benefit to case studies is evident in the ability to demonstrate how theory informs the pragmatic world, the reverse is quite possible. Case studies may provide important opportunities for deeper thinking (as opposed to superficial analysis typical of rote learning) that leads to further developing and improving theory. This is but one benefit of facilitating critical thinking that shows the interconnected relationship between theory and practice, though the two approaches may seem quite disconnected at times. Subsequently, understanding and appreciating key concepts, as well as applying key principles, can often occur simultaneously while benefiting the individual inside and outside the classroom.

Disadvantages. Although many disciplines that integrate case studies as teaching tools highlight their ability to blend the theoretical and practical, case studies can lack such integration. Sypher (1990) noted that "case studies have been thought of as a weaker or less reliable research method," more so because it appears "the real weakness of case studies seems to be too little research on what constitutes a good case" (p. 5). Further exploring which components contribute to strong case study development is an area worthy of scholarly attention. This issue relates well to other criticisms of case studies, including effective assessment of outcomes when using case studies.

Newey (1987) cited student interest as a factor to gauge effectiveness. Proceeding further, he argued that although case studies seek to represent reality, they are often viewed as contrived situations that are designed to promote rote learning processes. Notwithstanding the strength of case studies' perceived ability to bridge the theoretical and pragmatic, some criticism recognizes the failure to achieve this goal (Argyris, 1980). In light of such concerns, some teacher-scholars are invested in further examining how to include case studies in teaching and how such insights from students might impact teaching effectiveness (Scott, 2007).

Cullen et al. (2004), for example, concluded that despite "strong support within academic environment[s] to use case studies more" such widespread changes "would require changes in curriculum, learning, and assessment" (p. 253). Scott (2007) stated that the use of case studies "requires considerable student contact time for discussion and interaction" in addition to being "time intensive" (p. 24). Thus, this approach may represent a larger change in conventional teaching methods than originally perceived, despite being considered useful and effective to many teacher-scholars. Perhaps this is an indication that individual teacher-scholars may be faced with determining whether case studies would serve a certain audience well depending on the specific class and its logistics.

Summary

Case studies, particularly in health communication, can serve as powerful tools for instructors and students as they navigate the health care system and converse with others about health-related issues. Instructors employ case studies to achieve various instructional goals. Overall then, although instructors may justify the use of case studies with reference to a range of educational goals, an overarching goal with case study pedagogy is to privilege students' *active* learning. An instructor's incorporation of the case study method indicates her/his initiative to de-emphasize the conventional lecture-based teaching style in favor of students' engagement with life-like examples. The use of case studies aligns with the pedagogical philosophy that views students' grappling with, and arriving at resolutions for, real-world problems, as one of the most effectual means of learning.

NOTES

1   For various definitions, see Centers for Disease Control and Prevention (n.d.); du Pré (2010); Geist-Martin, Ray, & Sharf (2003); Kreps & Thornton (1992); Northouse & Northouse (1998); Ratzan (1993); Ratzan, Payne, & Bishop (1996); Rogers (1996); Thompson, Robinson, Anderson, & Federowicz (2008).

2   Several influential publications, from the 1950s to the 1970s, served as catalysts for health communication's development as a field (see Barnlund, 1976; Korsch, Gozzi, & Francis, 1968; Korsch & Negrete, 1972; Ruesch, 1961, 1963; Ruesch & Bateson, 1951; Watzlawick, Beavin, & Jackson, 1967).

3   An interest group is a term often used by professional organizations and its members to describe a relatively small or modest number of faculty, practitioners, graduate students, and undergraduate students teaching, conducting research, or working in a particular content area.

4   Presented in this review is a selective list.

5   Three remaining health communication articles appeared in this volume.

6   A teacher-scholar is a faculty member who conducts research while also teaching. Although some faculty's primary responsibilities center on teaching and service, the bulk of faculty teaching master's students (one of our primary audiences) would likely be conducting research, serving on thesis committees, and teaching. Because many of the citations were authored by teacher-scholars, we use that phrasing here. In instances when we refer solely to teaching, we employ the more general term instructors.

7   We prefer to use some derivation of the term "resolve" to better reinforce that case studies should yield a variety of potential action steps. Since these are also dynamic and may change over time, the preceding term is more preferable than the static connotations of "solution(s)." The former term also denotes that most real-world problems may require multiple resolutions and not merely one "solution."

References

Argyris, C. (1980). Some limitations of the case method: Experiences in a management development program. *Academy of Management Review, 5*, 291–298.

Barnlund, D. C. (1976). The mystification of meaning: Doctor-patient encounters. *Journal of Medical Education, 51*, 716–725.

Barrows, H. S. (1986). A taxonomy of problem-based learning methods. *Medical Education, 20*, 481–486.

Berger, M. A. (1983). In defense of the case method: A reply to Argyris. *Academy of Management Review, 8*, 329–333.

Bloom, B. S., Jr. (1956). *Taxonomy of educational objectives. Handbook 1: Cognitive domain.* New York, NY: Longman.

Braithwaite, D. O., & Wood, J. T. (2000). Learning from case studies. In D. O. Braithwaite & J. T. Wood (Eds.), *Case studies in interpersonal communication: Processes and problems* (pp. 3–16). Belmont, CA: Wadsworth/Thomson Learning.

Braithwaite, D. O., & Wood, J. T. (Eds.). (2011). *Casing interpersonal communication: Case studies in personal and social relationships.* Dubuque, IA: Kendall/Hunt.

Brown, R. S., & O'Rourke, D. J. (Eds.). (2003). *Case studies in sport communication.* Westport, CT: Praeger.

Centers for Disease Control and Prevention. (n.d.). Health communication strategies. Retrieved from http://www.cdcnpin.org/scripts/campaign/strategy.asp

Christians, C. G., Fackler, M., McKee, K. B., Kreshel, P. J., & Woods, R., Jr. (2009). *Media ethics: Cases and moral reasoning* (8th ed.). New York, NY: Pearson.

Clift, E., & Freimuth, V. S. (1995). Health communication: What it is and what it can do for you? *Journal of Health Education, 26*(2), 68–74.

Cline, R. W. (2003). Everyday interpersonal communication and health. In T. L. Thompson, A. M. Dorsey, K. I. Miller, & R. Parrott, R. (Eds.), *Handbook of health communication* (pp. 285–313). Mahwah, NJ: Lawrence Erlbaum and Associates.

Colburn, J. M., Sowola, E., & Williams-Bader, J. (Eds.). (2007). *Cases in public health communication and marketing* (Vol. 1). Available from http://www.casesjournal.org

Cullen, J., Richardson, S., & O'Brien, R. (2004). Exploring the teaching potential of empirically-based case studies. *Accounting Education, 13*, 251–266.

Day, L. A. (2006). *Ethics in media communications: Cases and controversies* (5th ed.). Belmont, CA: Thomson Wadsworth.

Deetz, S. (1990). Foreword. In B. D. Sypher (Ed.), *Case studies in organizational communication* (pp. viii–x). New York, NY: The Guilford Press.

Donohew, L., & Ray, E. B. (1990). Introduction: Systems perspectives on health communication. In E. B. Ray and L. Donohew (Eds.), *Communication and health: Systems and applications* (pp. 3–8). Mahwah, NJ: Lawrence Erlbaum and Associates.

Dooley, A. R., & Skinner, W. (1977). Casing casemethod methods. *Academy of Management Review, 2*, 277–288.

Dreher, B., & Kreps, G. L. (1990). Balancing the human equation: An expanded case study method. *Gerontology and Geriatrics Education, 10*, 63–72.

Dunne, D., & Brooks, K. (2004). *Teaching with cases.* Halifax, Nova Scotia, Canada: Society for Teaching and Learning in Higher Education.

du Pré, A. (2008). Applied health communication [book review]. *Health Communication, 23*, 492–494.

du Pré, A. (2010). *Communicating about health: Current issues and perspectives* (3rd ed.). New York, NY: Oxford University Press.

Egbert, N, Query, J. L., Quinlan, M. M., Savery, C. A., & Martinez, A. R. (in press). (Re) Viewing health communication and related interdisciplinary curricula: Towards a transdisciplinary perspective. In T. L. Thompson, R. Parrott, & J. F. Nussbaum (Eds.). *The handbook of health communication* (2nd ed.). New York, NY: Routledge.

Fairbanks, J., & Candelaria, J. (1998). *Case studies in community health.* New York, NY: Sage.

Fortenberry, J. L., Jr. (2011). *Cases in healthcare marketing.* Sudbury, MA: Jones & Bartlett Publishers.

Freimuth, V. S., Massett, H. A., & Meltzer, W. (2006). A descriptive analysis of 10 years of research published in the Journal of Health Communication. *Journal of Health Communication, 11*, 11–20.

Geist-Martin, P., Ray, E. B., & Sharf, B. F. (2003). *Communicating health: Personal, cultural, and political complexities.* Belmont, CA: Wadsworth/Thomson Learning.

Gwayi-Chore, M. (Ed.). (2010). *Cases in public health communication and marketing* (Vol. 4). Available from http://www.casesjournal.org

Hallett, L., Padmanabhan, N., Pitorak, H., & Roberson, K. (Eds.). (2009). *Cases in public health communication and marketing* (Vol. 3). Available from http://www.casesjournal.org

Harrington, H. (1995). Fostering reasoned decisions: Case-based pedagogy and the professional development of teachers. *Teaching and Teacher Education, 11*, 203–214.

Harter, L. M., & Quick, B. L. (2006). Health communication in practice: A case study approach [book review]. *Health Communication, 20*, 201–203.

Hartman, L. D. (1992). Business communication and the case method: Toward integration in accounting and MBA graduate programs. *Bulletin of the Association for Business Communication, 55*, 41–45.

Joost, A. M., & Meerloom, D. (Eds.). (1963). Communication and mental health [Special issue]. *Journal of Communication, 13*(3).

Keyton, J., & Shockley-Zalabak, P. (2006). Teacher introduction: The case study method as a pedagogical technique. In J. Keyton & P. Shockley-Zalaback (Eds.), *Case studies for organizational communication: Understanding communication processes* (pp. 1–5). Los Angeles, CA: Roxbury Publishing Company.

Kimball, B. A. (1995). *The emergence of case method teaching, 1870s–1990s: A search for legitimate pedagogy.* The Poynter Center for the Study of Ethics and American Institutions, Indiana University.

Kirby, E. L., & McBride, M. C. (2009). Introduction. In E. L. Kirby & M. C. McBride (Eds.), *Gender actualized: Cases in communicatively constructing realities* (pp. xvii–xxiii). Dubuque, IA: Kendall/Hunt Publishing.

Korsch, B. M., Gozzi, E. K., & Francis, V. (1968). Gaps in doctor-patient communication: Doctor-patient interaction and patient satisfaction. *Pediatrics, 42*, 855–871.

Korsch, B. M., & Negrete, V. E. (1972). Doctor-patient communication. *Scientific American, 227*, 66–74.

Kreps, G. L. (Ed.). (1996). Messages and meaning in health communication and health psychology [Special issue]. *Journal of Health Psychology, 1*(3).

Kreps, G. L., Bonaguro, E. W., & Query, J. L., Jr. (1998). The history and development of the field of health communication. In L. D. Jackson & B. K. Duffy (Eds.), *Health communication research: A guide to developments and directions* (pp. 1–15). Westport, CT: Greenwood Press.

Kreps, G. L., & Lederman, L. C. (1985). Using the case method in organizational communication education. Developing students' insight, knowledge, and creativity through experience-based learning and systematic debriefing. *Communication Education, 34*, 358–364.

Kreps, G. L., Query, J. L., Jr., & Bonaguro, E. W. (2008). The interdisciplinary study of health communication and its relationship to communication science. In L. C. Lederman (Ed.), *Beyond these walls: Readings in health communication* (pp. 3–14). New York, NY: Oxford Press.

Kreps, G. L., Sparks, L., & Villagran, M. (Eds.). (2010). Communication education and health promotion [Special issue]. *Communication Education, 59*(3).

Kreps, G. L., & Thornton, B. C. (1992). *Health communication* (2nd ed.). Prospect Heights, IL: Waveland Press.

Lawrence, P. R. (1953). The preparation of case material. In K. Andrews (Ed.), *The case method of teaching human relations and administration* (pp. 215–224). Cambridge, MA: Harvard University Press.

Lynn, L. E., Jr. (1999). *Teaching and learning with cases: A guidebook.* New York, NY: Chatham House Publishers.

May, S. (Ed.). (2006). *Case studies in organizational communication: Ethical perspectives and practices.* Thousand Oaks, CA: Sage.

McAdoo, J., & Nelson, P. (1975). Teaching speech communication via the case method. *Communication Quarterly, 23*, 29–32.

Mier, D. (1982). From concepts to practices: Student case study work in organizational communication. *Communication Education, 31*, 151–154.

Mottern, A., Sogor, L., & Zarbalian, G. (Eds.). (2008). *Cases in public health communication and marketing* (Vol. 2). Available from http://www.casesjournal.org

Neal, H. (1962). *Better communication for better health.* New York, NY: Columbia University Press.

Newey, C. (1987). A case study approach to teaching of materials. *European Journal of Engineering Education, 12*, 59–68.

Noar, S. M., & Palmgreen, P. (2009). Evaluating health communication campaigns: Key issues and alternative approaches [Special issue]. *Communication Methods and Measures, 3*(1–2).

Northouse, L. L., & Northouse, P. G. (1998). *Health communication: Strategies for health professionals* (3rd ed.). Stamford, CT: Appleton & Lange.

Pagano, M. P. (2010). *Interactive case studies in health communication.* Sudbury, MA: Jones and Bartlett Publishers.

Parrott, R. (2004). Emphasizing "communication" in health communication. *Journal of Communication, 54*, 751–787.

Query, J. L. (Ed.). (2002). Health communication and public health: Pedagogical and research insights [Special issue]. *Communication Studies, 53*(4).

Query, J. L. (Ed.). (2003). *Communication Studies, 54*(1).

Query, J. L., Wright, K. B., Bylund, C., & Mattson, M. (2007). Health communication instruction: Towards identifying common learning goals, course content, and pedagogical strategies. *Health Communication, 21*, 133–141.

Ratzan, S. C. (1993). Health communication and AIDS: Setting the agenda. In S. C. Ratzan (Ed.), *AIDS: Effective health communication for the 90s* (pp. 1–11). Washington, DC: Taylor & Francis.

Ratzan, S. C. (Ed.). (1994). Health communication: Challenges for the 21st century [Special issue]. *American Behavioral Scientist, 38*(2).

Ratzan, S. C. (1996). Introduction. *Journal of Health Communication: International Perspectives, 1*, v–vii.

Ratzan, S. C., Payne, J. G., & Bishop, C. (1996). The status and scope of health communication. *Journal of Health Communication: International Perspectives, 1*, 25–41.

Ray, E. B. (Ed.). (1993). *Case studies in health communication.* Hillsdale, NJ: Lawrence Erlbaum and Associates.

Ray, E. B (Ed.). (1996). *Case studies in communication and disenfranchisement: Applications to social health issues.* Mahwah, NJ: Lawrence Erlbaum and Associates.

Ray, E. B. (Ed.). (2005). *Health communication in practice: A case study approach.* Mahwah, NJ: Lawrence Erlbaum and Associates.

Robinson, J. D. (1993). Case studies in health communication [book review]. *Health Communication, 5*, 309–310.

Robinson, J. D. (1998). Communication and disenfranchisement: Social health issues and implications/ Case studies in communication and disenfranchisement: Social health issues and implications [book review]. *Health Communication, 10*, 103–105.

Rogers, E. M. (1994). The field of health communication today. *American Behavioral Scientist, 38*, 208–214.

Rogers, E. M. (1996). An up-to-date report. *Journal of Health Communication, 1*, 15–23.

Ruesch, J. (1961). *Therapeutic communication.* New York, NY: Norton.

Ruesch, J. (1963). The role of communication in therapeutic transactions. *Journal of Communication, 13*, 132–139.

Ruesch, J., & Bateson, G. (1951). Values, communication, and culture. In J. Ruesch & G. Bateson (Eds.), *Communication: The social matrix of psychiatry* (pp. 3–20). New York, NY: Norton.

Schnell, J. A. (2003). *Case studies in culture and communication: A group perspective.* Lanham, MD: Lexington Books.

Scott, N. (2007). An evaluation of the effects of using case method on student learning outcomes in a Tourism strategic planning course. *Journal of Teaching in Travel & Tourism, 7*, 21–34.

Sharf, B. F. (1993). Reading the vital signs: Research in health care communication. *Communication Monographs, 60*, 35–41.

Smith, D. (Ed.). (1988). Valued in health communication [Special issue]. *Journal of Applied Communication Research, 16*(1).

Sypher, B. D. (1990). Introduction. In B. D. Sypher (Ed.), *Case studies in organizational communication* (pp. 1–13). New York, NY: The Guilford Press.

Sypher, B. D. (1997). Introduction. In B. D. Sypher (Ed.), *Case studies in organizational Communication 2: Perspectives on contemporary work life* (pp. 1–10). New York, NY: The Guilford Press.

Taylor, J. R., & Van Every, E. J. (2010). *The situated organization: Case studies in the pragmatics of communication research.* New York, NY: Routledge.

Thompson, T. L. (2010). Welcome to the 100th issue of *Health Communication! Health Communication, 25,* 483–486.

Thompson, T. L., Robinson, J. D., Anderson, D. J., & Federowicz, M. (2008). Health communication: Where have we been and where can we go? In K. B. Wright & S. Moore (Eds.), *Applied health communication* (pp. 3–33). Cresskill, NJ: Hampton Press.

U.S. Department of Health, Education, and Welfare. (1963). *Surgeon General's conference on health communication, November 5–8, 1962.* Public Health Service Publication 998. Washington, DC: United States Public Service.

Watzlawick, P., Beavin, J. B., & Jackson, D. D. (1967). *Pragmatics of human communication: A study of interactional patterns, pathologies, and paradoxes.* New York, NY: Norton.

Weil, S., Oyelere, P., Yeoh, J., & Firer, C. (2001). A study of students' perceptions of the usefulness of case studies for the development of finance and accounting-related skills and knowledge. *Accounting Education, 10,* 123–146.

Wright, K. B., & Moore, S. D. (Eds.). (2008). *Applied health communication.* Cresskill, NJ: Hampton Press.

SECTION I

Experiencing Challenging Provider-Patient Communication Interactions

CHAPTER 2

No Time to Grieve

Losing My Life's Love and Regaining My Own Strength

Maria Brann

KEY TERMS

Coping with loss

Traditional provider-patient roles

Active patient participation

Identity

Abstract

Miscarriage is one of the most common health experiences women (and men) face, and the loss of an unborn child can have far-reaching effects on those coping with the loss. The communication surrounding the loss, or impending loss, of a child can affect the psychological and physical well-being of those involved. Unfortunately, some health care providers often do not know how to communicate with patients who are experiencing loss or other traumatic events (Gillotti, Thompson, & McNeilis, 2002), which further supports the need for patients to take an active role in their health care interactions to guide providers and receive the care they need. This case study focuses on the traditional and active patient experiences of one woman seeking "care" from a health care provider during her most difficult time: the loss of an unborn child. This loss, and its communication, were my own.

Each day patients seek care from a health care provider, and in many instances, patients follow the same routine they have every time they visit: they passively follow the provider's instructions. As patients, many have been socialized to accept this traditional role, which may hinder us from participating, to the preferred extent, in our own health care interactions. This role, and its accompanying muted communication, could have negative physical and psychological outcomes. However, the onus is not on any one party. Health care providers and patients share responsibility for communicating effectively with one another, which is paramount, and exceptionally difficult, when coping during traumatic events. In this case study, I describe my experience of losing my life's love while regaining strength to endure and persevere during, and after, the loss of my first child. I briefly highlight the silenced topic of miscarriage; describe the participatory nature of active patients; give voice to the health care providers and myself by detailing our effective, and ineffective, communication; as well as discuss my transforming identity during, and after, the interaction.

The Overwhelming Silence

Miscarriage, the loss of a baby before 20 weeks' gestation, occurs daily. Every year, more than half a million pregnant women in the United States experience a miscarriage (Church, 2004). It has been reported that between 25% and 35% of pregnant women knowingly lose a child to miscarriage, particularly within the first 12 weeks of pregnancy (Church, 2004). However, the number of miscarriages may actually be more than 50% of pregnancies because nearly 25% of pregnant women lose babies before they realize that they are pregnant (i.e., first one to two weeks of pregnancy when there is a 75% chance of miscarriage; Wang et al., 2003). Given the alarming statistics, it is highly likely that a woman may experience a miscarriage, and that many women and men, knowingly or unknowingly, have communicated with someone who has had a miscarriage. It is the overwhelming silence society has placed on this topic that keeps many individuals from knowing, understanding, sharing, and being comforted during such a tragic event. Still, as noted by Ross and Geist (1997), "a loss, no matter when it occurs, deserves to be acknowledged" (p. 181), but the silence forces women to suffer alone, triggering even more pain (Church, 2004).

Although the physical body can heal from a miscarriage fairly quickly, the psychological pain usually takes longer for recovery. This psychological pain can affect every person touched by the loss of the child: mother, father, sibling, or friend. Relationships, in particular, have the potential to change—positively, ambiguously, and negatively—when experiencing and communicating about the loss. Specifically, mothers who lose children are said to be the most affected group of people to deal with loss and often experience deteriorating physical health and suffer from depression and its many effects (Znoj & Keller, 2002). Women who identify themselves as mothers experience similar emotional outcomes from the loss of a child even if others do not recognize the woman as a mother (e.g., pregnant women who have not yet given birth). Like others who must cope with death, mothers attempt to "make sense" of the loss (Shapiro, 1993), or the impending loss, through their communication with others. This process can help restore the physical, mental, and social health of the living.

During, and after, the loss of a child, parents often turn to loved ones and health care providers for understanding, empathy, and support. Unfortunately, some of those trained to provide care often do not have the interpersonal skills necessary to communicate effectively with individuals facing loss or other traumatic events (Gillotti et al., 2002). Thus, patients have a responsibility, to the extent possible, to communicate effectively during their health care interactions to influence the quality of care and outcomes of the interaction (Cegala & Post, 2009; Street, 2001). Such effectiveness may be an elusive goal, however, due to the particular trauma.

Challenging the Traditional Role

Cegala (2005) stated, "The process and outcomes of physician-patient encounters are a function of what *both* physicians and patients communicatively contribute to the event" (p. 8).

Much of the research focuses on the role and skills of physicians in the interaction (Street, 2001); however, knowing that health care processes and outcomes are dependent upon the behaviors of both parties provides a rationale for ideally encouraging patients to become active participants in their health care, especially when health care providers are not meeting the needs of the patient.

As Haidet (2010) notes, "To become an active participant is to challenge a role our society has constructed for patients" (p. 197), and that role is to be a passive recipient of information and treatment. Conversely, active health participation has been defined as a person's "degree of participation in his or her own health care and maintenance, including how engaged one is with her or his own illness or health conditions and how one negotiates control of health care decision making with health care providers" (Sharf, Haidet, & Kroll, 2005, p. 49). At least three variables (i.e., predisposing factors, enabling factors, and provider responses) influence the degree to which a patient becomes active in her/his health care interaction.

Patients can be predisposed to engage in active participation. Particularly salient is the belief in this type of communication, importance of the health issue, patient personality, and rapport with the health care provider (Street, 2001). Two enabling factors also influence patients' likelihood of being active in their health care: knowledge of the health issue and assertive communication skills (Street, 2001). Patients who have information about the health issue they are experiencing and knowledge about how to assertively and expressively communicate are more likely to engage in active participation behaviors. Finally, how a health care provider responds to a patient can affect patient behaviors. For example, providers who utilize a patient-centered approach and build partnerships with their patients encourage patients to be more active in their health care (Street, 2001). While all of these variables may influence patients' likelihood of being active participants, other factors may also influence this behavior. For example, patients and health care providers need to recognize the context of the situation (e.g., emergency, planned surgery), identify the type of trauma experienced (e.g., acute, chronic), and consider how the individuals' behaviors may be influenced.

Although there are different ways to be active, one of the most fundamental ways is through communication, which is essential for the progression of the interaction (Cegala & Post, 2009; Street, 2001). Patients can be active by seeking information (e.g., asking questions), providing information (e.g., sharing experiences), using assertive communication (e.g., stating preferences), and expressing concerns (e.g., disclosing emotions). Using these active participatory behaviors has been shown to have a positive impact on quality of care and health outcomes. For example, active participation has been linked with comfort, support, knowledge, satisfaction, and physical health improvements (Greenfield, Kaplan, & Ware, 1985).

Another positive outcome is a sense of ownership and empowerment that comes from the patient participating in her/his health care decisions. Even with the positive outcomes that can emerge from shared decision making, many patients are not as active in their health care decision-making processes as they would like to be. By being active participants, patients encourage health care providers to address patients' needs (Street, 2001). There is, therefore, a great need to educate, encourage, and motivate patients about how to be active participants to empower them and to complement health care providers' medical expertise (Sharf et al., 2005).

The Lamb Becomes the Lion

The cold air chilled my 28-year-old, best-shape-of-my-life body, as I was rushed lying on a stretcher in the middle of the dark night into a brightly lit ambulance with flashing red lights. It was April, and I was in a strange city 863 miles from home attending a professional conference. My pain was unbearable, and the blood pouring from my body was flowing bright red.

"What is happening? Be sensible; you are an educated woman; you know what could be happening. The 7-week-old baby growing inside you is in trouble. It will be okay; it will be okay. God is in control, and He works miracles. I know this doesn't look good, but this will be different; this won't happen to my baby."

The frigid air outside was replaced by the cold stares of strangers inside the hospital's waiting room who were also eager to get behind the double doors of the emergency room (ER). When it was my turn to go through those doors to receive "care," the chill of the night air and the strangers' curious stares were replaced with the cold bed where I lay waiting: bleeding the life out of me. After 13 long hours of being poked and prodded by men learning about my body and my baby, I met my nemesis. That is, the woman who would forever change my perspective of all women in health care, the woman who would influence me to doubt that women share an empathy for other women's pain, the woman who should never be allowed to practice medicine.

She was an obstetrics (OB) resident. Although I don't know how long she had been in this position, it was clear she wasn't a giddy new schoolgirl nor was she a tired, worn-out, ready-to-move-on-to-the-next-rotation resident. As she entered the room, she looked down at 8.5 x 11 white pieces of paper with all the information she thought she needed to know about me already printed. She barely glanced up toward my face as she moved closer, never making eye contact, and simply said, "So you are from out of town?"

"Yes."

"On business; and all alone?"

"Yes."

"So what do you do?"

"I'm a professor."

"Oh, in what?"

And as I started to say "Communication Studies," I quickly questioned myself:

"Do I tell her what I study (i.e., health care providers' communication)? Will this intimidate her and her obvious lack of communicative, both verbal and nonverbal, effectiveness that she has so quickly and clearly exhibited so far? Should I just be assertive and explain to her that I need her to be focused on my baby who appears to be in danger? Should I …?"

It didn't matter. Before I even had the chance to answer, she continued her own conversation. In less than a second from pretending to be concerned, she said, "So I guess your doctor back home told you this wasn't a viable pregnancy. We can go upstairs and take care of this right now."

She didn't want a pregnancy, or a "problem" as it clearly became to her, to interfere with my business *or* her business. This inconvenience could be "taken care of" so we could both continue about our respective careers; after all, we were career women.

As I lay there shocked—and I'm still unsure if it was a dumbfounded feeling I experienced or if I was entering into physical shock as the bright red blood continued to flow from my body—all I could think was: *"No! I just saw my doctor yesterday, and everything was normal. … Snap out of it. Come back. Focus. Tell her this."* So I did: "I just saw my doctor yesterday, and he said everything was normal."

"Oh. Well, I haven't looked at your lab results yet. Maybe I should do that first."

"What?!? Are you kidding me? You haven't even looked at my bloodwork."

And then she walked out the wide-open door into the flow of other health care providers walking back and forth in the hall as they, I assumed, were taking much better care of their patients. At least, I was certain, they were reviewing test results before telling their patients misleading information.

She returned to my room, in the same manner as before, staring at the white papers.

"I didn't realize that you weren't as far along in your pregnancy as I thought. So it is possible that you could be okay."

"Wait. So I am okay. You just told me that we—me and my baby—weren't okay."

I was confused and scared and wanted someone to help me understand. *"Why won't someone just help me?"*

And it was as if she heard my internal monologue. "I'll do an exam to make sure everything is okay, *or* if it's not, we'll know."

"I want to know if everything is okay, but does she really need to do another exam? Can't she just look at all the information collected when I first entered this nightmare from all those other exams from all those men who 'raped' me with their hands and their cotton swabs in the name of learning what is wrong?"

Again, she "heard" my conversation—well, not all of it, but the first question—"I really want to do an exam [*to figure out if she is right*] so just lie back and I'll get started."

She pushed me into doing an exam with her words and her hand as she pressed my right shoulder back to lay me down. Despite her lack of compassion, I still respected her medical expertise, and I wanted to know what was going on. I watched as she pulled long, cold, metal forceps out of a drawer, and I was reminded once again of the evening's chill. She began to open and close them inside of me, pulling blood clots out of my body. No one had ever done this before! Even the invasive male ER resident only used cotton swabs to remove the blood clots. I lay there numb, not saying anything since she was the one who knew what to do. Until, wait, *"Oww! What is going on? Should this be feeling like this?"*

I lay there letting big round tears that I could no longer hold back, trickle down the sides of my temples, and drip into my ear canals as she performed the most painful internal exam of my life. After what seemed like an eternity had passed ... with my legs spread for the entire world to peak in through the open door ... she casually said, "Well, it looks like I got some tissue, which is normal," and then she walked out once again.

"I know you got some tissue because it feels like you scraped my insides out!" As I lay there thinking about her plucking the tissue off of my organs, she slithered back into the room.

"Here is a prescription that will finish the abortion."

"What?" I couldn't move. My mind was frozen. My body had sunk into the bed and made a hole from which I couldn't escape. All I could do was lie there. I just stared at the white drop-ceiling and bright fluorescent lights with tears now streaming down the sides of my cheeks. I didn't hear a word she said. *"Was she still talking? Was she still there?"*

My thoughts became focused again as a short, somewhat rotund nurse shuffled her feet when she walked into the room. I had never seen her before. *"Who is she? Is it shift change, and now I'm going to have to tell a whole new set of nurses why I'm here? What time is it?"*

"Here is your prescription."

"For what?"

She didn't know how to tell me, but her wide eyes said it all. She quickly turned on her heals and nearly sprinted out of the room before I could ask again. *"Where is she going?"* She went to get the *"abortionist"* to explain it all to me again.

"Shut up! Just shut up! I can't listen to you say 'abortion' again. I can't listen to you say, 'Get this prescription filled and finish the abortion. There is no more pregnancy.' Just shut up!"

"I want a phone."

"I'm sorry?"

"I want a phone to call my physician back home. I want to know what is going on."

"Well, we'll see if we can get a nurse to help you out." And she turned and walked out again, but not before I heard her exhale that sigh of "this is going to be a long night." Or maybe it was a sigh of "at least another doctor can deal with her now."

As the nurse brought in the bright red phone with the long cord and the buttons that stuck with each push, I frantically rummaged through my purse to find my personal pocket calendar: the one with the ocean scene on the front that I had chosen because it was serene even if all the commitments inside were not. After I had quickly thumbed through the pages and found the ones with contact names and phone numbers, I forcefully pushed in each number and waited for the button to pop back up.

"Thank you for calling the Physician's Office. How may I help you?"

"Hi. I just saw the doctor yesterday. I'm seven weeks pregnant, and the doctor said everything was okay, but now I am in an ER out of state because I have been bleeding. And I want ..."

"Hold on just a second honey. I'll get the nurse." And I did hold on: to the phone, to the bed, and to hope as I felt like I was running out of things to hold onto in my confused state.

I didn't care that she called me "honey," which under any other circumstance I would have offered a polite, but just-as-condescending response; and I didn't care that she cut me off. I was thankful for the mothering pet name and hurried communication to get me the help I so desperately wanted.

"This is the nurse. How can I help you?"

"I'm seven weeks pregnant. I'm out of town, and I started bleeding so I came to the hospital, and the doctor here wants me to take a prescription. I can't pronounce the name. It is spelled …"

"Whatever you do, do not take that medicine ..."

"I don't want to …"

"It will abort your baby. What did they say?"

"That's what I thought she said. I don't want to. I don't know what to do. She said that the pregnancy wasn't viable and she scraped some tissue and …"

"You should have another ultrasound to see what happened."

"But I've already had one. But I shouldn't take the medicine, right? This will kill my baby, right?"

"Right. Don't take the medicine. If you can, I would come home."

"Okay. Thank you …"

And then the nurse started talking to someone else before completely hanging up the phone: "Oh, that poor girl is all alone in a strange city ..."

"Oh that poor girl. Wait, that poor girl is me." And suddenly I snapped out of it. *"Don't grieve. There's no time. You have to do something. And besides, you don't have anything to grieve about, except maybe the loss of your autonomy."* I couldn't push the nurse call button fast enough or hard enough; it seemed to be plagued with the same problem as the sticky buttons on the phone.

"I want another ultrasound."

"Well the doctor has to order it, and you have already had one."

"I WANT another ultrasound."

"But ..."

"I would like to speak to the physician then so that I can let her know that I would like for her to order another ultrasound for me."

"Let me go get the doctor again."

The OB resident finally came back into the room. "The nurse said you want another ultrasound. You know it will only show that the fetus has been aborted."

I didn't care what she said. I wanted to scream: *My baby is still in there. I would never agree to let you abort my baby. You never even asked!"* Instead, I said, "I know that is what you think, but I am still concerned about what is going on inside my body. I want to see for myself what is going on with my baby. When I visited my doctor yesterday, I told him that I was nervous about flying and traveling so far away. He did an ultrasound and said that everything was normal and I should not worry about traveling. I don't understand how things could change so quickly. I would like another ultrasound so I can see what is going on."

"You will be charged for it."

"I would like another ultrasound."

She didn't say yes, or no. But as the hours ticked away, I was even more determined not to leave until I had my ultrasound.

Finally, two younger nurses came into my room, and without saying a word, wheeled my bed down the hallway to a large elevator. As I listened to the ding of the passing of each floor, I couldn't help but think, *"These people hate me. They think I don't get it. But I don't care. I'm a mom, and like a lioness who will devour anything that threatens her cub, I must protect my innocent baby."*

I got the ultrasound I demanded, and the answer I was seeking: the baby was still there, unharmed, even with all of the poking, prodding, and scraping. The *"abortionist"* who wanted to end the problem quickly and swiftly had met her match—the determined mother and the strong baby.

Losing, Gaining, and Transforming Identity

My miracle and the ability to assertively communicate my needs, however, were short-lived. As I slowly walked to my own bed after an exhausting plane ride of 863 miles, I felt a release of my body. All hope was lost as the lifeless body inside of me slipped out of my womb and into the world. I sank to the floor, sobbing in my husband's cradled arms. I was no longer the woman who saw beauty in everything in the world, who enjoyed life's simple pleasures. I was now the woman who was "pissed off" at the world, and most importantly, enraged with the woman in the strange city who started this downward spiral of losing my identity as a confident mother to becoming an unsure woman. Much as I changed from the powerless patient to the assertive advocate in that distant city, I would also gain a new identity of someone who was powerful, but not all-powerful; of someone who was knowledgeable, but not all-knowing; of someone who loved, but was not all-loving.

I realize now that the moment when the nurse brought in the prescription and quickly left my room, I began to assert some control over my loss (and transform into the active patient), even though I didn't understand what loss there might be. In my mind, the greatest loss at the time was my autonomy. It had been stripped from me, and I wanted it back. That was when I began to actively communicate my needs (e.g., a telephone to call my physician). Overhearing the nurse on the phone helped me, as fortunately, I (the assertive woman) began to come back. Hearing the pity of the nurse and realizing that I didn't want to be "that poor girl" motivated me to snap out of my stupor and begin to take some control. The scared patient retreated, at least temporarily, and the patient advocate returned. I recognized my need to squelch the scared patient and make my voice heard in the silence surrounding me and every other person coping with an impending miscarriage. I was assertive in my request for another ultrasound, although "the expert" said that it would only show that the baby had been aborted. I didn't care what she said, and as an active patient participant, I had to make my voice heard. I had to be assertive, I had to ask questions and clarify information, I had to express my concerns, and I had to share my narrative.

As I was returning home early based on my physician's advice, I was still confused, unsure of whom I was or how my baby was doing, and the scared patient began to resurface once again. I began to think about, and try to make sense of, my experience on the long plane ride home. *"What just happened? What is going to happen?"* I was becoming the new me, and it was through this transformation of feeling alone, scared, powerless, confident, ashamed, and rejuvenated that I decided to make decisions that would benefit my life and health, and hopefully, the lives and health of other women as well. It was my decision to educate physicians about the importance of communication and empathy, but more importantly, to educate other women to take control, assert themselves, own their identities, and make empowering decisions (Sharf & Vanderford, 2003), particularly by being active patient participants.

I don't know if I would have recognized the need to be an active patient if I hadn't experienced such heartache, and I don't know if I was as active as I wanted to be given the trauma I was experiencing. It is my hope, though, that by sharing this loss and personal transformation, it may serve to further heal the teller. And by reflecting on this scholar's narrative, as well as her patient, wife, and mom roles, it may provide guidance to others who care for, and about, the human spirit. It is imperative that we recognize the stigma society has perpetuated by continuing to silence discussions of miscarriage, which erodes the compassionate communication that is so desperately needed during these types of traumatic events. Until these voices are heard, it will be difficult to actively participate in our own health care.

Discussion Questions

1. How would you feel if you were in this patient's situation? How would you have communicated with the health care provider (e.g., what would you have said? how would you have acted?)? Or how would you have reacted and communicated with the health care provider if it was your partner in the situation?

2. What specific communicative behaviors did the patient enact to illustrate active participation?

3. How did the differing communicative behaviors affect all of the parties involved in the interaction? How might the interaction have been altered if the patient would have shared her thoughts with the provider?

4. How could the outcomes (e.g., physical, mental, and social health) have been altered if active communicative behaviors were enacted earlier in the interaction?

5. How might the emotional intensity of coming to grips with the potential loss of a child affect the communicative behaviors of a patient? How might the communication be different with a less emotionally charged outcome?

6. How could the health care provider have encouraged the patient to be active in the health care interaction? How might the health care provider's experiences have affected her communication during the interaction?

References

Cegala, D. J. (2005). The first three minutes. In E. B. Ray (Ed.), *Health communication in practice: A case study approach* (pp. 3–10). Mahwah, NJ: Lawrence Erlbaum Associates.

Cegala, D. J., & Post, D. M. (2009). The impact of patients' participation on physicians' patient-centered communication. *Patient Education and Counseling, 77*, 202–208.

Church, L. (2004). *Hope is like the sun: Finding hope and healing after miscarriage, stillbirth, and infant death.* Hampton, VA: HopeXchange Publishing.

Gillotti, C., Thompson, T., & McNeilis, K. (2002). Communicative competence in the delivery of bad news. *Social Science & Medicine, 54*, 1011–1023.

Greenfield, S., Kaplan, S. H., & Ware, Jr., J. E. (1985). Patients' participation in medical care: Effects on patient outcome. *Annals of Internal Medicine, 102*, 520–528.

Haidet, P. (2010). No longer silent: On becoming an active patient. *Health Communication, 25*, 195–197.

Ross, J. L., & Geist, P. (1997). Elation and devastation: Women's journeys through pregnancy and miscarriage. In L. A. M. Perry & P. Geist (Eds.), *Courage of conviction: Women's words, women's wisdom* (pp. 167–184). Mountain View, CA: Mayfield.

Sharf, B. F., Haidet, P., & Kroll, T. L. (2005). "I want you to put me in the grave with all my limbs:" The meaning of active health participation. In E. B. Ray (Ed.), *Health communication in practice: A case study approach* (pp. 39–51). Mahwah, NJ: Lawrence Erlbaum Associates.

Sharf, B. F., & Vanderford, M. L. (2003). Illness narratives and the social construction of health. In T. L. Thompson, A. M. Dorsey, K. I. Miller, & R. Parrott (Eds.), *Handbook of health communication* (pp. 9–34). Mahwah, NJ: Lawrence Erlbaum Associates.

Shapiro, C. H. (1993). *When part of the self is lost: Helping clients heal after sexual and reproductive losses.* San Francisco: Jossey-Bass.

Street, Jr., R. L. (2001). Active patients as powerful communicators: The linguistic foundation of participation in health care. In W. P. Robinson & H. Giles (Eds.), *The new handbook of language and social psychology* (2nd ed., pp. 541–560). Chichester, UK: John Wiley.

Wang, X., Chen, C., Wang, L., Chen, D., Guang, W., & French, J. (2003). Conception, early pregnancy loss, and time to clinical pregnancy: A population-based prospective study. *Fertility and Sterility, 79*, 577–584.

Znoj, H. J., & Keller, D. (2002). Mourning parents: Considering safeguards and their relation to health. *Death Studies, 26*, 545–565.

CHAPTER 3

Problematic Interactions Between Physicians and Deaf Patients

Lance S. Rintamaki, David M. Peek, and Elizabeth Karras

KEY TERMS

Deaf

Health care

Physician-patient communication

Intergroup communication model

Abstract

Physician-patient communication is central to the field of health communication, with recent work in this area highlighting problems some patients experience during physician-patient interactions. This chapter presents a case about problematic interactions Deaf patients report having with physicians. The case was developed based on a combination of (a) existing literature on Deaf patient health care experiences, (b) findings from an ongoing study on problematic physician-patient interactions reported by Deaf individuals, and (c) the clinical experiences of a physician who regularly works with Deaf patients. This case study illustrates the complexity of these exchanges through multiple viewpoints. As the reader, your job will be to identify the multiple perspectives involved, the reasons why certain events may occur as they do, and the subsequent impact these exchanges have on the interactants' emotional and behavioral outcomes.

Physician-patient communication constitutes one of the oldest and most prominent genres of research within the field of health communication (e.g., Ong, de Haes, Hoos, & Lammes, 1995; Thompson, Robinson, Anderson, & Federowicz, 2008). Physician-patient interactions are particularly important as they shape the types and quality of patients' health behaviors (e.g., if patients properly take their medications), clinical outcomes (e.g., if patients remain healthy or unhealthy), satisfaction with care (e.g., if patients are happy or unhappy with their physicians), and pursuit of litigation (i.e., whether patients sue their physicians) (e.g., Brown, Stewart, & Ryan, 2003; Fiscella et al., 2004; Levinson, Roter, Mullooly, Dull, & Frankel, 1997; Topacoglu et al., 2004). Despite the vast literature already compiled on physician-patient communication, this body of work continues to expand and will play a central role in the future of health communication research (see Sparks & Villagran, 2010).

Problems and dilemmas experienced by disenfranchised minority group members in health care contexts (e.g., people from minority racial and ethnic groups, gays and lesbians, living with HIV) have received more research attention since the mid 1990s (e.g., Ray, 1996; Frey, Adelman, Flint, & Query, 2000; Rintamaki, Scott, Kosenko, & Jensen, 2007; Röndahl, Innala, & Carlsson, 2006; Trivedi & Ayanian, 2006). One context that involves a number of challenging, multi-faceted issues is Deaf people's experiences with health care and their accounts of interactions with physicians. For those who perceive their deafness as a way of life and major contributor to their sense of self, they identify as Deaf with a capital "D." In contrast, those who perceive their deafness as a medical problem requiring therapeutic intervention by the medical community identify as deaf with a lowercase "d." For consistency, cultural Deafness (Deaf with a capital "D") will be the label used to describe Deaf patients[1] throughout this chapter.

Up to 16% of Americans have some degree of hearing loss (Agrawal, Platz, & Niparko, 2008). As with many people who are physically, linguistically, and socially distinct from the larger population, this group has converged and developed its own community, giving rise to what is now recognized as Deaf culture (Coopman, 2003). Although some research exists on communication and disability (e.g., Thompson, 2000), which includes linguistic minorities (e.g., McIntosh, 2000; Rose & Smith, 2000), few investigations focus on the health communication needs of Deaf people (see Thompson et al., 2008).

Deaf individuals are highly reliant on health care, often more so than hearing-abled people.[2] Deaf people visit physicians more frequently, are impaired by illness and injury more often, and view themselves as less healthy than hearing-abled people (e.g., Zazove et al., 1993).[3] Increased reliance on health care heightens the importance of good working relationships and communication with physicians, which can lead to improved health and well-being (Brown et al., 2003). When patients can effectively communicate with their physicians, they are more likely to engage in important health behaviors, such as being screened for illnesses and taking their medications properly (e.g., Hajek, Villagran, & Wittenberg-Lyles, 2007); however, there are a number of daunting barriers facing Deaf patients when communicating with physicians.

Barriers to Effective Physician-Patient Communication

Many Deaf and hard of hearing people in the United States, for example, communicate primarily through American Sign Language (ASL). Although ASL is the fourth most common language in the United States, few health care professionals are proficient in ASL (Kaskowitz, Nakaji, Clark, Gunsauls, & Sadler, 2006). Similarly, few doctors receive training regarding Deaf cultural issues, which can leave many Deaf patients feeling misunderstood by their physicians (Harmer, 1999). Subsequently, some research suggests that Deaf people are the most likely of all non-English speaking minorities to report poor interactions with their physicians (McEwen & Anton-Culver, 1988).

In the absence of ASL interpreters or a physician who can sign, many Deaf patients struggle to understand their physicians (e.g., Zazove et al., 1993). These language barriers often make it difficult for physicians to understand and properly treat their Deaf patients (Barnett & Franks, 2002). ASL interpreters can be employed during appointments and eliminate some of the communication barriers present for Deaf patients and their physicians. Unfortunately, however, interpreter availability and cost can serve as a barrier to their use (Harmer, 1999). When trained ASL interpreters are unavailable, some doctors may urge friends or family who sign ASL to interpret during visits, which can disrupt the patient's privacy (See Chapter 4, this volume, for somewhat similar issues). Imagine, for instance, if you had to come in to discuss an issue of reproductive or sexual health with your physician, while your mom, dad, or a younger sibling was translating in place of a medical interpreter. As with other medical contexts in which people other than the patient can communicate directly with the physician (without an interpreter), having hearing-abled family members present can also result in physicians directing conversation at the family member or interpreter (those with whom the physician can communicate), which can leave Deaf patients feeling spoken about, rather than spoken to.

In addition to translation issues, a serious conflict arises regarding disparities in cultural and medical orientations toward Deafness. Culturally Deaf people perceive their Deafness as a trait and part of their identity, whereas physicians frequently perceive Deafness as a pathology to be cured (Barnett & Franks, 2002). These views can lead to mistrust of medical professionals by the Deaf community.

In addition, the modern health care system is based on efficiency, seeking to identify and address health concerns with an economy of time and effort (Miller & Ryan, 2001). Deaf culture, however, is the opposite with regards to directness and use of time. Deaf communication patterns are often circular in style; that is, they employ expansive story-telling and extensive emotional expressions to convey meaning (Frew, 2002). Tensions arising from these cultural differences may lead to considerable misunderstanding and frustration between Deaf patients and hearing-abled health care providers.

Physician-Patient Interaction as Intergroup Communication

Given the different social groups involved (i.e., Deaf patients and hearing-abled physicians), communication between Deaf patients and their physicians can be viewed from an intergroup perspective. Rintamaki and Brashers (2010) suggest an intergroup communication model for framing how members of disenfranchised social groups (e.g., Deaf patients) and more affluent groups (e.g., hearing-abled physicians) interact. Unlike previous intergroup work that tends to focus on the actions or motivations of only one group, this model emphasizes the need to understand the cognitive (i.e., feelings and perspectives) and behavioral (i.e., actions taken) processes from both groups during these problematic exchanges. As such, Rintamaki and Brashers use this model to encourage understanding and appreciation of the perspectives of patients and the physicians during these encounters, as well as explain why each participant engages in specific actions. In the current context, this model reveals the sensitivity and frustration experienced by Deaf patients during these interactions, as well as a more holistic appreciation for physicians' intentions and behaviors with their patients.

Some insight into Deaf patients' perspectives during these encounters can be gleaned from the current intergroup literature. Perhaps as a result of their experiences with bias and discrimination, individuals who belong to disenfranchised groups such as the Deaf are shown to develop a heightened sensitivity to behaviors that may indicate the presence of prejudice or discrimination (Frable, Blackstone, & Scherbaum, 1990). Disenfranchised individuals are more prone to interpret ambiguous behaviors as indicative of stigma rather than other equally plausible explanations (e.g., Crocker & Major, 1989). For instance, if one belongs to a disenfranchised group and first meets a physician who seems a little terse or despondent, the patient may interpret that behavior as stigmatizing and indicative of some bias, even though a variety of reasonable explanations exist such as: The physician has a headache, is having a bad day, has just received disturbing news (e.g., the death of another patient), and/or was recently reprimanded by an administrator for spending too much time with patients. As such, even well-intentioned physicians may, then, inadvertently exhibit behaviors that Deaf patients interpret negatively. Subsequently, Deaf patients' sensitivity to bias may lead them to interpret benign actions of physicians as discriminatory.

Understanding the physician perspective in these contexts is useful for a multitude of reasons. Physician perspectives can provide insight into the training medical professionals receive and systems in which they work, which may explain many health care provider behaviors that could appear odd to the nonclinical eye. Actions that may be perceived as problematic from the patient perspective may be done by clinicians specifically for the patient's benefit. In the context of HIV, for instance, clinicians often wear protective equipment designed to limit patient's risks for infection but failure to explain the purpose of these precautions can leave some HIV-positive patients feeling stigmatized and distrustful of their providers (Rintamaki et al., 2007). In addition, system constraints (e.g., a hospital failing to provide an ASL interpreter during consultations with Deaf patients) may be blamed on the clinical team, despite their best efforts to provide high quality care for their Deaf patients.

Problematic Physician-Patient Interactions

Accordingly, the purpose of the proposed case study is to depict problematic interactions (i.e., aspects of the physician-patient exchange that impair effective information transfer, violate professional standards of physician conduct, or provoke emotional upset in the patient) experienced by Deaf patients when working with physicians. The case revolves around the perspectives of two participants in the health care interaction. Presented first is Todd's perspective, a young Deaf man. Todd visits the general internal medicine department at a university hospital since he fears he may have cancer. The second perspective is that of David, a medical student in his fourth year of clinical training. David is part of the clinical team that provides care for Todd. The entire scene, including the problematic interactions experienced by Todd and the perceptions of David regarding these same events, is based on a combination of (a) the literature previously reviewed, (b) findings from an on-going study on problematic physician-patient interactions reported by Deaf patients,[4] and (c) the clinical experiences of a physician who, as a medical student, witnessed numerous problematic interactions between clinicians and Deaf patients (the second author).[5]

In an on-going study of problematic provider-patient interactions reported by Deaf patients, we conducted six focus group interviews ($n = 39$; average group size of six members), and administered surveys ($n = 366$) with Deaf people regarding their problematic experiences in health care contexts. Participants' responses to open-ended questions about the types of problematic interactions they had experienced with physicians were coded by two research team members using latent content and constant comparative techniques (Charmaz, 2006; Glaser, 1992). In sum, Deaf participants described eight problematic encounter types, including:

- physicians rushing through appointments,
- physicians failing to provide ASL interpreters during consultations,
- Deaf patients believing they were treated poorly by the physician specifically because they are Deaf (i.e., perceived intentional discrimination),
- Deaf patients believing they were treated by physicians as less important than hearing-abled patients,
- physicians sharing confidential medical information with third parties (e.g., family members) without first consulting the Deaf patient for permission,
- physicians not understanding Deafness,
- physicians failing to even attempt communication with Deaf patients, and
- physicians pressuring Deaf patients (e.g., regarding treatment options).

Several of these problematic interactions are presented during Todd's experience. Some of the problematic exchanges were the result of frustrated residents who were hurried or irritated at having to work with a Deaf patient. The second author also noticed events during his medical training that appeared to frustrate Deaf patients and may have been misattributed as degrading or stigmatizing but were, in fact, the product of good intentions or clinical need. Insights gained from his experiences are presented through the perspective of the medical student, David.

Throughout the case study, we strive to illustrate the complexity of these exchanges. As the reader, your job will be to identify the multiple perspectives involved, the reasons why certain events occur, and the subsequent impact these exchanges have on the interactants' emotional and behavioral outcomes. This approach underscores the importance of research and in-depth assessment of physician-patient communication, and seeks to demonstrate how single events can be widely and inaccurately interpreted.

Todd's Perspective

Early last week, Todd discovered a small lump just under the angle of his right jaw. As someone in his early twenties, his first impulse was to assume it was not serious and that it would go away on its own. As the days passed and the lump remained, however, he began to wonder if it could be something more serious. He hated visiting physicians, given the number of frightening memories he had of doctors from his childhood. Still, he knew having the lump checked was a smart decision, so he mustered the courage to use IP-relay (i.e., a video system through which a relay interpreter communicates to the voice caller and then signs the voice user's responses back to the Deaf caller; http://www.ip-relay.com/index.php) to set up an appointment the next morning at the University Hospital out-patient clinic.

Todd arrived at the hospital clinic the next morning 15 minutes early for his appointment. He approached the receptionist, handed her his cell phone and pointed to the message he had typed. The message stated his name, that he was Deaf, that he was there for his appointment, and the number for a medical ASL interpreter if they had not already called for one. The receptionist merely smiled and wrote down Todd's information before gesturing for him to have a seat. He found a chair and started texting friends to pass time, beginning with his brother. Todd let him know he had stopped by the hospital to have something checked out and not to expect him for their usual pick-up basketball game later that morning.

An hour passed, during which Todd watched as other patients who arrived after him were shown back to the examination rooms. He hated feeling paranoid, but he always wondered if he was made to wait longer than other patients because he was Deaf. Some time later, a tall man in a short, white coat walked into the waiting room. The man smiled at Todd and held the door open, nodding with his head and gesturing to welcome Todd back to the examination rooms. Given that an ASL interpreter was not with the tall man, Todd assumed one would not be coming. It was not the first time this had happened to him, and he knew it would make communicating with the doctor difficult. Still, he was eager to move ahead, even if it meant having to write out everything with the doctors.

The man took Todd to a bright, compact room, where a small and intense-looking woman sat at a desk, waiting for him. Todd sat along side the desk, facing the woman, while the tall man moved to sit on a stool along the wall. The woman, who Todd assumed was the physician, though she did not introduce herself, smiled briefly before pushing a piece of paper and pen towards him. Todd signed a greeting in ASL, but as he suspected, she looked apologetic and shook her head, indicating that she could not sign back. She then lifted up a piece of paper, on which were written a series of questions. She pointed to the top one, which read, "What brings you in today?"

Todd pointed to the small lump on his neck. The doctor rubbed her own throat, then mouthed the words, "sore throat?" Although Todd is not great at lip-reading, her words were as clear to Todd as the question was off-target. Todd shook his head and pointed again at his neck, trying to pinpoint the lump. The doctor paused for a moment, then scribbled on her pad, "feeling something stuck?" He shook his head again, trying once more to point out the lump, this time circling it with his finger. He leaned forward a little, offering his neck for her to feel it, but instead the doctor pointed to the paper, instructing him to write.

Following her terse expression and quick, jerky hand movements, Todd sensed she was already frustrated by this form of exchange. He sighed to himself but began writing out an explanation: About a week ago, he was shaving and discovered a small lump on his neck. The doctor watched every word as it was written, but interrupted him before he could complete his explanation. She scribbled out a series of yes or no questions on her own pad and placed it in front of him to answer. He was quick to respond, but these seemed mundane and unimportant compared to the question he most wanted to ask.

As the doctor reviewed his responses, Todd decided to raise his primary concern and wrote in large letters, "Do I have cancer?" He pointed again to the small lump on his neck. This time, the doctor looked at his neck and peered intently. She reached over and carefully inspected the lump, tenderly pressing her fingers against it, tracing its size and probing its edges. After the inspection, Todd watched her carefully, but she appeared calm. She raised her eyebrows and said something he could not make out, but her open hands seemed to ask, "Is that all?" Todd was relieved by her lack of concern over the lump, relaxing as he nodded his head.

Todd watched the physician place her hand against her temple, as though rubbing a stubborn headache, close her eyes, take a breath, and then say something to the tall man against the wall. As the two clinicians kept talking, Todd found himself becoming more anxious again. He motioned to her to write down what they were saying, but she just shook her hands as though to communicate, "you don't need to know this." Frustrated, Todd thought to himself, "*If I could hear and you two were whispering to each other, that would be rude. How's this any different?*" Todd persisted, his anxiety increasing, until the physician relented and turned to speak with him directly. She did not write anything down, instead mouthing her words slowly to allow him to read her lips. He did his best to follow; however, his ASL was much better than his lip-reading. Exasperated, he held up his finger as if requesting her to stop, then pointed to the paper.

The physician wrote on her pad of paper that he needed a series of tests and a referral to another doctor, but first she would need to complete a physical exam. After Todd sat on the examination table, the physician provided a series of simple, nonverbal instructions without using the notepad, such as opening her mouth wide when she wanted him to do the same. He followed along fairly well, only twice confused about what she needed. The first time was when she wanted him to take off his shirt (she gestured uselessly a few times before finally pulling up on his shirt hems). The second time was when she wanted him to lie on his back (she alternately stuck one hand up flat, tapped on his chest, and pushed him backwards before he understood her meaning).

Todd was lying on the examination table when the doctor stopped what she was doing and looked away. Then, to Todd's surprise, his mom and dad entered the room. While his dad began speaking with the physician, his mother came up and signed to Todd. "Are you feeling alright?" she asked. "Your brother told me you were at the hospital, so I worried there was something serious." Todd's aunt died of cancer two years ago, and he knew that event had devastated his mom. He did not want her to know about the lump because he did not want to scare her, especially since the physician's demeanor suggested it was nothing to be concerned about. He saw the doctor and his dad talking at length, and asked his mom what they were discussing. "He's telling her you had chronic bronchitis as a kid, you're allergic to bee stings, and about Aunt Sarah's death. Usual doctor stuff." Todd wanted to downplay any cancer concerns his mom might have, but before he could do so, his dad stepped in, signing,

"The doctor wants to biopsy that lump, just to make sure it's nothing serious." Todd and his mom exchanged looks, each quickly signing questions and reassurances to each other about what biopsies entail, the likely insignificance of the lump, and how the entire process would probably be finished quickly. Just then, Todd saw his parents' heads snap in the direction of the physician. Todd saw the physician speaking again, who then gestured to the tall man in the white coat before walking out the door. When he saw the looks on his parents' faces, he realized something might be very wrong.

David's Perspective

In the fourth year of his medical program, David was well accustomed to the quick pace of the typical rounds[6] at University Hospital. Nonetheless, David had to move at a brisk pace to keep up with the resident physician, Dr. Zee, to whom he was currently assigned. After three years of residency,[7] Dr. Zee had acquired a reputation for being fanatical about staying on schedule; however, David knew that being in charge of the hospital's outpatient clinic that day was sure to test her patience. The clinic often ran behind schedule for a variety of reasons, most of which were outside of Dr. Zee's control. As a testament to that, it was only 8:30 a.m., but the clinical team had already fallen behind, which David knew would place Dr. Zee in a foul mood for the remainder of the day.

With a quick glance at her watch, Dr. Zee scowled and snapped out a series of orders. "We need to be out by 12:30 today, people. David and Marie, you really need your A-games today. Dr. Ekes wants to start afternoon rounds at 1 p.m. on the dot." Without another word, she turned on her heel and set off towards the clinic, the rest of the team racing to keep up.

David set about organizing the medical charts for several patients scheduled that morning. He saw a post-it note on the chart for the 8:30 appointment, bearing the words "DEAF" and "interpreter called." Knowing the impact on Dr. Zee's disposition if the Deaf patient's appointment or waiting for the interpreter delayed the schedule any further, David turned apprehensively to the receptionist. "Patty? Has the interpreter for Todd Johnson arrived yet?" The receptionist's reply was little more than a bland stare. "*Not good*," David murmured to himself.

After bringing Dr. Zee the news, David watched small muscles twitch across her face. "Alright, let's see the 8:45 first." David did as instructed, but when the 8:45 patient was out the door, the interpreter still had not arrived. When David told Dr. Zee the news regarding the still-absent interpreter, she sighed and said, "It'll be hard both on the patient and us if we do this without an interpreter. Alright, let's see the 9:00 and pray that interpreter shows up before we're done." David knew delays with the interpreters were not uncommon, but he hoped this lapse would be shorter than most.

By the time they finished with the 9:00 patient, the interpreter still had not arrived and Dr. Zee did not bother hiding her irritation. She looked through the medical charts and the upcoming appointments and sighed. "David, why don't you go get the 8:30. We'll have to do this in writing. And tell Patty to get the paperwork ready to file another grievance about the ASL interpreters not showing up when they're supposed to."

David went to the lobby and gestured to the young man who was their 8:30 patient to accompany him to the examination room. David saw the weary expression on the young man's face and hoped his own expression showed the patient his sympathy for the delay. David brought him to the examination room, where Dr. Zee waited with a list of anticipated questions. David felt certain she prepped those questions to improve the exam's efficiency so that they could be back on schedule if the exam, and follow-up paperwork, lasted less than 15 minutes (a duration typical of managed care often found in HMOs).

At the start of the consultation, David watched Dr. Zee and the patient scribble messages back and forth, coupled with varied gestures from the patient towards his neck. Then Dr. Zee read one of the messages aloud: "Do I have cancer?" The patient pointed again to his neck, which Dr. Zee inspected. She maintained her demeanor, but David had worked with her long enough to detect the shift in her voice as she asked, "Is that the only one?" The patient nodded his head.

Dr. Zee turned to David and told him to prepare paperwork for a referral, instructing him on which forms he needed and how to organize them. The patient waved to attract their attention, pointing to the pad in front of Dr. Zee. She half-smiled, then waved her hand and said, "It's just administrative stuff." The patient frowned slightly, apparently unsure about what she said, then shook his head. David heard Dr. Zee sigh softly. Yet, she set aside her need to keep on schedule to fully attend to the patient. She then wrote out a complete description of the referral process and why it needed to be done. David felt badly for her. He felt certain she had already spent too much time with this one patient to stay on schedule. The lobby was now likely crowded and the nurses would complain about clinic running past lunch time again. The attending physician[8] would also scold Dr. Zee about poor time management skills, regardless of these circumstances.

Dr. Zee was completing the abdominal exam when she and David heard a knock at the door. Patty popped her head in and said, "Mr. Johnson's parents are here." David breathed a sigh of relief, silently thanking the powers that be. He knew the parents could quickly help him fill in gaps in the patient's medical history and could likely translate in place of the medical interpreter. The parents entered just after Patty. The mother went to her son as the father began speaking with Dr. Zee about his son's well-being. David listened as Dr. Zee avoided answering the initial question about prognosis, then addressed a number of medical history questions she did not cover in-depth with the patient. He noticed her pause when the father mentioned how his sister-in-law died of cancer. When asked again what his son was in for, Dr. Zee explained that their son had a small lump in his neck and she needed to refer him for further exams. This disclosure caught David by surprise because such information is usually not revealed until permission is given explicitly by the adult patient.

"It's most likely benign," Dr. Zee explained, "but it's good just to be certain. I want to get a biopsy today and send it to the lab." The family then began to sign, becoming animated in the process. David watched the resident physician closely, seeing the tension mount in her facial expression as the seconds, then minutes, ticked by. What she said next further startled David, "I'm concerned this might be cancer. I want to rule it out." She told the truth, but David wondered if part of this delivery was out of spite for derailing her schedule. The parents were both stunned by the news, which they slowly signed to their son, who looked shocked and confused. Dr. Zee arose and, before walking out the door, explained that David would assist them with the referral process for the lab work. She exited without shaking anyone's hands. A fourth-year medical student was then left to pick up the pieces of a distraught family in need of answers and support.

NOTES

1 This phrasing is typically used in clinical contexts.

2 A review of the literature will show that hearing people are labeled in a variety of ways. In the prevailing health communication literature, however, we champion the term "able-bodied" for those without impairment and, for this reason, use "hearing-abled" throughout the chapter. This choice, however, is not without controversy. For instance, to avoid any inference of (dis)advantage with this phrasing, when one says "hearing-abled," does it not follow to say "Deaf-abled?" In addition, when speaking with members of the Deaf community, this minor modification is rarely used. It is commonplace to thus refer to people as "Deaf" or "hearing." There is no insult implied by either label. Ultimately, the reader may decide for himself or herself which terminology he or she finds most appropriate.

3 We recognize that the Zazove et al. (1993) citation may appear dated. As we note in the chapter, very little research is actually done with the Deaf population. There are few studies period, let alone those that make these specific claims. To our knowledge, we are providing the most recent citations that support claims made throughout this chapter.

4 The authors possess a combined 15 years of experience working with members of the Deaf community in research or clinical roles.

5 This case study is built, in part, upon data gathered as part of a larger, ongoing study, the full results of which are reported elsewhere (Karras, Rintamaki, & Peek, under review). As such, detailed explanation of the methods and results of this study are not included in the current chapter.

6 Medical rounds are scheduled patient visits from a team of physicians and other health care providers, usually conducted in hospitals or clinical settings.

7 In the United States, medical school provides physicians with a broad understanding of medicine. Medical residency is typically a three- or four-year period following medical school, during which physicians receive in-depth training on a specialized area of medicine (e.g., oncology, surgery, pediatrics).

8 In the United States, attending physicians have completed residency training and practice in a specialized area of medicine, usually in a hospital or clinic setting, where they oversee the provision of all health care for their medical specialty at that facility.

Discussion Questions

1. Why is culture a central factor for physicians to consider when interacting with their Deaf patients?

2. What are ways physicians can communicate and/or demonstrate ally behaviors to their Deaf patients (i.e., verbal and nonverbal strategies that communicate that the physician wants what's best for the patient)? Why do you recommend these behaviors? How are these behaviors culturally competent?

3. Identify and describe one problematic physician-patient interaction for the Deaf. Is it possible for other groups to experience this problem? Could a hearing-abled patient encounter this problematic interaction as well? Explain why.

4. What role does non-verbal communication play in problematic provider-patient interactions for the Deaf?

5. Describe the clash that occurs between the Deaf community and physicians regarding cultural and medical orientations toward deafness and its implications.

References

Agrawal, Y., Platz, E. A., & Niparko, J. K. (2008). Prevalence of hearing loss and differences by demographic characteristics among US adults: Data from the National Health and Nutrition Examination Survey, 1999–2004. *Arch Internal Medicine, 168,* 1522–1530.

Barnett, S., & Franks, P. (2002). Health care utilization and adults who are Deaf: Relationship with age at onset of deafness. *Health Services Research, 37,* 103–118.

Brown, J. B., Stewart, M., & Ryan, B. L. (2003). Outcomes of patient-provider interaction. In T. L. Thompson, A. M. Dorsey, K. I. Miller, & R. Parrott (Eds.), *Handbook of health communication* (pp. 141–161). Mahwah, NJ: Erlbaum.

Charmaz, K. (2006). *Constructing grounded theory: A practical guide through qualitative analysis.* Thousand Oaks, CA: Sage Publications.

Coopman, S. J. (2003). Communicating disability: Metaphors of oppression, metaphors of empowerment. In P. Kalbfleisch (Ed.), *Communication Yearbook 27* (pp. 337–394). Mahwah, NJ: Lawrence Erlbaum Associates.

Crocker, J., & Major, B. (1989). Social stigma and self-esteem: The self-protective properties of stigma. *Psychological Review, 96,* 608–630.

Fiscella, K., Meldrum, S., Franks, P., Shields, C. G., Duberstein, P., McDaniel, S. H., et al. (2004). Patient trust: Is it related to patient-centered behavior of primary care physicians? *Medical Care, 42,* 1049–1055.

Frable, D. E., Blackstone, T., & Scherbaum, C. (1990). Marginal and mindful: Deviants in social interactions. *Journal of Personality & Social Psychology, 59,* 140–149.

Frew, A. W. (2002). Signing and deaf culture. *American Annals of the Deaf, 11,* 24–28.

Frey, L. R., Adelman, M. B., Flint, L. J., & Query, J. L. (2000). Weaving meanings together in an AIDS residence: Communicative practices, perceived health outcomes, and the symbolic construction of community. *Journal of Health Communication, 5,* 53–72.

Glaser, B. (1992). *Basics of grounded theory analysis.* Mill Valley, CA: Sociology Press.

Hajek, C., Villagran, M., & Wittenberg-Lyles, E. (2007). The relationship among perceived physician accommodation, perceived outgroup typicality, and patient inclinations toward compliance. *Communication Research Reports, 24,* 293–302.

Harmer, L. M. (1999). Health care delivery and Deaf people: Practice, problems, and recommendations for change. *Journal of Deaf Studies and Deaf Education, 4,* 73–110.

Kahana, E., & Kahana, B. (2007). Health care partnership model of doctor-patient communication in cancer prevention and care among the aged. In H. D. O'Hair, G. L. Kreps, & L. Sparks (Eds.), *The handbook of communication and cancer care* (pp. 37–54). Cresskill, NJ: Hampton Press.

Karras, E., Rintamaki, L. S., & Peek, D. M. (under review). Problematic physician-patient interactions reported by deaf college students.

Kaskowitz, S. R., Nakaji, M. C., Clark, K. L., Gunsauls, D. C., & Sadler, G. R. (2006). Bringing prostate cancer education to deaf men. *Cancer Detection Prevention, 30,* 439–448

Kreps, G. L. (1988). Relational communication in health care. *Southern Speech Communication Journal, 53,* 344–359.

Levinson, W., Roter, D. L., Mullooly, J. P., Dull, V. T., & Frankel, R. M. (1997). Physician-patient communication: The relationship with malpractice claims among primary care physicians and surgeons. *Journal of the American Medical Association, 277,* 553–559.

McEwen, E., & Anton-Culver, H. (1988). The medical communication of deaf patients. *Journal of Family Practice, 26,* 289–291.

McIntosh, A. (2000). When the deaf and hearing interact: Communication features, relationships and disability issues. In D. O. Braithwaite & T. L. Thompson (Eds.), *Handbook of communication and people with disabilities: Research and application* (pp. 353–368). Mahwah, NJ: Lawrence Erlbaum Associates.

Miller, K. I., & Ryan, D. J. (2001). Communication in the age of managed care: Introduction to the special issue. *Journal of Applied Communication Research, 29,* 91–96.

Ong, L. M., de Haes, J. C., Hoos, A. M., & Lammes, F. B. (1995). Doctor-patient communication: A review of the literature. *Social Science & Medicine, 40,* 903–918.

Query, J. L., & Wright, K. B. (2003). Assessing communication competence in an online study: Toward informing subsequent interventions among older adults with cancer, their lay caregivers, and peers. *Health Communication, 15,* 205–219.

Ray, E., B. (1996). *Communication and disenfranchisement: Social health issues and implications.* Mahwah, NJ: Erlbaum.

Rintamaki, L. S., & Brashers, D. E. (2010). Stigma and intergroup communication. In H. Giles, S. Reid, & J. Harwood (Eds.), *The dynamics of intergroup communication* (pp. 155–166). New York: Peter Lang.

Rintamaki, L. S., Scott, A. M., Kosenko, K. A., & Jensen, R. E. (2007). Male patient perceptions of HIV stigma in health care contexts. *AIDS Patient Care And STDs, 21,* 956–969.

Röndahl, G., Innala, S., & Carlsson, M. (2006) Heterosexual assumptions in verbal and non-verbal communication in nursing. *Journal of Advanced Nursing, 56,* 373–381.

Rose, H., & Smith, A. (2000). Sighting sound/sounding sight: The "violence" of deaf-hearing communication. In D. O. Braithwaite & T. L. Thompson (Eds.), *Handbook of communication and people with disabilities: Research and application* (pp. 369–388). Mahwah, NJ: Lawrence Erlbaum Associates.

Sparks, L., & Villagran, M. (2010). *Patient and provider interaction: A global health communication perspective.* Cambridge, UK: Polity Press.

Thompson, T. (2000). Introduction: A history of communication and disability research. In D. O. Braithwaite, & T. L. Thompson, (Eds.) *Handbook of communication and people with disabilities: Research and application* (pp. 1–16). Mahwah, NJ: Lawrence Erlbaum Associates.

Thompson. T. L., Robinson, J. D., Anderson, D. J., & Federowicz, M. (2008). Health communication: Where have we been and where can we go? In K. B. Wright & S. Moore (Eds.), *Applied health communication* (pp. 3–33). Cresskill, NJ: Hampton Press.

Topacoglu, H., Karcioglu, O., Ozucelik, N., Ozsarac, M., Degerli, V., Sarikaya, S., et al. (2004). Analysis of factors affecting satisfaction in the emergency department: A survey of 1019 patients. *Advances in Therapy, 21*, 380–388.

Trivedi, A. N., & Ayanian, J. Z. (2006). Perceived discrimination and use of preventive health services. *Journal of General Internal Medicine, 21*, 553–558.

Zazove, P., Niemann, L., Gorenflo, D., Carmack, C., Mehr, D., Coyne, J., et al. (1993). The health status and health care utilization of deaf and hard-of-hearing persons. *Archives of Family Medicine, 2*, 745–752.

CHAPTER 4

Meaning in Context

The Real Work of Medical Interpreters

Meagan J. Araujo and Lori A. Roscoe

KEY TERMS

Medical interpreters

Health literacy

Patient/provider communication

Free clinics

Abstract

Large numbers of patients are relying increasingly on not-for-profit clinics as a primary source for health care for a variety of reasons. The case study presented here describes the situation of a non-English-speaking older patient seeking medical care at a not-for-profit clinic where he utilized the services of a volunteer interpreter, with mixed results. The analysis highlights the potential communication blunders that stem from language as well as cultural differences between healthcare providers and patients, as well as the implications of limited health literacy (Ad Hoc Committee on Health Literacy for the Council on Scientific Affairs, American Medical Association, 1999; Nielson-Bohlman, Panzer, & Kindig, 2004). The formidable challenge for medical interpreters in clinical settings is to attempt to bridge these language, literacy, and health literacy gaps for patients, while fulfilling a key communication role that medical providers recognize and accept. Each of the possible models for shaping the primary function of medical interpreters has potential risks and benefits for patients, as well as for the relationship between the interpreter and the medical provider.

The health care system in the United States is a bewildering array of institutions, insurance plans, and options for care (du Pré, 2009; Geist-Martin, Berlin Ray, & Sharf, 2003; Wright, Sparks, & O'Hair, 2008). Long gone are the days when family physicians took care of patients from birth to death. While health care reform efforts may improve insurance coverage and thus access to care for more Americans (U.S. Department of Health and Human Services, n.d.), it is unlikely to simplify the choices and decisions that characterize the health care landscape. For English-speaking patients with insurance coverage, medical care is usually accessible, although a number of difficult choices need to be made. These can include whether to use a walk-in clinic, physician's office, specialty practice, or emergency room. Other "thorny" dilemmas could involve obtaining prescription refills through mail order, a retail chain pharmacy, or a neighborhood pharmacy. Deciding to use generic or name-brand drugs? Adopting a wait-and-see approach (e.g., regarding prostate cancer treatment options) or opting for high-technology screening? Determining when to obtain mammograms, that is, every year, at two- or five-year periods? The case presented here highlights these difficult choices when compounded by differences in language and culture. The case highlights the complex role of the medical interpreter and explores these interactions from the interpreter's perspective.

According to the 2000 U.S. Census, Hispanics/Latinos accounted for 12.5% of the U.S. population, which represents a 61% increase since 1990 (Ramirez, 2004).[1] The 2010 U.S. Census is almost certain to reveal the continuing rapid growth of the Hispanic/Latino population. Of the 18% of the U.S. population age five and older who speak a language other than English at home, 60% speak Spanish, and 40% rate their ability to speak English as "less than very well" (Ramirez, 2004). Patients with limited English proficiency (LEP) can be challenging for health care providers to treat effectively, especially since language barriers are often accompanied by other factors such as uncertain immigration status, inadequate or non-existent insurance coverage, limited health literacy, and other cultural stumbling blocks (Ad Hoc Committee on Health Literacy for the Council on Scientific Affairs, American Medical Association, 1999; Angelelli, 2004; Betancourt, Green, & Ananeh-Firempong, 2003; Nielson-Bohlman et al., 2004).

A growing number of LEP patients in the United States rely on not-for-profit health institutions for their healthcare needs. Since most medical clinics that serve this population do not receive federal funding, they are not required to provide medical interpreters, although the patients they serve are predominantly non-English speaking (Singy & Guex, 2005). Even facilities that are required to provide medical interpretation may not be able to do so in optimal ways; some rely on medical interpretation services over the telephone, or on family members or available staff members (Green et al., 2005; Elderkin-Thompson, Silver, & Waitzkin, 2001).

Green et al. (2005) conducted a cross-sectional survey of 2,715 LEP Chinese and Vietnamese immigrant adults who received care at 11 community-based health centers across the U.S. More than two-thirds (67%) of the study population were female and the mean age of the participants was 53.4 years old. On average, the respondents had been in the United Stated for 11.4 years. According to survey data collected after the patients sought heathcare, patients who had an interpreter posed more questions than language-concordant respondents (30.1% vs. 20.9%, $p < .001$). Elderkin-Thompson et al. (2001) explored the dual roles bilingual nurses play as health care providers and interpreters. Their analysis of 21 video recorded encounters with Spanish-speaking patients revealed interpretation errors in more than half the cases. Patient outcomes and provider satisfaction are likely affected by the availability and level of training of medical interpreters (Angelelli, 2004; Baker, Parker, Williams, Coates, & Pitkin, 1996; Baker, Hayes, & Fortier, 1998; Dysart-Gale, 2005; Jacobs et al., 2001; Karliner, Jacobs, Chen, & Mutha, 2007). The differential impact of using chance interpreters (i.e., hospital staff or a bystander in the waiting room), untrained interpreters, bilingual health care providers, on-site interpreters, and telephone interpreters is not well understood. Understanding these differences may be an important step in developing a coherent theory of bilingual health communication (Hsieh, 2006b). Hsieh interviewed 26 professional interpreters, 17 of whom had completed a 40-hour training course offered by the Cross Cultural Health Care Program (CCHCP), an industry leader in training medical interpreters. The remaining interpreters (n = 9) passed a local certification program or had trained interpreters before education programs for medical interpreters were offered. This study found that speaker and contextual factors, such as level of training, relationship to the patient, and professional background, impacted interpreters' communicative strategies, management of role conflicts, and effectiveness. Even when medical interpreters are available, lack of agreement about their role and responsibilities in specific clinical settings, and differences in training can lead to problematic interactions and outcomes (Hsieh 2006a, 2006b, 2008).

Until recently, there was no national certification program for medical interpreters. Founded in Seattle in 1992, the CCHCP became the first organization to create a national certification program for medical interpreters. In addition to providing training and certification, the CCHCP has attempted to identify and clarify possible models for medical interpretation. The CCHCP identified a continuum of four overlapping roles for medical interpreters: conduit, clarifier, cultural broker, and advocate (Roat, Putsch, & Lucero, 1997). In the conduit role, the interpreter is expected to provide a complete, direct, word-for-word translation of the speech between patient and medical provider. Ideally, in this role, the provider addresses the interpreter as the patient. For example, instead of "Ask him if he has pain," the provider asks the interpreter, who in turn asks the patient, "Do you have pain?" The clarifier and cultural broker roles recognize the interpreter's need to ask clarifying questions and deviate from a word-for-word translation if he or she does not believe a direct translation exists or is appropriate. A cultural broker role acknowledges that culture, in addition to language, shapes one's understandings of health and healing, thereby granting the interpreter much greater flexibility in asking and answering questions. For example, the Hmong culture typically explains epilepsy as "the spirit catches you and you fall down" (Fadiman, 1997, p. 20). This interplay of spiritual causes and physical symptoms cannot be accurately conveyed using a word-for-word translation; thus, an interpreter acting as a cultural broker would know to translate this phrase from a Hmong patient as epilepsy for an English-speaking medical care provider. The cultural exchange is somewhat circular. The interpreter acting as cultural broker, for example, would also be able to explain to Western health care providers that the spiritual dimension of human experience must be acknowledged to increase the likelihood of a trusting relationship between a Hmong patient and his or her English-speaking, Western-trained medical care provider. An interpreter taking on the role of advocate might create a space for the patient to ask the health-care provider questions, even if not prompted by the provider or patient.

These models of medical interpretation and resulting roles for interpreters are based on the belief that the skills of medical interpreters are limited to their linguistic and cultural knowledge and do not take their professional presence into account (Bolden, 2000; Davidson, 2000).

Hseih (2007) believes that medical interpreters should be acknowledged as equal members of the health care team, in particular as co-diagnosticians. Hsieh's roles overlap and exceed the roles described by the CCHCP. Hsieh's description of interpreter roles can be conceptualized along a continuum beginning with the conduit role, and moving to the clarifier and cultural broker roles and then beyond to advocate, manager, and professional roles. Manager and professional roles expand previous CCHCP role definitions by emphasizing that medical interpreters are part of the healthcare team and not merely an invisible human machine, as in the conduit and clarifier models (Dysart-Gale, 2005). In the manager role, medical interpreters "assume roles that are complementary and/or supplementary to other health care providers, regulate appropriate and ethical performances, manage problematic behaviors of other speakers, and manage the content and flow of information to be culturally appropriate to provide optimal care" (Hseih, 2008, p. 1370). Finally, the professional role emphasizes that the work of medical interpreters often overlaps with the work of providers; and therefore, interpreters should be acknowledged as an integral part of the healthcare delivery team (Dysart-Gale, 2005; Hsieh, 2006a, 2008).

Hsieh's research recognizes the crucial role interpreters can play in improving a non-English speaking patient's health literacy. The term "health literacy" describes the set of individual literacy capacities that influence the relationships between low literacy, patient decision-making, disease prevention and self-care, and adherence with health care providers' recommendations (Baker, 2006). Citing the work of Ratzan and Parker (2000), the Institute of Medicine report defined health literacy as "the degree to which individuals have the capacity to obtain, process, and understand basic health information and services needed to make appropriate health care decisions" (Nielson-Bohlman et al., 2004, p. 2).

Literacy in one's native language, as well as some proficiency in the English language, is a key component of health literacy for residents in the United States (Green et al., 2005). This definition emphasizes health literacy as a personal capacity, but health literacy is also context-specific and dependent on the relationship between individual communication abilities, characteristics of the health care system, and the constraints on broader society (Ad Hoc Committee on Health Literacy for the Council on Scientific Affairs, American Medical Association, 1999; Nielson-Bohlman et al., 2004). Attempting to navigate the health care system in a foreign language is difficult at best, and an individual patient's health literacy can be improved by access to medical interpreters who can interpret language and cultural differences (Angelelli, 2004; Davidson, 2000; Hseih, 2006b; Karliner et al., 2007).

The case study described here highlights the complex role of the medical interpreter by exploring interactions from the interpreter's perspective, which is largely absent in the health communication literature (Thompson et al., 2008; Thompson, Dorsey, Miller, & Parrott, 2003). The case highlights the sensitive and complex nature of medical interpretation and raises new questions about how health care providers evaluate and value the work of medical interpreters. The role and impact of medical interpretation in clinical settings is thus an emerging area for research in health communication, and an area that has pressing practical significance.

Case Summary

The Health Outreach Clinic, located in a mid-sized metropolitan area, offers comprehensive, free healthcare to low-income patients who are not eligible for healthcare from other social service agencies.[2] Health care is provided by a volunteer workforce of doctors, dentists, nurses, therapists, pharmacists, nurse practitioners, technicians, and other health care professionals. The Clinic completes 27,000 appointments and estimates treating between 8,000 and 10,000 patients each year, the majority of whom are Spanish-speaking and have limited proficiency in English. Since this facility does not receive federal funding, it is not required to abide by Title VI of the 1964 Civil Rights Act, which prohibits institutions from discriminating on the basis of race, ethnicity, or country of origin, nor is it required to provide interpreter services for LEP patients. Some patients are accompanied by family members who can serve as interpreters; when no one is available to interpret, healthcare providers are left to practice what they sometimes refer to as "veterinary medicine." Veterinary medicine applies to situations when patients and their healthcare providers cannot communicate verbally using a common language. In these cases, providers often rely on extra diagnostic tests, non-verbal cues, and descriptions provided by others to make diagnoses and devise treatment plans (Hampers, Cha, Gutglass, Binns, & Krug 1999; Sarver & Barker, 2000; Waxman & Levitt, 2000; Woloshin, Schwartz, Katz, & Welch, 1997).

As part of her doctoral program, one of the authors (Meagan) interviewed volunteer healthcare providers and observed clinical interactions between healthcare providers and LEP patients at the clinic. Meagan spent approximately six to eight hours each week at the clinic. Due in part to her fluency in Spanish, she offered to interpret when needed, and her dual role as a researcher and volunteer interpreter appeared to positively impact the relationships she developed with the volunteer providers at the clinic. For example, some health care providers, like the nurse practitioner in this case, were generous with their explanations and time, often describing their work in more detail than might have been likely had she been there solely as an interpreter or researcher. Meagan often perceived that since she identified herself as a communication scholar, the providers emphasized how difficult communication with LEP patients was and perhaps reflected more on their own communication practices.

One afternoon, Sr. Gomez, an 85-year-old man, was driven to the clinic by his teenage granddaughter, Maria, so he could refill his prescription for blood pressure medication. After reading the patient's last name on the medical chart, Lydia, the Nurse Practitioner, asked Meagan to accompany her into the exam room. Meagan had worked with Lydia as an interpreter since starting her research project at the clinic months earlier. Since patients need to make an appointment at the clinic to have their prescriptions refilled, Meagan expected this interaction to go smoothly. Meagan greeted Sr. Gomez in Spanish and quickly realized that he was hard of hearing since he leaned closer, stared intently at her mouth, and focused on reading her lips. Meagan repeated her greeting, "Buenas tardes. ¿Como está usted?" [Good afternoon. How are you?][3] Lydia quickly read through Sr. Gomez's medical chart and told Meagan that he had been seen in the clinic a month ago for dizziness. Lydia asked Meagan to ask him if he still felt dizzy. Sr. Gomez replied, "Yes, I feel dizzy and sometimes I fall when getting up." Lydia noted this continuing symptom in Sr. Gomez's chart, which seemed consistent with his previous complaint, and then shifted the conversation to questions about Sr. Gomez's social history. Through this conversation, Lydia, speaking through Meagan, established that he had recently moved to Florida from his home country, Colombia. He was now living with his family in the local metropolitan area served by the clinic.

Lydia then requested Meagan to ask Sr. Gomez more specific questions about his legal status in the United States in an attempt to determine his eligibility for federal programs like Medicaid.

Lydia to Meagan:	Ask him if he sees another doctor at a hospital.
Meagan to Sr. Gomez:	¿Señor Gomez, usted tiene otro médico en algun otro lugar, en un hospital, por ejemplo? [Mr. Gomez, do you have another doctor in some other place in a hospital, for example?]
Sr. Gomez to Meagan:	No, no tengo otro médico. Mi família me lleva aqui.
Meagan to Lydia:	No, he doesn't have another doctor. His family brings him here.
Lydia to Meagan:	Well, does he have a green card or a passport?
Meagan to Sr. Gomez:	¿Señor Gomez, Usted tiene una tarjeta de Residencia americana o un pasaporte americano? [Mr. Gomez, do you have an American residency card or an American passport?]
Sr. Gomez to Meagan:	Yo tengo un pasaporte colombiano.
Meagan to Lydia:	He has a Colombian passport.
Lydia to Meagan:	I didn't ask you to ask him what kind of passport he has.

This exchange emphasizes the frequent, tedious nature of interpreted communication. At this juncture, Lydia became frustrated that the exchange was taking such a long time and that Meagan and Sr. Gomez were not answering the questions she asked. As the interview continued, Sr. Gomez did not answer questions about his legal status in the United States even after Meagan emphasized that the Nurse Practitioner was inquiring about his ability to access government health programs, not about whether he was in the United States legally. After several unsuccessful attempts to ascertain if he would be eligible for federal assistance, Lydia then asked if his granddaughter, Maria, was in the waiting room.

Maria then entered the exam room. From that point on, Lydia directed all questions to her and seemed relieved to be able to continue the conversation entirely in English. Although she seemed embarrassed to answer some of the questions about her grandfather, Maria was able to clarify that Sr. Gomez was not a citizen of the United States, and ineligible for federal programs. Although Lydia had already requested Meagan to ask Sr. Gomez about the medication he was taking, she asked Maria as well. While staring at her feet, Maria mumbled, "I don't know. My mom just told me to bring him here for a refill. I don't know for which one." Lydia responded, "Well, since your grandpa lives with you, it's important that you keep your home safe for him. Get rid of the area rugs, he could slip and fall. If there are dark hallways, make sure you leave lights on, in case he has to get up and go." Maria, still staring at the floor, seemed relieved when Lydia then thanked her and told her she could go back to the waiting room. Maria turned and left without another word.

Unlike moments earlier when Meagan and Sr. Gomez were responding to Lydia's questions, if Maria didn't know the answer, Lydia didn't press for more information. Since their exchange was entirely in English, Lydia was in control of asking questions and could easily understand Maria's answers, even if they were incomplete. Adding an interpreter to the exchange and conducting the conversation in Spanish meant adding another possible "poor historian" to the case. That is, it was difficult for Lydia to determine if Sr. Gomez was not answering the question she asked, or if Meagan was not relaying it accurately.

Lydia refocused her attention on Sr. Gomez's medical chart, and on her recent notes concerning his health status and social history. When Lydia instructed Meagan to ask Sr. Gomez if he brought his medications with him, he pulled out two prescription bottles. She took the bottles and, nodding her head, told Meagan to tell him she would write prescription refills. However, the clinic pharmacy was already closed for the day. Lydia asked if he would like to fill his prescriptions with generic medications that were part of Walmart's five-dollar prescription plan, since this option would allow Sr. Gomez to fill his prescriptions immediately.[4] Meagan explained that the pills might look different, but that they would do the same thing. He would, however, have to pay five dollars for each medication, rather than receiving them from the clinic pharmacy for no charge. Sr. Gomez shook his head and said, "No puedo rellenar el medicamento en Walmart. No puedo usar la farmacia de Walmart." [I cannot refill the medicine at Walmart. I cannot use Walmart's pharmacy.] Sr. Gomez thus explained that he only could receive care at the clinic, since he did not understand that citizenship was not a prerequisite for utilizing another pharmacy's services. Meagan also observed the growing look of concern in his eyes that he might be refused treatment at the one clinic with which he was becoming familiar.

Sensing Sr. Gomez's concern, Lydia had Meagan tell Sr. Gomez that it would be alright for him to fill his prescriptions tomorrow at the clinic, at which point he seemed visibly relieved, and said "ok, ok." Lydia then continued to ask Meagan to ask Sr. Gomez health-related questions about his daily life. Meagan's initial approach, in line with the conduit model, was to translate the questions as directly and accurately as possible. For example, when Lydia asked "Do you have enough to eat?" Meagan asked Sr. Gomez, in Spanish, "¿Tiene sufiente para comer?" being sure to relay Sr. Gomez's "si" and "no" replies, even though Lydia told Meagan she understood her patient's "yes" and "no" responses. The interaction went smoothly for several questions: with Lydia asking questions in English, Meagan translating into Spanish, Sr. Gomez answering in Spanish, and Meagan proceeding to translate his answers into English. Then, in an attempt to inquire about possible prostate symptoms, Lydia had Meagan ask Sr. Gomez: "Can you write your name in the snow when you pee?"

This is one of the moments most interpreters dread. Adopting the role of conduit would have required Meagan to translate word-for-word, but after considering the direct interpretation of Lydia's question, Meagan realized how confusing this would be for Sr. Gomez. How would Sr. Gomez make sense of this question? Had he ever seen snow? Why will he think that the nurse practitioner wants to know if he can write his name? Is she challenging his intelligence or competence? After a moment's hesitation, which drew a side-long glance from Lydia, Meagan chose to deviate from the conduit model and attempted to find a culturally appropriate interpretation that would reveal the information being sought. This approach is risky for interpreters, especially since many health care providers often assume that the interpreter is acting merely as a conduit. Another potential pitfall is that interpreters have varying knowledge levels about various medical symptoms.

> Meagan to Sr. Gomez: ¿Usted tiene que orinar frequentamente y al orinar, es el flujo débil o fuerte? [Do you have to urinate frequently, and when you urinate, is the flow weak or strong?]
>
> Sr. Gomez to Meagan: Yo tengo que orinar frequentamente pero poco. Muy poco. [I have to urinate frequently, but just a little. Very little.]

Meagan then relayed this information to Lydia in English, who scribbled this response in his chart. Lydia moved on to the next question. There was no indication that Lydia perceived the question to be culturally, linguistically, and medically inappropriate. It was also unclear what answers she recorded in the chart. Lydia wrote a referral and instructed Meagan to tell Sr. Gomez she was recommending that he see the urologist at the clinic next week. Sr. Gomez nodded to Meagan and Lydia, then he went to rejoin his granddaughter in the waiting room. Back in the hallway, Lydia signed off on Sr. Gomez's chart. She placed it on top of a growing pile to be filed, and picked up the next patient's chart without any comment about the interaction that just occurred.

Summary and Implications

The role of the interpreter deserves a closer comprehensive examination as health communication scholars continue to explore the impact of power dynamics and hierarchical differences in patient/provider interactions, as well as intraprofessional communication among members of the healthcare team. Specifically, to allow medical interpreters to fulfill and navigate the roles proposed by the CCHCP and Hseih (2008), healthcare providers will need to learn to work with interpreters and allow and encourage them to move between the conduit role and roles of advocate, manager, and professional when necessary and legally appropriate. The growing numbers of LEP patients lend urgency to these pressing issues and subsequent interventions.

NOTES

1   We acknowledge that individuals may identify with Hispanic, Latino, or both terms. We use Hispanic/Latino to be inclusive.

2   We use a pseudonym to ensure confidentiality and to comply with Institutional Review Board guidelines. The name and location of The Health Outreach Clinic are not revealed; however, the mission, number of patients, and demographic information are based on interviews with clinic administrative staff.

3   Usted (Ud.) is used in Spanish to show respect and indicate a formal relationship. As a general rule, older people, especially family members are referred to as usted. Usted is also used when meeting a person for the first time. In this case, I used usted because the patient was an elderly man and I had never met him before.

4   Our mention of Walmart is in no way intended to reinforce any of its questionable organizational practices.

Discussion Questions

1. What barriers prevent interpreters from discussing expectations for their role in clinical settings with medical care providers?

2. What risks do interpreters take when they deviate from a conduit model of translation?

3. Why shouldn't family members, including children, interpret medical information for their family members with limited English proficiency (LEP)?

4. What factors should an interpreter consider when facilitating communication between healthcare providers and patients?

5. From the vantage point of a family member or friend of this family, did Sr. Gomez receive good care at the clinic? Why or why not?

References

Ad Hoc Committee on Health Literacy for the Council on Scientific Affairs, American Medical Association. (1999). *Journal of the American Medical Association, 281*, 552–557.

Angelelli, C. V. (2004). *Medical interpreting and cross-cultural communication*. Cambridge, UK: Cambridge University Press.

Baker, D. W., Parker, R. M., Williams, M. V., Coates, W. C., & Pitkin, K. (1996). Use and effectiveness of interpreters in an emergency department. *Journal of the American Medical Association, 275*, 783–788.

Baker, D. W., Hayes, R., & Fortier, J. P. (1998) Interpreter use and satisfaction with interpersonal aspects of care for Spanish-speaking patients. *Medical Care, 36,* 1461–70.

Baker, D. W. (2006). The meaning and measure of health literacy. *Journal of General Internal Medicine, 21*, 878–883.

Betancourt, J. R., Green, A. R., & Ananeh-Firempong, O. (2003). Defining cultural competence: A practical framework for addressing racial/ethnic disparities in health and health care. *Public Health Reports, 118*, 293–302.

Bolden, G. B. (2000). Toward understanding practices of medical interpreting: Interpreters' involvement in history-taking. *Discourse Studies, 2*, 387–419.

Davidson, B. (2000). The interpreter as institutional gatekeeper: The socio-linguistic role of interpreters in Spanish-English medical discourse. *Journal of Sociolinguistics, 4*, 379–405.

du Pré, A. (2009). *Communicating about health: Current issues and perspectives*. New York: Oxford University Press.

Dysart-Gale, D. (2005). Communication models, professionalization, and the work of medical interpreters. *Health Communication, 17*, 91–103.

Elderkin-Thompson, V., Silver, R. C., & Waitzkin, H. (2001). When nurses double as interpreters: A study of Spanish-speaking patients in a U. S. primary care setting. *Social Science and Medicine, 52*, 1343–1358.

Fadiman, A. (1997). *The spirit catches you and you fall down: A Hmong child, her American doctors, and the collision of two cultures*. New York: Farrar, Straus and Giroux.

Geist-Martin, P., Berlin Ray, E., & Sharf, B. (2003). *Communicating health: Personal, cultural, and political complexities*. Belmont, CA: Wadsworth/Thompson Learning.

Green, A. R., Ngo-Metzger, Q., Legends, A. T. R., Massagli, M. P., Phillips, R. S., & Iezzoni, L. I. (2005). Interpreter services, language concordance, and health care quality. *Journal of General Internal Medicine, 20*, 1050–1056.

Hampers, L. C., Cha, S., Gutclass, D. J., Binns, H. J., & Krug, S. E. (1999). Language barriers and resource utilization in a pediatric emergency department. *Pediatrics, 103*, 1253–1256.

Hsieh, E. (2006a). Conflicts in how interpreters manage their roles in provider-patient interactions. *Social Science and Medicine, 62*, 721–730.

Hsieh, E. (2006b). Understanding medical interpreters: Reconceptualizing bilingual health communication. *Health Communication, 20*, 177–186.

Hsieh, E. (2007). Interpreters as co-diagnosticians: Overlapping roles and services between providers and interpreters. *Social Science and Medicine, 64*, 924–937.

Hsieh, E. (2008). "I am not a robot!" Interpreters' views of their roles in health care settings. *Qualitative Health Research, 18,* 1367–1383.

Jacobs, E. A., Lauderdale, D. S., Meltzer, D., Shorey, J. M., Levinson, W., & Thisted, R. A. (2001). Impact of interpreter services on delivery of health care to limited-English-proficient patients. *Journal of General Internal Medicine, 16*, 468–474.

Karliner, L. S., Jacobs, E. A., Chen, A. H., & Mutha, S. (2007). Do professional interpreters improve clinical care for patients with limited English proficiency? A systematic review of the literature. *Health Services Research, 42*, 727–754.

Nielson-Bohlman, L., Panzer, A. M., & Kindig, D. A. (2004). *Health literacy: A prescription to end confusion.* Washington, DC: Institute of Medicine of the National Academies Press.

Ramirez, R. (2004). We the people: Hispanics in the United States. U.S. Census Bureau special report. Retrieved from [*usa.usembassy.de/etexts/soc/we_hispanics_2000.pdf*]

Ratzan, S. C., & Parker, R. M. (2000). Introduction. In C. R. Selden, M. Zorn, S. C. Ratzan, & R. M. Parker (Eds.), *National Library of Medicine Current Bibliographies in Medicine: Health Literacy* (pp. v-vii) (NLM Pub. No. CBM 2000–1). Bethesda, MD: National Institutes of Health, U.S. Department of Health and Human Services.

Roat, C. E., Putsch, III, R. W., & Lucero, C. (1997). *Bridging the gap over the phone: A basic training for telephone interpreters serving medical settings.* Seattle, WA: Cross Cultural Health Care Program.

Sarver, J., & Baker, D. W. (2000). Effect of language barriers on follow up-appointments after an emergency department visit. *Journal of General Internal Medicine, 15*, 256–264.

Singy, P., & Guex, P. (2005). The interpreter's role with immigrant patients: Contrasted points of view. *Communication and Medicine, 2*, 45–51.

Thompson, T. L., Dorsey, A. M., Miller, K. I., & Parrott, R. (Eds.). (2003). *The handbook of health communication.* Mahwah, NJ: Lawrence Erlbaum Associates.

Thompson, V. L., Cavazos-Rehg, P. A., Jupka, K., Caito, N., Gratzke, J., Tate, K. Y., Deshpande, A. & Kreuter, M. W. (2008). Evidential preferences: Cultural appropriateness strategies in health communications, *Health Education Research, 23*, 549–559

U.S. Department of Health and Human Services. (n.d.) HealthCare.gov. Retrieved from http://www.healthcare.gov/

Waxman, M. A., & Levitt, M. A. (2000). Are diagnostic testing and admission rates higher in non-English speaking versus English speaking patients in the emergency department? *Annals of Emergency Medicine, 36,* 456–461.

Woloshin, S., Schwartz, L. M., Katz, S. J., & Welch, H. G. (1997). Is language a barrier to the use of preventative services? *Journal of General Internal Medicine, 12*, 472–477.

Wright, K. B., Sparks, L., & O'Hair, H. D. (2008). *Health communication in the 21st century.* Malden, MA: Blackwell Publishing.

SECTION II

Communicating Social Support During Daunting Life Events

CHAPTER 5

When Love Is Not Enough

Communication Challenges and Social Support Experienced When Placing a Spouse with Dementia in a Residential Care Facility

Mindi Ann Golden

KEY TERMS

Social support

Dementia

Caregiving

Residential placement

Abstract

Negative health impacts of caregiving for a person with dementia are well established, and placing a person with dementia in a residential care facility may become a necessary option. The decision to place a spouse with dementia in a residential care facility, and the difficult relational dynamics that can result, is one of the most significant periods that a support group can help a caregiver navigate. This case study focuses on support group interactions during a caregiver's decision-making process and her experience moving her spouse to a residential care facility. The potential for social support to mediate negative health impacts is discussed.

Estimates indicate that 5.3 million persons in the United States have Alzheimer's disease and that, currently, every 70 seconds one person in the United States develops Alzheimer's (Alzheimer's Association, 2010). Alzheimer's is the leading cause of dementia, a progressive decline in memory and cognitive ability. The likelihood of developing Alzheimer's and other dementia-causing diseases (e.g., vascular dementia) increases with age, with high blood pressure, heart disease, and diabetes being additional risk factors (Alzheimer's Association, 2010). Older African Americans and Hispanics are also at greater risk of developing dementia-causing diseases, likely due to the greater prevalence of other risk factors (e.g., diabetes) in these populations (Alzheimer's Association, 2010). Hence, with the population aging, increasing levels of risk-factor diseases, and no cure in sight, an estimated 11 to 16 million Americans will be diagnosed with Alzheimer's by the year 2050 (Alzheimer's Association, 2008a).

Dementia begins mildly. For instance, an individual might become confused during a routine chore or become lost in a familiar place. As dementia progresses, confusion can trigger wandering, hoarding, suspiciousness, and combativeness (Mace & Rabins, 1991). Eventually, script knowledge (i.e., recall and comprehension of sequences of action needed to complete a task) is impaired (Kemper & Lyons, 1993), disrupting the ability to carry out activities of daily living, such as bathing and dressing. Communicatively, mild-to-moderate dementia can result in the repetition of questions and statements, as well as common words being forgotten (Alzheimer's Association, 2009). A person with severe dementia becomes incontinent, loses the capacity for recognizable speech, and may not recognize those around him or her (Alzheimer's Association, 2009).

As dementia progresses, the emotional and physical toll on caregivers increases as they take on tasks formerly handled by the person with dementia, manage challenging behaviors, and provide physical assistance and care. Negative psychological and physical consequences of caregiving for a person with dementia are well established (FACCT & Robert Wood Johnson Foundation, 2001; Family Caregiver Alliance, 2006). Caregiving for a person with dementia is also a risk factor for premature mortality (Schultz & Beach, 1999). Despite negative impacts on caregivers, 70% of persons with Alzheimer's reside at home, cared for by family and friends (Alzheimer's Association, 2008b); however, 69% of nursing home residents suffer from cognitive impairment (Alzheimer's Association, 2008b). These numbers suggest that although caregivers keep a loved one at home for as long as possible, placement may become an excruciating, but necessary option.

Considerable research suggests that social support can buffer (i.e., protect against) negative mental and physical health impacts in the face of stressors (Cohen & Wills, 1985; Hsieh, 2004; MacGeorge, Samter, Feng, Gillihan, & Graves, 2007; Segrin, 2003; Wills, 1985). Cutrona and Russell (1990) identify five general types of social support: (a) emotional support—comfort in times of stress; (b) network support—social integration, feeling a part of a group; (c) esteem support—the bolstering of one's confidence and self-esteem; (d) tangible aid—instrumental assistance; and (e) informational support—advice or guidance regarding a problem. Social support, then, may have a "buffering effect" for caregivers of persons with dementia, particularly in the context of placement.

A support group is one place a caregiver can find needed social support. In support groups, persons managing similar health-related circumstances emphasize informational, emotional, and network support (Coulson, Buchanan, & Aubeeluck, 2007; Eichhorn, 2008; Frost & Massagli, 2008; Ginossar, 2008; Sharf, 1997). An extensive body of literature regarding caregiver support groups indicates that these supportive dynamics result in increased knowledge, a sense of universality (i.e., not being alone with caregiving problems), the opportunity to share feelings, mediation of negative emotions, and improved self-identity (see, for example, Cuijpers, Hosman, & Munnichs, 1996; Glosser & Wexler, 1985; Gonyea, 1989). In a broader sense, social support may also help support group members navigate uncertainty

(Brashers, Neidig, & Goldsmith, 2004; Shaw, McTavish, Hawkins, Gustafson, & Pingree, 2000) and manage dialectical tensions (i.e., unified opposites) experienced in the context of dementia caregiving (Baxter, Braithwaite, Golish, & Olson, 2002).[1] This case study focuses on support group interactions regarding one caregiver's experiences with decision-making and placing her spouse in residential care.

Making the Most Difficult Decision

Faye and Irv[2] have been married for 51 years. After Irv was diagnosed with Alzheimer's disease five years ago, Faye joined a support group for spouses of persons with dementia. Today, as Faye pulls into the parking lot of the adult day care and counseling center where her support group meets, she wonders how Rose, the group's leader, and the rest of the group will respond to what she has to share.

Rose: (looking around the room) The gang's all here! Who would like to start, today?

Faye: I would, if no one minds. I got some news the other day.

Rose: What's going on, Faye?

Faye: Well, I've had a lot of pain in my shoulder, so I went to see an orthopedist. He says I've torn my rotator cuff in five places, and I need surgery to repair it.

Elizabeth: Oh, Faye! You just finished recovering from your neck surgery.

Faye: I know. The thing is it'll be a long recovery and I'll need a caregiver to help me. I won't be able to shower myself or drive, and I'll need help doing exercises to rebuild my strength. My doctor said that I should think about placing Irv. His thinking is that, if I don't have to take care of Irv, I'll be able to take care of myself.

Rose: What do you think about that?

Faye: Well, it isn't that simple. The responsibility for Irv would still be there. And it's almost the holidays, then Irv's birthday. And I'd have to find a place for him. I'm worried that Irv is better physically than most people living in care facilities.

Doris: Could you move him somewhere temporarily, while you recover?

Faye: I can't imagine going through the difficulty of moving him somewhere, then moving him home again. He is getting worse. The other day he came out of the bathroom and he had rubbed sunblock all over his hair! He wants me with him all of the time. If I'm doing paperwork or talking on the phone, he is right there saying, "Where are you? I want you." I have to watch him like a hawk if we're in a store because he'll take things and put them in his pockets. But, at the same time, he's still better than so many people in care homes.

Rose: There's a lot to think about, but I think you'll reach a point where you know that you have to do something. For some people here, they reached a point where they knew that they had to get away for a break. Maybe in your case it will be knowing when placement is the right thing for you and Irv.

Faye: I was remembering that when I first came here to see the adult day care, I was worried that Irv would get depressed seeing people in wheelchairs, but he comes here and he loves it. So, maybe I should go forward with looking for a place for him. But, the doctor said if I can live with the pain, there's no rush for surgery. Maybe I should wait.

Rose: None of this will be easy, no matter what you decide. I think you're going to have to deal with your ambivalence about placing Irv, then you'll be able to make decisions.

Three weeks later during Faye's support group meeting:

Faye: I have, without a doubt, decided I am going to place Irv. I have to. I realize that I'm breaking myself down. And, the doctor says it's time.

Rose: This is a big decision. It won't be easy, on you or Irv.

Faye: It won't. We had to place my mother years ago. It was awful. I'm lucky that Irv has long-term care insurance, so I'm sorting through the paperwork, trying to figure out what he's entitled to. It's all very overwhelming. I visited one facility by my house, but I walked right out. It had a funny smell. I went to another facility near the university, Park House. They have forty residents. The people there seem very nice.

Rose: The owner there has a good reputation.

Faye: I met him. He seemed very caring. I'm just finding it so difficult with Irv. I think it's time, especially with my surgery. I don't think I could handle taking care of Irv and myself. But, this is devastating to me. And, I'm worried about how he'll respond.

Mike: Have you thought about how you'll prepare him?

Faye: Well, I don't see much point in saying anything ahead of time. He'll just forget.

Mike: When I placed Lynn, I think her major concern was that she would be abandoned. I started talking well ahead of time about the move, saying that she needed better care than I could give her, but that she would not be abandoned. I would be there.

Faye: But won't he forget?

Mike: I kept repeating it again and again, everyday. I don't think we can ignore that they still have feelings. I told Lynn that she was going to be someplace where they could give her the care she deserved, but I would visit. I would be there. She was not being abandoned.

Rose: There's no way to anticipate how Irv will respond, but how you prepare him is important.

Abby:	When I moved Bill to the nursing home, he was able to understand that I couldn't physically help him, and I was hurting myself trying. Are you getting the message that you are worn down across to Irv?
Faye:	I don't know. It's hard to tell what he thinks.
Rose:	I think what Abby is saying is that if you haven't directly begun the conversation with him, you need to bring it up.
Faye:	Won't telling him that I can't handle him anymore be hurtful?
Frank:	It was hard for me to tell Linda that I was getting worn down, but I had to. The only alternative is for you to just drop him off one day. That would be worse.
Mary:	I wouldn't say, "I can't handle you." Maybe, "I can't give you the care you deserve."
Rose:	Right. The important part is that you start preparing him. It won't be easy on either of you.

Reflecting on Decision-Making Support

Faye voices emotional difficulties as she contemplates placing Irv in a residential care facility, and she indicates practical challenges regarding timing and facility choice. In the language of relational dialectics, Faye is communicating autonomy (i.e., she must care for herself; Irv has increasing individual needs) and connection (i.e., the desire to spend holidays together; the devastation of being separated; not wanting to hurt Irv) (Golden, 2010). Faye is struggling with how to meet both needs. Faye's support group does not take a position when she first discusses the possibility of placement. The members realize that placement is a highly personal decision that only Faye can make. However, Faye is a long-time member of the support group, and she has watched other members place their spouses. Over time, a sense of similarity has been created among the group members (i.e., their spouses are in different stages of dementia-causing diseases, but group members will all face various problems and decisions) (Golden & Lund, 2009). The sense of similarity, created over time, constitutes network support, which provides a comfortable place for discussing an emotional issue and possibly eases Faye's progress toward a heart-wrenching, yet necessary decision.

When Faye decides to place Irv, the group communicates the informational, emotional, and network support common in support groups. Group members reflect upon similar experiences when placing their spouses (i.e., network support). Their advice for preparing Irv constitutes informational support. Emotional support is also evident as the group acknowledges the difficulties posed by Faye's decision and of telling Irv. Social support offered in the group acknowledges and addresses the issues of autonomy and connection that Faye voiced. The group tries to help Faye meet both needs: to do what is needed to take care of herself and to tend to her ongoing connection with Irv.

Uncertainty is central to Faye's interaction with her support group. Social support can help one manage uncertainty, but can also create uncertainty (Brashers et al., 2004). That is evident when Faye's group suggests that she must accept uncertainty regarding Irv's reaction, while simultaneously attempting to manage uncertainty by preparing him. The support group suggests Faye must manage an additional dialectic by accepting that there is no way to know how Irv will react to the move to a residential care facility, but also work out a specific message strategy for preparing Irv that might minimize a negative reaction. The group's emotional support also suggests that Faye must accept the certainty of emotional difficulties for herself; however, its degree (based on Irv's uncertain reaction) is uncertain. Thus, a support group can help a caregiver accept negative emotions, and offer informational support that may lessen the severity of negative outcomes and emotions.

The support offered in Faye's group relates to her physical and mental well-being. Faye is breaking down physically. Neck surgery and damage to her rotator cuff have resulted from Faye doing things as a caregiver beyond her physical capacities. Network support, a sense of connection to similar others, may have helped Faye make a challenging decision that will protect her from further physical harm. Once Faye has made her decision, social support within the group can help Faye manage her practical and emotional distress. Her support group's emotional support gives Faye a place to voice negative feelings and not feel alone in coping with caregiving problems (Cuijpers et al., 1996; Glosser & Wexler, 1985); the group's advice might also enhance Faye's sense of control and confidence in her ability to manage her caregiving situation (Cummings, Long, Peterson-Hazan, & Harrison, 1998; Kahan, Kemp, Staples, & Brummel-Smith, 1985). Hence, social support may be imperative to Faye's mental and physical well-being as a caregiver.

Making the Move

Faye moved Irv to Park House a month after making her decision. Four days after moving Irv, Faye talked about the experience with her support group.

Faye: It was very traumatic. In the car on the way there, I said, "Irv, you're going to be staying at a hotel for a while." He asked, "Why?" I said, "Well, you know I'm having surgery. I won't be able to take care of you. I've got to rest before and it will be a while after." He asked, "How long," so I said, "I don't know, but it will be a while." He said, "I don't wanna leave you," so I said, "I'll be there. I'll come and I'll be there." Well, we walked in and he was terrific. He says, "Hello everybody!" Then we went upstairs and I said, "Irv, look at the patio. You can sit there and look at the park and watch the kids." "Fine," he says, "where's my room?" So, I took him to his room. But then they started the entertainment downstairs and it all went downhill. Everybody was sitting down there and Irv tried to talk to a man who must have had a stroke. This man could hardly talk. Irv got up and said, "I want out. I want out!" I said, "Why? You liked it." He says, "I want out! They don't talk. I don't wanna stay here! I'm going home." I said, "I'd love to have you home if I could, but I can't." Then he looks at me and he says, (Faye starts to cry) "I'm going to cry if I don't go home." I have never, never seen Irv cry! Tears were coming to his eyes. It was awful. (Faye's crying tapers off, but her voice continues to crack) Anyway, Chuck, who is the owner, came up and he says, "We'll have to distract him and you'll leave." Chuck came outside afterward and said, "We'll call you after dinner." When he called, Chuck said that after I left they still had the music and one of the caregivers danced with Irv. He said that Irv ate well at dinner, and then he watched television afterward. So, that was positive. Chuck said not to visit for a week, so Irv could settle in, but I've called. The caregivers say Irv is doing well, but he's asking for me.

Rose: It's probably as difficult for you, Faye, as it is for Irv. But hang in there; he will adjust.

Faye: What did I do to him?! He's the most active one there. He's not happy. And I'm not happy. I know I shouldn't feel guilty, but I do.

Rose: Go back. What was the original reason for placement?

Faye: I was breaking down.

Rose: What you did was something that you needed for yourself. There was a reason.

Abby: I can certainly relate to what you're saying. Of the people at the nursing home where Bill lives, most of the men are out of it altogether, and some of the women are too. Many of them are in reclining wheelchairs. My heart is so heavy when I leave there. And the other night I had the fireplace on in the living room and I thought, *Bill used to love to sit here and relax.* And now he's in this crummy place, which isn't crummy, but it is crummy. It breaks my heart.

Faye: It's very hard. I go to bed at one, one-thirty in the morning. And I wake up about four.

Rose: Give yourself some room here, Faye. Give yourself some time. Be a little bit more-

Abby: Patient with yourself.

Elizabeth: Understanding.

Rose: It's the first week. It is going to be a huge adjustment.

Mike: Placing Lynn brought a great sense of relief, and that made me feel guilty. But, it all comes back to why I did it. I was headed, as you were, for physical and mental disaster. You gotta fall back, as Rose says, on why you did it. You did it for yourself and you did it for him.

Faye: I didn't do it for him. I don't feel I did it for him.

Mike: You did it for him, indirectly. Because, if you hadn't done it, then you would have suffered for it and you would not have been there to take care of him.

Faye: It just breaks my heart. I feel like I want to take him home. Then I think to myself, *What am I gonna gain if I take him home*? But I look at him and I think,

How can I do this to my husband? From a nice home to this?! It's heart breaking. And, to hear him say how much he wants to be with me. And how much he loves me. I can understand how he feels.

Reflecting on the Group's Support

Faye's interaction with Irv on the day of placement reflects distinct orientations to the autonomy-connection dialectic (Golden, 2010). Faye emphasizes ongoing relational continuity or connection (i.e., "I'll be there") in the context of their autonomous needs being met via a practical change. Irv fights to select connection to Faye and the continuity of home. Although feelings of guilt are quite typical following placement of a spouse, Irv's resistance likely exacerbates Faye's pervasive feelings of guilt. Faye perceives herself as doing something for herself (i.e., selecting autonomy) at the cost of Irv's happiness and their connection.

Faye's support group addresses the difficulties she faces as she wrestles with autonomy and connection. Abby and Mike genuinely acknowledge Faye's feelings and create a sense of shared experience in the group (i.e., network support) by describing feelings of guilt and sadness related to placing their spouses. Rose, Abby, and Elizabeth also sympathetically acknowledge Faye's feelings, offering comfort and hope, suggesting that Irv will adjust, as will Faye. In addition to the support group creating a sense of universality (i.e., network support), providing a place to voice negative feelings, and offering emotional support, Mike invites Faye to reframe and view autonomy as connection. Faye has a choice: she can view her actions as selecting autonomy over connection, or she can view autonomy as connection. By reframing, Faye can discern and appreciate that taking care of her own needs is taking care of Irv as she is more likely to avert a mental and physical disaster that could take her from him permanently.

Reframing as a form of emotional support offers caregivers a positive coping strategy (Cummings et al., 1998) that can mediate negative mental and emotional health impacts. Coping is an ongoing process of appraisal and reappraisal that can help one reduce stress (Lazarus & Folkman, 1984). Some stressors, such as a dementia-causing disease, cannot be mastered or "solved"; therefore, coping is central to an individual managing emotions, maintaining self-esteem, and maintaining a positive outlook given irremediable situations (Lazarus & Folkman, 1984). Social support is one resource that can facilitate coping, by helping an individual change subjective meanings or engage in positive reappraisal (Folkman & Lazarus, 1991). Negative mental and emotional impacts of placing a spouse with dementia in a care facility may be unavoidable; however, social support within a group of similar others can offer positive reappraisals that, if internalized by a caregiver, can help ease the negative impacts of placement over time.

NOTES

1   Extensive bodies of research exist regarding uncertainty management in health contexts and dialectical approaches to relationships. Babrow and Kline (2000), Babrow, Kasch, and Ford (1998), and Albrecht and Adelman (1987) provide excellent starting points for further reading regarding forms and causes of uncertainty in health contexts, and social support's impact on uncertainty. The September 2001 special issue of *Journal of Communication*, guest edited by Austin Babrow, is also an excellent resource regarding the shift from uncertainty reduction theory to uncertainty management theory in health and other contexts. For an overview of dialectical theory, see Baxter and Montgomery (1998). Also see Baxter (1990) for an overview of primary relational dialectics.

2   All proper names in the narrative portions of this case study are pseudonyms. This case is based on participant observation data collected by the author in a support group for spouses of persons with dementia. See Golden and Lund (2005–2006) for more information regarding the group.

Discussion Questions

1. What are your experiences with dementia-causing diseases? What symptoms of dementia have you observed and what impacts have you seen on a primary caregiver (e.g., yourself, a parent, a grandparent)? In what ways do you believe the five different forms of social support have made a difference in these situations?

2. With Cutrona's and Russell's definition of five types of social support in mind, review line by line the support group's interactions regarding Faye's decision and the day of placement. Discuss how each member's contributions reflect various types of social support. What forms are emphasized? What factors may have shaped using some forms of support more than others?

3. Irv needs assistance with all of his activities of daily living (e.g., bathing, dressing) and he requires supervision, but he can still speak and has a strong sense of home and his relationship with Faye. How might a person with dementia communicate resistance to a move if his or her condition was further progressed than Irv's? What responses have you observed in your family or in the family of someone you know? What message strategies could a caregiver employ prior to a move to residential care if the person with dementia could not understand the caregiver's needs?

4. To what degree do you think Faye waiting until the day of the move to tell Irv played a role in Irv's reaction? How do you think Irv would have responded if Faye, as the group suggested, began talking to him about the move two weeks earlier? When Faye does tell Irv about the move, what is the significance of Faye calling the residential care facility a "hotel"? Some people would likely label Faye's word choice a "lie." How would you respond to that? Would your response be different if this occurred in your own family?

5. Residential care facilities can be prohibitively expensive, and research suggests that many individuals hold different cultural attitudes toward caregiving and placement. How might distinct cultural beliefs and the absence of long-term care insurance lead to different conversations regarding Faye's situation? Assuming Faye does not have other family who can help with Irv's care, what other choices could she make that would meet both her and Irv's needs?

6. What factors do you think will impact whether Faye is able to reframe placement as "for Irv," not just for herself?

7. Faye's support group acknowledges uncertainty and tries to help Faye manage uncertainty. How is encouraging acceptance of uncertainty in the context of dementia caregiving and placement a positive form of social support? What factors might influence how a caregiver responds to advice that is intended to help him or her manage uncertainty?

References

Albrecht, T. L., & Adelman, M. B. (1987). *Communicating social support*. Thousand Oaks, CA: Sage.

Alzheimer's Association. (2008a). *2008 Alzheimer's Disease Facts and Figures*. Chicago, IL: Author. Retrieved from http://www.alz.org/national/documents/report_alzfactsfigures 2008.pdf

Alzheimer's Association. (2008b). *2008 Alzheimer's Disease Facts and Figures*. Chicago, IL: Author. Retrieved from http://www/alz.org/national/documents/topicsheet_2008_facts_figures.pdf

Alzheimer's Association. (2009). Stages of Alzheimer's. Retrieved from http://www.alz.org/alzheimers_disease_stages_of_alzheimers.asp

Alzheimer's Association. (2010). Alzheimer's disease facts and figures. Chicago, IL: Author. Retrieved from http://www.alz.org/alzheimers_disease_facts_figures.asp

Babrow, A. S. (Ed.). (2001). Uncertainty, evaluation, and communication [Special issue]. *Journal of Communication, 51*(3).

Babrow, A. S., Kasch, C. R., & Ford, L. A. (1998). The many meanings of uncertainty in illness: Toward a systematic accounting. *Health Communication, 10*, 1–23.

Babrow, A. S., & Kline, K. N. (2000). From "reducing" to "managing" uncertainty: Reconceptualizing the central challenge in breast self-exams. *Social Science and Medicine, 51*, 1805–1816.

Baxter, L. A. (1990). Dialectical contradictions in relationship development. *Journal of Social and Personal Relationships, 7*, 69–88.

Baxter, L. A., Braithwaite, D. O., Golish, T. D., & Olson, L. N. (2002). Contradictions of interactions for wives of elderly husbands with adult dementia. *Journal of Applied Communication Research, 30*, 1–26.

Baxter, L. A., & Montgomery, B. M. (1998). A guide to dialectical approaches to studying personal relationships. In B. M. Montgomery & L. A. Baxter (Eds.), *Dialectical approaches to studying personal relationships* (pp. 1–15). Mahwah, NJ: Lawrence Erlbaum.

Brashers, D. E., Neidig, J. L., & Goldsmith, D. J. (2004). Social support and the management of uncertainty for people living with HIV or AIDS. *Health Communication, 16*, 305–331.

Cohen, S., & Wills, T. A. (1985). Stress, social support, and the buffering hypothesis. *Psychological Bulletin, 98*, 310–357.

Coulson, N. S., Buchanan, H., & Aubeeluck, A. (2007). Social support in cyberspace: A content analysis of communication within a Huntington's disease online support group. *Patient Education and Counseling, 68*, 173–178.

Cuijpers, P., Hosman, C. M. H., & Munnichs, J. M. A. (1996). Change mechanisms of support groups for caregivers of dementia patients. *International Psychogeriatrics, 8*, 575–587.

Cummings, S. M., Long, J. K., Peterson-Hazan, S., & Harrison, J. (1998). The efficacy of a group treatment model in helping spouses meet the emotional and practical challenges of early stage caregiving. *Clinical Gerontologist, 20*(1), 29–45.

Cutrona, C. E., & Russell, D. W. (1990). Type of social support and specific stress: Toward a theory of optimal matching. In B. R. Sarason, I. G. Sarason, & G. R. Pierce (Eds.), *Social support: An interactional view* (pp. 319–366). New York, NY: John Wiley & Sons.

Eichhorn, K. C. (2008). Soliciting and providing social support over the internet: An investigation of online eating disorder support groups. *Journal of Computer Mediated Communication, 14,* 67–78.

FACCT, & Robert Wood Johnson Foundation. (2001). *A portrait of informal caregivers in America.* Portland, OR: Author.

Family Caregiver Alliance. (2006). *Caregiver assessment: Voices and views from the field.* Report from a National Consensus Development Conference (vol. II). San Francisco: CA: Author.

Folkman, S., & Lazarus, R. S. (1991). Coping and emotion. In A. Monat & R. S. Lazarus (Eds.), *Stress and coping: An anthology* (3rd ed. 207–227). New York: Columbia University Press.

Frost, J. H., & Massagli, M. P. (2008). Social uses of personal health information within PatientsLikeMe, an online patient community: What can happen when patients have access to another's data. *Journal of Medical Internet Research, 10*(3): e15.

Ginossar, T. (2008). Online participation: A content analysis of differences in utilization of two online cancer communities by men and women, patients, and family members. *Health Communication, 23,* 1–12.

Glosser, G., & Wexler, D. (1985). Participants' evaluation of educational/support groups for families of patients with Alzheimer's disease and other dementias. *The Gerontologist, 25,* 232–236.

Golden, M. A. (2010). Dialectical contradictions experienced when placing a dementing spouse in a residential care facility. *Qualitative Research Reports in Communication, 11,* 14–20.

Golden, M. A., & Lund, D. A. (2005–2006). Positioning in a support group for spouses of persons with dementia. *International Journal of Self Help & Self Care, 4,* 119–134.

Golden, M. A., & Lund, D. A. (2009). Identifying themes regarding the benefits and limitations of caregiver support group conversations. *Journal of Gerontological Social Work, 52*(2), 154–170.

Gonyea, J. G. (1989). Alzheimer's disease support groups: An analysis of their structure, format, and perceived benefits. *Social Work in Health Care, 14*(1), 61–72.

Hsieh, E. (2004). Stories in action and the dialogic management of identities: Storytelling in transplant support group meetings. *Research on Language and Social Interaction, 37,* 39–70.

Kahan, J., Kemp, B., Staples, F. R., & Brummel-Smith, K. (1985). Decreasing the burden in families caring for a relative with a dementing illness: A controlled study. *Journal of the American Geriatrics Society, 33,* 664–670.

Kemper, S., & Lyons, K. (1993). The effects of Alzheimer's dementia on language and communication. In M. L. Hummert, J. M. Weimann, & J. F. Nussbaum (Eds.), *Interpersonal communication in older adulthood: Interdisciplinary theory and research* (pp. 58–82). Thousand Oaks, CA: Sage.

Lazarus, R. S., & Folkman, S. (1984). *Stress, appraisal, and coping.* New York: Springer.

Mace, N. L., & Rabins, P. V. (1991). *The 36-hour day* (Rev. ed.). Baltimore, MD: The Johns Hopkins University Press.

MacGeorge, E. L., Samter, W., Feng, B., Gillihan, S. J., & Graves, A. R. (2007). After 9/11: Goal disruption, emotional support, and psychological health in a lower exposure sample. *Health Communication, 21,* 11–22.

Schultz, R., & Beach, S. R. (1999). Caregiving as a risk factor for mortality: The caregiver health effects study. *Journal of the American Medical Association, 282,* 2215–2219.

Segrin, C. (2003). Age moderates the relationship between social support and psychosocial problems. *Human Communication Research, 29,* 317–342.

Sharf, B. F. (1997). Communicating breast cancer on-line: Support and empowerment on the internet. *Women & Health, 26,* 65–84.

Shaw, B. R., McTavish, F., Hawkins, R., Gustafson, D. H., & Pingree, S. (2000). Experiences of women with breast cancer: Exchanging social support over the CHESS computer network. *Journal of Health Communication, 5,* 135–159.

Wills, T. A. (1985). Supportive functions of interpersonal relationships. In S. Cohen & S. L. Syme (Eds.), *Social support and health* (pp. 61–82). New York: Academic Press.

CHAPTER 6

Friendship When Facing Infertility
Challenges and Dilemmas of Social Support

Jennifer J. Bute and Jennifer S. Somerville

KEY TERMS

Social support

Friendship

Infertility

Disclosure

Abstract

Communication about health often occurs in our everyday conversations with friends and family members. The communication of social support is one particular type of everyday talk that has important consequences for physical and psychological health. The following case study explores some of the challenges and dilemmas that characterize the communication of social support in health-related situations. Through exploring the experiences of Stacey, a woman experiencing infertility, and her best friend and confidant, Sharon, we discern that even when social support is an expectation of close relationships, actually talking about some health topics can be problematic. In particular, the person coping with the health challenge and that person's loved ones might struggle with what to say and how to say it. In this case study, we use Goldsmith's (2004) theory of social support to explore the difficulties that relational partners might encounter during everyday interactions about health and encourage readers to contemplate their own experiences with such conversations.

Social support is one of the most studied communication topics of the past several decades (Goldsmith, 2004), and the study of support is particularly relevant to scholars, teachers, and students of health communication (Albrecht & Goldsmith, 2003). People define social support in a variety of ways. As Albrecht and Goldsmith (2003) explained, social support is "an umbrella term for providing a sense of reassurance, validation, and acceptance, the sharing of needed resources and assistance, and connecting or integrating structurally within a web of ties in a supportive network" (p. 265). One way of thinking about social support is to consider what individuals say and do to help the people they care about when those loved ones need guidance, information, advice, or a chance to vent. As we handle everyday hassles, such as dealing with a troublesome roommate, *and* cope with major life events, like managing a serious illness, we might actively seek support from those in our social network. In other cases, those close to us might sense that we need a little extra help or encouragement, even when we have not asked for it.

Our goal in this case study is to explore the complex nature of social support in close personal relationships as individuals navigate the terrains of health and illness. More specifically, this case centers on the communication of social support in the context of infertility. Infertility is a growing reproductive health concern in the United States (Chandra, Martinez, Mosher, Abma, & Jones, 2005), and women, in particular, might seek social support in their conversations with others as they cope with a fertility problem (e.g., Greil, 1991). Such conversations are also an important site for everyday talk about health and health-related issues.

Everyday Talk about Health

Health and illness are inherently social phenomena. Individuals' understandings of health and illness are socially constructed, and our experiences of health and illness are shaped by and, in turn, shape our communicative practices (Babrow & Mattson, 2003). As individuals form beliefs about health, seek to maintain a healthy lifestyle, experience sudden health events, cope with a diagnosis, or manage a chronic condition or disability, they do so in connection with others (e.g., friends, family members, peers, coworkers). Although a wealth of research in health communication focuses on teachable moments, such as patient-health care provider interactions or health education campaigns, much of the ongoing talk about health and illness is woven into our daily lives in the form of everyday conversations (Cline, 2003; Parrott, 2004).

Cline (2003) noted that health communication scholars should devote greater attention to informal conversations about health. Indeed, coping with a health issue, such as infertility, can have a profound effect on communication in interpersonal relationships (Duggan, 2006; Lyons, Sullivan, Ritvo, & Coyne, 1995). For instance, spouses might begin focusing much of their talk around one partner's health issues. Or friends might feel uncertain about how to broach a particular health topic, like a serious diagnosis, during a typical phone conversation. By focusing this case study on everyday interactions, rather than conversations with health care providers or health communication campaigns, we aim to draw attention to the growing body of work (e.g., see Beach & Good, 2004; Bylund & Duck, 2004; Goldsmith, Lindholm, & Bute, 2006; Haas, 2002) that addresses this neglected area in health communication (also see Cline, 2003).

Social Support and Health

The communication of social support in personal relationships is linked to a wide range of health-related outcomes, such as coping behaviors, levels of physical and psychological well-being, uncertainty management efforts, and adoption of a healthy lifestyle (Albrecht & Goldsmith, 2003; Goldsmith, 2004; Goldsmith et al., 2006; Thompson, & O'Hair, 2008). In some cases, social support can have positive effects—helping to improve the health of people managing an illness (Goldsmith, 2004). In other cases, attempts at social support can backfire, or be detrimental to someone's health (Goldsmith, 2004). Much of the research on social support indicates that communicating supportive messages to friends and loved ones can be challenging as individuals search for the "right" words to say, handle the potential awkwardness of sensitive conversations, and manage individual preferences for support (Burleson, 2003, 2008; Goldsmith, 2004; Silver, Wortman, & Crofton, 1990). For example, Silver and colleagues (1990) suggested that discussing a serious health issue is difficult for the person experiencing that issue (e.g., a person who has been diagnosed with cancer) and for those who provide support. Such discussions can highlight the emotional vulnerability and discomfort of potential support providers, including spouses, friends, relatives, and coworkers.

The Infertility Context

The challenges of communicating social support are particularly important for the growing number of women coping with infertility. According to the most recent National Survey of Family Growth, 7.3 million women ages 15 to 44 years reported a physical difficulty with getting pregnant or carrying a baby to term (Chandra et al., 2005). In fact, infertility is so prevalent that many of us are likely to know someone who has coped with this issue, like a friend, sibling, cousin, or acquaintance, even if we personally have never experienced it. And infertility usually comes as a shock to most people who struggle with it. Because many of us might make determined efforts to avoid pregnancy during young adulthood, we might be shocked if we discover that we cannot become pregnant once a decision is made to try to conceive.

Infertility has been described as a major life stressor for men and women (Malik & Coulson, 2008); however, it seems to have a particularly profound effect on women, perhaps because feminine identity is often closely associated with mothering and motherhood (Abbey, 2000). A wealth of research has suggested that talking about infertility can be highly unpleasant for women experiencing infertility, as well as their family members, friends, and acquaintances. For example, many women with a fertility problem have reported feeling uncomfortable discussing the intimate details of their situation (e.g., bodily functions, sexual relationships), yet sensing pressure to reveal their condition to curious others who might want to know why they do not have children (Bute, 2007; 2009; Letherby, 1999; Sandelowski & Jones, 1986). Women have also reported an obligation to hide negative feelings in particular social situations and make diligent efforts to manage the social stigma associated with infertility (Miall, 1986; Whiteford & Gonzalez, 1995). At the same time, supportive others might feel uncomfortable as well; they, too, might be reluctant to discuss the intimate details of testing and treatment for infertility and might grapple with whether and how to inquire about the fertility problem more generally (Bute, 2007). The overall discomfort often associated with talking about infertility is one possible explanation for the many embarrassing and insensitive comments those dealing with infertility might receive (Bute, 2007, 2009; Greil, 1991; Letherby, 1999; Sandelowski & Jones, 1986). For example, women and couples often receive advice like, "You should just adopt;" "Just try to relax;" or "Maybe it just wasn't meant to be" (see Bute, 2007; Greil, 1991).

Yet for the millions of women coping with infertility, the ability to discuss their fertility problem with others is associated with a host of key outcomes. Social support has been associated with better levels of adjustment to infertility (Gibson & Meyers, 2002), decreased infertility-related stress, and greater levels of overall well-being (Abbey, Andrews, & Halman 1991). In a similar manner, negative social interactions have been associated with adjustment problems and could potentially activate maladaptive coping, such as dwelling incessantly on the issue (Mindes, Ingram, Kliewer, & James, 2003). Thus, it is imperative for students and scholars to better understand and appreciate the problems that undergird the communication of social support in the infertility context. The following case study draws attention to a socially significant health concern while also highlighting the challenges of providing, eliciting, and receiving social support.

Understanding Social Support

Our approach to this case study is based on Goldsmith's (2004) theory of social support, which focuses on the meanings and dilemmas associated with troubles talk in close interpersonal relationships. Three key assumptions of Goldsmith's theory are particularly relevant to this case. First, the theory focuses on troubles talk as a "key location" (p. 6) for the communication of social support. Second, the theory focuses on enacted support, or what people actually say to one another in conversations. Finally, the theory centers on social support in close personal relationships. These three assumptions are explained in the paragraphs that follow.

Troubles talk. One important premise of this theory is that we often engage in troubles talk in which we share our problems (i.e., troubles) with those closest to us. For instance, many of us rely on friends and family members when we want to discuss stressors ranging from the daily hassles we encounter, like getting a flat tire on the way to campus or waiting in line at the campus health center, to major sources of distress, like life-altering health problems (e.g., infertility). We count on our loved ones to give us advice, encouragement, or a chance to blow off steam, all of which are examples of social support.

Enacted support. Another assumption of Goldsmith's theory is that the way we enact support is important: what you say and how you say it matters. Some ways of communicating social support in personal relationships are more satisfying and successful than others. That is, the theory is based on the premise that some supportive messages do a better job of accomplishing the task of communicating support while also attending to what talk means for identities (e.g., does asking for support mean looking weak because you have to admit that you need help? Does admitting a fertility problem make a woman seem less feminine?) and relationships (e.g., is social support an expectation in certain types of relationships?).

In the context of infertility, Goldsmith's theory helps emphasize that some ways of asking about a person's experiences with a fertility problem or her plans to have children in general can come across as particularly face-threatening and insensitive (e.g., "So, why don't you have children yet?"), but other ways of asking can build close relationships and provide an appropriate conversational moment for discussing emotions and concerns (e.g., "I know you've been trying to get pregnant for awhile. Is there anything you'd like to talk about?"). Some ways of offering advice to a woman dealing with infertility can also seem pushy or invasive (e.g., "Stop trying so hard, and you're bound to get pregnant!"), but other ways of suggesting advice can express sincere caring and encourage positive coping (e.g., "I'm concerned for you. Maybe we could get online together and check out some resources."). The friendship explored in this case study highlights the delicate balancing act of trying to communicate social support while still honoring valued identities and relational qualities.

Close personal relationships. Finally, Goldsmith argues that our close relationships with others serve as the primary context for troubles talk and enacted support. Thus, we are likely to share our problems and receive support from those close to us. Moreover, we might expect that certain friends and relatives will be there to support us. We might also be disappointed or hurt if they fail to do so, or if they make attempts at support that are deemed thoughtless or insensitive. The situation facing Stacey and Sharon provides an exemplar of the challenges that come along with enacting social support during troubles talk in close personal relationships.

The Case of Stacey and Sharon

The case of Stacey and Sharon is based on a recent study of 23 women coping with infertility. Based on in-depth interviews with study participants, we developed composite cases (see, for example, Ford & Christman, 2005) that represent the overall experiences described by women in the sample (see Bute, 2007; 2009; Bute & Vik, 2010 for details on the methods used in the study). Stacey represents the experiences of women managing the day-to-day struggles of a fertility problem. Her friend, Sharon, represents the supportive others who try to assist a loved one in coping with infertility. We have chosen to emphasize the perspectives of both parties who could potentially take part in supportive conversations to more fully illuminate the potential challenges and dilemmas faced by both individuals.

Stacey's Background

Stacey is 30 years old and has been married to her husband, Jack, for two years. Shortly after they married, Stacey and Jack started trying to become pregnant. Both of them had always wanted children, so they did not delay their efforts to start a family. After a year of trying without success, Stacey consulted her family practitioner, who referred her to a fertility specialist. Ever since, Stacey and Jack have endured a series of tests and treatments, including a recent attempt at *in vitro* fertilization, a costly procedure that involves fertilizing eggs outside the womb and then transferring an embryo (or embryos) to a woman's uterus.

The journey on their quest to have a child has been emotionally taxing for both of them, especially for Stacey, whose best friend, Sharon, recently had a baby. Talking about her fertility problem has always been a sensitive issue for Stacey. She feels ashamed, frustrated, and embarrassed to admit that she cannot become pregnant. And she is not fond of discussing the intimate details of her sex life and her body, even with her closest friends. On the other hand, Stacey often feels a need to vent and wants to be reassured that pursuing treatment is the "right" thing to do. She especially wishes she could talk to Sharon; however, since Sharon had her daughter, their relationship has seemed tense. The last time they talked on the phone, Stacey sensed that Sharon was uncomfortable. She often pondered a particularly awkward moment in their conversation:

Sharon: So, things are going okay for you and Jack?

Stacey: Yeah, I guess so. No real news to report on our end.

Sharon: No news, huh? Well, you know I'm always thinking about you.

Stacey: Thanks. How is Madison doing? I haven't seen her since she was born.

Sharon: Oh, fine. Tell me what's up at work. How's your new boss working out?

The entire conversation had seem forced and strained, and now Stacey regretted not taking the opportunity to talk to Sharon about the depression and anxiety she had been feeling as she and Jack contemplated whether to keep pursing fertility treatments. It seemed that Sharon had either been trying to inquire about her struggles to get pregnant in sort of a roundabout way, or had attempted to change the subject abruptly to avoid dwelling on the matter. In either case, Stacey felt frustrated that she was too embarrassed to talk about the painful treatment procedures and the heartbreaking news that their last attempt had failed. And Stacey had always viewed herself as an independent person, so it was difficult for her to admit that she needed some help coping with her inability to conceive. Meanwhile, Stacey felt even worse that Sharon obviously tried to talk about anything but her new baby—she asked Stacey about her job, then went on to inquire about her dog, her husband, and some recent home improvement projects. Only once during the conversation did Sharon mention her daughter, Madison. Stacey knows that Sharon is trying to protect her by avoiding the topic of babies, but regrets that she cannot share more fully in her best friend's joy. Stacey also feels that she has lost a valuable source of support. Indeed, all their conversations feel so awkward now that Stacey does not even know how to bring up her fertility problem without sounding silly, rude, or self-centered.

Sharon's Background

Sharon is a new mom and has been best friends with Stacey since college. The two live only an hour apart and have stayed in close contact through email, phone calls, and weekend lunches. When Stacey first confessed to Sharon that she was having trouble becoming pregnant, Sharon had no idea how to react. Stacey had said to Sharon, "Jack and I have been trying to get pregnant, and we're having some problems." As she spoke, Stacey played with her food, barely made eye contact, and looked visibly uncomfortable. Sharon had never known anyone in that situation before. Rather than elaborate much on the topic or press Stacey for more information, she tried to offer some encouraging words by saying, "I'm sure everything will work out."

But Sharon knew that she had not found the right thing to say; Stacey had not broached the subject since. Now every time they talk, Sharon wonders if she should bring up the topic and has even tried on a couple of occasions, usually asking indirect questions like, "How are things with you and Jack?" Sharon wonders if she should ask more direct questions: Are you still trying to get pregnant? Have you thought about adoption? Would you be happy remaining childless? But those questions just seem so invasive. She struggles with how to express her willingness to be there for Stacey without being too nosy. It also occurs to her that talking about the fertility problem might compel Stacey to dwell on the issue more than she desires.

And now that she has her daughter, Madison, the situation seems even worse. Stacey had been so brave—helping to coordinate a baby shower and visiting Sharon in the hospital when her daughter was born, but the two of them have never discussed how Sharon's pregnancy made Stacey feel. Telling Stacey she was pregnant was one of the most challenging conversations Sharon had ever had. Sharon remembers the conversation vividly:

Sharon: So, I've got some news to share with you.

Stacey: What's that?

Sharon: I just found out that I'm pregnant!

Stacey: That's great news!

Sharon: I hope that doesn't upset you.

Stacey: No, why would it?

Sharon: Um, no reason. Just let me know if you want to talk about it, okay?

Stacey: Okay.

Sharon cringed whenever she recalled this conversation. Once again, instead of asking her friend directly about her struggles, she had beat around the bush. Yet, she wanted to avoid embarrassing Stacey or bringing up a potentially painful topic since she did not want to hurt her friend, and she did not know how to respond. And she worried that by assuming Stacey would be upset by her news, she had unintentionally implied that Stacey was some kind of emotional basket case. No wonder Stacey did not talk about her infertility with her! The more she thought about it, the more Sharon felt that to preserve their friendship, she had to find a way to reach out to her friend.

The Lunch Date

Sharon finally decided to email Stacey and schedule a lunch date for the following Saturday. When Stacey received the brief message ("Noon on Saturday at Gabe's Place?"), she eagerly replied, "Sure" and hit the send key. As Saturday approached, both women pondered whether and how to bring up the topic of Stacey's fertility problem during their conversation.Maybe I should just say, "I have some things I'd like to talk through with you," thought Stacey. This approach would allow her to ease into the topic with Sharon. Meanwhile, Sharon wondered if she should simply say, "I've been thinking about you and Jack and wondering how the fertility treatments are going." She reasoned that the statement was not overly intrusive like a question might be and would allow Stacey to decide whether to open up.

When Saturday finally arrived, Stacey and Sharon pulled into the parking lot at almost the same time. The two women quickly parked, exited their cars, and embraced before walking into Gabe's, both looking forward to a much-needed conversation.

After entering the restaurant, the two spent some time catching up since they last visited. Sharon then decided to carefully approach the subject of Stacey's fertility problem:

Sharon: Stacey, I have to be honest. I have been scared to talk to you about your efforts to get pregnant. I was afraid that I would upset you, especially after I found out I was pregnant. But your friendship means the world to me, and I feel like the issue is causing tension between us. If my perception is wrong, please tell me. And, please tell me how you feel.

By not directly asking Stacey about her infertility, Sharon gave Stacey the opportunity to reflect on her feelings and how she would like to proceed with her answer to Sharon. Stacey felt a huge weight begin to lift as she told Sharon how painful it has been for her:

Stacey: I'm so glad you brought that up. Jack and I really want a baby, and the last several months have been just awful …

She then proceeded to tell Sharon about their recent *in vitro* failure, her feelings of shame and guilt, as well as her mixed emotions about discussing the issue with Sharon.

As the two women continued to talk, they expressed the complexity of the situation and their reluctance to bring up the topic previously. They also reinforced the importance of their friendship and vowed to keep working on strengthening their friendship. Yet, as they left the restaurant later that afternoon, both wondered whether and how they would continue to discuss Stacey's infertility and Sharon's new motherhood in the future.

Discussion Questions

1. Goldsmith's approach to social support says that what you say and how you say it matters. Reread the conversations that Stacey and Sharon recall throughout the case study. In what ways does Goldsmith's idea apply to these conversations?

2. Goldsmith's theory suggests that we might be concerned about the identity we portray in our conversations with others. What evidence of Stacey's identity concerns is present in this case study? What identity concerns does Sharon face?

3. Infertility is only one of many subjects that is deemed difficult to talk about in our society. What are some other health issues that you can think of that would be difficult to bring up in conversation with a friend? Why are they difficult to discuss?

4. Why do you think health topics related to sexuality and reproduction, like infertility or sexually transmitted infections (STIs), are considered taboo topics?

5. What types of communication skills do you think are needed or could be taught to help eliminate the stigma surrounding difficult-to-discuss topics?

6. How do you define social support? Social support has been found to have many benefits to health and well-being in individuals' lives. Based on your own experiences, do you agree that social support is beneficial? How so?

7. Where would you go for support when coping with a health challenge? How available do you think support is for potentially stigmatizing health conditions (e.g., infertility, STIs)?

References

Abbey, A. (2000). Adjusting to infertility. In J. H. Harvey & E. D. Miller (Eds.), *Loss and trauma: General and close relationship perspectives* (pp. 331–341). Philadelphia: Brunner-Routledge.

Abbey, A., Andrews, F. M., & Halman, L. J. (1991). The importance of social relationships for infertile couples' well-being. In A. L. Stanton & C. Dunkel-Schetter (Eds.), *Infertility: Perspectives from stress and coping research* (pp. 61–86). New York: Plenum Press.

Albrecht, T. L., & Goldsmith, D. J. (2003). Social support, social networks, and health. In T. L. Thompson, A. M. Dorsey, K. I. Miller, & R. Parrot (Eds.), *Handbook of health communication* (pp. 263–284). Mahwah, NJ: Erlbaum.

Babrow, A. S., & Mattson, M. (2003). Theorizing about health communication. In T. Thompson, A. M. Dorsey, K. Miller, & R. Parrot (Eds.), *Handbook of health communication.* (pp. 35–61). Hillsdale, NJ: Erlbaum.

Beach, W. A., & Good, J. S. (2004). Uncertain family trajectories: Interactional consequences of cancer diagnosis, treatment, and prognosis. *Journal of Social and Personal Relationships, 21*, 8–32.

Burleson, B. R. (2003). Emotional support skills. In J. O'Green & B. R. Burleson (Eds.), *Handbook of communication and social interaction skills* (pp. 551–594). Mahaw, NJ: Erlbaum.

Burleson, B. R. (2008). What counts as effective emotional support? Explorations of individual and situational differences. In M. T. Motley (Ed.), *Studies in applied interpersonal communication* (pp. 207–227). Thousand Oaks, CA: Sage.

Bute, J. J. (2007). *Talking about infertility: A conceptual model.* Unpublished doctoral dissertation.

Bute, J. J. (2009). "Nobody thinks twice about asking:" Women with a fertility problem and requests for information. *Health Communication, 24*, 752–763.

Bute, J. J., & Vik, T. A. (2010). Privacy management as unfinished business: Shifting boundaries in the context of infertility. *Communication Studies, 61*, 1–20.

Bylund, C. L., & Duck, S. (2004). The everyday interplay between family relationships and family members' health. *Journal of Social and Personal Relationships, 21*, 5–7.

Chandra, A., Martinez, G., Mosher, W., Abma, J., & Jones, J. (2005). *Fertility, family planning, and reproductive health of U.S. women: Data from the 2002 National Survey of Family Growth.*: National Center for Health Statistics.

Cline, R. J. W. (2003). Everyday interpersonal communication and health. In T. L. Thompson, A. M. Dorsey, K. I. Miller & R. Parrot (Eds.), *Handbook of health communication* (pp. 285–318). Mahwah, NJ: Erlbaum.

Duggan, A. (2006). Understanding interpersonal communication processes across health contexts: Advances in the last decade and challenges for the next decade. *Journal of Health Communication, 11*, 93–108.

Ford, L. A., & Christmon, B. C. (2005). "Every breast cancer is different": Illness narratives and the management of identity in breast cancer. In E. B. Ray (Ed.), *Health communication in practice: A case study approach* (pp. 157–169). Mahwah, NJ: Erlbaum.

Gibson, D. M., & Myers, J. E. (2002). The effect of social coping resources and growth-fostering relationships on infertility stress in women. *Journal of Mental Health Counseling, 24*, 68–80.

Goldsmith, D. J. (2004). *Communicating social support*. Cambridge: Cambridge University Press.

Goldsmith, D. J., Lindholm, K. A., & Bute, J. J. (2006). Dilemmas of talking about lifestyle changes among couples coping with a cardiac event. *Social Science and Medicine, 63*, 2079–2090.

Greil, A. L. (1991). *Not yet pregnant: Infertile couples in contemporary America*. New Brunswick: Rutgers University Press.

Haas, S. M. (2002). Social support as relationship maintenance in gay male couples coping with HIV or AIDS. *Journal of Social and Personal Relationships, 19*, 87–111.

Letherby, G. (1999). Other than mother and mothers as others: The experience of motherhood and non-motherhood in relation to "infertility" and "involuntary childlessness." *Women's Studies International Forum, 22*, 359–372.

Lyons, R. F., Sullivan, M. J. L., Ritvo, P. G., & Coyne, J. C. (1995). *Relationships in chronic illness and disability*. Thousand Oaks, CA: Sage.

Miall, C. E. (1986). The stigma of involuntary childlessness. *Social Problems, 33*, 268–282.

Malik, S., & Coulson, N. (2008). Computer-mediated infertility support groups: an exploratory study of online experiences. *Patient Education & Counseling, 73*(1), 105–113.

Mindes, E. J., Ingram, K. M., Kliewer, W., & James, C. A. (2003). Longitudinal analyses of the relationship between unsupportive social interactions and psychological adjustment among women with fertility problems. *Social Science and Medicine, 56*, 2165–2180.

Parrott, R. (2004). Emphasizing "communication" in health communication. *Journal of Communication, 54*, 751–787.

Sandelowski, M., & Jones, L. C. (1986). Social exchanges of infertile women. *Issues in Mental Health Nursing, 8*, 173–189.

Silver, R. C., Wortman, C. B., & Crofton, C. (1990). The role of coping in support provision: The self-presentational dilemma of victims of life crises. In B. R. Sarason & I. G. Sarason (Eds.), *Social support: An interactional view* (pp. 397–426). New York: Wiley.

Thompson, S., & O'Hair, H. (2008). Advice-giving and the management of uncertainty for cancer survivors. *Health Communication, 23*, 340–348.

Whiteford, L. M., & Gonzalez, L. (1995). Stigma: The hidden burden of infertility. *Social Science and Medicine, 40*, 27–36.

CHAPTER 7

Cultural Issues and Coping with Critical Illness of a Female Malay Cancer Survivor in Singapore[1]

Angela Ka Ying Mak and Suwichit (Sean) Chaidaroon

KEY TERMS

Cancer survivor

Cultural diversity

Social support

Self-advocacy

Abstract

This case study presents a story of Aminah[2], a Malay-Muslim Singaporean, who was diagnosed with second-stage breast cancer[3] in June 2009. Based on kampong spirit, a unique cultural belief of the Malay-Muslims in being a cohesive part of the community, Aminah has been supported spiritually through her daunting times. While this cancer survivor demonstrates a positive attitude through a strong sense of self-advocacy (see Brashers, Hass, & Neidig, 1999) unlike the majority of Singaporean patients, this case presents the key challenges Aminah faces including the misunderstanding of the Malay cultural values and people surrounding her. The case also illustrates a lack of awareness, appreciation, and knowledge of the healthcare benefits in her country.

This case aims to illustrate that culture is an important issue in health communication inquiry and pedagogy. Each ethnicity has its distinct interpretations and concepts of health, disease, and healing (Galanti, 1991; Spector, 1996). Thus, the negotiation of meanings of health issues is a complex process in a culturally diverse context (Wright, Sparks, & O'Hair, 2008). This case also highlights the diversity issue in health communication from an ethnic group's perspective in Singapore. This Asian country, in particular, offers a unique view on healthcare issues as the country's population of nearly 5 million consists of diverse races/cultures including Chinese, Malay, Indian, and Eurasian. Also, expatriates and foreigners comprise 30% of the country's population (Singapore Department of Statistics, 2009).[4] Therefore, while the country maintains its uniqueness of Asian cultural heritage, Singapore can also represent many developed, non-Asian countries based on its advanced economic system and multicultural population. The health communication issues illustrated in this case thus demonstrate distinct practices and lessons learned from working with culturally specific groups, which should help increase cultural sensitivity levels of health communication practices.

In addition, while mainstream health communication literature addresses primarily issues of health campaigns and provider-patient interactions, health communication permeates into all parts of our lives (Thompson, Robinson, Anderson, & Federowicz, 2008). This case, for example, illustrates an issue of health communication and its effects on one's employment, revealing that cancer survivorship can be viewed as a form of "disability" stigmatizing those undergoing treatments and affecting their lives afterwards. Therefore, health communication research and education should extend beyond the hospital, clinics, or campaign settings (Cline, 2003).

Literature Review

Cancer, a life-threatening illness, affects and shapes identities of individuals who discover that they have such a disease (Anderson & Geist-Martin, 2008). The term "cancer survivor" is attributed to an individual the moment s/he is diagnosed with cancer and for the rest of her/ his life, "regardless of whether death was ultimately due to cancer or some unrelated cause or event" (Rowland, Hewitt, & Ganz, 2006, p. 5101). It is frequently challenging to identify whether a patient still has cancer, or whether a patient has a precise prognosis following the successful treatment of the disease (see Kreps & Massimilla, 2002; O'Hair, Kreps, & Sparks, 2007). In addition, some individuals may decide not to receive any treatments and, thus, labeling them as patients could be misleading. Therefore, the term "cancer survivor" is more appropriate than "cancer patient" in general (du Pré & Ray, 2008).

In this section, a brief discussion on cancer in the workplace and in Singapore is provided as background before a review of relevant concepts including social support, self-advocacy, the Malay's notion of kampong spirit, and the circuit of culture theory/framework.

Cancer in the Workplace

Employment provides a means for cancer survivors to enhance their quality of life, as it fulfills the need to support their families, and provides them with a sense of identity, purpose, and social support. Peteet (2000) studied various cases of cancer survivors, including a middle-aged single mother, a divorced factory owner with lung cancer, a married sales consultant with multiple myeloma, a Christian industrial arts teacher who developed pancreatic cancer shortly after retirement, and a divorced middle-aged breast cancer manager who accepted a promotion that involved relocation to different state. Peteet (2000) concluded that "continuing or returning to the workplace allows many patients to maintain a sense of normalcy or control" (p. 202). In addition, returning to paid employment after a cancer diagnosis and treatment is an important transformation from patients to survivors. Bradley and Bednarek (2002) conducted a study among 253 patients ($n = 58$ lung cancer, $n = 53$ colon cancer, $n = 73$ breast cancer, and $n = 69$ prostate cancer). Most patients, at the time of the interview, were in their early sixties with the exception of prostate cancer patients. The majority were Caucasians and about 20% of the sample was African American. The findings indicated that some cancer survivors were persistent in remaining at work "to save for potential future medical expenses as well as keeping health insurance, even though their health status is compromised" (p. 194). As this study suggested, this transition back to the workplace is not without problems.

Bennett et al. (2008) examined employment problems faced by 68% cancer survivors (6–24 months since diagnosis). This research team found that the difficulties cancer survivors encountered were mostly in two areas: physical difficulties and attitudes of employers. Very often, cancer survivors experience physical fatigue, which can affect their performance at work (Stanton et al., 2005). In a similar manner, colleagues' and employers' perceptions of the cancer survivors' physical health, side and after effects of cancer treatments, as well as potential biases may influence the likelihood of some cancer survivors gaining re-employment. Other factors found to influence the likelihood of return to work include whether work involves a large amount of physical effort and side effects of the cancer and treatment (Spelten, Sprangers, & Verbeek, 2002). Cancer survivors thus face unique workplace challenges, further exacerbated by a high level of uncertainty pertaining to curability and relapse, posing questions of risk pertaining to the hiring of survivors. It is also important to note that an individual's risk for developing another type of cancer increases dramatically once a person becomes a cancer survivor (Curtis et al., 2006).[5] This risk of a second cancer may affect the perception of employers and co-workers when hiring cancer survivors.

Cancer in Singapore

Chen et al. (2006) conducted a survey assessing the perceptions about cancer survivors in Singapore. Findings from this study indicated that although the majority of respondents had positive attitudes toward working with cancer survivors, approximately 90% of 62 respondents did not believe that they deserved equal opportunities at work. Notably, more than 80% of the respondents would not hire a cancer survivor if they were in the position to hire regardless of the status of their treatment.

In 2000, the World Health Organization (WHO) ranked Singapore sixth out of 191 countries on overall health system performance in its World Health Report (Ministry of Health, 2007). Singapore adopts a mixed financing system,[6] which ensures that no Singaporean is denied access to healthcare due to financial concerns. The cost of cancer treatments differs with the types of cancer and depends on whether the individual requires chemotherapy, radiotherapy, surgery, or a combination of two or more of these methods. The average medical bill in Singapore is very affordable for average citizens.[7] For example, removing breast lumps in a public hospital costs less than a thousand U.S. dollars while it would cost at least double that amount in the United States. Although the Singaporean citizens enjoy great healthcare benefits, the patient advocacy movement is still in its infancy (Ting & Yen, 2008) due in part to the paternalistic government structure and low social capitalism.

Social Support

Social support is an essential form of communication that plays an integral role in the survival of cancer patients as well as their lives after cancer (see Wright, 2002). Social support can be defined as "verbal and nonverbal communication between recipients and providers that helps manage uncertainty about the situation, the self, the other or the relationship and functions to enhance a perception of personal control in one's life experience" (Albrecht & Adelman, 1987, p. 19). Friends, families, colleagues, and co-workers can provide support to cancer survivors during their life-threatening moments in various ways (Goldsmith, 2004). They can offer tangible assistance or *instrumental support*. They can also listen to and encourage the patients and provide *emotional support*. This dimension, in particular, has been consistently and empirically linked with health outcomes (Broadhead et al., 1983; Wills & Fegan, 2001). *Esteem support* can also be provided by helping the patients feel that their problems are validated and legitimized. Finally, a common form is giving advice or *informational support* to the patients (see Wills, 1985). Nowadays, social support can be sought not only from people surrounding the patients but also online, especially in the case of cancer (Query & Wright, 2008; Wright, 2002). It is imperative to note, however, that such well-intended supportive communication may also lead to negative consequences if such interactions are perceived as unwanted, intrusive, or patronizing (Goldsmith & Fitch, 1997; La Gaipa, 1990). As you peruse the case, consider different forms of social support the character received and to what extent each supportive act was presented to her effectively.

Self-advocacy in Cancer Patients and Survivors

Self-advocacy is the degree of willingness and active participation of a patient in three dimensions: "increased illness and treatment education, increased assertiveness in health care interactions, and increased potential for nonadherence" (Brashers et al., 1999, p. 97). The concept of patient advocacy has been discussed and developed to include the areas of self, organizational, and public policy contexts (Leigh, 2008). As proposed by the National Coalition for Cancer Survivorship (NCCS; 2009), advocacy exists at different levels. It starts with the individual seeking to ensure that s/he receives quality care. In addition, patient advocacy can exist for others in the same community/situation. Finally, the largest scale of patient advocacy can be initiated and supported by organizations that campaign for improvements at the national level.

Self-advocacy is about equipping oneself with the necessary tools and skills to assert the individuals' rights, communicate their needs, and take control of their situation (NCCS, 2009). In an ideal situation, cancer patients and survivors should have the right to self-advocate (Hoffman & Stovall, 2006). Patient empowerment should not be predefined by healthcare professionals, or limited by the disease or illness. Rather, it should be negotiated to the extent possible, to suit the patients' circumstances and lifestyle (Aujoulat, d'Hoore, & Deccache, 2007). As you read the following case, consider the levels of advocacy at the individual, organizational, and national levels in Singapore.

Cancer and the Kampong Spirit

In the past, when Singaporeans lived in *kampongs* (i.e., Malay term for villages), members of the community used to know each other very well and neighbors were close-knit much like a family.

There existed a **kampong spirit**, or what is commonly known to Malays as the spirit of *gotong royong*, a Javanese term that literally means "to share a burden" (Sullivan, 1986). The concept of community self-help or mutual self-help (Bowen, 1986; Hawkins, 1955; Sullivan, 1986) embodied in the term indicates there is a collective sense of responsibility toward the community, and it is believed to have "good" societal and sociological benefits (Chia & Tan, 2004).

Among the Malays in Singapore, the kampong spirit is apparent where members of the community largely benefit from the sharing of resources, in which individualism is downplayed, and all work should be achieved together (Rahardjo, 1994). However, as the monetary and contractual relationships between individuals increased, the custom of *gotong royong* also declined (Van der Kroef, 1960). Despite this decrease, today, many Malays have retained this kampong spirit through community involvement and offering support across major life incidents, such as cancer.

The unique cultural value of each community can lead to different interpretations of illness as well as different views on treatments. For example, members in many individualistic cultures may feel comfortable sharing openly with strangers about their illness and may be less likely to seek help from others in fighting the battle. In contrast, among the collectivistic cultures like Asians, the ways in which individuals cope with life-threatening disease is different. For example, many Chinese typically prefer not to disclose their major illness beyond close family units since they believe that it is bad luck which could also pass onto others. For many Japanese individuals, they often do not want others to visit them in the final stage of life as a way to maintain their self-pride.

The Circuit of Culture Framework

As culture is an important theme of the present case, it is paramount to analyze how cultural values shape the way in which health issues are interpreted and understood (Dutta & Zoller, 2008). Subsequently, the analysis of a cancer survivorship topic is discussed next, based on the **circuit of culture** framework (Curtin & Gaither, 2005). This approach is designed to delineate the complications of the case when different components of cultural values and expectations clash.

To interpret more effectively how culture influences communicative practices and the converse, Curtin and Gaither (2005) propose that individuals consider the *holistic* picture of how culture operates through five components (or "moments") simultaneously. First, *regulations* refer to any norms, rules, and policies that regulate communicative practices in the particular society. Second, *representation* consists of any symbols and language that illustrate ideology and value. Third, *production* is the process of making meanings through the use of symbols. Fourth, *consumption* includes the process in which societal individuals make sense of and adopt the symbols as a part of their daily lives. Fifth, *identity* encompasses the meanings that are accrued, adopted, and shared by an overwhelming number of network members.

Unlike other frameworks that mostly attempt to compare different cultures in respective societies, the "circuit of culture" model offers a lens to view each culture *within* its particular context. As they developed this framework, Curtin and Gaither (2005) took into consideration that *unequal power* exists in most societies and this imbalance impacts the way individuals view different cultures. As you move through the following case, you should discern that Malay culture can be viewed through these five principles, while the majority of Singaporeans may have their own set of principles.

The Case Study

A day after celebrating her 31st birthday in June 2009, Aminah met misfortune. After two initial operations to remove the supposedly benign lump on her right breast, her doctor informed her that that lump had been cancerous. Aminah pursed her lips and told herself that everything would be "fine." She remembered purchasing an enhancement to her Medishield, a government health insurance policy, to cover any emergencies such as cancer. She later became dismayed, however, when the Central Provident Fund (CPF) Board[8] informed her that the policy she had would only take effect if her bill had reached $2,125[9] for the year, which it had not.

Aminah panicked. She was very worried about the high cost of cancer treatment and how her insurance would not cover all the expenses. Her chemotherapy treatment in the National Cancer Center (NCC) Singapore was estimated to last for six months, with the total cost estimated at least $5,700. Aminah was at a loss. Although the lump removal had depleted her Medisave, a compulsory medical account, she still had to undergo eight chemotherapy sessions which would also be a massive financial burden to her. Further worsening the situation, there was only $1,420 in her husband's Medisave account.

Aminah still had three young school-aged children to feed. Pressing questions began to pop up in her mind. For example, should her children be told? Should she agree to the chemotherapy? What would chemotherapy mean to her ability to support her family financially and emotionally? Would she have to stop working? Aminah furrowed her eyebrows and decided to first speak to her husband. After some at-length discussion, Aminah finally decided to receive treatments hoping she would survive this disease.

Aminah was residing in a small two-room apartment with her family. When speaking with her children and others about her condition, she was amicable and upfront about it. Although her experience with cancer had started only recently, Aminah was treating her life positively and taking each day as it came. For Aminah, the cancer had been a surprise. Her family did not have any history of cancer, and she was unprepared as she did not have prior knowledge about the effects of cancer and treatment costs.

Already into her third out of eight treatments scheduled, Aminah rested at home on a no-pay leave following the advice of her employer, Melissa, and her doctor's orders. Aminah closed her eyes and thought of her predicament. She felt she was blessed to have an employer who understood her condition, and who allowed her to take time off for cancer treatment. Melissa's understanding was essential, more so since every chemotherapy session was taking its toll on Aminah. Aminah counted her blessings as she appreciated her supervisor's empathy. Regrettably, however, with no official legislation in place currently to protect the rights of cancer survivors in terms of employability, not all cancer patients were as fortunate as Aminah.

Aminah was also puzzled by all the myths that defined what a cancer patient should or should not do. She hoped someone could help separate fiction from truth. In her line of work as a beauty therapist, for instance, she had to handle slimming equipment that emitted radio frequency waves. According to her Chinese colleague, Tingting, she could not use the equipment since radio frequency waves could trigger the dormant cancer cells in her body. Aminah was also advised by her friends to refrain from cooking, but she could not understand their rationale. It was also something that she could not afford to do on a long-term basis due to financial considerations and her dedication to ensure her children had proper meals prepared by her.[10]

After her cancer had been confirmed, Aminah had been automatically referred to NCC by the Singapore General Hospital (SGH). The entire process, however, up to the day of her first appointment, was painstakingly slow. She did not complain though as she was already thankful she would be receiving assistance from NCC with regards to medical costs. With time being the key to a cancer patient's chances of survival, the medical social worker who helped Aminah with her case was shocked to learn that Aminah had yet to start her chemotherapy sessions, even though four weeks had lapsed since her last contact with NCC. Upon guidance from her social worker, Aminah called the NCC to schedule her chemotherapy sessions herself, when it should have been already done. Aminah's colleagues and friends perceived that NCC's response was sluggish due to Aminah's status as a subsidized patient leading to the impression that she was treated as a second-class patient. Aminah believed this unfounded information and grudgingly accepted the slow process.

Aminah's doctor had also advised her to stop working due to her chemotherapy treatments in which she was injected with anti-cancer drugs. Not working would allow her to recuperate after each chemotherapy session (i.e., "chemo") to better cope with side effects. Many factors shape the intensity of chemo's after effects, including the primary site of the cancer, stage of the disease, age and health of the individual, as well as type of treatments. For Aminah, side effects typically did not happen immediately, and could last for up to a week or so. Aminah resented that she felt weak and tired, also suffering hot flashes after each chemo session despite these being quite common. She could not even step out of her apartment as the sunlight, which seemed blinding, contributed to her feeling nauseous. She also suffered from an uncomfortable cold sensation in her nose. Despite these challenges, she still continued doing housework at her own pace, with her husband and oldest daughter "chipping in."

Aminah's Employer and Workplace

Aminah defied the stereotype that Malays are lazy.[11] She was eager to work again. After marrying, Aminah stopped working to take care of her family and children. As her children grew, she rejoined the workforce in 2000 by working as a temporary sales associate at established retailers and department stores in local shopping malls. It was only in 2008, when she enrolled in a skills upgrading course, that she chanced upon the beauty treatment class. After completing her course in March 2008, Aminah worked as a full-time beauty therapist at Melissa's salon. As part of her job's scope, Aminah worked at least 10 hours daily, six days a week. Aminah was the first employee of the salon to be diagnosed with cancer. Although the salon is a small start-up with only two other beauty therapists, the impact of her cancer has reverberated on the business' operations and job routines.

In May 2009, when Aminah was officially diagnosed with cancer and before her chemotherapy sessions began, Melissa made some provisional changes to accommodate Aminah's illness by changing Aminah's full-time contract to a part-time one. The new contract required for Aminah to work only three times a week. It was only when Aminah started her chemotherapy treatments in September that she stopped working completely. She had also been told by her doctor that she would only be able to return to work after having completed all chemotherapy treatments. This process might take several months and her doctor set a tentative completion date for April 2010.

In addition to immense support from her family members, Aminah's employer, Melissa, was equally thoughtful when she heard that Aminah had been stricken with cancer. Not only did she highlight Aminah's financial dilemma to a local newspaper in hope of raising awareness about Aminah's plight, Melissa personally organized a fundraiser with her church for Aminah. As of this writing, $1,000 has been raised and Melissa hoped that the rest of the treatment costs could be borne by the premiums Aminah had paid. Aminah's support network was undeniably strong, as her family members and her employer stood by her through those difficult months. Aminah showed resilience in spite of all the setbacks that she was facing. She maintained a positive attitude and carried on her daily activities including household chores and daily shopping. She told herself daily that she was unafraid of the illness and she would conquer it eventually.

Melissa, a Eurasian Christian, has two salons employing less than eight people. Aminah's departure left Melissa with a serious personnel shortage. The search for Aminah's replacement has also been time-consuming as the new beauty therapists needed to be trained. Special arrangements were made though, and Melissa had her staff cover Aminah's duties. Extra workloads and longer working hours for Aminah's co-workers were thus necessary.

While still working part-time at the salon, one of Aminah's workers, Tingting, lamented to Aminah that she had to assume more responsibilities and was tired from attending to so many customers. Although Aminah felt bad that she was unable to help out more during peak periods, she was unable to do so due to the physical post-surgery side effects. For example, massaging a customer for two hours with continuous force was no longer an option for her as it could aggravate her incisions.

Yielding to Chemo's Intensity and Ongoing Employer Support
Although Aminah was no longer working at the salon, Melissa still called on her to check on her well-being. She even visited Aminah with the rest of the workers from the salon for the

recent *Hari Raya Aidilfitri* celebration (i.e., a festivity celebrated by all Muslims). Aminah received overwhelming support from her co-workers and good wishes were also in abundance from her regular customers. Melissa reinforced that Aminah was welcome to return to work after her chemotherapy treatments.

Melissa had gone well beyond the call of duty as an employer in providing so many accommodations for Aminah. She had the option of firing Aminah; however, Melissa understood that there was more to running a business than bringing in sales and earning profits. For Melissa, although the accommodations she made were centered on Aminah, she could now set her own company guidelines and policies to help other employees faced with similar situations involving major forms of illnesses or disability.

NOTES

1   We want to thank our undergraduate students Mohamad Heikel Bin Kharsani, LIM Shu Yin, Manjit Kaur d/o Mon Singh, TAN Jia Hao, and Sharifh Nadzirah Binte Syed Zulkifli for their assistance in conducting the interview with Aminah and drafting this case.

2   This case is based on a true story of a Malay woman in Singapore from a casual interview. Although the primary aim of this interview was to develop a larger research project and the interview was not treated as data gathering for research analysis, the interviewee agreed to be recorded prior to the interview and her identity has been protected. The character's name is a pseudonym.

3   Stages of cancer indicate severity of a case and help both patients and caregivers determine appropriate treatments. In general, stages of cancer are determined by the cancer type and the spread of the tumor(s) (National Cancer Institute, 2004). The severity of each case can be identified in five stages, ranging from 0, where cancer is found only on the layer of cells in a specific organ, to IV, where the cancer has already spread to other organs in an individual's body.

4   Among its population of 4.16 million, 77% are Chinese, 14% Malays, and 8% Indians, with the remaining 1% consisting of people from international backgrounds including Eurasians and Caucasians. English has become the language of administration, while Malay, Chinese, and Tamil are the other official languages (Singapore Department of Statistics, 2009).

5   Empirical studies have been conducted to confirm the risk of developing a second type of cancer among cancer survivors. Among many types of cancer that lead to the second malignancies are cancer of buccal cavity and pharynx, digestive tract, respiratory tract, cervix uteri, uterine corpus, male genital tract, bone and soft tissue, skin, eye, brain, thyroid, etc. (see Curtis et al., 2006)

6   The healthcare system in Singapore lies between both ends of the spectrum of complete privatization and being state-funded. Singapore adopts the "3M" system to finance healthcare, based on the premise of a shared responsibility between individuals and the state. This "3M" system is a co-payment system and is comprised of Medisave (a compulsory medical savings account), MediShield (a low cost catastrophic medical insurance scheme), and Medifund (a medical endowment fund for those who cannot afford insurance) (Central Provident Fund Board, 2010).

7   The median monthly income level in Singapore stands at US$3,420 in 2009 (Singapore Department of Statistics, 2010) versus US$4,335 in the United States (US Census Bureau, 2010). Among the blue-collared workers, a majority of the production craftsmen earned a monthly income of $1,410–$2,115 making them the highest earners

among blue-collared workers. In contrast, the majority of cleaners and laborers earned $350–$704 monthly (Singapore Department of Statistics, 2005).

8   The Central Provident Fund (CPF) in Singapore is similar to Social Security in the U.S.

9   All currencies in this paper have been converted from Singapore's dollars to current U.S. dollars as of 2010.

10 When Aminah kept preparing food for her children, she demonstrated a deep Asian cultural value, especially among Malays. In particular, she exemplified that it is an utmost duty of a mother to solely prepare good meals for her children.

11 In general, the Malays are a minority group (15%) in Singapore. Most of them have less educational preparation when compared to the Chinese and thus occupy blue collar jobs in the country.

Discussion Questions

1. Compare the National Coalition for Cancer Survivorship (NCCS) with similar organizations in your country such as the American Cancer Society, National Cancer Institute, and Centers for Disease Control and Prevention. Discuss the levels of advocacy the organizations provide to cancer patients and cancer survivors. Identify and explain at least three pressing needs cancer patients and survivors have in your community. How would you, as a health communication major/minor or specialist attempt to address the preceding needs?

2. If a similar case happened in other countries including the United States, do you believe a cancer patient would accept the status of "subsidized patient" and then be unlikely to question the slow bureaucratic process? What cultural and societal norms shape and inform your response?

3. Identify all types of support provided to Aminah by people surrounding her and provide specific evidence from the case. Then, classify the social support that was effectively, ambiguously, and ineffectively provided to Aminah. Justify and support your analysis.

4. In your country, what is your sense about the overall attitude of employers toward retaining and hiring cancer patients as well as cancer survivors? If employers and co-workers learn that there are cancer survivors or cancer patients in their workplaces, how would they likely treat them? Compare your answers with Aminah's case.

5. If you were Aminah's supervisor, how would you respond to the situation? Why?

References

Albrecht, T. L., & Adelman, M. B. (1987). Communicating social support: A theoretical perspective. In T. L. Albrecht & M. B. Adelman (Eds.), *Communicating social support* (pp. 18–39). Newbury Park, CA: Sage.

Anderson, J. O., & Geist-Martin, P. (2008). Finding hope and healing: Composing and re-composing survivors identities. In L. Sparks, H. D. O'Hair, & G. L. Kreps (Eds.), *Cancer, communication, and aging* (pp. 115–146). Cresskill, NJ: Hampton Press.

Aujoulat, I., d'Hoore, W., & Deccache, A. (2007). Patient empowerment in theory and practice: Polysemy or cacophony? *Patient Education and Counseling, 66*, 13–20.

Bennett, J. A., Brown, P., Cameron, L., Whitehead, L. C., Porter, D., & McPherson, K. M. (2008). Changes in employment and household income during the 24 months following a cancer diagnosis. *Supportive Care in Cancer, 17*, 1057–1064.

Bowen, J. R. (1986). On the political construction of tradition: Gotong Royong in Indonesia. *The Journal of Asian Studies, 45*, 545–561.

Bradley, C. J., & Bednarek, H. L. (2002). Employment patterns of long-term cancer survivors. *Psycho-Oncology, 11*, 188–198.

Brashers, D. E., Hass, S. M., & Neidig, J. L. (1999). The patient self-advocacy scale: Measuring patient involvement in health care decision-making interactions. *Health Communication, 11*, 97–121.

Broadhead, W. E., Kaplan, B. H., James, S. A., Wagner, E. H., Schoenbach, V. J., Grimson, R., et al. (1983). The epidemiologic evidence for a relationship between social support and health. *American Journal of Epidemiology, 117*, 521–537.

Central Provident Fund Board. (2010). Understanding medisave and medishield. In *My cpf-providing for your healthcare needs...stretching your medisave dollars.* Retrieved from http://mycpf.cpf.gov.sg/CPF/Templates/MyCPF_PrinterFriendly_Template.aspx?NRMODE=Published&NRORIGINALURL=%2FCPF%2Fmy-cpf%2FHealthcare%2FPvdHC3.htm&NRNODEGUID=%7B2562D1D0-1A35-4330-B06A-9025D7E8D99F%7D&NRCACHEHINT=Guest

Chen, H. M. K., Tan, W. H., Tan, W. C., Yu, C. K. E., Lim, T. H. J., Tay, M. H., & See, H. T. (2006). Attitudes towards cancer survivors: A small survey. *Singapore Medical Journal, 47*, 143–146.

Chia, V., & Tan, R. (2004, July 20). *Disappearance of the kampong spirit: An economic explanation.* Retrieved from http://www.oaktree-research.com/index2.php?option=content&do_pdf=1&id=131

Cline, R. J. W. (2003). Everyday interpersonal communication and health. In T. L. Thompson, A. M. Dorsey, K. I. Miller, & R. Parrott (Eds.), *Handbook of health communication* (pp. 285–313). Mahwah, NJ: Lawrence Erlbaum Associates.

Curtin, P. A., & Gaither, T. K. (2005) Privileging identity, difference, and power: The circuit of culture as a basis for public relations practice. *Journal of Public Relations Research, 17*, 91–115.

Curtis, R. E., Freedman, D. M., Ron, E., Ries, L. A., Hacker, D. G., Edwards, B. K., Tucker M. A., & Fraumeni, J. F., Jr. (Eds.). (2006). *New malignancies among cancer survivors: SEER cancer registries*, 1973–2000. Bethesda, MD: NIH Publications.

Dutta, M. J., & Zoller, H. M. (2008). Theoretical foundations: Interpretive, critical, and cultural approaches to health communication. In H. M. Zoller & M. J. Dutta (Eds.), *Emerging perspectives in health communication: Meaning, culture, and power* (pp. 1–27). New York, NY: Routledge.

du Pré, A., & Ray, E. B. (2008). Comforting episodes: Transcendent experiences of cancer survivors. In L. Sparks, H. D. O'Hair, & G. L. Kreps, G.L. (Eds.), *Cancer, communication, and aging* (pp. 99–114). Cresskill, NJ: Hampton Press.

Galanti, G. (1991). *Caring for patients from different cultures: Case studies from American hospitals.* Philadelphia, PA: University of Pennsylvania Press.

Goldsmith, D. J. (2004). *Communicating social support.* Cambridge, England: Cambridge University Press.

Goldsmith, D. J., & Fitch, K. (1997). The normative context of advice and social support. *Human Communication Research, 23*, 454–476.

Hawkins, E. D. (1955). Prospects for economic development in Indonesia. *World Politics, 8*, 91–111.

Hoffman, B., & Stovall, E. (2006). Survivorship perspectives and advocacy. *Journal of Clinical Oncology, 24*, 5154–5159.

Kreps, G. L., & Massimilla, D. C. (2002). Cancer communications research and health outcomes: Review and challenge. *Communication Studies, 53*, 318–336.

La Gaipa, J. J. (1990). The negative effects of informal support systems. In S. Duck & R. C. Silver (Eds.), *Personal relationships and social support* (pp. 122–139). Newbury Park, CA: Sage.

Leigh, S. (2008). Cancer survivorship: Advocacy organizations and support systems. *Hermatology/ Oncology Clinics of North America, 22*, 355–363.

Ministry of Health. (2007). *Healthcare financing: What others said of us.* Retrieved from http://www .moh.gov.sg/mohcorp/hcsystem.aspx?id=22966

National Cancer Institute. (2004). *Staging: Questions and answers.* Retrieved from http://www.cancer .gov/cancertopics/factsheet/Detection/staging

National Coalition for Cancer Survivorship. (2009) *Self-advocacy: A cancer survivor's handbook.* Silver Spring: MD.

O'Hair, H. D., Kreps, G. L., & Sparks, L. (2007). Conceptualizing cancer care and communication. In H. D. O'Hair, G. L. Kreps, & L. Sparks (Eds.). *The handbook of communication and cancer care* (pp. 1–10). Cresskill, NJ: Hampton Press.

Peteet, P. (2000). Cancer and the meaning of work. *General Hospital Psychiatry, 22*, 200–205.

Query, J. L., Jr., & Wright, K. B. (2008). Online support groups among older adults with cancer and their lay caregivers. In L. Sparks, H. D. O'Hair, & G. L. Kreps (Eds.), *Cancer, communication, and aging* (pp. 189–213). Cresskill, NJ: Hampton Press.

Rahardjo, S. (1994). Between two worlds: Modern state and traditional society in Indonesia. *Law & Society Review, 28*, 493–502.

Rowland, J. H., Hewitt, M., & Ganz, P. A. (2006). Cancer survivorship: A new challenge in delivering quality cancer care. *Journal of Clinical Oncology, 24*, 5101–5104.

Singapore Department of Statistics. (2005). *General household survey.* Retrieved from http://www .singstat.gov.sg/pubn/popn/ghsr1/t54–61.pdf

Singapore Department of Statistics. (2009). Retrieved from http://www.singstat.gov.sg/stats/keyind .html#demoind

Singapore Department of Statistics. (2010). *Household income in 2009 lower than in 2008 but still higher than in earlier years.* Retrieved from http://www.singstat.gov.sg/news/news/ op19022010.pdf

Spector, R. (1996). *Culture and diversity in health and illness.* Stamford, CT: Appleton Lange.

Spelten, E. R., Sprangers, M. A., & Verbeek, J. H. (2002). Factors reported to influence the return to work of cancer survivors: A literature review. *Psycho-oncology, 11*, 124–131.

Stanton, A. L., Ganz, P. A., Rowland, J. H., Meyerowitz, B. E., Krupnick, J. L., & Sears, S. R. (2005). Promoting adjustment after treatment for cancer. *Cancer Supplement, 104*, 2608–2613.

Sullivan, J. (1986). Kampung and state: The role of government in the development of urban community in Yogyakarta. *Indonesia, 41*, 63–88.

Thompson, T. L., Robinson, J. D., Anderson, D. J., & Federowicz, M. (2008). Health communication: Where have we been and where can we go? In K. B. Wright & S. Moore (Eds.), *Applied health communication* (pp. 3–33). Cresskill, NJ: Hampton Press.

Ting, G. S., & Yen, J. L. (2008). Patient advocacy and its role in Singapore. *Ethics and Healthcare SGH Proceeding, 17*(1), 3–8.

US Census Bureau. (2010). *State and county quickfacts.* Retrieved from http://quickfacts.census.gov/ qfd/states/00000.html

Van der Kroef, J. M. (1960). The changing pattern of Indonesia's representative government. *The Canadian Journal of Economics and Political Science, 26*, 215–240.

Wills, T. A. (1985). Supportive functions of interpersonal relationships. In S. Cohen & S. L. Syme (Eds.), *Social support and health* (pp. 61–82). New York: Academic.

Wills, T. A., & Fegan, M. F. (2001). Social networks and social support. In A. Baum, T. A. Revenson, & J. E. Singer (Eds.), *Handbook of health psychology* (pp. 209–234). Mahwah, NJ: Lawrence Erlbaum Associates.

Wright, K. (2002). Social support within an on-line cancer community: An assessment of emotional support, perceptions of advantages and disadvantages, and motives for using the community from a communication perspective. *Journal of Applied Communication Research, 30*, 195–209.

Wright, K. B., Sparks, L., & O'Hair, H. D. (2008). *Health communication in the 21st century.* Malden, MA: Blackwell Publishing.

SECTION III

Identifying Multiple Influences Affecting Health and Decision-Making

CHAPTER 8

When Obesity Is a Crime
Family Communication and Individual Member Health

Elizabeth A. Baiocchi-Wagner

KEY TERMS

Socio-ecological model

Obesity

Health behaviors

Family

Abstract

It is often difficult to tease out the specific influence of individual factors on one's health behaviors. Given that individual differences, conversations with peers and relatives, media messages, and environmental issues might have mixed effects on our health across the lifespan, a theory explaining health behaviors in more holistic ways is merited. The socio-ecological model (McLeroy, Bibeau, Stekler, & Glanz, 1988) serves this purpose by investigating individual health behaviors at the intrapersonal, interpersonal, institutional, community, and societal levels. Although focused on the family, the case study and accompanying discussion questions invite examination of the situation at each level of the socio-ecological model to guide evaluation of the case's narrative comprehensively. In particular, this case study depicts the real-life events surrounding a mother's debatable legal responsibility for her teenage son's weight—555 pounds—and enables one to reflect on various contributing factors to health behavior by illustrating multiple, interlocking levels of influence.

Consider what you ate for lunch yesterday. Whether you sat down to a spinach salad, paired a greasy burger with a soda, or grabbed a granola bar on the run, it is highly unlikely that you made this meal choice completely on your own. Naturally, personal factors influenced your decision: You may hold the personal belief that eating nutritiously is important, or perhaps fast-food dining is "the norm" in your family or social network. Maybe you have little confidence in your ability (also referred to as *self-efficacy*, see Bandura, 1977) to select produce (e.g., fresh spinach, ripe fruit) and make your own lunch with it; furthermore, you may find it easier to grab quick snacks instead of full plates at mealtimes. Although several theories explain the impact of individuals' attitudes and beliefs on (un)healthy eating behaviors (e.g., Theory of Reasoned Action, Theory of Planned Behavior, Self-Efficacy Theory; see Ajzen, 2002; Bandura, 1977; 1995), a theory that might offer a more complete understanding of these choices is the socio-ecological model of health behaviors (McLeroy et al., 1988). This model is particularly helpful in understanding and classifying how *multiple factors*, not merely individual preferences, influence individual health behaviors and those of others.

Socio-Ecological Model of Health Behavior

According to Hayden (2009), socio-ecological theories explain health behavior in a comprehensive way (see also chapter 20 of this volume). Specifically, the socio-ecological model moves past an individual-focused perspective on health behavior by accounting for *additional* levels of influence on an individual's health, including the interpersonal level (e.g., relationships with relatives or friends), institutional level (e.g., rules and regulations of informal structures[1] such as school and the office), community level (e.g., standards and norms espoused by a particular group or organization), and societal level (e.g., policies or laws placed into practice by governing bodies). The use of the socio-ecological model for understanding health behaviors (e.g., alcohol use, cigarette smoking, overeating) and outcomes is prevalent in multiple health-related disciplines (e.g., Public Health, Medicine, Health Journalism) and is becoming more recognized in the health communication field specifically (Sallis & Owen, 1997). This is especially true in the area of community organizing (i.e., the process of changing individual health behavior by changing the community; for a review, see Dearing, 2003). Each of the five levels of the model is reviewed below.

At the innermost area of the socio-ecological model (Hayden, 2009) is the intrapersonal level. Examples of intrapersonal-level factors include an individual's own attitudes, beliefs, and personality traits; that is, what we think and value often influences the behaviors we adopt. Research and theory, focused on explaining health behaviors, examines these individual factors (e.g., Burt, Dinh, Peterson, & Sarason, 2000; Byrne, Byrne, & Reinhart, 1995). For instance, research indicates that adolescents (recruited from a Midwestern and a Southwestern university; $N = 659$, *mean age* = 20.5 years, $SD = 2.56$; 63% female, 75% White) with high sensation-seeking personalities often engage in more risk-taking behaviors, such as substance abuse (Miller & Quick, 2010).

Arguably, the interpersonal level of influence is one of the most easily identifiable and relatable sources of influence in the socio-ecological model (see Ackerson & Viswanath, 2009). The interpersonal level of the model demonstrates how peers and loved ones influence health behaviors. Several studies, for instance, show that if an individual smokes, his or her friends most likely smoke (e.g., Pollard, Tucker, Green, Kennedy, & Go, 2010). Similarly, in their review of research assessing behavioral factors that influence children's food intake, Birch and Fisher (1998) suggested that parents who preferred not to eat junk food had children who followed suit.

Some factors influence well-being at an institutional level. These include rules and regulations of structures in individuals' lives, such as the work place and school. For instance, many companies now offer their employees the opportunity to participate in wellness programs

(Geist-Martin, Horsley, & Farrell, 2003). Most programs include some combination of a health report, educational materials, and fitness plan (Harding, 2009).

When social networks or local groups and organizations influence our health, community-level factors are at work. What becomes the norm for a community may impact the daily health behaviors of its residents. In my hometown of Columbia, Missouri, for example, a local nonprofit in the area sponsors a community-wide event called "Bike, Walk, and Wheel Week," which encourages citizens to consider active transportation as an alternative to a vehicle. The organization also offers classes to teach individuals how to bike safely and confidently on city streets (PedNet, 2008).

Finally, the societal level targets the broadest level of the model. Countries' economies, cultural norms, and social policies greatly, and sometimes unwittingly, influence health behaviors. An example of health being influenced at the societal level is the continued existence of female genital manipulation (FGM). FGM is a procedure, often performed in African regions, that intentionally alters and/or injures the female's genital organs. The procedure is painful, and health consequences include severe bleeding, infertility, newborn sickness, and/or death (World Health Organization, 2010). Causes for FGM, however, are non-medical: cultural and religious norms of these societies perpetuate the practice (World Health Organization, 2010).

Having reviewed each level of the model, let's return to yesterday's lunch example: What other factors might have influenced your meal decision? At the interpersonal level, maybe you ate a salad because a friend or family member suggested you make a healthy lunch together. If your university forbids food in the classroom, an institutional level limitation, squeezing in a granola bar between your noon and one o'clock classes might be the most practical choice. Individuals living in more populated and health-minded communities might possess easier access to healthier, whole food products, while others' food choices are predominantly buffets and fast-food establishments. Finally, the societal level, which explores the influence of economics, social policies, and cultural attitudes on health, has some influence too. If you are like many in our nation and around the globe, you may not be able to afford organic produce or other expensive health foods. As you may have already concluded, often times, your health behaviors—even minor choices like yesterday's lunch—are influenced by several, if not all, of these levels simultaneously.

In summary, the socio-ecological model attempts to explain the interplay of internal, personal factors and external, social factors on our health behaviors. Seemingly, if multiple factors contribute to health deterioration and disease, then multiple factors should also be at the root of better health and/or disease prevention. Thus, it is essential that researchers actively investigate how individual, interpersonal, institutional, community, and societal levels *work together* to influence health. Findings about these multiple levels of influence could lead to increased health awareness, improved innovations in health literacy, and more informed health interventions (Stokols, 1996; Street, 2003). One particular area of application for the socio-ecological model in health communication research is obesity prevention.

An Overweight Nation

The prevalence of overweight and obesity in Western society in the last decade continues to grow (Flegal, Carroll, Ogden, & Johnson, 2002; Ogden et al., 2006). Recent estimates suggest that 68% of adults in the United States are classified as overweight or obese (Flegal, Carroll, Ogden, & Curtin, 2010). Among the young adult population (ages 18–29), obesity rates tripled between 1971–1974 and 2005–2006 with approximately 28% of young adults currently obese and an additional 28% overweight (National Center for Health Statistics, 2009). The rate of increased obesity in children is also alarming. During the past 30 years, the number of overweight children has more than tripled; studies show that nearly 34% of children and teens in America are either overweight or at risk of becoming overweight (Office of the Surgeon General, 2008; Ogden et al., 2006). Using data from the National Health and Nutrition Examination study (NHANES) collected from children, adolescents, and adults between the 1970s and 2004, a research team estimated that by 2030, a shocking 86% of Americans will be obese (Wang, Beydoun, Liang, Cabellero, & Kumanyika, 2008)![2] Obesity also disproportionately affects African Americans and Hispanics (compared to Whites), as well as those living in Southern and Appalachian regions (arguably, impoverished populations) versus other areas of the nation (Centers for Disease Control and Prevention [CDC], 2009).

It is the consequences associated with obesity that are truly frightening. The U.S. Department of Health and Human Services (DHHS), in cooperation with the National Heart, Lung, and Blood Institute (1998), found obese individuals at higher risk for heart disease, hypertension and stroke, cancer, and diabetes. According to CDC (2007) estimates, 1 in 3 children born in the year 2000 will likely develop diabetes. Add in the fact that our nation's obesity-related medical costs typically amount to around $93 billion (Herper, 2006) and there is no question that obesity, officially declared a national epidemic by CDC, is a major problem (Koplan & Dietz, 1999).

Certainly, each summary statistic above links to various levels of the socio-ecological model. A pressing question then arises: How much variance in one's health behaviors is explained, for example, by his/her own beliefs and attitudes, community, or interpersonal influences? As the following case will illustrate, some believe that family communicative influence is so pivotal to health behaviors that family members ought to share the responsibility for our mixed health outcomes. As the case in this chapter emphasizes a mother-son dynamic, it is important to first review research specific to family communication and health—an area that is gaining increased recognition in health communication research and education (see Jones, Beach, & Jackson, 2004 for a review).

Family Communication and Individual Member Health

Many scholars agree that families represent one of the most important socializing agents (Baxter & Braithwaite, 2006). It follows, then, that families' communicated attitudes, beliefs, and behaviors about health often, and substantially, affect individual family members' health behaviors (e.g., Flora & Schooler, 1995; Rimal & Flora, 1998). For example, families may teach health-promoting behaviors such as nutritious eating and exercise habits by modeling appropriate behaviors (see Kunkel, Hummert, & Dennis, 2006 for a review of social cognitive theory in family studies).

A family's influence on an individual member's diet and physical activity behaviors is largely communicative, as communication exists as the main mechanism through which family members offer words of caution, give advice, provide support, create health-based rules, and so on (Baxter, Bylund, Imes, & Sheive, 2005). A small amount of research on family communication and parental communication in particular, has attempted to unravel a part of the process by examining "family norms" regarding diet and physical activity. For instance, if you're like most kids, your parents were probably your most important role model during childhood (e.g., Hart, Herriot, Bishop, & Truby, 2003). If you grew up watching your caregivers enjoy healthy foods and engage in physical activity, you are more likely to do the same today (Office of the Surgeon General, 2008). Did your mother ever discuss healthful eating with you? If she did, and you perceived it as an important value to her, it is likely that you ate more fruits and vegetables than other kids (Boutelle, Birkeland, Hannan, Story, & Neumark-Sztainer, 2007).

Conversely, while parents and/or other close family members influenced your eating and physical activity habits (e.g., Sallis, Prochaska, & Taylor, 2000), other studies also show the influential power of *your* health communication on your *parents'* health behaviors (Rimal & Flora, 1998). Subsequently, scholars from various disciplines acknowledge the importance of continued scholarly attention to family influence on individual member health (e.g., Bylund & Duck, 2004; Epstein, 2006; Kreps, O'Hair, & Clowers, 1994; Schrodt, Ledbetter, & Ohrt, 2007). Basically, this pool of research illustrates how the health behaviors you perform today most likely reflect the communication you received from your parents and other family members about those topics in years past. Keep this information in mind as you read the following case.

Case Study

In May 2009, a search began for a missing mother, Jerri Gray, after she and her teenage son, Alexander, fled their home in South Carolina. Jerri, a 49-year-old African American woman and South Carolina resident, took flight as she had been charged with felony neglect of Alexander and was in danger of losing her son. Jerri's case, however, was unlike most parental neglect situations. Law enforcement charged the mother on the grounds of child neglect due in part to her son's weight, which had reached a life-threatening 555 pounds by the boy's 14th birthday (Faure, 2009).

CBS news reported that the South Carolina authorities caught up with Jerri and Alexander outside of Baltimore, Maryland, and arrested her ("Mom of 555-pound Teen Speaks Out," 2009). Jerri was immediately distraught and officials took her to the hospital for fear that she would physically harm herself. Jerri's nightmare, however, was only beginning. The media caught wind of the saga, and soon her and Alexander's story spread throughout the nation.

Speculation arose immediately around the circumstances of Alexander's excessive weight. How did Alexander gain access to so much food? Jerri, a fairly heavy-set woman, attempted to explain how her son's weight, which had always been above average, managed to spiral out of control. She explained that as a single mother (Alexander's father left about 10 years prior) with a limited income, finding the time to practice a healthy lifestyle just was not an option. She swore that she never kept fattening snacks, such as sweets or sodas, in the house: "A lot of times I had to work fulltime, second shift or fulltime, third shift, and I wasn't home a lot" ("Mom of 555-pound Teen," 2009). She also acknowledged that the occasional, more convenient fast-food meal occurred when she would need to sleep between work shifts. Ultimately, then, she had little opportunity to discuss and monitor Alexander's eating habits.

Still, blaming Alexander's weight on the occasional fast-food meal or Alexander's sneaky indulgences did not seem to satisfy media viewers, or the courts. Jerri found herself in need of legal counsel. South Carolina attorney Grant Varner (and his father, Kim) offered to take on Gray's case pro bono. On a talk show appearance, Grant Varner offered additional explanations for Alexander's size. For example, apparently Alexander (who, like most teenagers, attended school all day) ate multiple lunches while at school and the least expensive menu items ranged from pizza to fried chicken (C. G. Varner, personal communication, April 16, 2010). His friends also contributed, often giving Alexander sugary snacks during the day. At home alone, Alexander ate whatever food he wanted and in unhealthy quantities (Miller, 2009).

Many inquired as to what steps Jerri wished she would have taken to prevent her son's obesity. Worse yet, law enforcement continued to insist that opportunities to treat Alexander's obesity had arisen, but they claimed Jerri never took advantage of these possibilities. Jerri felt defeated. She had tried to prevent this situation. For instance, she followed the nutrition guidelines set for her son by the Department of Social Services (Child and Adult Care Food Program, n.d.), and at one time, Jerri became very serious about helping Alexander combat obesity. Jerri received a $30,000 scholarship[3] for a specific medical treatment center in North Carolina. Upon arrival, however, the center informed her they were unaware of Alexander's enormous size and, thus, he was not a candidate for the particular treatment. The two were turned away and sent back to South Carolina, unable to use the funding (C. G. Varner, personal communication, April 16, 2010).

Despite these efforts, Jerri acknowledged that had she not been a single mother working additional shifts, she could have spent more time talking about the importance of low-fat, nutritious meals with Alexander. Since the trip to North Carolina, Jerri insisted that she could not afford treatments for her son (Cox, 2009).

Other factors make this a difficult case to prosecute. First, according to the Garners, Alexander was never tested for genetic abnormalities that may have predisposed him to excessive weight gain, more so because Jerri could not afford it. Genetic defects, such as a leptin protein deficiency, may explain why some individuals tend to overeat and never feel full (Bochukova et al., 2010; O'Rahilly & Farooqi, 2008). Additionally, some argue that one must consider Jerri's socio-economic status before blaming her parenting skills. In a review of research addressing economic disadvantage in the family, Barnett (2008) highlighted how living in poverty creates psychological distress in parents. This life circumstance, in turn, correlates with more instances of negative parental communication (i.e., coercive, harsh, or unresponsive parenting), which can lead to less positive outcomes for children. Finally, according to Richard Balnave, a law professor, rarely is obesity considered an imminent threat, as many health problems associated with childhood obesity do not surface until adulthood in most cases (cited in Barnett, 2009).

The last paradox begs an investigation of another related issue of debate in this case—assessing state courts' level of power and intervention. A 2008 report from the Child Welfare League of America, one year shy of Jerri and Alexander's case, reviewed recent court cases in which a parent (or parents) was accused of neglect due to a child's excessive weight. Similar cases to Jerri's arose in New York, Texas, Pennsylvania, California, and Indiana. Due in part to these instances, the states (with the exception of California) expanded their definition of statutory neglect to include morbid obesity (Darwin, 2008). Most cases resulted in interventions such as nutritional counseling, daily work-outs, and cooking classes for the child and family member(s). However, two state courts, California's and Indiana's, filed criminal charges against the parent(s), although no one was jailed (Darwin, 2008). In Jerri's case, if she is found guilty of child medical neglect, according to the state of South Carolina, she could be punished by spending 10 years in prison (*Gray v. South Carolina*, 2009, J991098). She would then be the first woman convicted of felony charges, not misdemeanors, for this type of offense.

Summary

According to Barnett (2009), the South Carolina DHHS sought custody of Alexander after health care providers confirmed that the boy was in serious harm. Counsel for the DHHS, Virginia Williamson, claimed that Alexander should be removed from the home, not because of his weight, but based on the fact that Jerri "was not meeting his medical needs" (Barnett, 2009, p. 1D). Jerri, however, deeply loves her son and believes that Alexander should remain with her: "Mentally he needs to be with me. We both need to be included together in whatever program that they have to offer so that we both can benefit from it. So as our lives go on together, then we will have learned how to control it and keep it under control" (Colb, 2009).

In the end, the South Carolina Department of Social Services determined that Jerri was more a part of Alexander's *problem* and less a part of his *solution*. Alexander was removed from Jerri's custody. He currently resides with Jerri's sister in her home, where Jerri is allowed to visit Alexander for a few hours on a weekly basis (Faure, 2009). At the time of this case's writing, Jerri's trial is pending.

NOTES

1   Although use of the term "informal structures" to refer to schools and the work place is debatable, Hayden (2009) specifically uses this term.

2   Wang et al. (2008) do not provide the NHANES sample characteristics in their article.

3   The term "scholarship" is unrelated to Alexander's academic performance; Grant Varner, as well as other sources, specifically utilized this term to refer to the funding.

Discussion Questions

1. Do you and your family members discuss health issues? If so, what topics are most common? How have these conversations contributed to your current health behaviors?

2. This case predominantly focuses on the interpersonal level of influence on one's health. Take a moment to consider the other levels of the model as they relate to this case. Where do you discern intrapersonal factors coming into play? Institutional messages? Community messages? Societal messages?

3. In cases of morbidly obese children and adolescents, what role do you believe family communication should play in correcting/improving children's health behaviors? What about the role of the government?

4. Imagine if you had a morbidly overweight family member. How might you discuss healthy eating and physical activity behaviors with that person?

5. Do you think the jury should find Jerri Gray guilty of child neglect? Would your response change if factors in the situation changed (e.g., Alexander was younger or weighed less; Jerri was wealthy and/or White/Hispanic/Asian; Alexander's father was in the picture)?

6. How do you think the outcome of this case will impact other parents of obese children? Parents of anorexic or bulimic children?

7. To what other health behavior contexts could you extend the socio-ecological model?

References

Ackerson, L., & Viswanath, K. (2009). The social context of interpersonal communication and health. *Journal of Health Communication, 14*, 5–17.

Ajzen, I. (2002). Perceived behavior control, self-efficacy, locus of control and the theory of planned behavior. *Journal of Applied Social Psychology, 32*, 1–20.

Bandura, A. (1977). Analysis of self-efficacy theory of behavior change. *Cognitive Therapy and Research, 1*, 287–310.

Bandura, A. (1995). *Self-efficacy in changing societies.* Cambridge: Cambridge University Press.

Barnett, M. (2008). Economic disadvantage in complex family systems: Expansion of family stress models. *Clinical Child and Family Psychology Review, 11*, 145–161.

Barnett, R. (2009). *Is child obesity child abuse?* Retrieved from *USA Today* http://www.usatoday.com/printedition/life/20090721/obesityparents21_cv.art.htm

Baxter, L., & Braithwaite, D. (2006). Metatheory and theory in family communication research. In D. Braithwaite & L. Baxter (Eds.), *Engaging theories in family communication: Multiple perspectives* (pp. 1–15). Thousand Oaks, CA: Sage.

Baxter, L., Bylund, C., Imes, R., & Sheive, D. (2005). Family communication environments and rule-based social control of adolescents' healthy lifestyle choices. *The Journal of Family Communication, 5*, 209–227.

Birch, L. L., & Fisher, J. O. (1998). Development of eating behaviors among children and adolescents. *Pediatrics, 101*(suppl), 539–549.

Bochukova, E., Huang, N., Keogh, J., Henning, E., Purmann, C., Blaszczyk, K., et al. (2010). Large, rare chromosomal deletions associated with early-onset obesity. *Nature, 463*, 666–670.

Boutelle, K., Birkeland, R., Hannan, P., Story, M., & Neumark-Sztainer, D. (2007). Associations between maternal concern for healthful eating and maternal eating behaviors, home food availability, and adolescent eating behaviors. *Journal of Nutrition Education Behavior, 39*, 248–256.

Burt, R., Dinh, K., Peterson, A., & Sarason, I. (2000). Predicting adolescent smoking: A prospective study of personality variables. *Preventive Medicine, 30*, 115–125.

Bylund, C. L., & Duck, S. (2004). The everyday interplay between family relationships and family members' health. *Journal of Social and Personal Relationships, 21*, 308–313.

Byrne, D., Byrne, A., & Reinhart, M. (1995). Personality, stress, and the decision to commence cigarette smoking in adolescence. *Journal of Psychosomatic Research, 39*, 53–62

Centers for Disease Control and Prevention. (2009). Differences in prevalence of obesity among black, white, and Hispanic adults—United States, 2006–2008. *Morbidity and Mortality Weekly Report, 58*(27), 740–744.

Centers for Disease Control and Prevention. (2007). *National diabetes fact sheet, 2007.* Retrieved from http://www.cdc.gov/diabetes/pubs/pdf/ndfs_2007.pdf

Child and adult care food program. (n.d.). Retrieved from South Carolina Department of Social Services https://dss.sc.gov/content/customers/food/cacfp/index.aspx

Colb, S. (2009). *Child obesity as child neglect: Is the standard American diet dangerous?* Retrieved from http://writ.news.findlaw.com/colb/20090722.html

Cox, L. (2009). *Courts charge mother of 555 lb boy*. Retrieved from *ABC News* http://abcnews.go.com/Health/WellnessNews/story?id=7941609&page=1

Darwin, A. (2008, July/August). *Childhood obesity: Is it abuse?* Retrieved from *Children's Voice* http://www.cwla.org/voice/0807obesity.htm

Dearing, J. W. (2003). The state of the art and the state of the science of community organizing. In T. Thompson, A. Dorsey, K. Miller, & R. Parrott (Eds.), *Handbook of health communication* (pp. 207–220). Mahwah, NJ: Lawrence Erlbaum.

Epstein, R. M. (2006). Making communication research matter: What do patients notice, what do patients want and what do patients need? *Patient Education and Counseling, 60*, 272–278.

Faure, G. (2009, October). Should parents of obese kids lose custody? Retrieved from *Time* http://www.time.com/time/health/article/0,8599,1930772,00.html#ixzz0m3rp4s00

Flegal, K. M., Carroll, M. D., Ogden, C. L., & Curtin, L. R. (2010). Prevalence and trends in obesity among US adults, 1999–2008. *Journal of the American Medical Association, 303*, 235–241.

Flegal, K. M., Carroll, M. D., Ogden, C. L., & Johnson, C. L. (2002). Prevalence and trends in obesity among US adults, 1999–2000. *Journal of the American Medical Association, 288*, 1723–1727.

Flora, J., & Schooler, C. (1995). Influence of health communication environments on children's diet and exercise knowledge, attitudes, and behavior. In G. Kreps, D. O'Hair, J. Flora, & C. Schooler (Eds.), *Communication and health outcomes* (pp. 187–213). Cresskill, NJ: Hampton Press.

Geist-Martin, P., Horsley, K., & Farrell, A. (2003). Working well: Communicating individual and collective wellness initiatives. In T. Thompson, A. Dorsey, K. Miller, & R. Parrott (Eds.), *Handbook of health communication* (pp. 423–443). Mahwah, NJ: Lawrence Erlbaum.

Gray v. South Carolina, No. I431153. Retrieved April 18, 2010 from Greenville County 13th Judicial Circuit Public Index Search http://www.greenvillecounty.org/scjd/publicindex/SCJDPublicIndex23/PISearch.aspx?CourtType=G (June 17, 2009)

Gray v. South Carolina, No. J991098. Retrieved April 18, 2010 from Greenville County 13th Judicial Circuit Public Index Search http://www.greenvillecounty.org/scjd/publicindex/SCJDPublicIndex23/PISearch.aspx?CourtType=G (June 17, 2009)

Harding, A. (2009). Company wellness programs improve health, cut costs. Retrieved from CNN http://www.cnn.com/2009/HEALTH/09/01/hcif.healthy.living/

Hart, K., Herriot, A., Bishop, J., & Truby, H. (2003). Promoting healthy diet and exercise patterns amongst primary school children: A qualitative investigation of parental perspectives. *Journal of Human Nutrition and Dietetics, 16*, 89–96.

Hayden, J. (2009). *Introduction to health behavior theory*. Sudbury, MA: Jones and Bartlett.

Herper, M. (2006). *The hidden costs of obesity*. Retrieved from *Forbes*, http://www.forbes.com/2006/07/19/obesity-fat-costs_cx_mh_0720obesity.html

Jones, D., Beach, S., & Jackson, H. (2004). Family influences on health: A framework to organize research and guide intervention. In A. Vangelisti (Ed.), *Handbook of family communication* (pp. 647–672). Mahwah, NJ: Lawrence Erlbaum.

Koplan, J., & Dietz, W. (1999). Caloric imbalance and public health policy. *Journal of the American Medical Association, 282*, 1579–1581.

Kreps, G., O'Hair, D., & Clowers, M. (1994). The influences of human communication on health outcomes. *The American Behavioral Scientist, 38*, 248–256.

Kunkel, A., Hummert, M. L., & Dennis, M. R. (2006). Social learning theory: Modeling and communication in the family context. In D. Braithwaite & L. Baxter (Eds.), *Engaging theories in family communication: Multiple perspectives* (pp. 260–275). Thousand Oaks, CA: Sage.

McLeroy, K., Bibeau, D., Stekler, A., & Glanz, K. (1988). An ecological perspective on health promotion. *Health Education Quarterly, 15*, 351–377.

Miller, T. (2009). *Is child obesity abuse? Court to decide if S.C. mom Jerri Gray neglected 555-pound, 14-year-old son.* Retrieved from *The NY Daily News* http://www.nydailynews.com/lifestyle/health/2009/07/22/2009-07-22_is_obesity_child_abuse_court_to_decide_if_sc_mom_jerri_gray_neglected_555pound_1.html

Miller, C., & Quick, B. (2010). Sensation seeking and psychological reactance as health risk predictors for an emerging adult population. *Health Communication, 25*, 266–275.

Mom of 555-pound teen speaks out. (2009, June). Retrieved from http://www.cbsnews.com/stories/2009/06/25/earlyshow/main5112393.shtml

National Center for Health Statistics. (2009). *Health, United States, 2008 with chartbook.* Retrieved from http://www.cdc.gov/nchs/data/hus/hus08.pdf

National Heart, Lung, and Blood Institute. (1998). Clinical guideline on the identification, evaluation, and treatment of overweight and obesity in adults: The evidence report. *US Department of Health and Human Services, National Institutes of Health, National Heart, Lung, and Blood Institute.* Bethesda, MD. (NIH Publication No. 98-4083).

Office of the Surgeon General. (2008). *Healthy youth for a healthy future.* Retrieved from http://www.surgeongeneral.gov/obesityprevention/factsheet/index.html

Ogden, C., Carroll, M., Curtin, L., McDowell, M., Tabak, C., & Flegal, K. (2006). Prevalence of overweight and obesity in the United States, 1999–2004. *Journal of the American Medical Association, 295*, 1549–1555.

O'Rahilly, S., & Farooqi, S. (2008). Human obesity as a heritable disorder of the central control of energy balance. *International Journal of Obesity, 32*, S55–S61.

PedNet. (2008). Programs: *What we do.* Retrieved from http://www.pednet.org/programs/

Pollard, M., Tucker, J., Green, H., Kennedy, D., & Go, M. (2010). Friendship networks and trajectories of adolescent tobacco use. *Addictive Behaviors, 35*, 678–685.

Rimal, R. N., & Flora, J. A. (1998). Bidirectional familial influences in dietary behavior: Test of a model of campaign influences. *Human Communication Research, 24*, 610–637.

Sallis, J., & Owen, N. (1997). Ecological models of health behavior. In K. Glanz, B. Rimer, & F. Lewis (Eds.), *Health behavior and health education* (3rd ed., pp. 462–484). San Francisco: Jossey-Bass.

Sallis, J., Prochaska, J. J., & Taylor, W. C. (2000). A review of correlates of physical activity for children and adolescents. *Medicine and Science in Sports and Exercise, 32*, 963–975.

Schrodt, P., Ledbetter, A. M., & Ohrt, J. K. (2007). Parental confirmation and affection as mediators of family communication patterns and children's mental well-being. *Journal of Family Communication, 7*, 23–46.

Stokols, D. (1996). Translating social ecological theory into guidelines for community health promotion. *American Journal of Health Promotion, 10*, 282–298.

Street, R. L. (2003). Communication in medical encounters: An ecological perspective. In T. Thompson, A. Dorsey, K. Miller, & R. Parrott (Eds.), *Handbook of health communication* (pp. 63–89). Mahwah, NJ: Lawrence Erlbaum.

Wang, Y., Beydoun, M., Liang, L., Cabellero, B., & Kumanyika, S. (2008). Will all Americans become overweight or obese? Estimating the progression and cost of the U.S. obesity epidemic. *Obesity, 16*, 2323–2330.

World Health Organization. (2010). Female genital mutilation. Retrieved from http://www.who.int/mediacentre/factsheets/fs241/en/

CHAPTER 9

Medical Decisions in Older Age
Managing Complexities, Uncertainties, and Social Relationships

Jennifer E. Ohs

KEY TERMS

Medical decisions

Older adulthood

Ecological perspective
on decision-making

Uncertainty
management

Abstract

Medical decisions in older adulthood frequently entail consideration of a variety of health issues and social relationships relevant to the decision (Hummert & Nussbaum, 2001). The case presented illustrates the decision-making process of a 69-year-old woman considering a surgical procedure. Although not immediately life threatening, her decision arouses anxiety and uncertainty which are revealed and managed through her interactions. By examining her decision-making process from an ecological perspective, an understanding of the profound complexities, uncertainties, and influences associated with medical decisions in older adulthood can be realized.

Making decisions involving one's health and medical care can be a complicated and challenging process. Persons facing a major medical decision may cope with illness-related uncertainty, process complicated medical information, and consider numerous treatment alternatives. The complexities associated with medical decisions are amplified for older adults, who often experience multiple diseases, disability, and frailty concurrently (Fried, Ferrucci, Darer, Williamson, & Anderson, 2004), which may require management of numerous treatment regimens. Decisions about medical care can have far reaching effects for the well-being and survival of older adults (Park, 1999). The following review of literature positions medical decision-making at the latter end of the lifespan as situated in an ecology of interconnected communication contexts that affect medical decisions in older adulthood. The case that follows illustrates the process of medical decision-making of an older adult woman in such a way that demonstrates the various complexities and interactions associated with a medical decision in older adulthood.

Ecological Perspective

An ecological perspective on medical decision-making views the interactions involved in the decision through a reciprocal model of influence involving various interdependent contexts of communication. Street (2003) proposed that the interpersonal communication in medical

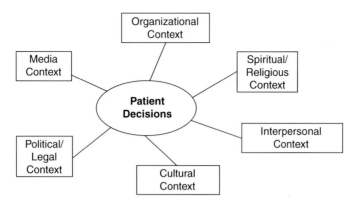

FIGURE 9.1 Contextual influences posed by an ecological model.

encounters is affected by various social contexts, including the organizational, political-legal, cultural, and media contexts. Similarly, medical decision-making is situated within a highly complex ecology in which interpersonal, cultural, spiritual/religious, political-legal, organizational, and media contexts of communication can be influential and pivotal in understanding the processes and outcomes of the decision (see **FIGURE 9.1**) (adapted from Street, 2003).

Organizational Context[1]

In the organizational context of communication, the relationship between a physician and patient has important implications. Provider-patient interactions have been researched extensively and the interaction has an impact on outcomes such as adherence to treatment, patient satisfaction, and symptom resolution (for review, see Brown, Stewart, & Ryan, 2003; Sparks & Villagran, 2010). The value of quality communication between physicians and patients is widely recognized (e.g., Roter & Hall, 2006), and various attempts at communication skills training for physicians (e.g., MD Anderson Cancer Center, n.d.) and patients (e.g., Cegala, Marinelli, & Post, 2000) have been developed. Research on the efficacy of such programs has been mixed, perhaps due in part to the widespread failure to integrate communication theory in the development and execution of such programs (Cegala & Broz, 2002). In one study, the knowledge of appropriate provider-patient communication of first-year medical students ($n = 71$) one year into a four-year interdisciplinary course emphasizing communication skills training was not significantly different from the knowledge of fourth-year students ($n = 47$) who had completed the training (Wright et al., 2006). As the interaction and information exchange between providers and patients is crucial to informed decision-making (Street, 1992), understanding the impact of communication education and training on effective medical decision-making is vital.

Older adults have unique medical and interpersonal needs during interactions with their health care providers (Nussbaum, Ragan, & Whaley, 2003; Thompson, Robinson, & Beisecker, 2004). As noted previously, older adults are more likely than younger adults to experience multiple health issues concurrently. Further, older adults tend to have different needs for information during medical encounters and attitudes about medical care and physicians than their younger counterparts (see Thompson et al., 2004). Communication education and training programs for physicians specializing in geriatrics are not prolific, although communication skills training for older patients has been found to enhance information seeking and providing of older adults during medical encounters (Cegala, Post, & McClure, 2001). Given the potential complexity of the medical encounter and medical decisions for older adults, communication between physicians and older patients may be of particular consequence for their medical decision-making.

There is a current trend of shared decision-making between patients and providers which purportedly has positive impacts on patient adherence to treatment regimens (e.g., Ong, de Haes, Hoos, & Lammes, 1995) and health (e.g., Brody, Miller, Lerman, Smith, & Caputo, 1989). Patient involvement in medical decision-making has also been found to decrease decisional uncertainty for patients making decisions about treatment for HIV/AIDS (Kremer, Ironson, Schneiderman, & Hautzinger, 2007) and lower depression for patients with breast cancer (Vogel, Leonhart, & Helmes, 2009). Less joint decision-making, however, occurs between older patients and their physicians than between younger patients and their providers (Thompson et al., 2004). Some researchers view older adults' participation in medical decision-making negatively because older adults could have difficulties comprehending and remembering medical information (Liu & Gonzalez, 2007). However, the likelihood of experiencing age-related cognitive impairment varies greatly during the course of older adulthood. The "young-old" (frequently identified as those between 65 and 75; Suzman & Riley, 1985) may be less subject to the effects of cognitive decline than those 75 and older (see Busse, Bischkopf, Reidel-Heller, & Angermeyer, 2003; Schönknecht, Pantel, Kruse, & Schröder, 2005). The "young-old" may benefit from participation in their medical decisions, especially given that patient-centered approaches encouraging patient participation in medical encounters have been linked to positive health outcomes such as increases in self-management of chronic illness and facilitation of disease control (e.g., Epping-Jordan, Pruitt, Bengoa, & Wagner, 2004).

Interpersonal Context

In addition to consultations with physicians, individuals often tap into their informal, interpersonal social network when faced with decisions regarding health (Tardy & Hale, 1998). This may be particularly true for older adults, who are often accompanied by a family member or friend when visiting a physician (Beisecker & Thompson, 1995; Nussbaum et al., 2003). Older adults' relationships with their adult children have been noted as particularly influential in the decision-making process, as older adults may need to rely on their children for support or help after a decision is made (Hummert & Morgan, 2001). The social support and opinions of friends who have faced similar situations can also shape the decision-making process for older adults, as friends are important sources of information and support in understanding health experiences (e.g., Cline, 2003).

Political-Legal Context

The political-legal context in which health care decisions are situated impact medical decisions as well. Health insurance provisions, availability of medical services and resources, as well as the overarching system of managed care can affect communication surrounding a medical decision (see Miller & Ryan, 2001). For example, the advent of managed care in the United States affects the length of the physician-patient office visit (Greene & Adelman, 1996) and has been shown to affect where and when patients seek treatment, as in the case of some asthma patients who found that managed care authorization procedures destabilize medical conditions and health care practices (Gillespie, 2001). The political environment in which medical decisions are made can certainly influence the process and outcomes of decision-making.

Media Context

In terms of the media context, the Internet and related media sources present consumers with more available health-related resources than ever before (Korp, 2006). The media context could include a myriad of sources of information including pamphlets, advertisements for medications or medical procedures, and books. The medium that has received most attention in recent years with reference to health care is the Internet. Adults over the age of 60 are increasingly using the Internet to search for health information (Wright & Query, 2004; Ybarra & Suman, 2008). Older individuals are accessing the Internet to research health and medical care, wellness, and disease (Lindberg, 2002), and the information available online can vary in credibility and quality. The Internet clearly has consequences for the health and health care decisions of older adults.

Religious/Spiritual Context

Religion and spirituality may be especially important in the medical decisions of older adults. Not only does religion/spirituality surface in conversations of those in the late stages of terminal illness (Keeley, 2004), but many older adults have been shown to raise religion as a topic of conversation during visits with internal medicine physicians for routine monitoring of one or more chronic conditions (Robinson & Nussbaum, 2004). Religion and spirituality can affect how patients make medical decisions, particularly as they pertain to chronic and terminal illness (Wennberg, 1989). Older adults may be more likely to tap into their religion and spirituality when making medical decisions, if only because religious belief and motivation tend to increase in older age (Koenig, Kvale, & Ferrel, 1988).

Cultural Context

Although somewhat indiscriminate due in part to the symbolic and subconscious nature of its influence in human life, culture may have an important influence on medical decisions. Culture can include a group's collective values, beliefs, norms, rules, communicative behavior, social institutions, and media channels (Pecchioni, Ota, & Sparks, 2004) and is connected to persons' definitions of health (Dutta & Zoller, 2008; Witte & Morrison, 1995). For example, some cultures define health on only physiological terms, whereas other cultures include psychological and spiritual components when referring to health. Religion and spirituality, which is part of one's culture, may be linked to race, ethnicity, religion, and health in meaningful ways for older adults. For example, religion plays an important role on the physical and mental health of older African American adults in ways unique to their religious participation (Taylor, Chatters, & Levin, 2004). The ways in which culture can be independently influential on health and medical decisions and also intertwined with other contexts of communication, such as religious/spiritual or interpersonal, may be meaningful in understanding such decisions.

Problematic Integration Theory

The influences posited by an ecological perspective have the potential to inform a medical decision and affect uncertainty related to the decision. Uncertainty is widely recognized as a central feature of illness (e.g., Babrow, Hines, & Kasch, 2000) and can arise from various characteristics of an illness experience, including the complexity of illness and quality of available information about a disease (Babrow et al., 2000). Problematic Integration (PI) theory (Babrow, 1992, 1995, 2001, 2007) is useful in illuminating the uncertainty management processes involved in medical decisions. According to PI theory, individuals tend to develop probabilistic orientations, or beliefs and expectations that involve likelihood. For instance, a person deciding whether to take a particular medication may examine the likelihood the behavior or medication will have the purported effects. PI theory also posits that evaluative orientations or understandings of the world that project a sense of "goodness/badness" or "desirability/undesirability" arise in individuals. For example, a person may consider whether the effects of a particular medication would be desirable, or if returning to work promptly after a surgical procedure would be a viable option. A person's probabilistic and evaluative orientations are integrated in experience and interdependent. Sometimes an individual's view of what is likely can affect assessment of value, and value judgments can affect probability estimates. Integrating probabilistic and evaluative orientations can be problematic, as they are incorporated within broader complexities of knowledge, feelings, and behavioral intentions.

Problematic integration is particularly challenging if probabilistic and evaluative orientations are *divergent*, if what a person believes and desires is in sharp contrast, if a person faces *ambiguity*, if a person experiences *ambivalence*, or if a person has an *impossible* desire (Babrow, 2001). The experience of uncertainty further complicates PI (Babrow, 2007). Babrow (1992, 1995) asserted that the degree of integrative difficulty is predicted by the location of a particular expectancy in one's system of beliefs and value. Health tends to be a central value in human belief systems, and thus, it naturally follows that medical decisions have the potential to involve high degrees of problematic integration.

According to PI theory, communication is central to the ways that PI is formed and transformed (Babrow, 2001). Specifically, communication is a *source* of PI, communicative acts *are* probabilistic and evaluative orientations, communication is the *medium* by which PI spreads, and communication is a *resource* in experiences with PI. Hines (2001) specifically explicated the role of communication in coping with illness-related uncertainties. In efforts to cope with serious illness, individuals must manage multiple and interrelated sets of uncertainty. Thus, communicatively, probabilistic assessments occur for one to understand the outcomes of medical treatment, and evaluative judgments are generated to discern the desirability level of probable outcomes.

The following case illustrates the decision-making process of a Caucasian older adult woman facing multiple chronic health issues. Her story illustrates her management of information and uncertainty surrounding her decision, as well as her interactions with health professionals and social network members.

Case Study

"What time is your appointment tomorrow, Liz?" Eli asked, gazing across the living room at his wife from where he stood in the front hallway of their home.

Lizzie Gill was so absorbed sorting through her medical files in preparation for her appointment with her primary care physician (PCP) she hadn't noticed that her husband had come in. "Golly, Eli, I just lost track of time," Lizzie said with a chuckle. "Let me put these files away and I'll put on some tea." Lizzie took one last glance at the file folder that lay open in her lap. On the coffee table in front of her sat a pad of paper with notes, and beside it, a portable file box. Lizzie jotted additional notes on her pad. "You realize that it's been over two years since I got Lyme disease?" Lizzie carefully returned the file to the box. "It is hard to keep track of all of the dates and procedures and prescriptions and treatments. Thank goodness I have a system!" Lizzie closed the lid and lifted the box from the table. Eli came over to her and took the box from her. "So what time is your appointment tomorrow?"

"Just put the box near the door. I'll need it at the appointment. This sinus infection isn't going away and I think the Lyme is complicating things and the doctor may need some of the records."

"Do you need me to drive you tomorrow then?" asked Eli.

"No, no. I'll be okay. Thanks, though," she said, making her way to the kitchen.

A Visit with the PCP

"What is going on with you today, Mrs. Gill?" asked the nurse as she closed the door to the visiting room.

Before Lizzie could respond, the nurse sat down on a stool and swiveled around to face a computer sitting on a desk across from Lizzie's chair. *"Do I answer her or wait until she turns back to me?"* "Mrs. Gill, what brings you in today?" the nurse said with her back still turned to her, now typing away at the keyboard.

"Oh. Well. I was in a few weeks ago with sinus pressure and a cold of sorts. Dr. Tierney prescribed some antibiotics. My sinuses are still pretty clogged, though," said Lizzie.

"Okay," said the nurse as she clicked through various screens and typed a note into what Lizzie assumed was her chart. "Let's take your vitals." As the nurse took her blood pressure,

Lizzie almost dropped the two file folders she had brought with her. *"I should have brought the file box,"* Lizzie thought as she caught the folders. *"I was too tired to drag it with me."*

"I suspect my Lyme disease may be interfering," said Lizzie, while the nurse took her blood pressure. "I've been feeling fatigued lately."

The nurse finished taking her vitals and typed a note on the computer. "Okay, Mrs. Gill. The doctor will be in to see you soon."

A few minutes later, Dr. Tierney entered the room. "Hello, Mrs. Gill. How are you today? I understand that you haven't gotten much relief from the treatment we gave you last time you were in," said Dr. Tierney as she sat down at the computer and logged in.

"No, not very much," said Lizzie.

"I'm concerned that the treatment hasn't improved your symptoms. Have you had sinus troubles before?" asked Dr. Tierney.

"Well, yes. About 30 years ago I had sinus surgery. I haven't had much trouble since."

"I see," said Dr. Tierney, turning to face her. "Let's take a look," she said. After Dr. Tierney had examined her, she told Lizzie that she would have expected her to have more relief as a result of the treatment.

"You think my Lyme disease is interfering with things, Dr. Tierney?" asked Lizzie.

"The symptoms you have could be anything from a simple cold to a cancerous growth. I recommend having a CT scan and seeing an otolaryngologist. Dr. Wu is the local specialist, but there are a number of others in the Springfield area," said Dr. Tierney turning back to the computer.

"Oh gosh, what a drive. I'm sure Dr. Wu is fine, if you recommend him."

"I'll write you a referral and have you scheduled for the CT scan," said Dr. Tierney. She turned around and stood up. She smiled and said, as she opened the door, "You can pick up the information when you check out. The computer system makes things so easy around here!"

"Oh, that's great. Thanks so much," said Lizzie, standing up.

A Visit with the Otolaryngologist (i.e., Ear Nose Throat Specialist)

Lizzie parked her car across the street from a building that used to be the town's abortion clinic. *"Of all places. I never thought I would step foot in that building."* Lizzie fingered the medallion she wore on a chain around her neck: Mary, the mother of Jesus. *"Oh holy Mary, mother of God, I was nervous enough about this appointment without it being at the old clinic."* Lizzie entered the doctor's office, checked in, and sat down in the waiting room. She was relieved that she was in the company of two other women, one around her age and one a bit younger. *"Thank you, Jesus, that I don't have to sit here alone with my thoughts!"* "Have you been here before?" Lizzie asked them.

"Yes," replied the older woman. "I am following up after sinus surgery."

The younger woman looked up from a magazine and nodded. "I am too."

"Oh really?" said Lizzie. "How did it go?"

The older woman replied, "Oh, just fine. Dr. Wu is a real fine surgeon."

"Oh, that's good to hear," said Lizzie. "What about you?" she asked the younger woman.

The younger woman shrugged. "I don't have anything to compare to," she said. "But there are more ear, nose, and throat specialists in Springfield."

Lizzie chuckled. "I guess I would have to know that it was worth the effort. My husband, Eli, would have to take me and he's not keen on the drive. My kids don't live around here."

A nurse opened a door to the waiting area and called the younger woman back. The older woman commented, "He must be running behind today. We've both been here a little while. I guess when you're the only specialist in town that's what happens!"

"But you've liked Dr. Wu?"

"As I said, he's a real fine surgeon. I'm glad I had the procedure done," said the older woman. About 20 minutes later, Lizzie was taken back to a room, where she waited another 10 minutes before Dr. Wu came in.

"Hello hello!" said Dr. Wu as he entered the room. He spoke in a loud voice with an accent Lizzie couldn't place. "You must be Mrs. Gill! I am Dr. Wu!" He extended his hand, which Lizzie took. He shook it with enthusiasm. "I have reviewed the files Dr. Tierney sent over and your CT scan. You have had sinus surgery before, yes?"

"Yes, about 30 years ago. I haven't had any trouble since. I wondered if …" Lizzie began when Dr. Wu interrupted.[2]

"Yes, yes. We need to remove whatever coagulated during that surgery."

"Coagulated?"

"Yes. Here is a pamphlet on the procedure," said Dr. Wu, handing her a brochure. Lizzie took it and leaned back, realizing she needed her glasses to read the print. She shuffled through her bag to find them as Dr. Wu continued to talk.

"… Endoscopic surgery is really the best course of action. The procedure will help your sinuses to better do their job."

Lizzie placed her glasses on her nose and fumbled with the pamphlet. "Does the fact that I have Lyme disease present complications?" she asked.

"This is not a problem. You are a good candidate for the procedure. They'll go over all of your medical history at the pre-operation meeting at the hospital, of course. The nurse will be in to give you pre-surgery instructions. She will explain everything you need to know."

"Oh my gosh! This sounds like a done deal!" "Well, what kind of recovery time could I expect? I will need to make arrangements with my family," said Lizzie, her voice anxious.

"No need to worry, Mrs. Gill. This is an out-patient surgery. You will be able to go home the day of the surgery. You can read all about it in your pamphlet, okay?" said Dr. Wu as he stood up. "You look it over and the nurse will be right in. We're here to answer all of your questions."

After Dr. Wu left, Lizzie took a deep breath. *"Oh, God, this isn't what I expected. Will I need someone to help me, God? Eli will help me, but he keeps so busy."* She tried to read the brochure, but she was distracted by the sound of Dr. Wu's voice floating through the walls as he talked in the next room. Though most of his conversation was muffled, she heard him laugh and say loud and clear, "Oh Mrs. Jones, you know I'm a surgeon. I love to get in there and cut. But I really do not think your husband would benefit. In his condition, I just do not recommend it."

Lizzie shuddered. *"For some reason, Dr. Wu makes me uncomfortable. This whole place makes me uncomfortable. I just want to get out of here."*

The nurse opened the door. "Okay, Mrs. Gill. We've scheduled you for surgery in three weeks over at Middletown Hospital. I have everything you need to know on your pre-surgery instructions so you won't forget," she began.

"Okay …" Lizzie said apprehensively. *"I'll consider all of this when I get home."*

Conversations at Home

That evening, Lizzie read the brochure and the pre-surgical instructions carefully. "Eli, I'm just not sure about all of this," she murmured. "It says here that I risk permanent blindness in having this done. What do you think of that?" Eli looked down at his hands. Before he could respond, the telephone rang. He rose from his chair to get it.

"Hello? Oh, hi James. How are you doing?" Eli asked. After a moment he followed, "Oh we're doing just fine. Mom just went to the doctor today. An ear, nose, and throat specialist … Yep. Pain in her face, headaches, and congestion for a while now. He has her scheduled for surgery in a few weeks. She's not sure about it …" Eli turned to Lizzie after a moment. "He wants to talk to you," said Eli.

Lizzie took the phone. "Hi, James. How are you?"

"I'm good, Mom. Tell me how you're doing."

"I'm fine. I've just been having some sinus trouble and I went in to see a specialist today. He recommended that I have surgery to help my sinuses to do their job better."

"Is it an endoscopic procedure, Mom?"

"Yes. Why?"

"That's what I had done three years ago when I was having all of those headaches."

"Oh! I forgot that you had that surgery back then. You had just gotten married to Carla, so I didn't need to be there. How was the recovery? Did you need a lot of help?"

"The recovery was okay. I had the surgery on a Friday morning and went back to work on Monday. It didn't really help. I felt just as awful afterwards. I'm not sure it's really worth it."

"No kidding! One of the risks is permanent blindness!"

"Right. Let me look some things up for you on the procedure and I'll e-mail you later tonight, okay Mom?"

"Okay, sweetie. Thank you."

Lizzie enjoyed the rest of her conversation with James. He reminded her that her grand-daughter, Lilly, would be celebrating her second birthday in four weeks and was looking forward to seeing her. *"That's just a week after I'm supposed to have the surgery,"* thought Lizzie.

That night, Lizzie had trouble falling asleep. *"God, I'm really nervous about this. I have been really looking forward to seeing Lilly and being with her for her birthday. Seeing her with my own two eyes is so important to me God."* Lizzie blinked away her tears.

The next day Lizzie went to mass, a daily ritual for her. She stayed then to volunteer at the rectory office as she did each Wednesday morning. Afterwards, she was always tired. Lyme disease slowed her down. When she arrived at home, she wanted to do nothing except take a nap. She had a message from her daughter, Jenah, on her answering machine.

Jenah picked up her phone right after Lizzie dialed. "Hi Mom. I got an e-mail from James. He told me about the surgery. Have you read the e-mail he sent about the success rates?"

"Hi Jenah. Word travels so fast these days. No, I haven't read the e-mail."

"You should take a look at it. The articles indicate that the procedure is relatively minor. The doctor will probably check the polyps for cancerous growths, which is important. But it has its risks. You must have been in pain for a while, Mom. I wish you would've told me."

Lizzie laughed. "Compared to how I feel with the Lyme disease, a bit of sinus pressure is hardly something to complain about!"

"So you're going to go in for the procedure?"

"Well, I guess so. That's what the doctor recommended."

"When is it scheduled?"

Lizzie swallowed. "Three weeks from today."

"Okay. Well. Keep me posted. I'll be thinking about you."

"I will, sweetheart."

An Evening Chat with Eli

That evening after Eli got in from his outdoor work, Lizzie asked him to look at James' e-mail with her. "I don't know, Eli. The success rates seem convincing, but the risks are questionable," said Lizzie. "I wish I could get a second opinion. There's so much I don't know."

"Well, there's not much of a chance for that unless we want to drive to the city."

"Yes, I guess so," said Lizzie. She waited for Eli to reply, but he simply turned off the computer. Lizzie sighed. *"I don't want to pester him to drive to Springfield. That's just silly. Dr. Wu is a fine surgeon."*

Lizzie got in bed that night feeling troubled once again. *"God? I don't feel any better about this tonight than I did last night. I don't really want to have this surgery. I'm not sure what to do. Please help me."*

NOTES

1. Although this section is longer than the other model components (e.g., interpersonal, media), the length was necessary to respond effectively to editorial requests.

2. See Cegala (2005) concerning medical consult interruptions.

Discussion Questions

1. In what ways does Lizzie's case exemplify the various contexts of the ecological perspective? How are the various contexts individually distinct and influential? How are they embedded within each other and intertwined?

2. In what ways was the cultural context of communication encompassed by the ecological perspective illustrated in the case? What influences could culture have on a medical decision? What could constitute culturally related communication?

3. How do Lizzie's interactions attempt to manage the uncertainty surrounding her decision?

4. Reflecting on the medical decisions and featured health care interactions, what unique needs of older adults are illustrated in the case? Were these needs attended to effectively by individuals in the case? If yes, how so? If no, how could Lizzie's experience have been improved?

5. Who is ultimately responsible for the medical decision illustrated in the case? Who do you think should be responsible for the decision? Who do you believe was most influential in Lizzie's decision-making? Who would you contend should be the most influential in the decision-making process?

References

Babrow, A. S. (1992). Communication and problematic integration: Understanding diverging probability and value, ambiguity, ambivalence, and impossibility. *Communication Theory, 2*, 95–130.

Babrow, A. S. (1995). Communication and problematic integration: Milan Kundera's "Lost Letters" in *The Blue Book of Laughter and Forgetting. Communication Monographs, 62*, 283–300.

Babrow, A. S. (2001). Uncertainty, value, communication and problematic integration. *Journal of Communication, 51*, 553–73.

Babrow, A. S. (2007). Problematic integration theory. In B. B. Whaley & W. Samter (Eds.), *Explaining communication: Contemporary theories and exemplars* (pp. 181–200). Mahwah, NJ: Lawrence Erlbaum Associates, Inc.

Babrow, A. S., Hines, S. C., & Kasch, C. R. (2000). Illness and uncertainty: Problematic integration and strategies of communicating about medical uncertainty and ambiguity. In B. B. Whaley (Ed.), *Explaining illness: Messages strategies, and contexts* (pp. 41–67). Hillsdale, NJ: Erlbaum.

Beisecker, A. E. & Thompson, T. L. (1995). The elderly patient-physician interaction. In J. F. Nussbaum & J. Coupland (Eds.), *Handbook of communication and aging research* (pp. 397–416). Mahwah, NJ: Lawrence Erlbaum and Associates.

Brody, D. S., Miller, S. M., Lerman, C. E., Smith, D. G., & Caputo, G. C. (1989). Patient perception of involvement in medical care: Relationship to illness attitudes and outcomes. *Journal of General Internal Medicine, 4*, 506–511.

Brown, J. B., Stewart, M., & Ryan, B. L. (2003). Outcomes of patient-provider interaction. In T. L. Thompson, A. M. Dorsey, K. I. Miller, & R. Parrott (Eds.), *Handbook of health communication* (pp. 141–161). Mahwah, NJ: Erlbaum.

Busse, A., Bischkopf, J., Riedel-Heller, S. G., & Angermeyer, M. C. (2003). Mild cognitive impairment: Prevalence and incidence according to different diagnostic criteria. *British Journal of Psychiatry, 182*, 449–545.

Cegala, D. J. (2005). The first three minutes. In B. E. Ray (Ed.), *Health communication in practice: A case study approach* (pp. 3–10). Mahwah, NJ: Erlbaum.

Cegala, D. J., & Broz, S. L. (2002). Physician communication skills training: A review of theoretical backgrounds, objectives, and skills. *Medical Educations, 36*, 1004–1016.

Cegala, D. J., Marinelli, T., & Post, D. (2000). The effects of patient communication skills training on compliance. *Archives of Family Medicine, 9*, 57–64.

Cegala, D. J., Post, D. M., & McClure, L. (2001). The effects of patient communication skills training on the discourse of older patients during a primary care interview. *Journal of the American Geriatrics Society, 49*, 1505–1511.

Cline, R. J. W. (2003). Everyday interpersonal communication and health. In T. L. Thompson, M. Dorsey, K. I. Miller, & R. Parrott (Eds.), *Handbook of health communication* (pp. 285–313). Mahwah, NJ: Erlbaum.

Dutta, M. J., & Zoller, H. M. (2008). Theoretical foundations: Interpretive, critical, and cultural approaches to health communication. In H. M. Zoller & M. J. Dutta (Eds.), *Emerging* perspectives in health communication: Meaning, culture, and power* (pp. 1–27). New York, NY: Routledge.

Epping-Jordan, J. E., Pruitt, S. D., Bengoa, R., & Wagner, E. H. (2004). Improving the quality of health care for chronic conditions. *Quality and Safety in Health Care, 13*, 299–305.

Fried, L. P., Ferrucci, L., Darer, J., Williamson, J. D., & Anderson, G. (2004). Untangling the concepts of disability, frailty, and comorbidity: Implications for improved targeting and care. *Journal of Gerontology Series A: Biological Sciences and Medical Sciences, 59*, 255–263.

Gillespie, S. R. (2001). The politics of breathing: Asthmatic Medicaid patients under managed care. *Journal of Applied Communication Research, 29*, 97–116.

Greene, M. G., & Adelman, R. D. (1996). Psychosocial factors in older patients' medical encounters. *Research on Aging, 18*, 84–102.

Hines, S. C. (2001). Coping with uncertainties in advance care planning. *Journal of Communication, 51*, 1–14.

Hummert, M. L., & Morgan, M. (2001). Negotiating decisions in the aging family. In M. L. Hummert & J. F. Nussbaum (Eds.), *Aging, communication, and health* (pp. 177–201). Mahwah, NJ: Erlbaum.

Hummert, M. L., & Nussbaum, J. F. (2001). Introduction: Successful aging, communication, and health. In M. L. Hummert & J. F. Nussbaum (Eds.), *Aging, communication, & health: Linking research and practice for successful aging* (pp. xi–xix). Mahwah, NJ: Lawrence Erlbaum and Associates.

Keely, M. P. (2004). Final conversations: Survivors' memorable messages concerning religious faith and spirituality. *Health Communication, 16*, 87–104.

Koenig, H., Kvale, J., & Ferrel, C. (1988). Religion and well-being in later life. *The Gerontologist, 28*, 18–27.

Korp, P. (2006). Health on the Internet: Implications for health promotion. *Health Education Research, 21*, 78–86.

Kremer, H., Ironson, G., Schneiderman, N., & Hautzinger, M. (2007). "It's my body:" Does patient involvement in decision making reduce decisional conflict? *Medical Decision Making, 27*, 522–532.

Lindberg, D. A. B. (2002). Older Americans, health information, and the Internet. In R. W. Morell (Ed.), *Adults, health information, and the World Wide Web* (pp. 13–19). Mahwah, NJ: Erlbaum.

Liu, L. L., & Gonzalez, R. (2007). Judgment and decision processes in older adults' compliance with medical regimens. In D. C. Park & L. L. Liu (Eds.), *Medical adherence and aging* (pp. 201–232). Washington, DC: American Psychological Association.

MD Anderson Cancer Center. (n.d.). Interpersonal Communication and Relationship Enhancement: I*CARE. Retrieved from http://www.mdanderson.org/education-and-research/resources-for-professionals/ professional-educational-resources/i-care/

Miller, K., & Ryan, D. (2001). Communication in the age of managed care: Introduction to the special issue. *Journal of Applied Communication Research, 29*, 91–96.

Nussbaum, J. F., Ragan, S., & Whaley, B. (2003). Children, older adults, and women: Impact on provider-patient interaction. In T. L. Thompson, A. M. Dorsey, K. I. Miller, & R. Parrott (Eds.), *Handbook of health communication* (pp. 183–204). Mahwah, NJ: Erlbaum.

Ong, L. M. L., de Haes, J. C., Hoos, A. M., & Lammes, F. B. (1995). Doctor-patient communication: A review of the literature. *Social Science Medicine, 40*, 903–918.

Park, D. C. (1999). Aging and the controlled and automatic processing of medical information and medical intentions. In D. C. Park, R. W. Morrell, & K. Shifren (Eds.), *Processing of medical information in aging patients: Cognitive and human factors perspectives* (pp. 3–22). Mahwah, NJ: Erlbaum.

Pecchioni, L. L., Ota, H., & Sparks, L. (2004). Cultural issues in communication and aging. In J. F. Nussbaum & J. Coupland (Eds.), *Handbook of communication and aging research* (pp. 167–207). Mahwah, NJ: Erlbaum.

Robinson, J. D., & Nussbaum, J. F. (2004). Grounding research and medical education about religion in actual physician-patient interaction: Church attendance, social support, and older adults. *Health Communication, 16*, 63–85.

Roter, D. L., & Hall, J. A. (2006). Doctors talking with patients/patients talking with doctors: Improving communication in medical visits (2nd ed.). Westport, CT: Praeger.

Schönknecht, P., Pantel, J., Kruse, A., & Schröder, J. (2005). Prevalence and natural course of aging-associated cognitive decline in a population-based sample of young-old subjects. *American Journal of Psychiatry, 162*, 2071–2077.

Sparks, L., & Villagran, M. (2010). *Patient and provider interaction: A global health communication perspective*. Cambridge, UK: Polity Press.

Street, R. L. (1992). Analyzing communication in medical consultations: Do behavioral measures correspond to patients' perceptions? *Medical Care, 30*, 976–989.

Street, R. L. (2003). Communication in medical encounters: An ecological perspective. In T. L. Thompson, A. M. Dorsey, K. I. Miller, & R. Parrott (Eds.), *Handbook of health communication* (pp. 63–93). Mahwah, NJ: Erlbaum.

Suzman, R., & Riley, M. W. (1985). Introducing the "oldest old." *Milbank Memorial Fund Quarterly: Health and Society, 63*, 177–185.

Taylor, R. J., Chatters, L. M., & Levin, J. S. (2004). *Religion in the lives of African Americans: Social, psychological, and health perspectives*. Newbury Park, CA: Sage.

Tardy, R. W., & Hale, C. L. (1998). Bonding and cracking: The role of informal, interpersonal networks in health care decision making. *Health Communication, 10*, 151–173.

Thompson, T. L., Robinson, J. D., & Beisecker, A. E. (2004). The older patient-physician interaction. In J. F. Nussbaum & J. C. Coupland (Eds.), *Handbook of communication and aging research* (2nd ed., pp. 451–477). Mahwah, NJ: Erlbaum.

Vogel, B. A., Leonhart, R., & Helmes, A. W. (2009). Communication matters: The impact of communication and participation in decision making on breast cancer patients' depression and quality of life. *Patient Education and Counseling, 77*, 391–397.

Wennberg, R. N. (1989). *Terminal choice: Euthanasia, suicide, and the right to die*. Grand Rapids, MI: Erdmans.

Witte, K., & Morrison, K. (1995). Intercultural and cross cultural health communication: Understanding people and motivating health behaviors. In R. L. Wiseman (Ed.), *Intercultural communication theory* (pp. 216–246). Thousand Oaks, CA: Sage.

Wright, K. B., & Query, Jr., J. L. (2004). Online support and older adults: A theoretical examination of benefits and limitations of computer-mediated support for older adults and possible health outcomes. In J. F. Nussbaum & J. Coupland (Eds.), *Handbook of communication and aging research* (2nd ed., pp. 499–519). Mahwah, NJ: Lawrence Erlbaum Associates.

Wright, K. B., Bylund, C., Ware, J., Parker, P., Query, J. L., & Baile, W. (2006). Medical student attitudes toward communication skills training and knowledge of appropriate provider-patient communication: A comparison of first-year and fourth-year medical students. *Medical Education Online, 11*. Available: http: www.med-ed-online.org.

Ybarra, M., & Suman, M. (2008). Reasons, assessments, and actions taken: Sex and age differences in uses of Internet health information. *Health Education Research, 23*, 512–521.

CHAPTER 10

To Use or Not to Use, That Is the Question

Applying the Theory of Planned Behavior to Understand Diabetics' Intentions to Engage in Insulin Pump Therapy

Corey Jay Liberman

KEY TERMS

Attitudes

Diabetes

Perceived behavioral control

Subjective norm

Abstract

The purpose of this chapter is to explain how one's decision to begin using insulin pump therapy as a form of diabetes management can be explained by the major tenets of Ajzen's (1985) theory of planned behavior. The chapter begins with a brief introduction to diabetes and how insulin pump therapy works. An introduction to the theory of planned behavior follows, where three variables that often predict one's behavioral intentions are discussed: attitude, subjective norm, and perceived behavioral control (Ajzen, 1985). The majority of the chapter is devoted to explaining how these three variables have been studied previously, from a health communication perspective, as well as why the theory would be applicable to the study of insulin pump therapy. The chapter concludes with some final implications regarding the link between attitude and behavior and how difficult the process of persuasion can be in the realm of health communication.

Three years ago, Thomas, a high school freshman with a stellar health record, suddenly fainted during his gym class. After a series of questions, his school nurse suspected that perhaps Thomas' blood sugar level was too high. As Thomas thought about the few weeks preceding this incident, he shared with the nurse that he had been extremely thirsty, had lost approximately 20 pounds without cutting back, and was urinating quite frequently. Based on her medical training, the nurse decided to give Thomas a routine blood sugar test to determine if the level of glucose in his blood was elevated. Thomas' blood sugar reading that morning was 758: approximately 643 units higher than the average person's level (i.e., 115). The nurse scheduled an emergency appointment with an endocrinologist (i.e., a physician who specializes in the diagnosis and treatment of diseases affecting the endocrine system) at a local hospital so that Thomas could receive immediate care for the disease with which he had just been diagnosed: diabetes. Thomas was in the hospital for seven days, during which time he met with doctors, nurses, certified diabetes educators, dieticians, and psychologists, all of whom wanted to help Thomas appreciate the nature of diabetes and how he could take charge of the condition as much as possible.

Now, three years later, Thomas is very knowledgeable about diabetes, though he is still somewhat psychologically damaged. He oftentimes still asks the "why did this happen to me" question. Recently, however, Thomas' life took a turn for the better. A week ago, Thomas was both upset and excited when he left his routine appointment with his endocrinologist. He was upset because his blood work revealed that his A1C level (i.e., a person's average blood glucose level during a three-month period) was 10.3% (approximately three percentage points higher than it should be) and he had just received a prescription for 540 syringes, the number of needles needed for injection during the next three months. He was also excited, however, as his doctor informed him about a technological device that would dramatically improve his quality of life and lessen the nuisance of the everyday pain, physical and psychological, associated with diabetes, more so since the technology requires only a single needle every three days.

Thomas' endocrinologist gave him literature about the device, as well as a contact number to speak to a representative to gain additional information. As Thomas recalled his experiences since being diagnosed three years ago, this was the first time that he was truly excited about a medical breakthrough (one that occurred approximately three decades ago, but that he had just recently learned about) in the world of diabetes. After taking a week to read all about this technological device, as well as speaking with a product representative, he was convinced that this device would change his life for the better. Notwithstanding his enthusiasm, many questions were brought to the forefront. For example, what were the drawbacks of this device? What would others think about it? Would he be able to realistically afford the device? What if something went wrong with the technology while he was sleeping? What if the device was recalled by the manufacturer? What if the needle hurt? Thomas quickly realized that his decision-making process was going to be more difficult than he could have possibly imagined.

Have you ever attempted to convince a close friend or family member to do something? Perhaps to stop smoking cigarettes, start exercising more frequently, begin taking vitamins, stop drinking alcohol so often, visit a doctor on a more routine basis, start taking a certain medication, or become an organ donor? If you answered yes to any of these questions, you have likely discovered many of the formidable challenges involved in persuasive interactions. Why is this process so difficult? At least one reason is that there are many steps involved in the process of persuasion. The purpose of this case study is to examine how someone might use communication in an effort to convince individuals living with diabetes, like Thomas, to consider adopting a new form of health management known as insulin pump therapy. By the end of this chapter, you, ideally, should understand and appreciate what insulin pump therapy is, how it works, and why it is considered to be beneficial. Additionally, you should have a better grasp of why the process of persuasive communication is so involved, detailed, multifaceted, and, perhaps most importantly, daunting.

Diabetes: An Overview of Insulin Pump Therapy

According to the American Diabetes Association, nearly 23.6 million Americans suffer from diabetes, a chronic illness whereby one's body is unable to produce, or unable to metabolize, the human hormone insulin (American Diabetes Association [ADA], 2007). Those with this chronic disease do not have a functional pancreas, prohibiting the production of human insulin, a bodily hormone that is necessary for the breakdown of glucose in the bloodstream. Without the constant flow of insulin, the amount of sugar in one's bloodstream becomes too elevated which, if not treated, can ultimately lead to death. Prior to the early 20th century, there was no medical treatment for diabetes, meaning that there was no tactic for lowering one's blood sugar except constant aerobic exercise (see Colberg & Walsh, 2002). Nearly 85 years ago, however, a group of four medical researchers discovered a way to create a synthetic version of human insulin: one that mimics the naturally produced hormone and provides a medicinal treatment for individuals living with both **type 1** (i.e., the body is unable to produce insulin) and **type 2** (i.e., the body is able to produce insulin but not enough to break down the glucose in the human bloodstream) diabetes. As the ADA (2010) reports, those with type 1 diabetes, which constitutes approximately 5% to 10% of those diagnosed with this chronic illness, do not have a functional pancreas and, as a result, require synthetic insulin. Additionally, those with type 2 diabetes, which constitutes approximately 90% to 95% of those diagnosed, have a semi-functional pancreas, which either does not produce enough insulin or the human insulin is ignored by the body. Although type 1 diabetes cannot be prevented, a healthy diet, physical activity, and a healthy body weight can collectively help prevent the onset of type 2 diabetes. Certain ethnic groups, including African Americans, Native Americans, Latinos, Asian Americans, and Native Hawaiians, are at a higher risk for the disease as compared to Caucasians (ADA, 2010). Although a cure for this disease still does not exist, the use of synthetic insulin (when properly regimented) enables one to live a more "diabetic-free" life by tricking the body into believing that the synthetically produced insulin is the real, bodily created hormone. This synthetic insulin is injected into the diabetic's body periodically throughout the day in an effort to break down the glucose present in his/her bloodstream. Thus, although there is still no cure for this chronic disease, there is a treatment available to control, manage, and monitor one's blood sugar levels (i.e., the amount of glucose in the human bloodstream at any given time).

There was a time, approximately 30 years ago, when individuals could only administer insulin into the body via a method known as multiple daily injection (MDI), whereby individuals living with diabetes would inject insulin first thing in the morning (i.e., long-acting insulin to help break down blood glucose throughout the course of the day), before bedtime (i.e., long-acting insulin to help break down glucose while the individual was asleep), and at each meal time throughout the course of the day (i.e., breakfast, lunch, mid-day snack, dinner, evening snack) (see Weissberg-Benchell, Antisdel-Lomaglio, & Seshadri, 2003). However, during the late 1970s, a treatment regimen known as insulin pump therapy was introduced, which has greatly facilitated the process of insulin injection. Also known as continuous subcutaneous insulin infusion (CSII), insulin pump therapy allows an individual living with diabetes to use a reservoir (i.e., a device that holds enough synthetic insulin for approximately three days) and an infusion set (i.e., a tiny tube that remains inside the individual's abdomen, waist-side, or buttocks) to automatically administer daily insulin (see Plotnick, Clark, Brancati, & Erlinger, 2003). In short, the insulin pump is a small, battery-operated device that is programmed to periodically administer synthetic insulin to the body, released from the reservoir, and entered into the bloodstream via the infusion set (see Lavin-Tompkins, 1997). The insulin pump is programmed so it periodically administers synthetic insulin to the body throughout the course of the day, thereby mimicking the process of long-acting insulin creation in the body of a non-diabetic and then requiring the insulin pump user to manually program the device at meal times (Boland, Grey, Oesterle, Frederickson, & Tamborlane, 1999; Pickup & Keen, 2002; Weissberg-Benchell, Antisdel-Lomaglio, & Seshadri, 2003).

Overall, the use of insulin pump therapy, as opposed to MDI, features personal and medical benefits. For example, insulin pump therapy has lessened the amount of daily injections that one must administer, requiring only one injection every two to three days, as opposed to four to six times daily using the MDI technique (see Plotnick et al., 2003). Furthermore, insulin pump therapy allows for more flexibility in what food one consumes and the timing of one's meals, providing individuals living with diabetes with a world of change (see Chantelau, Schiffers, Schutze, & Hansen, 1997). Past research has demonstrated the therapeutic value of insulin pump therapy. For example, insulin pump therapy has improved overall blood glucose levels among users (DeVries, Snoek, Kostense, & Heine, 2002). It has also led to a statistically significant decrease in insulin requirements among pump users (Weissberg-Benchell, Antisdel-Lomaglio, & Seshadri, 2003) and an overall decrease in the occurrences of extremely high blood sugar levels (Pickup & Keen, 2002). Insulin pump therapy has yielded better overall levels of blood glucose when one first awakens in the morning (DeVries et al., 2002) and has produced an overall decrease in the occurrences of extremely low blood sugars (Pickup & Keen, 2002). Finally, this medical intervention has improved energy levels (Bech, Gudex, & Staehr-Johansen, 1996) and has facilitated greater flexibility in lifestyle among individuals living with diabetes (Chantelau et al., 1997). In light of the preceding benefits of insulin pump therapy, it is surprising that more Americans with this disease have not moved from MDI treatment to CSII treatment during the past several decades. Of the approximately 23.6 million Americans who suffer from diabetes, only approximately 320,000 people living in the United States have shifted from daily injection therapy to insulin pump therapy (ADA, 2010). These numbers indicate that only a small percentage of all individuals living in the United States that require daily insulin are using insulin pump therapy, mainly due to lack of information, the expense of this medical device, and/or fear of technology (see Weissberg-Benchell, Antisdel-Lomaglio, & Seshadri, 2003).

Health Communication: An Application of the Theory of Planned Behavior

The previous statistic (that only a small percentage of individuals living with diabetes in the United States are using insulin pump therapy) provides health communication scholars with a difficult task. In particular, how can communication function to persuade non-pump-users to adopt this technological device? The theory of planned behavior, which was first proposed by Icek Ajzen in 1985, helps explain how, through communication, one might be persuaded to engage or disengage in particular [mostly health-related] behaviors. As such, this theory can help explain one's decision to switch from MDI to insulin pump therapy. According to Ajzen (1985), one's decision to engage in a particular behavior is a function of three interdependent variables: one's attitude (i.e., is this behavior a "good" idea?), one's subjective norm (i.e., would others agree that this behavior is a good idea?), and perceived behavioral control (i.e., if I think that this behavior is a good idea, and others concur, then do I have both the ability and the necessary resources to perform this behavior?). Each of these three variables is discussed next.

Attitude

First, there exists ample research in the field of health communication that indicates a correlation between attitude and behavior (Conner & Armitage, 1998; Courneya, 1995; Lowe, Bennett, Walker, Milne, & Bozionelos, 2003). For example, many students who hold an attitude that earning high grades in school is desirable are likely to study diligently before exams. Based on several health-related studies that have used Ajzen's (1985) theory, attitude accounts for a large portion of one's reason to engage in a particular behavior. For instance, Sutton, McVey, and Glanz (1999) studied 949 individuals (approximately 59% female, 41% male), ranging in age from 16 to 24, who had heterosexual intercourse at least once in their lives, in an effort to assess condom use. They discovered that one's attitude about using condoms during sexual intercourse (i.e., I think that using a condom is a good idea) was related to one's intention to use this contraceptive device ($\beta = 0.31$, $p < .001$).[1] Similarly, Johnston and White (2003) studied 289 first-year undergraduate students in an Australian university (approximately 80% female, 20% male), ranging in age from 18 to 59 ($M = 26$, $SD = 9.66$), in an effort to assess binge-drinking behavior. They found that one's attitude about engaging in binge-drinking activities (i.e., binge-drinking is a good idea) was related to one's intention to engage in this type of behavior ($\beta = 0.32$, $p < .001$).

Although these two examples do not address the issue of diabetes management, it is likely that similar results might surface when considering one's intention to engage in insulin pump therapy, as one's attitude will likely influence intention to adopt. That is, if one has a positive attitude about using insulin pump therapy as a way of managing this chronic disease, he/she is more likely to engage in this behavior. For example, individuals living with diabetes who understand the positive effects, personal and medical, of insulin pump therapy are likely to have a high intention to engage in this behavior. What becomes equally (if not more) important for health communication scholars is to determine key factors that might influence an insulin-dependent individual to develop a negative attitude about using an insulin pump. For example, it is possible that some individuals might question the longitudinal effects of using insulin pump therapy, because it might increase the possibility of having lasting scar tissue buildup in the abdomen, waist-side, and/or buttocks (see Plotnick et al., 2003). Furthermore, some might question the medical utility of using insulin pump therapy among individuals who exercise frequently: arguing that using an insulin pump is likely to lead to many more instances of hypoglycemia (i.e., too little glucose in the blood) and could ultimately become a nuisance (see Colberg & Walsh, 2002). It is also possible that some individuals could have several psychosocial concerns regarding insulin pump therapy. These could include the stigma of having an infusion set inserted daily into one's body, possible fear of technology, or potential fear of being constantly connected to a medical device (see Boland et al., 1999).

Thus, although on the surface level it seems as though individuals living with diabetes should, largely, have a positive attitude about insulin pump therapy, it is possible that some unforeseen, or possibly ignored, variables might produce certain hesitations. According to Ajzen's (1985) theory, intention to behave begins with one's attitude toward the behavior; if one thinks that insulin pump therapy is a good idea, he/she will be much more likely to use it as a form of diabetes management. From a communication perspective, it is likely that two social agents would be at work when attempting to create a positive attitude of insulin pump therapy in the mind of the potential adopter: one's doctor and marketing campaigns. One's physician is likely going to be the strongest persuasive agent in the health communication process, due in part to the positive medical benefits associated with insulin pump therapy (see Pickup & Keen, 2002). From a patient perspective, however, marketing on behalf of the companies that produce insulin pumps (i.e., Minimed, Deltec, Animas, Insulet) also becomes an agent in the health communication process. Therefore, doctors and insulin pump distributors have the potential to be influential in creating a positive attitude in the minds of individuals living with diabetes who are contemplating insulin pump therapy. Thus, it becomes important for health communication scholars to ascertain how doctors and companies can use persuasive strategies to strengthen one's positive attitude about, and mitigate one's hesitations toward, insulin pump therapy, especially given its demonstrated therapeutic merits.

Relating this back to the example at the beginning of the chapter, Thomas, before he intends to begin insulin pump therapy, must have a positive attitude about it. Again, after reading the literature about the device, and speaking with a representative from the company, Thomas was convinced that this form of diabetes management would provide a world of difference. That is, his positive attitude regarding insulin pump therapy had emerged. He realized that he would only need to inject himself once every three days, which translates into 17 fewer injections over that same three-day period. He further realized that his lifestyle would become much more flexible because he could go an entire day (from work to the gym and back home) without having to bring extra needles and his necessary bottle of insulin. He realized that, although technologies might "fail," individuals have been using this form of diabetes management, insulin pump therapy, for quite a while; during the past 30 years, many prior issues have been addressed through updating and refurbishing. He realized that, although scar tissue buildup is among the negative ramifications of insulin pump therapy, having one needle injected every three days, instead of 18, dramatically reduces that likelihood. In the end, Thomas had formed a positive attitude about insulin pump therapy.

Subjective Norm

The second variable, according to Ajzen (1985), is subjective norm; do others with whom I share an important relationship believe that a given behavior is a good idea? This variable has its roots in social psychology, specifically in the realm of social influence and how salient others influence our attitudes. For example, if one's network of friends all think that smoking is a good idea, one might be more inclined to engage in this behavior. A large body of research in the world of health communication and persuasion has focused on subjective norms (see Armitage & Conner, 2001). For instance, Conn, Tripp-Reimer, and Maas (2003) studied 225 women living in a community-dwelling, ranging in age from 65 to 92 ($M = 74.33$, $SD = 6.50$), in an effort to determine intentions to begin routine exercise. Results from the study indicated that subjective norm was a key predictor of one's intention to begin exercising regularly ($\beta = 0.47, p < .05$). Likewise, McMillan and Conner (2003) studied 461 undergraduate students at a university in England (approximately 55% female, 45% male), ranging in age from 17 to 54 (although no means or standard deviations were reported, most students were between the ages of 19 and 22), to assess illicit drug use. Results indicated that one's subjective norm was a significant predictor of one's intention to engage in illegal drug use ($\beta = 0.133, p < .01$ for LSD; $\beta = 0.095, p < .05$ for Amphetamine; $\beta = 0.216, p < .001$ for Cannabis; $\beta = 0.151, p < .001$ for Ecstasy). McMillan and Connor (2003) thus concluded that "in relation to the decision to use [drugs], it is social pressure from knowing salient others who use the drugs that is important" (p. 1677).

Based on the results from these studies, it becomes essential to recognize the influence that salient others have on human decision-making processes. Relating back to the study of insulin pump therapy, it is thus crucial to know not only who might be considered salient for individuals living with diabetes, but also whether these salient others have a positive attitude toward the use of such medical technologies. As a great number of biomedical scholars have noted over the years, diabetes impacts the life of the individual and those affiliated with him/her, such as significant others, siblings, parents, colleagues, coworkers, friends, neighbors, and doctors. Therefore, it is likely that many of these individuals are going to impact, to some degree, one's intention to engage in insulin pump therapy. For example, it is likely that salient others will begin to exert a certain amount of influence when they discover that the utilization of an insulin pump can lead to better blood glucose control and can allow for more flexibility in one's eating schedule. These salient others may also attempt to influence the potential adopter when they realize that insulin pump therapy can result in fewer episodes of hypoglycemia and hyperglycemia (i.e., too much glucose in the blood) and can result in more precise insulin dosing.

This second variable presents health communication scholars with a strikingly different goal. Rather than figuring out how to frame a communication message that may foster a positive attitude in the mind of the patient, this variable requires one to determine how to frame a communication message that may engender a positive attitude in the minds of the patients' salient others. The key, then, is to have salient others positively frame insulin pump therapy by emphasizing key benefits about this medical technology. Such an approach is similar to the two-step flow model of communication proposed by Elihu Katz and Paul Lazarsfeld (1955), where a source creates a message, sends this message to an intermediary source (or opinion leader), and then this intermediary source sends the message to the desired recipient. This two-step model is how the process of influence oftentimes functions in society. What is paramount, then, is to identify and encourage those who have the most capability of influence so that they can attempt to persuade others. In this case, the intermediary sources would be what Ajzen (1985) called salient others: parents, family members, friends, colleagues, coworkers, and physicians. According to the theory of planned behavior, it is these individuals who are best positioned to influence the individual living with diabetes contemplating insulin pump therapy (Ajzen, 1985). If the "right" salient other constructs the "right" message, the likelihood of persuading an individual living with diabetes to adopt insulin pump therapy increases. Again, it is the power of persuasive communication by a persuasive source that might be the difference between behavior adoption and behavior avoidance.

Thomas' endocrinologist was the first salient other who entered the decision-making process and, because she was the one to initially suggest insulin pump therapy, she certainly approved. When Thomas spoke to his parents about the insulin pump, and explained to them all of the benefits of such a device, they also concurred. Jacob, his workout partner, was a bit skeptical, asking him what would happen when he ran on the treadmill, lifted heavy weights, or went swimming. After Thomas reassured him that the insulin pump would not get in the way of any of the preceding activities, and that he could easily disconnect the device when he wanted to swim, Jacob also approved. Other friends, close coworkers, and family members were also all in agreement; if the device would change Thomas' life for the better, there was no better thing for him to do. Now, not only did Thomas have a strong, positive attitude about insulin pump therapy, but he also had the support of salient others in his network(s).

Perceived Behavioral Control

The final variable that predicts one's intention to engage in a given behavior, according to the theory of planned behavior, is perceived behavioral control (Ajzen, 1985). In short, this is the idea that to perform a given behavior, an individual must have the necessary resources to do so, and must have the self-assurance that behavioral engagement is possible. For example, it would be lovely for some to retire to a warm destination at 50 years of age, only to relax and play golf for the rest of one's life. However, even if one has a positive attitude about this behavior (i.e., moving to a warm destination and playing golf is a great idea) and salient others agree, one might not realistically be able to retire at age 50, perhaps due to a lack of financial resources and/or the negative repercussions associated with leaving one's family behind. This variable, too, has received much attention in the health communication literature. For example, Johnston, Johnston, Pollard, Kinmonth, and Mant (2004) studied 597 individuals from the United Kingdom with coronary heart disease (approximately 71% male, 29%female), the average age being 63.4 ($SD = 10.0$), to determine the cardiovascular risk behaviors in which people engage one year after diagnosis. Results indicated that individuals who thought that they were capable of exercise were more likely to engage in this behavior since they had two resources (confidence and ease) that provided behavioral control ($\beta = .26$, $p < .001$). Similarly, Norman, Conner, and Bell (1999) studied 84 smokers attending health promotion clinics (approximately 55% female, 45% male), ranging in age from 19 to 69 ($M = 43.42$, $SD = 12.48$), to determine the likelihood of smoking cessation. Results indicated that smokers were more likely to quit if they thought that they had control over ceasing the behavior and replacing the behavior with another ($\beta = 0.69$, $p < .001$).

Since the theory of planned behavior (Ajzen, 1985) has not yet been applied to the study of insulin pump therapy, there are no data that can support the existence of perceived behavioral control as a variable predicting behavioral intention. Certain resources are also necessary if one is to adopt this form of medical technology. One necessary resource that is likely to impact one's intention to begin insulin pump therapy is money. Although the insulin pump has been on the market for nearly three decades, its price has not decreased at a high enough percentage to allow all those living with type 1 diabetes to own this medical device (Pickup & Keen, 2002). Unfortunately, financial constraints and/or inadequate medical insurance might prohibit interested patients from engaging in insulin pump therapy. According to DeVries et al. (2002), another resource that one living with diabetes must have is an extensive education regarding all aspects of this chronic illness. To utilize an insulin pump, individuals living with diabetes must understand (a) how insulin works in a non-diabetic body, (b) how synthetic insulin is supposed to be used, (c) how to resolve both hypoglycemic and hyperglycemic occurrences, and (d) the difference between a bolus (short-acting insulin) and a basal (long-acting insulin) rate. Thus, knowledge and education regarding the disease in general, and insulin in particular, are necessary before using insulin pump therapy.

Another resource necessary for the use of insulin pump therapy, according to DeVries et al. (2002), is motivation. Individuals living with diabetes should realize that insulin pump therapy differs dramatically from MDI therapy and must be ready and willing to change their present insulin treatment regimen. They must be motivated to learn about this technology and must also be encouraged to keep constant tabs on the insulin pump, on the daily delivery of insulin, and on daily blood sugar logs. Without motivation, which is similar to other areas of health communication (e.g., people attempting to stop smoking, people attempting to stop using illegal drugs, people attempting to make healthier eating decisions), one's perceived behavioral control is negatively impacted. According to Prochaska, Norcross, and DiClemente's (1994) updated Stages of Change Model, which elucidates certain independent variables that predict one's intention to alter an existing behavior, or begin a new behavior, a motivated individual would likely be in the preparation stage of the insulin pump therapy process, as he/she would have self-verified the necessary skills for behavioral change.

An additional variable that is associated with perceived behavioral control is a patient's age (Plotnick et al., 2003). Although insulin pump therapy is safe for children and adolescents, some suggest this demographic population might have a more difficult time using the infusion set and the reservoir, and they might need the assistance of others. Therefore, even if one decides that he/she wants to begin insulin pump therapy, age might become a prohibitive variable. In the end, perceived behavioral control becomes as important as attitude and subjective norm in predicting one's intention to engage in a given behavior (Ajzen, 1985).

Now that Thomas had a positive attitude, and the support from others, did he have perceived behavioral control over starting insulin pump therapy? Because Thomas had been extensively educated about diabetes for the past three years, he believed he knew about every single aspect of this disease. As such, he had the educational prerequisite for insulin pump therapy. Thomas was also a very motivated individual; no matter what he decided to do, he knew that he would do it well. Not only was Thomas motivated to lower his A1C, which is among the many benefits of the insulin pump, but he was also motivated to start a new life that made the management of diabetes much easier and more tolerable.

NOTE

1   β = the *Beta Coefficient* derived from performing the regression analyses. These findings also occurred more than chance alone would predict since $p < .05$, which is the social science standard for hypothesis testing. For a more detailed discussion about how to use and interpret regression, see Frey, Botan, and Kreps (2000).

Discussion Questions

1. Why is the process of persuasive health communication so difficult? Are there ways to make the process more manageable?

2. What are the pros and cons of using the theory of planned behavior to explain one's behavioral intentions? What variables are excluded that become important to understand and predict one's behavioral decision-making?

3. Which of the three variables involved in one's decision-making process, as presented in the theory of planned behavior (attitude, subjective norm, perceived behavioral control), is most important in predicting one's behavioral intentions? Why is it the most important?

4. Why is it necessary to target attitudes when attempting to persuade someone to adopt, change, or modify behavior? What are the implications of this view?

5. Although some of the examples, throughout this case study, focus on distinct health behaviors (e.g., smoking, condom use, drug use), why are these types of behavior similar to one's decision to begin insulin pump therapy? Compare and contrast the respective persuasion processes.

6. Is it more difficult to foster and engender an attitude that does not yet exist, or to change an existing attitude? Why? What are some key implications of the preceding objectives for the study of health communication?

References

Ajzen, I. (1985). From intentions to actions: A theory of planned behavior. In J. Kuhl & J. Beckman (Eds.), *Action control: From cognition to behavior* (pp. 11–39). New York, NY: Springer-Verlag.

American Diabetes Association. (2007). *National diabetes fact sheet.* Retrieved from http://www.diabetes.org/diabetes-basics/diabetes-statistics/?utm_source=WWW&utm_medium=DropDownDB&utm_content=Statistics&utm_campaign=CON

Armitage, C. J., & Conner, M. (2001). Efficacy of the theory of planned behavior: A meta-analytic review. *British Journal of Social Psychology, 40*, 471–499.

Bech, P., Gudex, C., & Staehr-Johansen, K. (1996). The WHO (ten) well-being index: Validation in diabetes. *Psychotherapy and Psychosomatics, 65*, 183–190.

Boland, E. A., Grey, M., Oesterle, A., Frederickson, L., & Tamborlane, W. V. (1999). Continuous subcutaneous insulin infusion: A new way to lower risk of severe hypoglycemia, improve metabolic control, and enhance coping in adolescents with type one diabetes. *Diabetes Care, 22*, 1779–1784.

Chantelau, E., Schiffers, T., Schutze, J., & Hansen, B. (1997). Effect of patient-selected intensive insulin therapy on quality of life. *Patient Education and Counseling, 30*, 167–173.

Colberg, S. R., & Walsh, J. (2002). Pumping insulin during exercise. *The Physician and Sports Medicine, 30*, 1–8.

Conn, V. S., Tripp-Reimer, T., & Maas, M. L. (2003). Older women and exercise: Theory of planned behavior beliefs. *Public Health Nursing, 20*, 153–163.

Conner, M., & Armitage, C. J. (1998). Extending the theory of planned behavior: A review and avenues for further research. *Journal of Applied Social Psychology, 28*, 1429–1464.

Courneya, K. S. (1995). Understanding readiness for regular physical activity in older individuals: An application of the theory of planned behavior. *Health Psychology, 14*, 80–87.

DeVries, J. H., Snoek, F. J., Kostense, P. J., & Heine, R. J. (2002). Randomized trial of continuous subcutaneous insulin infusion and intensive injection therapy in type one diabetes for patients with long-standing poor glycemic control. *Diabetes Care, 25*, 2074–2080.

Frey, L. R., Botan, C. H., & Kreps, G. L. (2000). *Investigating communication: An introduction to research methods* (2nd ed.). Needham Heights, MA: Allyn & Bacon.

Johnston, D. W., Johnston, M., Pollard, B., Kinmonth, A. L., & Mant, D. (2004). Motivation is not enough: Prediction of risk behavior following diagnosis of coronary heart disease from the theory of planned behavior. *Health Psychology, 23*, 533–538.

Johnston, K. L., & White, K. (2003). Binge-drinking: A test of the role of group norms in the theory of planned behavior. *Psychology and Health, 18*, 63–77.

Katz, E., & Lazarsfeld, P. (1955). *Personal influence.* New York, NY: Free Press.

Lavin-Tompkins, J. (1997). Insulin pump therapy: Situations and solutions. *Lippincott's Primary Care Practice, 1*, 519–526.

Lowe, R., Bennett, P., Walker, I., Milne, S., & Bozionelos, G. (2003). A connectionist implementation of the theory of planned behavior: Association of beliefs with exercise intention. *Health Psychology, 22*, 464–470.

McMillan, B., & Conner, M. (2003). Applying an extended version of the theory of planned behavior to illicit drug use among adolescents. *Journal of Applied Social Psychology, 33*, 1662–1683.

Norman, P., Conner, M., & Bell, R. (1999). The theory of planned behavior and smoking cessation. *Health Psychology, 18*, 89–94.

Plotnick, L. P., Clark, L. M., Brancati, F. L., & Erlinger, T. (2003). Safety and effectiveness of insulin pump therapy in children and adolescents with type one diabetes. *Diabetes Care, 26*, 1142–1146.

Pickup, J., & Keen, H. (2002). Continuous subcutaneous insulin infusion at 25 years: Evidence base for the expanding use of insulin pump therapy in type one diabetes. *Diabetes Care, 25*, 593–598.

Prochaska, J. O., Norcross, J., & DiClemente, C. C. (1994). *Changing for good: The revolutionary program that explains the six stages of change and teaches you how to free yourself from bad habits.* New York, NY: Morrow.

Sutton, S., McVey, D., & Glanz, A. (1999). A comparative test of the theory of reasoned action and the theory of planned behavior in the prediction of condom use intentions in a national sample of English young people. *Health Psychology, 18*, 72–81.

Weissberg-Benchell, J., Antisdel-Lomaglio, J., & Seshadri, R. (2003). Insulin pump therapy: A meta-analysis. *Diabetes Care, 26*, 1079–1087.

SECTION IV

Recognizing and Addressing Campaign Challenges Through Formative Research

CHAPTER 11

Caring for Yourself is Caring for Your Child

Helping Parents of Children with Eating Disorders Seek Health Care for Themselves

Sheetal J. Patel, Autumn Shafer, Nancy L. Zucker, and Cynthia M. Bulik

KEY TERMS

Eating disorders

Self-care

Formative research

Caregiver

Abstract

It is not always easy to change health behaviors. Just imagine how many times you have been told to do something "good" for your health, and you have ignored the message. The purpose of the "Caring for Yourself is Caring for Your Child" case study is to demonstrate that formative research is an important part of developing effective messages to motivate behavior change. Formative research helps trained communicators know what might change their target audience's behavior. This case focuses on how students created messages to motivate parents of children with eating disorders, in particular, attempting to promote stress reduction strategies among parental caregivers. Decreasing parents' stress and anxiety levels can ultimately aid in a child's recovery because many parents are more likely to be energized, confident, and better able to administer prescribed treatments.

Some parents, however, are often resistant to messages that encourage them to reduce their stress (e.g., take a walk, join a support group) because they often feel selfish taking time for themselves and may not appreciate the benefits of self-care for themselves. Graduate students conducted focus groups, interviews, and an experiment[1] to develop health communication messages that would help encourage parents to engage in self-care practices for themselves. Findings from the formative research informed the content and presentation of messages, which were used in a subsequent health communication campaign. During the formative phase, many parents and experts informed the students that featured messages had to be credible and reinforce that parental self-care could help their child recover.

The Challenge

As students in a graduate-level interdisciplinary health communication course, we were excited to learn that we would be tasked with creating persuasive messages for a "real world" client. In this case, the client was the director of a local university-affiliated eating disorder program. The director explained that we needed to develop messages that could be displayed at the clinic to encourage parents to engage in healthy adaptive behaviors (i.e., self-care) to reduce their stress and negative emotions. Adaptive behaviors are activities a person does to cope with stress that are healthy (e.g., exercising, listening to music, talking to a friend) rather than maladaptive (e.g., denying stress, avoiding others, losing sleep) (Glanz & Schwartz, 2008). For parents of children with eating disorders (ED), healthy adaptive behaviors can be simple activities, such as taking five minutes of personal time to go for a walk or engaging in a hobby, or they can involve more complex activities, such as attending a parent support group.

The challenge in creating messages was presented by a mother of a child with an ED who accompanied the director. When this parent shared her experiences, we immediately understood the importance of this project. She recounted years of sitting with her daughter at every meal; the emotions of fear, guilt, and stress she felt on a daily basis; and the internal struggle to take care of her own well-being while caring for her ill child. It never occurred to her that she should take care of herself. Indeed, even when the director suggested that necessity, she did not believe it. Another mother experienced a similar struggle:

> You know, you're there beating yourself up thinking, going over the last number of years trying to figure out where you messed up. I think everything works against it. Your worry, your sadness, your depression about it, works against care-taking. It's almost like I can't think of one thing that would lead one to say, "ah, this is a good time for me to take care of myself."

The challenge presented to the class was to determine how to persuade parents to care for themselves, while also caring for their sick children. Caring for a child with an ED, even in the best of circumstances, is stressful and often like being on an "emotional roller-coaster." When parents do not engage in self-care at the same time, the child's recovery can be adversely affected because parents may be overwhelmed with stress and anxiety and unable to plan and carry out their child's treatment to the best of their abilities (e.g., Zucker, Ferriter, Best, & Brantley, 2005). The director described the situation:

> Recovery from an eating disorder can take place over years. Parents do a lot to help their child recover, and over time, it can take a toll on their stress levels and their physical health. We want to let parents know that as caregivers they need to take care of themselves to maintain the ability to best care for their child over the long recovery process.

As students, we decided conducting formative research about what could motivate parents to engage in self-care would be the best first step towards developing effective messages. We would then be able to understand and appreciate parent's ED-related experiences and thoughts as well as identify potential persuasive strategies promoting care for themselves.

We soon discovered that convincing parents to take time away from their children to engage in self-care would be no easy feat, and so we continued the formative research process after the health campaigns course concluded. The purpose of this case study is to describe the formative research conducted to develop the messages for the "Caring for Yourself is Caring for Your Child" health communication campaign. Formative research helps health communicators better understand their target audiences and the messages that may persuade them (see Witte, Meyer, & Martell, 2001 for a detailed discussion). The proceeding formative research process can be adapted and applied to message development for other health topics.

The Health Problem

More than 11 million people in the United States suffer from an ED, such as anorexia nervosa, binge eating disorder, and bulimia nervosa that can have serious, even fatal health complications (National Eating Disorders Association, 2005).[2] Many EDs begin in adolescence (Engel, Staats Reiss, & Dombeck, 2007). EDs can become chronic and treatment-resistant, often leaving millions of parents of children with EDs involved in a prolonged, challenging, expensive, emotional, and sometimes unsupported process of care (e.g., Graap et al., 2008). As illustrated by the mother quoted earlier, many parents frequently report feelings of distress, guilt, helplessness, and uncertainty about how to help their child. Although parental involvement in a child's treatment improves ED outcomes, parents often neglect their own health when caring for their ill child, which can impede the child's recovery process (e.g., Kyriacou, Treasure, & Schmidt, 2008; Zucker et al., 2005). For example, high levels of stress and anxiety can hinder a parent's ability to quickly and confidently make treatment decisions, manage treatments his/her child may resist such as refeeding, or can influence the parent to become hyper-vigilant (Zucker et al., 2005).

Some parents resist self-care for a number of reasons. First, people who misunderstand EDs may incorrectly blame parents for causing the ED and for not being able to compel their children to eat or stop eating, or may be skeptical that an ED is a mental illness. Due to the stigma and nature of this psychiatric illness, patients often want their illness to remain a secret, which may stop parents from obtaining help when they need it. Furthermore, treatment of children with EDs is time-consuming and emotionally demanding on parents. For example, parents of children with any type of ED are often responsible for planning and overseeing meals, and they must also ensure the child receives psychiatric therapy. Depending on the severity of their illness, some children must be hospitalized multiple times during the recovery process.[3] Finally, health care for EDs can be expensive and may not be reimbursed by insurance companies.[4] Due to the resulting financial burden and time-consuming nature of effective treatments, parents often juggle their job and time spent with their child (Haigh & Treasure, 2002). If parents have other children, they may also struggle to attend to the family as a whole. All of these competing time demands restrict parents' time for themselves. The problems many parents encounter when trying to engage in healthy adaptive behaviors are known as barriers, and such obstacles must be addressed in an effective health communication campaign.

Moving from Heath Problem to Action: Formative Research

To develop effective messages that resonate with the target audience, pre-campaign research is necessary (e.g., Noar, 2006). Such investigations should be systematic and theory-based. The former term, systematic, indicates there is an organized and methodical plan. A theory is a general set of principles and/or propositions that may help explain a social phenomenon. These principles can then provide guidance for what message features look like and suggest levels of emphasis. Without systematic, formative research undergirded by relevant theories, messages may have no effect, or unintended effects, on the target audience (Whittingham, Ruiter, Zimbile, & Kok, 2008).

Systematic formative research is typically conducted at the preproduction and production phases of campaign development. Preproduction research focuses on the target audience's perspectives and current behavior. It is useful for ascertaining health message components. Production research is the study of the target audience's subsequent responses to developed concepts and messages (Atkin & Freimuth, 2001). Applying relevant theory to both preceding phases can help create the most effective communication campaign.

Theoretical Integration

The first step we took was to find previous research about parents of children with EDs in the fields of health communication, psychology, and psychiatry. Conversations with the director confirmed that the findings in the studies (e.g., parents' severe emotional changes, parents' self-blame and guilt, problems with services and treatment, deterioration of family relationships) also existed in other treatment situations. This search for germane research directed us to three relevant theoretical frameworks that were used to guide message development: Transactional Model of Stress and Coping (Stress and Coping Model; Glanz, Rimer, & Viswanath, 2008), Transtheoretical Model of Behavior Change (Transtheoretical Model; Prochaska, Redding, & Evers, 2008), and Prospect Theory (Kahneman & Tversky, 1979).

The first two frameworks provided some insights into parental experiences and which behavioral motivators would be important. According to the Stress and Coping Model (Glanz et al., 2008), when a person encounters a stressful event, he/she first considers the significance, controllability, and potential impact of the stressor. Second, a person assesses his/her own ability and options for coping with the stressor (Glanz et al., 2008). The present formative research indicated that parents are likely in this second step as they may know they are stressed; however, many perceive nothing can be done because there are too many barriers to self-care, or because they lack adaptive coping skills. This theory suggested that messages should emphasize that parents have the ability to cope with their stress and they have access to coping resources (e.g., therapists, easy and quick self-care activities, parent support groups).

The Transtheoretical Model describes stages of readiness that a person may be experiencing during the process of behavior change (Prochaska et al., 2008). The model posits that a target audience, in this case parents of children with EDs, may not be at the same stage in recognizing the need to practice self-care. Previous research (e.g., Zucker et al., 2005) indicated parents were most likely in the first three stages: (a) precontemplative (no intention to engage in adaptive self-care), (b) contemplative (intention to engage), and (c) preparation (has taken some planning steps towards action). We expected that very few parents would initially reside in the final two stages: action (has engaged in adaptive self-care) and maintenance (engages on a regular basis) due in part to the information we received from one ED program director. It is important to note that some versions of the Transtheoretical Model also include a sixth stage (termination), where total behavior change is complete and there is no chance of relapse into the former unhealthy behavior (Prochaska et al., 2008). For the purposes of this case, we were only interested in parents who still engaged in maladaptive coping and had not yet reached termination. At any stage in the model, it is possible for a person to relapse back to unhealthy behaviors as opposed to ever reaching the termination stage.

The Transtheoretical Model also delineated the processes of change, as to what types of feelings and thoughts are likely to move parents from one stage to the next (Prochaska et al., 2008). For example, if a parent learns new information that supports self-care (i.e., consciousness raising), he/she may be more likely to move from the precontemplative stage to the contemplative stage. The information may prompt parents to start thinking about engaging in self-care. If parents can actually imagine themselves taking a short walk (i.e., self re-evaluation, or changing a person's self-image), for example, they may be more likely to move from the contemplative stage to the preparation stage. The Transtheoretical Model also includes consideration of how people tend to weigh the pros and cons of engaging in a health behavior, referred to as decisional balance (e.g., Prochaska et al., 2008). For parents of children with EDs, decisional balance is especially important, as time for self-care behavior is time away from the child. Self-care time could thus be viewed as detrimental to their child's health rather than beneficial for the parent and, ultimately, the child.

The third theory used to develop messages described potential persuasion strategies that might be effective (Kahneman & Tversky, 1979). Prospect Theory provided a technique that could influence this decisional balance analysis through gain and loss frames (Kahneman & Tversky, 1979). Gain frames emphasize the benefits of a recommended health behavior, and loss frames emphasize the consequences or risks of not practicing that healthy behavior (Rothman, Bartels, Wlaschin, & Salovey, 2006). It is unclear which type of frame is most effective (O'Keefe & Jensen, 2007, 2009). Previous research has focused on prevention (i.e., stop an illness from occurring) and detection (i.e., determine if an illness is present) of health behaviors when discussing gain and loss frames as opposed to adaptive health behaviors. There have been only small differences found for very specific health behaviors (e.g., breast cancer detection, dental hygiene), and it is argued that it is not possible to make a general statement concerning when gain versus loss frames will be more persuasive (O'Keefe & Jensen, 2007, 2009). Thus, formative research was necessary to determine the best framing strategy for parents of children with EDs.

Preproduction Research

To inform the content of the campaign messages, we conducted three focus groups (5–9 parents per group) with 19 parents of children with EDs (4 fathers and 15 mothers; age of children varied substantially from teenagers to full-grown adults), and 19 in-depth interviews with experts specializing in EDs (i.e., 8 clinical psychologists, 3 nurses, 2 dietitians, 2 general practitioners, 2 family social workers, and 2 psychiatrists). Preproduction and production testing research were conducted with some of the same participants due to the scarcity of, and difficulty in recruiting, parents willing to speak about their experiences with their children. The first focus group was purely preproduction research, as these parents did not evaluate any message concepts. In the second and third focus groups, the first half of the session was preproduction research, while the second half of the discussion was production research. Parents were recruited by referral through clinicians and posted fliers. Experts were recruited with help from the directors of the ED programs and e-mail solicitations that explained the purpose of the project. This research required a modest budget.[5] All research was authorized by the university's Institutional Review Board (IRB).[6]

The focus group and interview protocol guides were similar. Each assessed concepts that would be helpful in message development: (a) parents' and experts' experience with EDs; (b) impact of the ED on parents' lives; (c) coping strategies, as well as barriers and motivators to using these strategies; (d) preferred sources for information; and (e) types of self-care messages as well as distinct gain and loss frames that would be convincing to parents. The director, a clinical psychologist, conducted the focus groups (average length 1.6 hours), while students observed. Students conducted the interviews (average length 45 minutes). Once transcripts of the focus groups and interviews (totaling 321 single-spaced pages) had been culled, the data were coded using a constant comparative method to create a codebook and systematically analyze the data (Lindlof & Taylor, 2002). This type of coding involves searching through the transcripts for instances that represent concepts of interest and comparing each instance until saturation (i.e., when no new insights are gained by further categorization or comparison) (Creswell, 2007). We focused on uncovering any themes in the responses that related to our theoretical concepts (see Hruschka et al., 2004; Rothman et al., 2006). For example, the graduate student co-authors, who were also the coders, noted every time a parent gave a reason why he/she did not or could not engage in self-care (i.e., barriers to self-care) and grouped those reasons into categories. Inter-coder reliability, which refers to the degree of agreement between raters, was 60% for the focus groups and 90% for the interviews.[7] In cases where the graduate coders disagreed, coders would speak about their justification for the selected code (theme) until they came to a consensus. We analyzed parents' responses by interpreting the coded transcripts while considering both how often, to what degree, and in what context certain experiences, emotions, barriers, and motivators were mentioned. We used Atlas.ti, a qualitative analysis software, which allows multiple researchers to analyze data through organizing of transcriptions and codebooks, make coded data searchable, and build visual networks that allow researchers to connect selected passages and codes (Creswell, 2007).

We were able to affirm that most parents were in the early stages of change and identify key barriers and motivators to self-care. The main barrier was parents' belief that engaging in self-care activities involved risking their child's recovery process. As such, parents could be motivated to overcome this barrier if we re-framed the issue by encouraging parents to focus on how increasing adaptive behaviors could help their child recover. Messages emphasized that parents would be better able to administer treatment and would be setting a "good" example for their child regarding how to adapt to stress in a healthy way. Framing self-care as important for their children's recovery gave parents the permission they needed to focus on their own well-being without feeling as if they were neglecting their children. As one mother who had been in a parent support group said, "The fact that I knew that it [my self-care] would model for her [daughter], it gave me permission to do it. Maybe I needed that."

Another key finding was that parents and experts rated the impact of certain barriers differently. Parents identified psychological barriers, such as the need for obtaining permission from clinicians and other parents, as paramount. Experts thought logistical barriers, such as lack of time and financial burden, were the greatest barriers. An interdisciplinary perspective (i.e., researchers from two fields of study working together to solve a problem or conduct research) helped to reconcile differences among the research findings gathered from experts and parents. The research team, which included ED clinicians and communication researchers, agreed that parents did need permission to engage in self-care because they often felt guilty and blamed themselves for their child's disease. Thus, in this particular case, seeking similarities between researchers' opinions helped resolve disagreements concerning disparate interpretations. Ultimately, the team agreed on the tagline "Caring for Yourself is Caring for Your Child" that served as the overarching campaign concept. One of the benefits of working with an interdisciplinary team is that different perspectives can later inform a successful health communication campaign.

We then integrated the theoretical concepts consistent with what parents and experts indicated in the messages (see **FIGURE 11.1** for examples of Transtheoretical Model concepts in the messages) (Prochaska et al., 2008). For example, the tagline is consistent with the concept of decisional balance in the Transtheoretical Model (Prochaska et al., 2008). It serves to re-frame self-care seen as a key barrier (e.g., feeling selfish for caring for themselves) to a key motivator (e.g., wanting to care for their child). Essentially, we re-framed what parents may have perceived as a disadvantage of self-care, taking time away from caring for their child, and presented it as the most important advantage, being better able to care for their child. Additionally, from the preproduction research, we were able to identify the sources of the message (i.e., other parents of children with EDs, an affected child, an ED clinician) parents would find most credible for giving them necessary permission. We were then able to

FIGURE 11.1   Example of how Transtheoretical Model (Prochaska et al., 2008) concepts were integrated into the messages.

Note: Similar messages were tested during the production research experiment.[8]

modify the messages to reflect these sources for production testing. Permission to engage in self-care from these sources should help parents move through stages toward taking action. In another example of message revision based on the Transtheoretical Model (Prochaska et al., 2008), we revised messages related to two of the processes of change by validating parents' feelings (dramatic relief) and directing parents to resources (e.g., ED program websites) for further information (consciousness raising). These revisions complemented the elements of the Stress and Coping Model by recognizing the stressor and then showing parents they have resources to help them change how they feel.

Production Testing Research

We showed parents and experts three to six message concepts printed on 11 × 17 color posters. Parents and experts were then asked to indicate what they thought the main message was, if the messages would be effective, what improvements were needed, and which photographs would be most attention-getting, relatable, and motivating. Message concepts were continually revised based on the feedback received from parents and experts about the messages' appeal, relevance, readability, attractiveness, central themes, and appropriateness (see **FIGURE 11.2** for how messages evolved during testing phases). We stopped revising messages once we stopped obtaining new information about message enhancements and the main message.

One goal of the production testing during the focus groups and interviews was to evaluate the effectiveness of potential photos and text in the messages. We asked participants about each potential photo (e.g., emotions it evokes, relevance, preference, appeal, feelings about the source) and examined their responses not by counting preference frequencies, but rather by considering the entire discussion of positive or negative thoughts and feelings related to the photos.

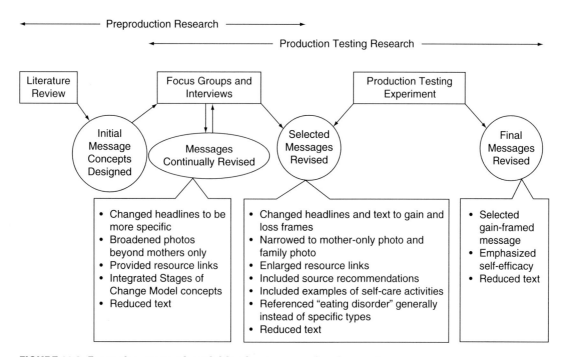

FIGURE 11.2 Formative research activities for message development.

The text was evaluated in the same way. Focus groups and interviews, in this case, helped assess why and how a photo may be effective and provided useful information about how the audience responded to featured messages beyond what a simple preference poll could offer.

Two message concepts emerged as the strongest in terms of appealing to parents, evoking positive emotions, and communicating our message of support (see Figure 11.1). One message focused on speaking out to overcome the stigma associated with EDs. The other message emphasized the importance of parents receiving self-care, enabling them to take better care of their family as a whole. The slogan "Caring for Yourself is Caring for Your Child" that was generated in the preproduction research was also tested in the production research (see Figure 11.2).

The first step of the production testing research revealed that parents were most receptive to messages that validated their feelings, cast parents rather than a recovered child as the source, and focused on the key barriers to acquiring permission to engage in self-care and resource access. The experts were sensitive to language in some of the messages that could be interpreted as blaming parents and stated that the messages should acknowledge self-care could be simple. Based on feedback from parents and experts, we were able to select two photos and headlines. These embodied the emotional connection parents needed to overcome barriers to the next stage in the Transtheoretical Model (Prochaska et al., 2008) and to streamline the message to be comprehensible and motivational.

Message attractiveness and appeal were also refined during this process. Elements related to the Transtheoretical Model (Prochaska et al., 2008) and Stress and Coping Model (Glanz et al., 2008) were also further improved. For example, parents wanted the website addresses (i.e., URLs) larger to improve visibility. The URLs helped parents progress through the stages in the Transtheoretical Model by serving as resource cues, which corresponds to the consciousness raising process of change (Prochaska et al., 2008), and discern there were resources to help manage their stress as related to the Stress and Coping Model (Glanz et al., 2008).

Based on the feedback from parents and experts in the second step of production research, we were confident about the message design and basic content. One question that was not clearly addressed in the focus groups or interviews was whether gain- or loss-framed messages were better at motivating parents to engage in adaptive self-care. Therefore, we conducted an experiment to address this question. A formative research experiment allows a researcher to change certain elements in a message to ascertain if different effects occur for distinct messages.[9] For example, we could test competing ideas about whether a message should have pictures or use one slogan instead of another.

We conducted an online experiment with 108 parents of children with EDs who were recruited through educational ED websites.[10] Parents were randomly assigned to one of three treatment conditions: In Condition 1, parents viewed gain-framed paragraphs that emphasized the advantages of engaging in self-care; in Condition 2, parents viewed loss-framed paragraphs that emphasized the disadvantages of failing to engage in self-care; and in Condition 3, the control condition, parents were asked the same questions, but did not view any messages (i.e., traditional control group).

After the parents viewed the paragraphs, their attitudes toward self-care, self-efficacy (belief they can practice self-care; see Bandura, 1997), decisional balance (beliefs about benefits and consequences), intentions to engage in self-care, and personality traits were assessed.[11] The personality trait measured was a person's tendency to want to either avoid something unpleasant or approach something pleasant. For example, some people love new adventures and challenges such as skydiving, while others would rather avoid any risks. These avoid/approach tendencies were measured by an established scale called the behavior inhibition/approach systems (BIS/BAS), which asks parents to rate their agreement with 24 statements about what motivates their general behavior (Carver & White, 1994).[12] Because a parent control group was compared to parent groups who viewed the gain and loss frames, no pretest (i.e., data collection measure assessing attitudes, beliefs, etc. before viewing any messages) was used. At the conclusion of the framing experiment, we obtained more feedback on message design by showing all parents the two strong message concepts that emerged from the first part of the production research (see Figure 11.1). We then asked parents to provide feedback about the photos, design, and motivational impact of each concept.

Results from the experiment showed that both gain and loss frames had favorable effects. We were able to obtain these results by conducting statistical tests that compare parents' answers between the three conditions employing analysis of variance and regression analysis.[13] By posing some questions about personality traits, we found that loss-framed messages were significantly worse than the control condition for parents who were fearful of bad things happening. Parents who tended to avoid risky situations and viewed a message about what they might lose if they did not practice self-care were less likely to have positive attitudes about self-care. In contrast, parents who were not highly fearful of negative outcomes did not experience an attitude shift after viewing the loss-framed messages.[14]

Gain-framed messages appeared more effective than loss-framed messages at making some of the benefits of self-care appear more influential in a parent's decision to engage in self-care. For example, there was an increase in how much parents thought the ability to feel less stressed would motivate them to engage in self-care.[15] Gain-framed messages were also more likely to evoke positive emotional reactions such as joy and less likely to influence parents to feel anxious.[16] This finding was important given the amount of stress and anxiety parents were already feeling. In an open-ended question, parents who viewed the loss-framed messages indicated they wanted to learn more about the benefits of self-care in the messages. The potential for gain-framed messages to alleviate stress and the fact that parents who viewed loss frames expressed a desire to know the gains/benefits of self-care ultimately supported the use of gain frames in the final campaign. Even a lack of differences between the frame conditions and the control condition was informative to message design. For example, neither gain- nor loss-framed messages yielded significant differences in self-efficacy to engage in self-care compared to the control condition.[17] Given that the Stress and Coping Model (Glanz et al., 2008) indicated self-efficacy was a key factor in parents' likelihood of practicing self-care, the results suggested that the messages should be changed to more clearly address self-efficacy.

The parents in the experiment reported that the messages were appealing and relevant. Of all parents, approximately 86% thought the stigma message was speaking to them and about 78% thought the character in the ad was similar to themselves. Additionally, about 81% thought the message was appealing. Some parents suggested, however, that the messages could be improved by clarifying how they can access parent services (e.g., is there a fee for resources?; what's the phone number?). We included these suggestions in the final messages. By the end of production testing, we had created empirically informed messages that should be effective in a health communication campaign for parents of children with EDs.

Transforming the Formative Research to Campaign Implementation

This case enabled the graduate students to address the challenge of creating effective health messages and learn how to do formative research. The focus groups with our target audience were helpful in culling and understanding parent experiences, current stages of readiness to engage in self-care, and feedback about what messages resonated with parents. The interviews with ED experts were valuable at revealing what experts found to be the most and least effective in communicating with parents and helping guard against potential harms tied to the forthcoming campaign. The experiment compared two competing ideas about the phrasing of key messages. It was important to conduct preproduction research to learn about the target audience and production testing yielded feedback concerning the messages.

Armed with campaign messages developed from the systematic, theory-based formative research, the campaign implementation could begin. The message concepts that were developed and tested during the formative research were incorporated into effective content and design elements for several different presentations that could be used in the ED clinic: posters, brochures, information packets for treatment teams, notepads in waiting rooms, buttons for clinicians and nurses, feature stories on parents willing to speak about their own experiences with self-care, blog posts, and a website[18] for parents of children with EDs that shared parent stories, expert recommended resources, and lists of different types of adaptive behaviors to serve as ideas for parents. Regardless of the type of message presentation, the graduate student health campaigners focused on framing the benefits of self-care as helpful to parents and their child's recovery and by granting parents "permission" to engage in self-care.

Editor's Note: For Endnotes 14–17, as this campaign is likely to yield multiple non-competing publications, the statistical findings are not reported. In this manner, the authors may publish those results in other outlets.

NOTES

1   The experiment was conducted online with participants randomly assigned to one of two treatment conditions or a traditional control group. See Frey, Botan, and Kreps (2000) for a further discussion on experimental design.

2   The prevalence is based on the most recent and reliable data. Recognizing the need for improved surveillance and data collection systems for tracking the prevalence and severity of eating disorders, the Federal Response to Eliminate Eating Disorders (FREED) Act was introduced in the U.S. Senate in 2010 and would require the Centers for Disease Control and Prevention to collect and track reliable data on prevalence and mortality of eating disorders.

3   This statement is based on the extensive treatment experience of the co-authors (Drs. Bulik and Zucker).

4   This information is based on one of the expert interviews with an eating disorder program in-take coordinator.

5   Approximately $2,500 was spent on conducting and analyzing the formative research with the majority of that money spent on transcription of the focus groups and interviews. We would like to thank Dr. Jane Brown and the School of Journalism and Mass Communication at the University of North Carolina at Chapel Hill for funding this research.

6   The IRB is responsible for ethical and regulatory oversight of research that involves human subjects. For further reading, refer to the *Journal of Applied Communication Research's* special issue on IRBs (2005, volume 33, issue 3).

7   After each interview and focus group was independently coded, simple percent agreement was measured and disagreements were discussed (Hruschka et al., 2006). Because focus group participants expressed a wider range of responses than experts, leaving more room for interpretation when coding, agreement levels were lower for focus groups than interviews. Every disagreement was discussed until consensus was reached. The consensus data was then used for analysis.

8   Due to copyright, photos in the advertisements in Figure 11.1 are not the images used during testing; however, they are similar in terms of style and mood projected by the models.

9   Many experiments involve manipulating an independent variable (e.g., message features) to assess potential impacts on predicted outcomes (i.e., dependent variables). This approach often establishes treatment groups (i.e., individuals who receive partial exposure to independent variable[s]). Traditional control groups do not receive exposure. See Frey et al. (2000) for a detailed discussion.

10 Parents' average age was 52 years old, most were married (77%), and some were divorced (17%). Nearly all parents were Caucasian (94%) and female (99%). The average age of the child with an eating disorder was 21 years old, and the child had been diagnosed for an average of 6 years.

11 To measure attitudes and self-efficacy, five-point Likert-type adapted scales were employed. The attitudes measure consisted of 10 items. The self-efficacy measure consisted of 9 items. Cronbach's Alpha for all scales discussed in this case were above .80. Note that the social science threshold for "satisfactory" reliability, using Cronbach's alpha, = .70.

12 The approach personality trait (BAS) scale consisted of 13 Likert-type items. The avoidance (BIS) scale consisted of 7 Likert-type items. Four items in the scale are fillers and not used in analysis.

13 We conducted a series of analysis of variance (ANOVA) tests. The reader is directed to Kranzler, Moursund, and Kranzler (2006) for a beginner's start to understanding ANOVAs. We also conducted hierarchical regression analyses (see Aiken & West, 1991).

14 We next conducted a series of hierarchical regression analyses (see Aiken & West, 1991). Regressions allow researchers to ascertain if one variable (predictor, an independent variable elsewhere) or characteristic predicts another variable (criterion, a dependent variable elsewhere). In addition, one can also find out if other variables serve as moderators. A moderator is a variable that affects the strength of the relationship between a predictor variable and a criterion variable. Intention to take personal time was predicted from (a) potential moderating variables (BIS and BAS scores), (b) experimental framing condition (gain vs. loss), and (c) the centered interaction of these two terms. An interaction signifies that an independent variable influences a dependent variable but that relationship is also influenced by a second independent variable. A significant interaction was found indicating that the result was more than mere coincidence. For the detailed statistics, please contact the first author.

15 We conducted an ANOVA where the independent variable was the condition (gain vs. loss vs. control) and the dependent variable was the importance of feeling less stressed to making a decision to engage in self-care. For detailed statistics, please contact the first author.

16 We conducted an ANOVA where the independent variable was the condition (gain vs. loss vs. control) and the dependent variable was the emotion in relation to the message felt by the parent. For detailed statistics, please contact the first author.

17 A hierarchical regression was conducted. Changes in self-efficacy were predicted from (a) potential moderating variables (BIS and BAS scores), (b) experimental framing condition (gain vs. loss), and (c) the centered interaction of these two terms. No significant results were found in the hierarchical model; i.e., the results did not occur more than chance alone would predict.

18 The campaign evaluation was in progress during the time of this book's publication. Part of the evaluation protocol was to track website hits, thus, the URL is not listed here.

Discussion Questions

1. What might have happened with the campaign design had the researchers failed to conduct systematic, theory-based formative research?

2. What was the purpose of conducting formative research with parents and experts in eating disorders?

3. Can you think of other possible methods that researchers could have used to conduct formative research? What might these additional methods contribute to an understanding of the key message elements?

4. Did you expect gain-framed messages to be more effective for adaptive behaviors? If so, why? In what health situations do you believe gain-framed messages are sometimes less effective than loss-framed messages with parents?

5. Think of an adaptive health behavior that might be important to college students (e.g., coping with the stress of finals week by adopting healthy behaviors, such as exercise, rather than unhealthy behaviors, such as excessive drinking). What formative research would you conduct for a campaign to promote that adaptive behavior?

References

Aiken, L., & West, S. (1991). *Multiple regression: Testing and interpreting interactions.* Thousand Oaks, CA: Sage Publications, Inc.

Atkin, C., & Freimuth, V. (2001). Formative evaluation research in campaign design. In R. Rice, & C. Atkin (Eds.) *Public communication campaigns* (pp. 125–145). Thousand Oaks, NJ: Sage Publications, Inc.

Bandura, A. (1997). *Self-efficacy: The exercise of control.* New York, NY: W.H. Freeman.

Carver, C., & White, T. (1994). BIS/BAS Scales. *Journal of Personality and Social Psychology, 67,* 319–333.

Creswell, J. (2007). *Qualitative inquiry & research design: Choosing among five approaches.* Thousand Oaks, CA: Sage Publications.

Engel, B., Staats Reiss, N., & Dombeck, M. (2007). *Prevalence, onset and course of eating disorders.* Retrieved from www.mentalhelp.net/poc/view_doc.php?type=doc&id=11746&cn=46

Frey, L., Botan, C., & Kreps, G. (2000). *Investigating communication: An introduction to research methods* (2nd ed.). Boston, MA: Allyn & Bacon.

Glanz, K., Rimer, B.K., & Viswanath, K. (2008). *Health behavior and health education: Theory, research, and practice* (4th ed.). San Francisco, CA: Jossey-Bass.

Glanz, K., & Schwartz, M. (2008). Stress, coping, and health behavior. *Health behavior and health education: Theory, research, and practice* (4th ed., pp. 211–236). San Francisco, CA: Jossey-Bass.

Graap, H., Bleich, S., Herbst, F., Trostmann, Y., Wancata, J., & de Zwaan, M. (2008). The needs of carers of patients with anorexia and bulimia nervosa. European Eating Disorders Review: *The Journal of the Eating Disorders Association, 16,* 21–29.

Haigh, R., & Treasure, J. (2002). Investigating the needs of carers in the area of eating disorders: Development of the Carers' Needs Assessment Measure (CaNAM). *European Eating Disorders Review: The Journal of the Eating Disorders Association, 11,* 125–141.

Hruschka, D., Schwartz, D., St. John, D., Picone-Decaro, E., Jenkins, R., & Carey, J. (2004). Reliability in coding open-ended data: Lessons learned from HIV behavioral research. *Field Methods, 16,* 307–331.

Kahneman, D., & Tversky, A. (1979). Prospect theory: An analysis of decision under risk. *Econometrica, 47,* 263–291.

Kranzler, G., Moursund, J., & Kranzler, J. (2006). *Statistics for the terrified.* Upper Saddle River, NJ: Prentice Hall.

Kyriacou, O., Treasure, J., & Schmidt, U. (2008). Understanding how parents cope with living with someone with anorexia nervosa: Modeling the factors that are associated with caregiver distress. *The International Journal of Eating Disorders, 41,* 233–242.

Lindlof, T. R., & Taylor, B. C. (2002). *Qualitative communication research methods.* Thousand Oaks, CA: Sage Publications.

National Eating Disorders Association. (2005). *Statistics: Eating disorders and their precursors.* Retrieved from http://www.nationaleatingdisorders.org/uploads/file/Statistics%20%20Updated%20Feb%2010,%20 2008%20B.pdf

Noar, S. (2006). A 10-year retrospective of research in health mass media campaigns: Where do we go from here? *Journal of Health Communication, 11*, 21–42.

O'Keefe, D., & Jensen, J. (2007). The relative persuasiveness of gain-framed loss-framed messages for encouraging disease prevention behaviors: A meta-analytic review. *Journal of Health Communication, 12*, 623–644.

O'Keefe, D., & Jensen, J. (2009). The relative persuasiveness of gain-framed and loss-framed messages for encouraging disease detection behaviors: A meta-analytic review. *Journal of Communication, 59*, 296–316.

Prochaska, J., Redding, C., & Evers, K. (2008). The transtheoretical model and stages of change. In R. Glanz, B. K. Rimer, & K. Viswanath (Eds.), *Health behavior and health education: Theory research and practice* (4th ed., pp. 97–122). San Francisco, CA: Jossey-Bass.

Rothman, A., Bartels, R., Wlaschin, J., & Salovey, P. (2006). The strategic use of gain- and loss-framed messages to promote healthy behavior: How theory can inform practice. *Journal of Communication, 56*, S202–S220.

Whittingham, J., Ruiter, R. A. C., Zimbile, F., & Kok, G. (2008). Experimental pretesting of public health campaigns: A case study. *Journal of Health Communication, 13*, 216–229.

Witte, K., Meyer, G., & Martell, D. (2001). *Effective health risk messages: A step-by-step guide.* Thousand Oaks, CA: Sage Publications.

Zucker, N., Ferriter, C., Best, S., & Brantley, A. (2005). Group parent training: A novel approach for the treatment of eating disorders. *Eating Disorders, 13*, 391–405.

CHAPTER 12

Implementing a Secondhand Smoke Intervention in Two Texas *Colonias*

Sabemos: Por Respeto, No Se Fuma Aquí (We Know: Out of Respect, Do Not Smoke Here)

Heather R. Clark, Julie Parrish St. John, Michael T. Stephenson, Michelle Dixon Johns, and Judy Berkowitz

KEY TERMS

Campaign

Cultural relevance

Hispanic

Secondhand smoke

Abstract

The purpose of this case study is to provide information to address the following question: What culturally appropriate, low-tech delivery methods are most effective for reaching Hispanic[1] populations living in *colonias*?[2] The target population for the health communication campaign discussed here is Hispanic residents living in the Rio Grande Valley along the Texas-Mexico border, and the message is reducing exposure to secondhand smoke. Hispanics are the fastest-growing cultural group in the United States and are projected to comprise nearly one-quarter of the total U.S. population by the middle of the twenty-first century (U.S. Census Bureau, n.d.). This growth rate places great pressure on public health officials to identify and determine this population's health needs and to provide effective disease prevention and treatment services. The target population, *colonia* residents, faces unique challenges such as living in unincorporated areas lacking basic infrastructure and lacking access to newer information dissemination methods.

"Don't pass gas."

This campaign slogan may not mean what you think it means! The American Legacy Foundation and the Ad Council jointly developed the "Don't pass gas" secondhand smoke campaign to target youth by "speaking" to them in a way that catches their attention (Ad Council, 2005). Research consistently shows that carefully designed and implemented mass media interventions like the "Don't pass gas" campaign can effectively reach large audiences by disseminating information, raising awareness, and promoting behavior change (Hopkins et al., 2001; Niederdeppe, Fiore, Baker, & Smith, 2008; Vallone,

Allen, & Xiao, 2009). When such campaigns are designed for populations with disparities (i.e., low economic status, low educational attainment, minority status), a common method used by the media is a supplemental interpersonal communication component (Hopkins et al., 2001). Importantly, these campaigns must consider cultural roles and norms in the design and development of these mediated and interpersonal components in these campaigns (Kreuter & McClure, 2004).

This case study describes a multi-faceted intervention targeted at the Hispanic parents of adolescents in Spanish-speaking *colonias* located in the Lower Rio Grande Valley on the Texas-Mexico border. Hispanics are the fastest growing cultural group in the United States, now surpassing African Americans to become the second-largest racial/ethnic group (after non-Hispanic whites). The number of Hispanics in the United States has doubled in recent decades (National Center for Health Statistics, 2009), and at the current growth rate, Hispanics are projected to compose nearly one-quarter of the total U.S. population by the middle of the 21st century (U.S. Census Bureau, n.d.; Ramirez & de la Cruz, 2003; Vega & Lopez, 2001). This growth rate places intense pressure on public health officials to identify this population's health needs and complicates their ability to provide effective disease prevention and treatment services. When considering how to most effectively reach this audience, health campaign planners must consider the vast range of barriers and cultural determinants to health care prevention and treatment.

Given the large number of Hispanics and their generally low economic and educational levels, which have been linked to tobacco and other substance abuse, as well as existing barriers to adequate treatment, one would expect an abundance of data about their use of alcohol, tobacco, and other drugs. Unfortunately, few health-related studies exist that are specifically related to this population (Flores et al., 2002; Vega & Lopez, 2001).

This case study describes the use of multiple delivery methods to provide culturally appropriate communication about secondhand smoke exposure to Hispanics residing in the Lower Rio Grande Valley along the Texas-Mexico border. The targeted population was Hispanic parents/caregivers of youth who were age 14 and younger. The intervention implemented, *Sabemos*, is a Centers for Disease Control and Prevention (CDC) developed program modified by the research team to specifically target residents in Hidalgo County, the seventh most populated county in the state of Texas. Hidalgo County houses more than 75% of Texas *colonias* (Texas Department of State Health Services, 2004).

Colonia residents face formidable health burdens that are unique compared to other populations. Largely inhabited by immigrants, *colonias* are unincorporated areas lacking a variety of basic infrastructure aspects such as paved streets, sidewalks, storm drainage, sewers, electricity, potable water, postal service, and telephone lines. Moreover, *colonias* house numerous undocumented residents and the largest group of migrant farm workers in the United States (State Energy Conservation Office, n.d.; Public Broadcasting Service, 2000). Due in part to their migrant status, residents may reside in the area for a short time before moving elsewhere to find employment; often such migration coincides with the types of crops, planting, and harvesting in specific areas. Approximately 90% of *colonia* residents speak only Spanish in their home (U.S. Census Bureau, 2000). Health campaign planning staff in this South Texas community are native to the area and have been working in a research capacity for more than 10 years allowing them to gain insight and extensive experience in working with the Lower Rio Grande Valley *colonias*. Residents within the *colonias* are highly connected, providing crucial social support to each other in their everyday life (e.g., carpooling with the one person on the block with a vehicle; multiple family use of scarce resources such as electricity, water, or appliances; and joint child care allowing for others in the community to work). These are only a few of the characteristics of *colonias* that health campaign planners must be mindful of and address when exploring appropriate types of campaign messages and dissemination methods.

These characteristics, however, are not unique to South Texas. *Healthy People 2010* emphasized that "people with the greatest health burdens have the least access to information, communication technologies, health care and supporting services" (U.S. Department of Health & Human Services [USDHHS], 2000; Freimuth, 1990). The digital divide is a term which describes the disparity in access to technology between the mainstream population and underserved populations (Lorence, Park, & Fox, 2006; see also Livingstone & Helsper, 2007). Similarly, Hispanic residents in communities such as *colonias* may lack access to computers and by extension, widely used information dissemination methods such as e-mail, social networking sites, and health organization web sites. Lorence et al.'s (2006) study indicated that, despite nationwide initiatives to reduce the digital divide, for low income populations, Hispanics, and other ethnic groups, the digital divide continues to be significant and persistent. Although this technological gap makes the distribution of health information much more difficult (Eng et al., 1998; USDHHS, 2000), it can be addressed creatively provided the campaign planning team considers a wide array of available resources for message dissemination.

Subsequently, the overarching question this case study tackles is: What culturally appropriate, low-tech delivery methods are most effective for reaching Hispanic populations living in *colonias*? The project team considered this issue when devising a message-dissemination strategy that would maximize the opportunity for the targeted audience to receive the health campaign messages.

The Campaign: *Sabemos*

Before we discuss the issues and challenges to disseminating a culturally appropriate campaign, a brief review is important to provide background information. *Sabemos: Por Respeto, No Se Fuma Aquí* ("We Know: Out of respect, do not smoke here") is a media campaign toolkit developed by the Office on Smoking and Health at the CDC. *Sabemos* focuses on reducing the number of children under 14 who are exposed to secondhand smoke in their homes, cars, and community. The *Sabemos* materials emphasize five behavioral components for adult caregivers: (a) begin by not smoking in your home and car, (b) talk to your children about the dangers of secondhand smoke, (c) keep your home and car smoke-free, (d) teach your children how to avoid secondhand smoke, and (e) support local restaurants and other businesses that have a smoke-free policy. The toolkit (available from the CDC at http://www.cdc.gov/tobacco/basic_information/secondhand_smoke/sabemos/) is a pre-packaged set of materials designed for local organizations interested in promoting smoke-free homes and communities by emphasizing the preceding five behavioral outcomes. These toolkits are especially useful to organizations with limited resources to develop campaign materials from scratch. CDC planners suggest those interested in using *Sabemos* may include local health care advocates or providers, church or religious organizations, local leaders and trusted advisors, community-based organizations, as well as community health workers.

The *Sabemos* toolkit provides an introductory letter from the CDC outlining the dangers of secondhand smoke exposure and strategies for creating a normative culture of smoke-free homes, cars, and communities for children under 14. The toolkit contains information on Hispanic culture, tips for how to broaden the reach of the messages, an Opinion-Editorial article, talking points and an interview guide that can be used for interviews or call-in shows, scripts for local announcers to record public service announcements (PSAs), and pre-recorded PSA audio files. The toolkit also includes a set of stickers that can be affixed to car bumpers or windows, and doors or windows of homes or businesses. Additionally, the toolkit has information cards that provide tips on how to create a smoke-free culture. All materials are in Spanish and English.

The research literature shows that most successful campaigns are those which are theoretically grounded (Atkin & Freimuth, 2001). CDC researchers, who extensively piloted message concepts and ideas, based the final set of *Sabemos* campaign materials on several theoretical foundations. First, utilizing the Theory of Reasoned Action (TRA; Ajzen & Fishbein, 1980), the campaign aims to promote an awareness of existing positive social norms regarding the protection of children in the home from exposure to secondhand smoke (CDC, 2007). The stickers provided in the toolkit were designed to target social norms regarding secondhand smoke, such that placing the stickers on car bumpers or on the front doors or windows of homes would communicate the message that local residents value a smoke-free environment for their children. Second, the campaign is based upon Hispanic cultural values of prioritizing family (*familia*) and respect (*respeto*) (Ellickson, Collins, & Bell, 1999; Hecht et al., 2003; Santiago-Rivera, 2003). A series of pre-campaign focus groups were conducted in different regions of the United States (New York, New Jersey, Texas, Illinois, and California), which indicated family and respect were highly valued cultural traits, particularly within families who migrate regularly to unfamiliar communities to find work. The campaign's tagline emphasizes the importance of not exposing younger children to secondhand smoke out of respect for their family ("*Por respeto, no se fuma aquí*"). All *Sabemos* communication materials contain the "*Por respeto*" tagline as well as

FIGURE 12.1 Sabemos logo.

a common logo, as seen in **FIGURE 12.1**, to build familiarity with the campaign. This practice is referred to as branding. Finally, the campaign relies in part upon Diffusion of Innovation theory (Rogers, 1995), specifically the opinion leader concept. Diffusion, defined by Rogers (1995), is "the process by which an innovation is communicated through certain channels over time among the members of a social system" (p. 35). Diffusion can be assisted when individuals who are regarded as opinion leaders are instrumental in introducing a campaign idea to the community. In *Sabemos*, the innovation is the idea that is being promoted, in this particular case, preventing secondhand smoke exposure to children ages 14 and under. The information in the toolkit encourages organizations to identify trusted community leaders, local media, and interpersonal channels to help launch the campaign, thereby fostering trusting relationships between the campaign's sponsors and the community.

Challenges and Questions for Culturally Adapting *Sabemos* to South Texas

A case study is designed optimally to review complex issues and challenges that individuals or planning teams face in specific situations, followed by the decision-making process that led to strategies designed to overcome those complex issues and challenges. The *Sabemos* campaign planning team had several complex challenges.

First, although the CDC version of *Sabemos* was created for a Hispanic audience, the broadcast materials were clearly not "local" or specific to the border community. Second, the target audience was low income, spoke only Spanish at home, and had little or no access to media other than radio. Therefore, the primary concern then became how the health campaign planning team could most effectively disseminate the *Sabemos* message. Third, several of the most effective health media campaigns relied heavily upon an interpersonal or community-education component. However, it was important to determine what would be the most effective and cost-efficient way to disseminate the *Sabemos* message to a target audience with such clearly defined characteristics; moreover, what source would be most effective? Finally, the project staff faced natural events that could have ended the project before its official launch: two hurricanes, Dolly and Ike, within a period of three months making landfall in the project area. In light of these problems, the question became how would the health campaign planning team proceed when much of the population had priorities other than worrying about exposure to secondhand smoke? What follows is a discussion of how these issues were addressed while remembering the main issue in this case study: What culturally appropriate, low-tech delivery methods are most effective for reaching Hispanic populations living in *colonias*?

The first major issue faced by the research team was adapting the CDC toolkit materials to the Hispanic culture in the Lower Rio Grande Valley of South Texas. Although CDC researchers conducted extensive pre-campaign research to develop the toolkit, the toolkit materials appropriately suggest that organizations should gain insight and knowledge of the culture's characteristics, values, and attitudes (CDC, 2007). Indeed, some research shows considerable variation within Hispanic language and culture (Varela et al., 2004). For example, El Paso, Texas Hispanic culture has variations that are unique and not shared by the culture in the Lower Rio Grande Valley (Alvaro, Jones, Robles, & Siegel, 2005; Gregory, 1983).

The project was implemented in three impoverished *colonias* on the Texas-Mexico border, where poverty is extensive and multiple members of families live together under one roof in substandard housing (U.S. Census Bureau, 2000). Hence, an exceptional amount of care was given to understand this audience to establish how best to approach the reduction of secondhand smoke with campaign messages (Parrott, Wilson, Buttram, Jones & Steiner, 1999; Piotrow & Kincaid, 2001). From these efforts, evidence suggested changes to the pre-packaged materials were needed to maximally adapt the content for the target community. For instance, the language used in the pre-recorded radio ads was not colloquial (e.g., conversational, rather than formal Spanish), and the announcer's voice on the ads did not "sound" like Spanish-speaking residents from South Texas. In light of the preceding information, the research team made minor changes to the public service announcement scripts and used a local announcer to voice a portion of the ads.

A second issue was how to reach *and* connect with individuals living in the *colonias*. A large advertising budget was not available to the health campaign planners; therefore, televised commercials and large print ads, which are typically very costly, were not feasible. Moreover, issues specific to the digital divide had to be considered. Specifically, few residents had computer or internet access since phone lines or internet connections do not always exist in the *colonias* or alternatively, the cost of such service was prohibitive where access would be available. Therefore, those media that would typically be relied upon heavily in most campaigns (e.g., social networking internet sites, television ads during cable television events) were not appropriate for this audience.

Spanish-language radio stations have been shown to be an attractive means through which to reach the targeted audience (Meyer, Roberto, & Atkin, 2003), and the health campaign planning team confirmed this finding through pre-campaign surveys with members of the targeted communities. As there were an abundance of Spanish-language radio stations in the area, the health campaign planning team had to determine which of the stations would be most effective at reaching the targeted audience. Once stations were identified from the pre-campaign surveys, we followed the lead of other campaign researchers (Palmgreen, Donohew, Lorch, Hoyle, & Stephenson, 2001; Palmgreen, Lorch, Stephenson, Hoyle & Donohew, 2007) and asked the preferred local radio stations to match the amount of time we purchased for radio ads with donated time. For example, if we purchased time for the PSA to air 30 times on a station, we asked if they would be willing to match and provide an additional 30 spots at no additional cost. Once finalized, the intervention consisted of a one-month radio advertising campaign initially conducted in *colonias* located in Alton and Progreso (both are in the same media market).

Challenges with the media campaign were not only due to limited campaign resources, but the economy was in a downward spiral and most radio stations' rates had increased. Negotiations for a lower advertising rate, in addition to donated airtime, were challenging. One member of the health campaign planning team, who resided in Hidalgo County, spent a considerable amount of time discussing the benefits of the campaign to the community with advertising managers and secured donations from the local stations.

Airtime alone, however, did not guarantee that our messages would either be received or resonate with the target audience. Flora (2001) discussed the importance of small-group educational sessions that are designed with the goal of facilitating exposure to health campaigns in addition to much needed social support to the targeted population. The health campaign staff thus utilized individual and group instruction methods to influence and emphasize the behavioral changes of the media campaign by employing a community health worker model (Culica, Walton, Harker, & Prezio, 2008; Southwell & Yzer, 2007). These interpersonal sessions reinforced the media messages targeting parental knowledge, attitudes, and behaviors (Stephenson, Quick & Hirsch, 2010) and about their role(s) in the exposure of their children to secondhand smoke. The expectation was that these additions to the media messages would not only help shape attitudes and behaviors, but through the interaction of individuals with others in their peer group, they would also influence social group norms.

Known by various names, such as lay health advisor, community health workers, or peer navigators, the Health Resources and Services Administration (HRSA) describes *promotor de salud* as:

> terms used in Mexico, Latin America and Latino communities in the United States to describe advocates of the welfare of their own community who have the vocation, time, dedication and experience to assist fellow community members in improving their health status and quality of life. (HRSA, 2007, p. 2)

Highly trusted, due in part to being indigenous to the community, *promotores*[3] provide much needed social support regarding health-related issues. Members of the *colonias* are familiar with these individuals as they frequent the *colonias* as health advocates for many organizations. Both paid and unpaid, *promotores* often fulfill roles in which they:

> offer interpretation or translation services, provide culturally appropriate health education and information, assist people in receiving the care they need, give informal counseling and guidance on health behaviors, advocate for individual and community health needs, and provide some direct services such as first aid and blood pressure screenings (HRSA, 2007, p. 2).

For the *Sabemos* campaign, *promotores* were trained to conduct the small group education sessions. *Promotores* engaged members of the target population through *charlas* (community meetings) held in the homes of *colonia* residents. *Promotores* are culturally relevant (Larkey, Gonzalez, Mar, & Glantz, 2009; Levine, Becker, & Bone, 1992; Richter et al., 1974), provide crucial social support to help the target population adopt behavioral change (Baquero et al., 2009; Heisler et al., 2009; Elder, Ayala, Slymen, Arrendondo, & Campbell, 2009; McCloskey, 2009; Medina, Blacazar, Hollen, Nkhoma, & Mas, 2007; Postma, Karr, & Kieckhefer, 2009), and are effective in working with Hispanic populations (Balcazar, Alvarado, Cantu, Pedregon, & Fulwood, 2009; Larkey et al., 2009).

While the *Sabemos* radio advertisements were being aired on local stations, the *promotores* scheduled *charlas*, prepared a meal for the participants who attended the *charlas,* and met with the participants for 30 to 45 minutes discussing the effects of secondhand smoke and how decision-makers and caregivers in the home can prevent secondhand smoke exposure. The *promotores* reviewed the five behavioral objectives emphasized in the *Sabemos* toolkit. Additionally, *promotores* provided *charla* participants with stickers to place on their cars and front doors or windows with the intent of encouraging an environment that was smoke-free for the children who resided there, as well as to establish smoke-free norms in the community. The *promotores* were particularly valuable since mistrust in the *colonia* culture is high, particularly given that many of the individuals are in the country illegally; thus, the health campaign team believed the use of *promotores* was paramount to effectively convey the message in the campaign.

Finally, during the intervention, two unpredictable, high-impact events occurred that led the health campaign planners to regroup: the arrival of hurricanes Dolly and Ike in South Texas in the exact region where the project was to be conducted, and the project's principal investigator was diagnosed with cancer, removing him from project management just prior to the campaign's roll out. Implications existed for the management of the campaign as well as the timeline of the project that few could have anticipated. In the case of the hurricanes, the health campaign planning team faced the reality that residents were going to be far more concerned with their own safety and welfare for an undefined period of time rather than worry about secondhand smoke exposure. The health campaign planners and *promotores* consulted and reached a solution that kept the campaign timeline manageable but allowed for the unplanned natural event to be dealt with by local residents so that appropriate attention could be given to the *Sabemos* campaign. Regarding the illness of the investigator, major decisions shifted to one of the co-investigators, and the health campaign team worked collectively to fill in the role until his return.

Research Design, Evaluation Methods, and Findings

The campaign was evaluated using a repeated-measures design where data was collected from the same individuals at multiple time periods throughout the campaign. The questionnaire contained items used in evaluating previous campaigns, but it was adapted for the purpose of this study (Potter, Judkins, Piesse, Nolin, & Huhman, 2008; Huhman et al., 2007). The questionnaire collected data on participant demographics, existing smoking and secondhand smoke behavior, and message exposure. The questionnaire also measured behaviors, attitudes, and intentions to perform behaviors that were targeted in the *Sabemos* intervention. Pretest data were collected six weeks prior to the media intervention. Two sets of posttest data were collected: the first about six weeks after the final media broadcast and *charlas,* and the second about three months after the campaign's conclusion. Using a systematic sampling with a random start,[4] data were collected from 400 adults who reside in a home with a child under the age of 14. Following the infusion of additional funds for the health campaign, a booster media campaign was completed at nine months following the initial campaign. One final posttest data collection was completed immediately following the end of the booster media campaign.

Despite the unusually high completion of pretest and both posttests by participants, data collection within the *colonias* presented its own challenges. *Colonias* are a unique culture with respect to household composition. Typically, more than one family lives in a household; therefore, surveys were conducted with one adult decision-maker in each of the sampled households. Researchers hypothesized a significantly greater change in the targeted *Sabemos* outcomes (knowledge, attitude, intentions, and behaviors related to secondhand smoke) in the *colonias* receiving the media campaign and educational sessions than the *colonia* receiving only the media campaign. Although the data analytic phase is ongoing, we have initial results on the original design comparing Alton (media + personal education intervention) to Progreso (media only). There were no significant differences on four key outcome variables for the *Sabemos* campaign.[5] However, the trends show nearly significant effects in Alton compared to Progreso, with individuals in Alton showing near-significant outcomes consistent with *Sabemos*.

Summary

This case study reviewed how a health campaign planning team adapted a pre-existing toolkit into a campaign that was both culturally appropriate and utilized non-traditional mechanisms through which to distribute the campaign messages. In this case study, the *Sabemos* campaign was adapted to meet the needs of the targeted audience: Hispanic parents and caregivers of children under 14 years of age who reside in Lower Rio Grande Valley *colonias*. Primarily at issue was selecting a culturally appropriate, low-tech delivery method through which to effectively reach the target audience. The toolkit was localized for the community, the digital divide had to be considered in devising a message dissemination strategy, and trusted community health workers, *promotores*, were utilized to reinforce the *Sabemos* messages that were airing concurrently on local radio stations.

This chapter was supported by Cooperative Agreement Number 5U48 DP000045 from the Centers for Disease Control and Prevention. The findings and conclusions in this report chapter are those of the author and do not necessarily represent the official position of the Centers for Disease Control and Prevention.

NOTES

1   The federal government defines Hispanic or Latino as a person of Mexican, Puerto Rican, Cuban, South or Central American, or other Spanish culture or origin regardless of race. Thus, Hispanics may be any race. The terms "Hispanic" and "Latino" are used by the U.S. Census Bureau; hereinafter in this chapter, the term "Hispanic" is used to refer to all individuals who reported they were Hispanic or Latino.

2   Meaning neighborhood in Spanish, a colonia is a tract of farm land bought by developers who divided the land and sold the sections without any improvements to most poor, Mexican Americans along the U.S.-Mexico border. Most colonias are unincorporated areas that lack the basic services taken for granted by most people in the United States, such as lacking water and sewage systems, electricity, paved roads, or safe and sanitary housing (State Energy Conservation Office, n.d.).

3   Given that the vast majority of people who fulfill this role are women, the traditional reference is to *promotoras*. However, given there are men who serve in this role, we use the inclusive term *promotores* throughout this chapter.

4   Systematic sampling is a method for generating a random sample of individuals to participate in the study. To generate a systematic sample, a skip interval was computed by dividing the total number of housing units by the total number of interviews needed for each *colonia* and then selecting the first household at random. For a more detailed discussion of stratified random sampling, see Frey, Botan, and Kreps (2000).

5   That is, they did not occur more than chance alone would have predicted. They also failed to be below $p < .05$, the social science standard for hypothesis testing. For a more detailed discussion, see Frey, Botan, and Kreps (2000)

Discussion Questions

1. Why would the campaign planners select *colonia* residents living on the Texas-Mexico border as a target population? What are the implications of selecting this region for public health and health communication interventions?

2. What additional channels can you identify to disseminate the campaign's message other than through radio and the *charlas* held by the project's *promotores*? Be able to support your reasoning focusing on salient advantages and potential pitfalls.

3. Could public events, such as a health fair or a school carnival, be effective at disseminating the campaign's message to the target audience? How would a campaign planner determine if a public event was worth the time and monetary investment to disseminate the messages, particularly if financial resources were limited?

4. An integral cultural element of this target audience was shared caregiving. Several adults in a household, besides the parents, often have authority over the children living there. How then can campaign planners disseminate the message to all of the adult caregivers, and how are the adult caregivers supposed to negotiate new secondhand smoke exposure rules for a given household? Additionally, how do campaign planners work with adult caregivers who are not the decision-makers of the household and have little to no authority about overall household decisions like smoking in the home?

5. Could the *Sabemos* campaign be implemented with a similar target audience in a large city? What would the research team need to do differently in terms of reaching the target audience and adapting the messages and mechanisms for distributing the messages?

6. Why might residents in the *colonias* be uninterested in reducing secondhand smoke exposure among the children under their care?

References

Alvaro, E. M., Jones, S. P., Robles, A. S., & Siegel, J. T. (2005). Predictors of organ donation behavior among Hispanic Americans. *Progress in Transplantation, 15*, 149–156.

Ad Council. (2005). American Legacy Foundation and the Ad Council launch first campaign to call attention to and education public about dangers of secondhand smoke. [Media release]. Retrieved from http://www.adcouncil.org/newsDetail.aspx?id=57

Atkin, C. K., & Freimuth, V. S. (2001). Formative evaluation research in campaign design. In R. E. Rice, & C. K. Atkin (Eds.), *Public communication campaigns* (pp. 125–145). Thousand Oaks, CA: Sage.

Ajzen, I., & Fishbein, M. (1980). *Understanding attitudes and predicting social behavior.* Englewood Cliffs, NJ: Prentice-Hall.

Balcázar, H., Alvarado, M., Cantu, F., Pedregon, V., & Fulwood, R. (2009). A promotora de salud model for addressing cardiovascular disease risk factors in the US-Mexico border region. *Preventing Chronic Disease, 6*, A02.

Baquero, B., Ayala, G. X., Arrendondo, E. M., Campbell, N. R., Slymen, D. J., Gallow, L., & Elder, J. P. (2009). *Secretos de la Buena Vida*: Processes of dietary change via a tailored nutrition communication intervention for Latinas. *Health Education Research, 24*, 855–866.

Centers for Disease Control and Prevention. (2007). *Sabemos: Por respeto, aquí no se fuma.* Retrieved from http://www.cdc.gov/tobacco/basic_information/secondhand_smoke/sabemos/

Culica, D., Walton, J. W., Harker, K., & Prezio, E. A. (2008). Effectiveness of a community health worker as sole diabetes educator: Comparison of CoDE with similar culturally appropriate interventions. *Journal of Health Care for the Poor and Underserved, 19*, 1076–1095.

Elder, J. P., Ayala, G. X., Slymen, D. J., Arrendondo, E. M., & Campbell, N. R. (2009). Evaluating psychosocial and behavioral mechanisms of change in a tailored communication intervention. *Health Education and Behavior, 36*, 366–80.

Ellickson, P. L., Collins, R. L., & Bell, R. M. (1999). Adolescent use of illicit drugs other than marijuana: How important is social bonding and for which ethnic groups? *Substance Use & Misuse, 34*, 317–346.

Eng, T. R., Maxfield, A., Patrick, K., Deering, M. J., Ratzan, S. C., & Gustafson, D. H. (1998). Access to health information and support: A public highway or a private road? *Journal of the American Medical Association, 280*, 1371–1375.

Flora, J. A. (2001). The Stanford community studies: Campaigns to reduce cardiovascular disease. In R. E. Rice, & C. K. Atkin (Eds.), *Public communication campaigns* (3rd ed, pp. 193–213). Thousand Oaks, CA: Sage.

Flores, G., Fuentes-Afflick, E., Barbot, O., Carter-Pokas, O., Claudio, L., Lara, M., McLaurin, J. A., Pachter, L., Ramos Gomez, F., Valdez, R. B., Villarruel, A. M., Zambrana, R. E., Greenberg, R., & Weitzman, M. (2002). The health of Latino children: Urgent priorities, unanswered questions, and a research agenda. *Journal of the American Medical Association, 288*, 82–89.

Freimuth, V. S. (1990). The chronically uninformed: Closing the knowledge gap in health. In E. B. Ray, & L. Donohew (Eds.), *Communication and health: Systems and applications* (pp. 171–186). Hillsdale, NJ: Lawrence Erlbaum Associates.

Frey, L., Botan, K., & Kreps, G. (2000). *Investigating communication: An introduction to research methods* (2nd ed.). Boston, MA: Allyn & Bacon.

Gregory, K. L. (1983). Native-view paradigms: Multiple cultures and culture conflicts in organizations. *Administrative Science Quarterly, 28*, 359–376.

Health Resources and Services Administration. (2007). *Community health worker national workforce study.* Retrieved from http://bhpr.hrsa.gov/healthworkforce/chw/

Hecht, M. L., Marsiglia, F. F., Elvira, E., Wagstaff, D. A., Kulis, S., Dustman, P., & Miller-Day, M. (2003). Culturally grounded substance abuse prevention: An evaluation of the *keepin' it R.E.A.L.* curriculum. *Prevention Science, 4*, 233–248.

Heisler, M., Spencer, M., Forman, J., Robinson, C., Shultz, C., Palmisano, G., et al. (2009). Participants' assessments of the effects of a community health worker intervention on their diabetes self-management and interactions with healthcare providers. *American Journal of Preventive Medicine, 37*(6- S1), S270–279.

Hopkins, D. P., Briss, P. A., Ricard, C. J., Husten, C. G., Carande-Kulis, V. G., Fielding, J. E., et al. (2001). Reviews of evidence regarding interventions to reduce tobacco use and exposure to environmental tobacco smoke. *American Journal of Preventive Medicine, 20(2S)*, 16–66.

Huhman, M. E., Potter, L. D., Duke, J. C., Judkins, D. R., Heitzler, C. D., & Wong, F. L. (2007). Evaluation of a national physical activity intervention for children: VERB™ campaign, 2002–2004. *American Journal of Preventive Medicine, 32*, 38–43.

Kreuter, M. W., & McClure, S. M. (2004). The role of culture in health communication. *Annual Review of Public Health, 25*, 439–455.

Larkey, L. K., Gonzalez, J. A., Mar, L. E., & Glantz, N. (2009). Latina recruitment for cancer prevention education via community based participatory research strategies. *Contemporary Clinical Trials, 30*, 47–54.

Levine, D. M., Becker, D. M., & Bone, L. R. (1992). Narrowing the gap in health status of minority populations: A community-academic medical center partnership. *American Journal of Preventive Medicine, 8*, 319–323.

Livingstone, S., & Helsper, E. (2007). Gradations in digital inclusion: Children, young people, and the digital divide. *New Media & Society, 9*, 671–696.

Lorence, D. P., Park, H., & Fox, S. (2006). Racial disparities in health information access: Resilience of the digital divide. *Journal of Medical Systems, 30*, 241–249.

McCloskey, J. (2009). Promotores as partners in a community-based diabetes intervention program targeting Hispanics. *Family & Community Health, 32*, 48–57.

Medina, A., Balcazar, H., Hollen, M. L., Nkhoma, A., & Mas, F. S. (2007). Promotores de salud: Educating Hispanic communities on heart-healthy living. *American Journal of Health Education, 38*, 194–202.

Meyer, G., Roberto, A. J., & Atkin, C. K. (2003). A radio-based approach to promoting gun safety: Process and outcome evaluation implications and insights. *Health Communication, 15*, 299–318.

National Center for Health Statistics. (2009). *Health, United States 2008 with Chartbook.* Retrieved from http://www.cdc.gov/nchs/data/hus/hus08.pdf#001

Niederdeppe, J., Fiore, M. C., Baker, T. B., & Smith, S. S. (2008). Smoking-cessation media campaigns and their effectiveness among socioeconomically advantaged and disadvantaged populations. *American Journal of Public Health, 98*, 916–924.

Parrott, R., Wilson, K., Buttram, C., Jones, K., & Steiner, C. (1999). Migrant farm workers' access to pesticide prevention and information: Cultivando buenos habitos campaign development. *Journal of Health Communication, 4*, 49–64.

Palmgreen, P., Donohew, L., Lorch, E. P., Hoyle, R. H., & Stephenson, M. T. (2001). Television campaigns and adolescent marijuana use: Tests of a sensation seeking targeting. *American Journal of Public Health, 91*, 292–296.

Palmgreen, P., Lorch, E. P., Stephenson, M. T., Hoyle, R. H., & Donohew, L. (2007). Effects of the Office of National Drug Control Policy's marijuana initiative campaign on high sensation-seeking adolescents. *American Journal of Public Health, 97*, 1644–1649.

Piotrow, P. T., & Kincaid, D. L. (2001). Strategic communication for international health programs. In R. E. Rice, & C. K. Atkin (Eds.), *Public Communication Campaigns* (pp. 249–268). Thousand Oaks, CA: Sage Publications.

Postma, J., Karr, C., & Kieckhefer, G. (2009). Community health workers and environmental interventions for children with asthma: A systematic review. *Journal of Asthma, 46*, 564–576.

Potter, L. D., Judkins, D. R., Piesse, A., Nolin, M. J., & Huhman, M. (2008). Methodology of an Outcome Evaluation of the VERB™ Campaign. *American Journal of Preventive Medicine, 34*(6S), 230–40.

Public Broadcasting Service. (2000). *The Forgotten Americans.* Retrieved from: http://www.pbs.org/klru/forgottenamericans/colonias.htm

Ramirez, R. R., & de la Cruz, P. G. (2003). *The Hispanic population in the United States: March 2002.* Retrieved from http://www.census.gov/prod/2003pubs/p20-545.pdf

Richter, R. W., Bengen, B., Alsup, P. A., Bruun, B., Kilcoyne, M. M., & Challenor, B. D. (1974). The community health worker: A resource for improved health care delivery. *American Journal of Public Health, 64*, 1056–1061.

Rogers, E. M. (1995). *Diffusion of innovations* (4th ed.). New York, NY: Free Press.

Santiago-Rivera, A. (2003). Latino values and family transitions: Practical considerations for counseling. *Counseling and Human Development, 35*, 1–12.

State Energy Conservation Office. (n.d.) *Colonias Projects.* Retrieved from: http://www.seco.cpa.state.tx.us/colonias.htm

Stephenson, M. T., Quick, B. L., & Hirsch, H. A. (2010). Evidence in support of a strategy to target authoritarian and permissive parents in anti-drug media campaigns. *Communication Research, 37*, 73–104.

Southwell, B. G., & Yzer, M. C. (2007). The roles of interpersonal communication in mass media campaigns. In C. S. Beck (Ed.), *Communication yearbook, 31* (pp. 420–455). New York, NY: Routledge.

Texas Department of State Health Services. (2004). *Selected Health Facts 2004: Hidalgo County.* Retrieved from http://www.dshs.state.tx.us/chs/cfs/cfs04/Hidalg04.pdf

U.S. Census Bureau. (2000). *State & County QuickFacts: Hidalgo County, Texas.* Retrieved from http://quickfacts.census.gov/qfd/states/48/48215.html

U.S. Census Bureau. (n.d.). *Hispanics in the United States.* Retrieved from http://www.census.gov/population/www/socdemo/hispanic/hispanic.html

U.S. Department of Health and Human Services. (2000). *Healthy People 2010.* Retrieved from http://www.healthypeople.gov/document/HTML/Volume1/11HealthCom.htm

Vallone, D. M., Allen, J. A., & Xiao, H. (2009). Is socioeconomic status associated with awareness of and receptivity to the truth® Campaign? *Drug and Alcohol Dependence, 104*, S115–120.

Varela, E. R., Vernberg, E. M., Sanchez-Sosa, J. J., Riverson, A., Mitchell, M., & Mashunkashey, J. (2004). Parenting style of Mexican, Mexican American, and Caucasian-Non-Hispanic families: Social context and cultural influences. *Journal of Family Psychology, 18*, 651–657.

Vega, W. A., & Lopez, S. R. (2001). Priority issues in Latino mental health services research. *Mental Health Services Research, 3*, 189–200.

SECTION V

Designing, Implementing, and Evaluating Effective Health Campaigns

CHAPTER 13

Engaging Motorcycle Safety in a University Community

Toward a Health Campaign Pedagogy Model for Community Advocacy

Marifran Mattson, Emily Joy Haas, Traci K. Gillig, and Carin L. Kosmoski

KEY TERMS

Health advocacy

Message development tool

Health communication pedagogy

Motorcycle safety

Abstract

Health campaign pedagogy can serve students and their communities as communication practice and advocacy. This chapter highlights the case of the Motorcycle Safety at Purdue (MS@P) campaign to build on and extend communication pedagogy as communication praxis (Barge & Shockley-Zalabak, 2008; Morreale & Pearson, 2008; Query, Wright, Bylund, & Mattson, 2007) by forwarding a health campaign pedagogy model for engaging students in community advocacy. Although the model is based on the social marketing framework (Kotler & Lee, 2008), the Message Development Tool (Mattson & Basu, 2010a, 2010b), and a unique campaign exemplar, the phases of the model are adaptable to other health issues, communities, and health communication curricula.

We begin by introducing the Motorcycle Safety at Purdue (MS@P) campaign case study. Then, we provide an overview of the theoretically grounded framework that guides the campaign. Finally, we argue for extending the campaign framework to promote a health campaign pedagogy model that engages students in communication practice and community advocacy.

Motorcycle Safety at Purdue Campaign

The MS@P campaign came about literally by accident. After their professor, Marifran Mattson, was seriously injured in a motorcycle accident, graduate students who were enrolled in her campaign evaluation class suspected that their university community needed motorcycle safety advocacy. The students convinced Mattson to allow the class to conduct a needs assessment. The assessment revealed that a health and safety campaign was warranted (Kosmoski, Mattson, & Hall, 2007). From that information, the MS@P campaign was conceived.

The resulting campaign seeks to raise awareness about motorcycle accident risks, increase safe driving behaviors, and promote communication about motorcycle safety in the greater university community. A health campaign framework that emphasizes the importance of effective messaging guides the campaign (Mattson & Basu, 2010a, 2010b).

Motorcycle Safety Risks in a University Community

University settings contain structural and logistical risk factors associated with motorcycle accidents. Purdue University, home of the MS@P campaign, is a mid-sized, upper-middle-class university town in the Midwest. Several poorly marked one-way streets run through the campus. Crowds of pedestrians often jaywalk across these and other campus streets. Additionally, thousands of new students as well as their friends and family members arrive on campus each year. Many of these individuals are unfamiliar with of the community's traffic regulations. Taken together, the confusing traffic patterns, the inconsistent movements of pedestrians, and the lack of understanding of traffic regulations can cause distractions for motorcyclists and drivers of cars and trucks which may compromise safety.

University demographics also exacerbate motorcycle safety risks. West Lafayette, Indiana, the city of Purdue University and the MS@P campaign, features a population in which more than 50% are between the ages of 18 and 24, and approximately 10% are under the age of 18 years old (Purdue University, 2009–2010). Due in part to the engineering, computer technology, and agriculture foci of this university, there are 137 males to every 100 females over the age of 18 (Purdue University, 2009–2010). Because vehicle accidents, and motorcycle accidents in particular, are highest among young males (Centers for Disease Control and Prevention, 2008; National Highway Transportation Safety Administration [NHTSA], 2010), a university community provides an appropriate environment within which to address this high-risk population.

Other motorcycle safety risk factors stem from an increase in the sale of motorcycles across the United States during the past several years (Motorcycle Industry Council, 2006). With more motorcycles on the roads, motorcycle accidents, injuries, and fatalities also have increased (NHTSA, 2010). In Indiana, motorcyclist fatalities have increased an average of 9.4% annually while other categories of traffic fatalities have decreased. The age groups most frequently involved in motorcycle accidents are 21–30 and 41–50 (NHTSA, 2010). In 2009, there were 100 motorcycle accidents reported in the county in which Purdue University is located (Nunn, 2009). Generally in this county, motorcycle accidents are "primarily due to driver error, failure to yield the right-of-way, or an unsafe speed by either the motorcyclist and/or other drivers involved" (Baldwin, 2007, p. 41). Thus, Purdue University and its surrounding community are an ideal setting for a motorcycle safety campaign.

Health Communication Campaign Framework

The MS@P campaign is grounded in an extension of the social marketing framework (Kotler & Lee, 2008) and the Message Development Tool (MDT) for health communication campaigns (Mattson & Basu, 2010a, 2010b). The MDT advanced the traditional social marketing framework by enhancing attention to relevant messaging components throughout the campaign process. As **FIGURE 13.1** of the Health Communication Campaign Framework (HCCF) depicts, the phases of a health communication campaign remain consistent with social marketing; however, communication theory-based messaging is foregrounded by emphasizing message effectiveness elements during the messaging process in Phase 2.[1] The messaging process is defined by Mattson and Basu (2010a, 2010b) as the dynamic and iterative practice of creating, disseminating, and sharing meaning through messages. Messaging is not restricted to assembling message variables for dissemination. Instead, the messaging process shares meaning and should involve cultural and organizational factors that shape messages and message dissemination choices as well as impact evaluation. In addition to the HCCF, the MS@P campaign applies the Extended Parallel Process Model (EPPM; Witte, 1992) as a guide for message development. Consistent with the EPPM, MS@P messages aim to balance fear and efficacy to encourage audience members to attend to and accept, rather than reject, the messages.

The MS@P campaign also utilizes research methods consistent with the HCCF phases of needs assessment, formative research of the messaging process, outcome evaluation, and feedback. Before committing to creating the campaign, an extensive, year-long needs assessment was conducted. It included a literature review and focus groups with motorcyclists. These focus groups consisted of motorcyclists who were University students, staff, and faculty. This needs assessment research was fundamental to the campaign's formation because most of the graduate students in the campaign class were not motorcyclists nor were they familiar with motorcycle riding culture or existing motorcycle safety campaigns. Focus group moderators thus probed motorcyclists about their beliefs and behaviors regarding safety practices, such as wearing safety gear and riding safely, as well as their opinions about what should be included in a motorcycle safety campaign. Ultimately, the needs assessment determined that three audiences warranted targeting by a motorcycle safety campaign: motorcyclists, friends and family of motorcyclists, as well as drivers of cars and trucks.

Next, during the formative research phase, the students and Mattson set out to understand the Purdue University community's requirements for a comprehensive motorcycle safety campaign. The campaign team used in-depth interviews and focus groups to gather data about the attitudes, beliefs, behaviors, and informational needs of each target audience. Focus groups also provided feedback on draft messages, promotional items, and ideas regarding campaign implementation.

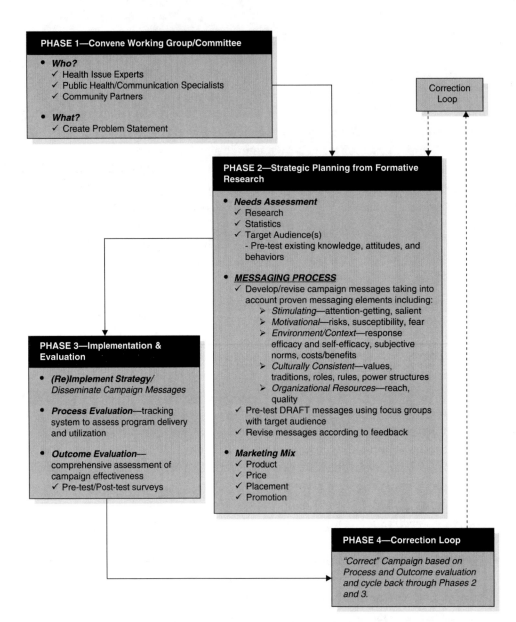

FIGURE 13.1 Health Communication Campaign Framework (HCCF; adapted from the Message Development Tool by Mattson & Basu, 2010a, 2010b)

Outcome evaluation of the campaign incorporates a pre-test/post-test survey. Prior to the campaign's implementation, a baseline pre-test survey of attitudes, beliefs, and behaviors regarding motorcycle safety was distributed across campus to students, staff, and faculty. Post-test surveys have been distributed to each target audience during the spring semester of every academic year since launching the campaign in 2006. Data from these surveys is analyzed to determine awareness of the campaign as well as attitudinal and behavioral impacts of campaign messages.

The MS@P campaign utilizes a variety of messages to encourage motorcycle safety among the three target audiences. One message reminds drivers of cars and trucks to "Watch for Motorcycles Everywhere." This message includes a caution sign emblazoned with a motorcyclist (**FIGURE 13.2**). Another message encourages motorcyclists to wear proper safety gear by comparing motorcycle safety gear to football safety gear (**FIGURE 13.3**). The idea of this message is that football players do not play football without wearing their safety gear for fear of being injured, so motorcyclists, who have similar safety gear for injury prevention, should wear their safety gear when motorcycling. Both of these messages were tested extensively with the target audiences during focus groups and have become effective messages for the campaign. However, even after thorough formative research testing not all MS@P messages have been effective during the campaign. If yearly outcome evaluation analyses reveal the need for new or revised messages or promotional strategies, target audience members are given the opportunity to analyze draft messages or strategies before they are re/implemented.

The next section describes how the MS@P campaign benefits students pursuing their degrees and in their job searches as well as promotes community health advocacy.

FIGURE 13.2 "Watch for Motorcycles Everywhere" message.

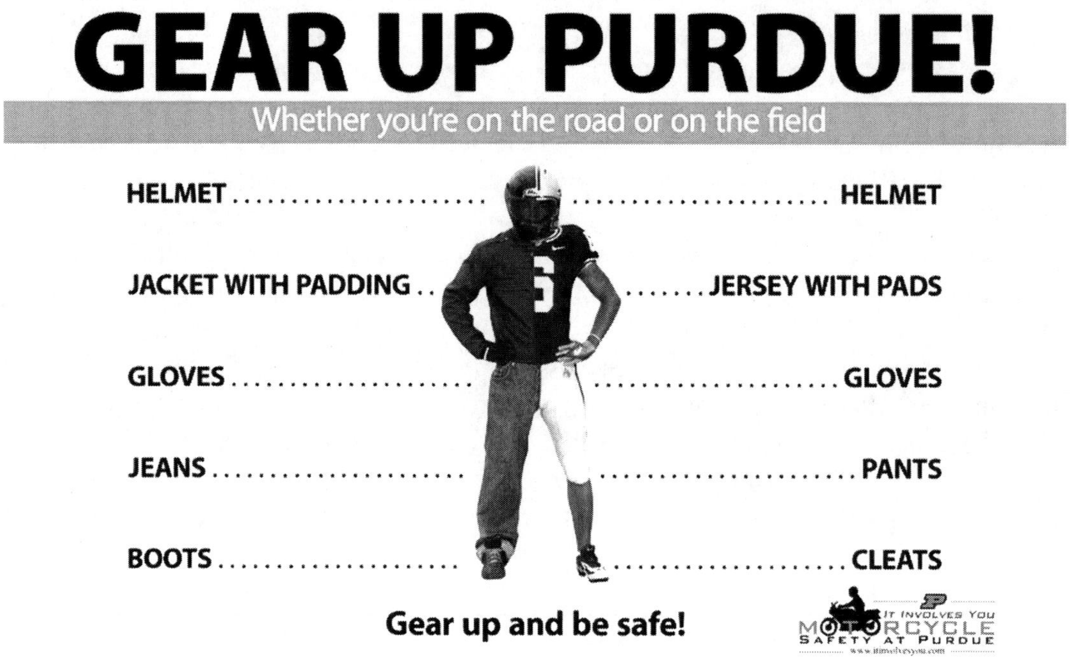
GEAR UP PURDUE!
Whether you're on the road or on the field
HELMET .... HELMET
JACKET WITH PADDING .... JERSEY WITH PADS
GLOVES .... GLOVES
JEANS .... PANTS
BOOTS .... CLEATS
Gear up and be safe!
It Involves You
MOTORCYCLE
SAFETY AT PURDUE

FIGURE 13.3 "Gear Up Purdue!" message.

Toward a Health Campaign Pedagogy Model for Community Advocacy

A unique aspect of the MS@P campaign is its roots in communication pedagogy (Barge & Shockley-Zalabak, 2008; Morreale & Pearson, 2008; Query et al., 2007). The MS@P campaign demonstrates how the HCCF can be extended to inform pedagogy practice. The HCCF established a process to engage students in communication practice and community advocacy and lead to the development of a pedagogy model. The MS@P campaign was created during a two-course, graduate-level sequence consisting of one course on campaign design and implementation and one course on campaign message evaluation. Students enrolled in this course sequence learned key concepts, principles, and strategies through readings and lectures as well as through hands-on campaign experience.

The ongoing MS@P campaign serves as a backdrop for campaign courses that have been offered since the initial course sequence. These courses provide a variety of students the opportunity to learn from and contribute to the growth of the campaign. Undergraduate students in courses such as Introduction to Health Communication and Small Group Communication work with the community on service-learning projects associated with the MS@P campaign. For example, a class of self-directed work teams in a Small Group Communication class partnered with the mayor's office to develop a proposal for how the mayor, who is an avid motorcyclist, could serve as a spokesperson for the campaign. The following semester another class designed public service announcements featuring the mayor and tested those messages with focus groups of target audience members. This campaign is fortunate to have a mayor who is a motorcyclist and is willing to serve as a spokesperson. Other individuals in a campus community can serve as spokespersons for campaigns when they have passion for and knowledge of the pertinent health issue. For example, campus representatives, local government officials, or any recognizable community members or former community members could serve as spokespersons for health communication campaigns.

The MS@P campaign provides valuable learning experiences for hundreds of graduate and undergraduate students. The campaign slogan, "It Involves You," reminds students that even though they may not be motorcyclists, this safety issue deserves community attention. In addition, many students have reported that working on the MS@P campaign was instrumental to securing a job within their career field. In each class that works on the campaign, at least one class session is devoted to discussing how students can incorporate their work on the MS@P campaign into their résumé or vita and practicing how they can talk about what they learned working on the campaign during a job interview. One student said that a recruiter for a business consulting firm asked if she rode a motorcycle. When she responded "no," the recruiter wondered why she had participated in a class project involving the MS@P campaign. This provided an opportunity to talk about the transferrable skills of project management, leadership, and network development she learned while interacting with community members to develop partnerships for the campaign. Ultimately, the company offered the student a position. In this way, classes involved with the campaign have short-term and long-term implications for students while benefiting the community.

Opportunities and challenges posed by the MS@P campaign are presented next. These opportunities and challenges, coupled with the HCCF previously discussed, provide the basis for a pedagogy model for engaging students in community advocacy.

Maximizing Campaign Opportunities and Minimizing Challenges

Although much time and attention is consumed by the many details of maintaining the MS@P campaign and corresponding coursework, writing about the campaign affords the luxury to pause from the usual busyness and reflect on and share the lessons learned from this experience. Designing, implementing, and evaluating a health campaign during the course of an academic term, or across terms, poses valuable opportunities for applied communication practice and community advocacy on any university or college campus. Such interventions, however, also present many challenges. Accordingly, we highlight a few opportunities and challenges advancing suggestions for maximizing the former while minimizing the latter.

Adopting a health campaign as a pedagogical tool adds considerable complexity that must be considered during course planning and execution. For instance, the instructor must strategically manage student turnover in working on the campaign from term to term to sustain the campaign's vitality. Interest in the campaign's health issue also is likely to wax and wane among some students and community partners. Subsequently, ongoing strategies for motivating and maintaining interest and relevance must be considered. The variety of research methods (e.g., focus groups to pre-test messages) and event-oriented projects (e.g., booths at community events) needed for a campaign helps alleviate diminishing attention spans. Also, as new students and community partners join the campaign, their enthusiasm tends to be infectious and invigorating to existing campaign members.

Another challenge and opportunity involves funding. As with all campaigns, funding can be a time-consuming, ongoing concern. Within university and college settings, small teaching and research grants may be available, and existing organizational (e.g., classroom space, graphic design expertise) and community resources (e.g., relevant advocacy organizations, in-kind donations[2] from area businesses) can be leveraged for the benefit of the campaign, students, and community. Funding source research and grant writing also can be incorporated into course assignments to provide learning experiences and résumé/vitae builders. In general, with some creativity and ingenuity, most campaign and coursework challenges can be turned into valuable opportunities. In addition, the amount of funding a campaign will need depends on the size of the university or college and its surrounding community as well as the scope of the campaign. For our large university within a mid-sized community, funding primarily is required for producing messages and promotional items. Smaller campuses and communities may require fewer resources to achieve saturation (i.e., diffusion of the campaign such that the campaign is recognizable to the majority of community members).

Health Campaign Pedagogy Model for Community Advocacy

Based on our experiences with the MS@P campaign, we conclude this chapter by extending the HCCF into a health campaign pedagogy model for engaging students in community advocacy. This practical model is designed for instructors, students, and scholars at both university and college campuses to follow in establishing a health campaign or other relevant coursework at the graduate and/or undergraduate levels.

As **FIGURE 13.4** illustrates, we build upon the HCCF to forward a Health Campaign Pedagogy Model for Community Advocacy. Instructors should be mindful that a sequence of health campaign courses could attempt to achieve the entire model, or each phase or major bullet point within the model could be accomplished by a term-long course or project. We commence Phase 1 by defining Advocacy as Passion + Action indicating that the instructor and the students need to have or infuse a sense of passion for the health issue and be ready to take action through a campaign focused on the health issue. To impart the passion to key audiences and share the action(s) necessary, the instructor and students should identify community partners and funding sources, and work together with these partners to create a problem statement that guides the campaign. This problem statement serves as the basis for the strategic planning process in Phase 2, which incorporates the needs assessment, the messaging process, attention to the 4 Ps in the marketing mix (i.e., product, price, placement, promotion), and the proposed

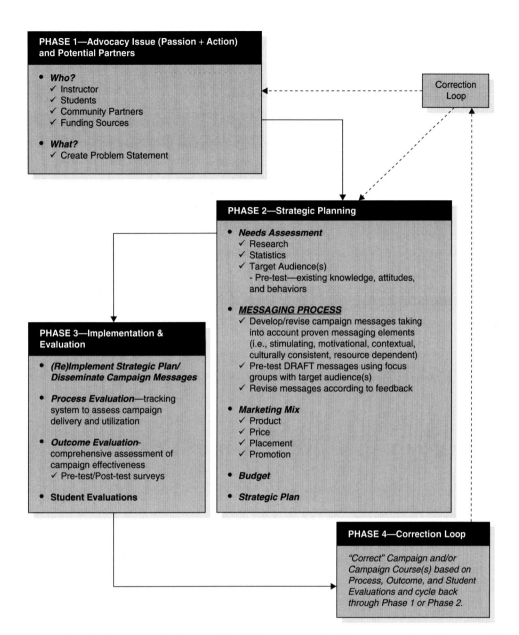

FIGURE 13.4 Health Campaign Pedagogy Model for Community Advocacy (adapted from the Health Communication Campaign Framework.)

budget, which all culminate in a strategic plan. In Phase 3, the strategic plan is implemented and evaluated through process and outcome evaluation. Student evaluations also play a role in determining how the course will progress or be changed. Based on campaign and course evaluations, Phase 4 formulates the correction loop which feeds back into Phase 1 and/or Phase 2.

Again, this cyclical process can inform either a single course or a course sequence working on a health issue through a health campaign.

Despite the inevitable frustrations encountered while campaigning for motorcycle safety or another health issue facing a university or college community, inspiration and strength can be found in the words of noted anthropologist Margaret Mead,

> "Never doubt that a small group of thoughtful, committed citizens can change the world. Indeed, it is the only thing that ever has."

Although the Motorcycle Safety at Purdue campaign came into existence because of an unfortunate and nearly fatal accident, the pedagogical, communication praxis, and community advocacy opportunities and benefits have been exceptionally enriching and life enhancing.

NOTES

1   Communication theory and research have indicated several elements of messages that increase message effectiveness. Mattson and Basu (2010a, 2010b) drew on this theory and research when they included the messaging elements of stimulating, motivational, environmentally and contextually appropriate, culturally consistent, and resource reliant when they developed the Message Development Tool.

2   In-kind donations refer to donations that are made in products or services rather than money. For example, a local motorcycle dealership donated a full set of safety gear (i.e., full-face helmet, padded jacket, gloves, padded pants, and boots) to the Motorcycle Safety at Purdue campaign instead of donating cash.

Discussion Questions

1. What are some health and/or safety issues relevant to your university, college, and/or community? Discuss the potential for developing a health and/or safety campaign to address each issue. Who might be potential community partners for each issue?

2. Why is a thorough needs assessment important in the campaign development process? What methods can be used to conduct a needs assessment?

3. The Motorcycle Safety at Purdue campaign had three target audiences. Discuss the importance of audience segmentation for campaign development.

4. What are some examples of formative research and why are they imperative to the development of a health and/or safety campaign and/or campaign messages?

5. The case study of the Motorcycle Safety at Purdue campaign indicated the use of a pre-test/post-test survey to evaluate the outcome or impact of the campaign. What are some of the pros and cons of this evaluation method? What are other methods that could be used to evaluate the impact of a health and/or safety campaign?

6. What is process tracking? Why is process tracking important? What are some process tracking methods?

7. One of the challenges of utilizing the health campaign pedagogy model elucidated in this chapter was turnover of campaign staff from semester to semester as different classes work on the campaign. Discuss some ways in which this challenge could be minimized. Discuss other challenges that might emerge when utilizing this approach to conducting a health campaign.

8. How do you think you, as a student, would benefit personally and professionally from working on an actual health and/or safety campaign?

References

Baldwin, M. (2007). *2006 Tippecanoe County Vehicle Crash Report*. Lafayette, Indiana: Area Plan Commission of Tippecanoe County.

Barge, J. K., & Shockley-Zalabak, P. (2008). Engaged scholarship and the creation of useful organizational knowledge. *Journal of Applied Communication Research, 36*, 251–265.

Centers for Disease Control and Prevention. (2008). *Teen Drivers: Fact Sheet*. Retrieved from http://www.cdc.gov/MotorVehicleSafety/Teen_Drivers/teendrivers_factsheet.html

Kosmoski, C. L., Mattson, M., & Hall, J. (2007). Reconsidering motorcycle safety at Purdue: A case study integrating campaign theory and practice. *Cases in Public Health Communication & Marketing, 1*. Retrieved from http://www.gwumc.edu/sphhs/departments/pch/phcm/cases journal/volume1/peer-reviewed/cases_1_07.cfm

Kotler, P., & Lee, N. R. (2008). *Social marketing: Influencing behaviors for good* (3rd ed.). Thousand Oaks, CA: Sage.

Mattson, M., & Basu, A. (2010a). Centers for Disease Control's DES Update: A case for effective operationlization of messaging in social marketing practice. *Health Promotion Practice, 11*, 580–588.

Mattson, M., & Basu, A. (2010b). The message development tool: A case for effective operationalization of messaging in social marketing practice. *Health Marketing Quarterly, 27*, 275–290.

Morreale, S. P., & Pearson, J. C. (2008). Why communication education is important: The centrality of the discipline in the 21st century. *Communication Education, 57*, 224–240.

Motorcycle Industry Council. (2006). *Motorcycle and scooter sales up for the 13th straight year.* Retrieved from http://www.mic.org/news021706.cfm

National Highway Transportation Safety Administration. (2010). *Traffic Safety Facts 2008: Motorcycles*. Retrieved from http://www-nrd.nhtsa.dot.gov/pubs/811159.pdf

Nunn, S. (2009). *Indiana Traffic Safety Facts: 2009*. Indianapolis: Indiana Criminal Justice Institute.

Purdue University. (2009–2010). *Purdue University Data Digest West Lafayette*. Retrieved from http://www.purdue.edu/DataDigest/

Query, J. L., Wright, K. B., Bylund, C. L., & Mattson, M. (2007). Health communication instruction: Toward identifying common learning goals, course content, and pedagogical strategies to guide curicular development. *Health Communication, 21*, 133–141.

Witte, K. (1992). Putting the fear back into fear appeals: The extended parallel process model. *Communication Monographs, 59*, 329–349.

CHAPTER 14

Health Communication in the Classroom and Community

Designing Theory-Driven Health Messages Using Effective Teaching Techniques

Brandi N. Frisby, Kerry Byrnes, and Maria Brann

KEY TERMS

ATV safety intervention

Theory of planned behavior

Experiential learning

Social marketing

Abstract

Disseminating safety messages is an important, yet sometimes difficult, task that should not be underestimated. The case study presented originated in a graduate-level health communication seminar in which the primary goal was the dissemination of potentially life-saving safety messages. The class was framed as an experiential learning experience (Steinaker & Bell, 1979), and utilized Kotler and Lee's (2008) social marketing steps and the Theory of Planned Behavior (TPB; Ajzen, 1985) to investigate a safety issue in the community. Specifically, students utilized these three frameworks (i.e., experiential learning, social marketing, and TPB) to address all-terrain vehicle (ATV) safety for middle school students through formative research, message design, campaign implementation, and campaign evaluation. This case delineates the benefits to the community and the middle school students including collaborative opportunities; dissemination of risk-related information to the community; and impacts on the knowledge, attitudes, and behaviors of middle school students.

The research team in this case study embarked on a journey to improve all-terrain vehicle (ATV) safety in the state of West Virginia, and on this journey, stories about ATV risks emerged which solidified the need for this type of safety campaign. For example, a middle school student recalled,

A girl in our school was in an ATV accident last year. Her dad died, and she was hurt so badly that she was out of school for the entire semester. She had broken bones and stitches. She is back now, but she still rides ATVs, and she isn't scared at all. She doesn't even wear a helmet.

To address the poor safety behaviors demonstrated in the previous story, students in a graduate-level health communication course designed a health intervention. The campaign followed experiential learning principles and was guided by underlying theory, which is characteristic of practical and successful health campaigns (Wang, 2009). The graduate students involved maintained a theory-driven approach using a social marketing plan (Kotler & Lee, 2008) to thoroughly assess, and determine how to best approach, the issue. Through the social marketing steps, the Theory of Planned Behavior (TPB; Azjen, 1985) was identified as a promising approach and used to research, develop, and implement an ATV safety campaign for middle school students. TPB (Azjen, 1985) argues that health messages should address the target audiences' attitudes, behaviors, perceived behavioral control, behavioral intent, knowledge, and norms of those who interact with the target audience. To develop a successful ATV safety campaign, the instructor and students traveled through a detailed process, which is described in this case study.

Getting the Key into the Ignition

This safety campaign began in a graduate classroom, and in order to begin the campaign, an understanding of the concerns and risks that plague health message design was necessary. Similarly, an ATV rider noted that riders should also be aware of the risks before riding an ATV, "I think everyone needs to pay attention to the (safety) messages. I view an ATV the same as I would a car. You need to understand that if you do not drive them safely, there are risks." In order to prepare for the potential risks associated with health message design, the graduate class became immersed in the project through the experiential learning stages.

Steinaker and Bell (1979) identified a series of stages which comprise experiential learning: exposure, participation, identification, internalization, and dissemination. Exposure is when students are introduced to a problem and their consciousness is heightened. After exposure, the participation stage occurs when students make a choice to become part of the experience. Identification involves students beginning to apply principles and experiences to the situation. After the first three stages, internalization is evident when students begin to make decisions based on these experiences; that is, the learning experience begins to affect their daily lives. Lastly, dissemination occurs when students begin to inform others about the experience.

Health communication courses are particularly situated for experiential learning projects due partially to the focus on increasing awareness and appreciation of healthy, safe behaviors, as well as communicating about those behaviors at the dyadic, organizational, and community levels. Experiential learning has become a popular pedagogical technique for enhancing education (Kolb & Kolb, 2005), and one that many students have requested as it provides real-world experience (Schultz & Higbee, 2007). The process through which students engage in experiential learning is one that includes converting knowledge to experience, and conversely, experience into knowledge. Presented in this case study are the steps taken to identify ATV safety as a pressing social problem, development of a safety campaign, and finally, implementation of the health messages in the community.

Experiencing the Ride

Preparation was essential in experiencing the "ride" that included researching, developing, disseminating, and evaluating the health campaign. This preparation, however, was not always matched by the ATV riders themselves as they experienced the ride,

> Facilitator: Why don't you take safety precautions?
>
> ATV Rider: I don't know; I guess because it's not readily available. When I really go riding there's not like helmets right there or gloves right there. We just jump on and go, we don't really think about it.

Kotler and Lee (2008) delineated a 10-step social marketing process to be used for the development of an effective health campaign. These steps include (1) describing the background, purpose, and plan; (2) conducting a situation analysis; (3) selecting a target audience; (4) setting objectives and goals; (5) analyzing target audiences and the competition; (6) crafting a desired position; (7) developing a marketing strategy; (8) creating a plan for evaluation and monitoring; (9) determining budgets and finding funding sources; and (10) completing an implementation plan. Each social marketing step provided the students with diverse experiential learning opportunities (see Witte, Meyer, & Martell, 2001 for similar steps).

An important precursor to the development of a health campaign and a social marketing plan is the identification of a target audience and target behaviors. Although several issues were considered, ATV safety was an issue that had been recognized as dangerous on a national level (ATV Safety Institute, n.d.). Moreover, the dangers of the recreational activity were especially salient in the community where the students resided (Helmkamp, 2009), and the legislation currently in place had been ineffective (Ross, Stuart, & Davis, 1999).

Nationally, ATV use is increasing in popularity. Approximately 25 million Americans ride ATVs and 70% are riding as a family recreational activity (ATV Safety Institute, n.d.). The high rates of morbidity and mortality for children under 16 years of age is especially alarming. A third of all fatal ATV accidents involved a child under the age of 16 (U.S. Consumer Product Safety Commission, 2008). Injuries also increased substantially across every driver age group including 76% for children ages 12 to 15, 23% for children ages 6 to 11, and 233% for children under 6 (Consumer Federation of America, 2003). While children under the age of 16 constitute 14% of all ATV drivers, they sustain 40% of all injuries (U.S. Consumer Product Safety Commission, 2008).

All states considered, West Virginia has been recognized as one of the most dangerous places to ride an ATV (Helmkamp, 2009). Despite the danger, the sale of ATVs has increased five-fold, and an estimated 460,000 ATVs are owned in West Virginia, with another 16,000 being purchased yearly (Helmkamp, Bixler, Kaplan, & Hall, 2008). This increase in the number of ATVs has led to an increase in the number of ATV accidents and fatalities. ATV injuries and fatalities in West Virginia have been well documented, with 15% of all ATV literature in the United States focusing on West Virginia alone (Criminal Justice Statistical Analysis Center, 2008). The number of reported deaths in West Virginia is, per capita, eight times higher than the national average, despite West Virginia's relatively smaller population (Helmkamp et al., 2008). The increasingly popular, and dangerous, ATV riding practices revealed a clear societal need for scholars and practitioners to address this problem.

After the enactment of ATV safety legislation in May 2004, West Virginia has averaged 45 deaths annually (Criminal Justice Statistical Analysis Center, 2008), which is a substantial increase in the number of deaths that were reported prior to the new legislation. Other states have experienced similar problems, noting that government regulations have not improved safety efforts (Ross et al., 1999). Given the evidence which suggests that government regulation is ineffective in numerous states, and the increase in deaths in West Virginia, new strategies to address this social issue needed to be considered.

The campaign design emerged through the simultaneous application of the experiential learning taxonomy and social marketing steps. The research team began formative research, completing the first six steps of Kotler and Lee's (2008) social marketing process. Throughout the completion of these steps, the research team also experienced Steinaker and Bell's (1979) exposure and participation stages. Formative research was conducted through (1) a review of the literature; (2) the organization, transcription, and analysis of 13 focus groups and 2 interviews; and after the class' completion, (3) quantitative pilot surveys. All formative research was guided by two research questions:

RQ1: What types of safe, and unsafe, riding behaviors do ATV riders practice?

RQ2: What influences, or could influence, ATV riders' (un)safe riding practices?

Support for Implementing a Safety Campaign

Past research found a moderate positive association between ATV safety training and practicing safe riding behaviors for adolescents and young adults (Burgus, Madsen, Sanderson, & Rautiainen, 2009). In a qualitative study, Caucasian adults ($M = 48$ years; *range* 30–60 years) and children ($M = 14$ years; *range* 12–18 years) ATV riders (60% male) suggested that training in educational settings, showing a realistic understanding of current ATV practices, and emphasizing consequences would exert the most influence over riders (Aitken et al., 2004). This information allowed the research team to further refine the target audience and guided the development of a safety training program. Additional formative research focused on gaining an understanding of riding practices and influences (e.g., media, social network, culture) on riders' behaviors.

Support from the Focus Groups and Interviews

Thirteen focus group discussions and two interviews were held with 79 ATV riders. Of the participants, 65 students (42 males, 23 females) participated in 10 face-to-face focus groups (with an average of 6 participants per focus group) and 1 face-to-face interview, 8 community members (2 males, 6 females) participated in 2 online focus groups (with 4 and 3 participants respectively) and 1 online interview, and 6 male employees of an ATV dealership participated in 1 face-to-face focus group. Diverse groups of ATV riders (e.g., varying ages, both sexes, differing riding experience levels) were chosen in an attempt to elicit multiple perspectives on ATV riding behaviors. The adult participants reported retrospectively on their ATV riding as adolescents, and some reported on their children's riding habits. The transcribed discussions resulted in 196 typed, single-spaced pages of transcripts with ATV riders. The transcripts were analyzed following standard qualitative research methods set forth by Strauss and Corbin (1998). Members of the research team read the transcripts and then began to sort the data into coding units (i.e., a basic unit of text that expressed a complete idea). The coding units were reread, along with the data, until "threads of meaning that recur" emerged (Baxter, 1991, p. 250). This approach delineated general, recurrent themes (Charmaz, 2002). Our team met to discuss emerging themes and then to recode all data based on those themes. Any disagreements were discussed among the team members and resolved.

Several themes were instrumental in designing the campaign. The data revealed that ATV riders were aware of safe and legal riding behaviors; however, they predominately engaged in unsafe behaviors. For example, many participants claimed that they did not wear helmets primarily due to discomfort or inconvenience. They also viewed those in their riding networks as engaging in the same unsafe behaviors, thus reinforcing that they are influenced to engage in similar unsafe behaviors practiced by their friends, siblings, and parents. Some participants noted that traumatic events had the potential to change their unsafe behaviors, as did ATV safety training. Behavioral changes which resulted from traumatic events, however, were short lived.

Switching Gears

Safe behaviors when riding an ATV, as noted, were not encouraged or even typical of the majority of riders and their social networks. In fact, practicing safe behaviors may require an attitude shift as mentioned by one ATV rider, "Never have I worn a helmet on an ATV. I'm not saying that's good, but no one ever put a helmet on me, but it's just not something we ever did."

Our team identified the most prevalent behaviors which were associated with ATV injury and deaths in the existing literature and in the focus groups, which included not wearing a helmet as suggested by this rider. These behaviors were used to develop a slogan and logo: "ATV Safety: You Make the CHOICE." This slogan addresses the following areas: Check Your Gear, Handle the Machine, Observe the Environment, Ignore Peer Pressure, Coach Others, and Enjoy the Ride (see **FIGURE 14.1** for logo). Curriculum and surveys were then developed with items that addressed each of the areas in CHOICE.

The surveys were discussed in small classes to improve the language and usability of the survey. As a result of these discussions, a finalized survey was created that included

FIGURE 14.1 ATV safety: You make the CHOICE logo

quantitative measures of attitudes, norms, behaviors, intentions, control, and knowledge, and open-ended questions to understand the audience and their behaviors. This survey was then pilot tested, discussed, refined, and tested again. As TPB (Ajzen, 1985) had not been used in this context, multiple discussions and revisions of the survey were deemed necessary to create the most appropriate survey for middle school-aged students and increase the validity of the items and scales to be used during the actual campaign.

Designing the Surveys

Attitudes, intent, knowledge, norms, control, and behaviors were initially measured using 5-item, 5-point, Likert-type scales ranging from *strongly disagree* (1) to *strongly agree* (5). Each attitude question referred to an attitude toward a specific behavior, and as such, each item was used independently in further analyses. Similarly, each specific knowledge item was used independently in further analyses. For *intent*, scale reliability was improved by dropping one item. For *norms*, two items were dropped to improve reliability, resulting in a 3-item scale. All scale reliabilities, means, and standard deviations are reported in **TABLE 14.1**.

Support from Pilot Surveys

Participants (N = 502, approximately 56% males and 44% females) completed the pilot survey designed to address specific ATV riding behaviors that included measures of each

TABLE 14.1 Pilot Survey Scale Reliabilities, Means, and Standard Deviations

Variable	α	M	SD
Attitude	–	–	–
Intent	.70	3.22	1.00
Knowledge	–	–	–
Norms	.80	2.70	1.35
Control	.77	3.63	.93
Behavior	.81	2.58	1.31

component of TPB (Azjen, 1985). On a 5-point scale, the majority of participants rated safety as very important ($n = 280$) or important ($n = 175$), ($M = 3.53$, $SD = .66$). Approximately 30% reported that they owned an ATV, only 19% had received safety training, and approximately 60% had begun riding ATVs prior to the age of 14.

An overwhelming percentage of participants reported riding ATVs mostly with friends. Results revealed that 93% of the participants reported riding with friends, followed by siblings (49%), cousins (42%), and parents (33%). The majority of participants also reported being most influenced by friends (79%), followed by parents (49%) and siblings (35%). Briefly, participants reported on 5-point scales that they were following laws which included riding on trails instead of streets ($M = 2.78$, $SD = 1.64$), riding the appropriately sized ATV ($M = 2.73$, $SD = 1.63$), and wearing a helmet ($M = 2.65$, $SD = 1.78$). However, riding with passengers, which is a negative, and illegal, riding behavior was still common ($M = 2.59$, $SD = 1.71$). Of particular interest in this study is the revelation that the behavior riders engage in the *least* is communicating with others about ATV safety ($M = 2.17$, $SD = 1.55$).

Taken together, key literature, focus groups, interviews, and quantitative data suggest that attitudes toward safety and the norms of an individual's social network are influential in current riding behaviors, and in potentially changing those behaviors, which provided support for using TPB (Ajzen, 1985) as a guiding theoretical framework. The research team then progressed from formative research into the final four steps of Kotler and Lee's (2008) social marketing plan.

Continuing on the Trail

After finalizing the survey, it was important that the research team determine how to move forward with the campaign for middle school students. In situations where ATV riders were in accidents, they too decided how to move forward. One ATV rider stated, "Personal experience gives you fear, so I feel after seeing what can happen after not riding safely, it makes me a better driver, because I don't want to get hurt."

Since one goal of this campaign was to keep adolescents from getting hurt, principals at local middle schools were contacted to determine their interest and perceived need for the campaign to be introduced to their students. As interest increased, the research team developed a draft of the proposed curriculum and submitted it to three counties' Boards of Education for approval. The research team worked closely with the schools to understand more about the middle school students' cognitive capacities and effective instructional practices for middle school-aged learners, developing surveys which then reflected these principles.

Following Board of Education approval, Phase One began in early February. During this phase, the primary goal was to administer a pre-test survey to the students to ascertain base levels of the components of TPB (e.g., attitudes, behaviors) (Ajzen, 1985) related to ATV safety. During this phase, informal conversations with students provided further evidence about the severity and frequency with which ATV accidents were impacting the middle school students' lives.

Phase Two began at the end of April, which was strategically chosen to deliver the safety messages before the primary riding season begins in May. It was during this phase that middle school students were exposed to the interactive safety presentation which focused on six topic areas (i.e., CHOICE) that emerged as themes in the focus group data and in the research on ATV safety, injuries, and fatalities. The students were informed about wearing proper safety gear, riding the appropriately sized ATV, observing the environment for potential hazards, ignoring negative peer pressure, discussing safety with other riders, and enjoying the ride in a safe way. The presentation lasted approximately 30 minutes and was immediately followed with a post-test survey which included the same items as the pre-test survey that was administered almost three months earlier. During the presentation, the graduate students experienced identification with the material, demonstrated internalization of the information, and disseminated the safety messages, completing the experiential learning process. The research team then examined the survey results to assess effectiveness of the safety program.

How Was the Ride?

The research team gained information about the students' riding behaviors through survey responses and informal conversations during the ATV safety campaign. Interestingly, when middle school students were presented with the opportunity to evaluate their own riding behaviors, their perceptions of safety differed from the safe behaviors that are legal and that were incorporated into the campaign. One student believed that they were being safe in the following exchange:

Presenter: Are you safe when riding an ATV?

Student: Yeah.

Presenter: What do you do to be safe?

Student: Well, my grandpa just tells me to hold on to him tighter.

Although this student believed that she was being safe, there appears to be a disconnect between this belief and actual ATV safety practices.

To understand the behaviors, attitudes, and cognitions of the middle school students, the pilot surveys were revised before administration to the target audience. Based on the qualitative discussions of the survey, suggestions from middle school personnel, and the scale reliability information, three changes were made to improve the survey. First, *attitudes* were measured using a semantic differential scale as suggested by Ajzen (2006). Second, *behaviors* were measured on a scale ranging from *never* to *always* to assess behavior frequency. Last, each scale utilized a 7-point scale instead of a 5-point scale to increase variance in the answers (Francis et al., 2004).

Campaign Instrumentation

Attitude was measured using a 5-item, semantic differential scale; intent, knowledge, norms, and control were measured using 5-item, 7-point, Likert-type scales ranging from *strongly disagree* (1) to *strongly agree* (7); and behaviors were measured using a 6-item, 7-point, Likert-type scale ranging from *never* (1) to *always* (7). For knowledge, each item measured knowledge about a different subject, thus, each specific knowledge item was used independently in further analyses. For norms, three items were dropped to improve reliability, resulting in a 2-item scale. For control, one item was dropped to improve reliability, resulting in a 4-item measure. All scale reliabilities, means, and standard deviations are reported in **TABLE 14.2**.

Phase One Results

Students reported on their ATV riding practices using semantic differential (i.e., attitudes) and 7-point, Likert-type scales (i.e., behaviors, knowledge, intent, norms, and perceived control;

TABLE 14.2 Campaign Data Scale Reliabilities, Means, and Standard Deviations

Variable	α	M	SD
Attitude	.82	5.73	1.06
Intent	.83	5.36	1.07
Knowledge	–	–	–
Norms	.74	4.20	1.91
Control	.63	5.98	.78
Behavior	.80	4.57	1.35
Learning	.90	5.67	1.11

see **TABLE 14.3** for means and standard deviations of student riding behaviors at Phase One). Students ($N = 99$, 41 males, 58 females) rated safety as very important ($n = 51$), important ($n = 24$), or somewhat important ($n = 13$), ($M = 6.11$, $SD = 1.26$). Of the middle school students, approximately 70% reported that their family owned at least one ATV, only 30% of the students had received ATV safety training, and approximately 98% of the students reported that they had ridden ATVs prior to the age of 12. They reported riding with their parents most frequently (69%), followed by their friends (67%), cousins (67%), and siblings (59%). Of the people with whom they ride, 71% reported that their parents have the most influence over their riding behaviors, followed by friends (61%), cousins (48%), and siblings (40%).

Phase Two Results

Although more students participated in the educational program and post-test survey, only students who completed both the pre-test and post-test survey were included in the Phase Two analyses. Students ($N = 90$, 39 males, 51 females) rated safety as very important ($n = 37$), important ($n = 30$), or somewhat important ($n = 17$), ($M = 6.15$, $SD = 1.07$). Of the participants, 76% reported that they owned an ATV and about 29% had received ATV safety training.

Students demonstrated a significant change in knowledge about riding the correct-sized machine. Levene's test indicated that equal variances were assumed, $t(176) = -5.08$, $p < .01$, with the students knowing more about machine size after the safety presentation ($M = 5.98$, $SD = 1.43$) than they did before ($M = 4.91$, $SD = 1.38$). Students also demonstrated an increase in knowledge about not riding with passengers on the same machine. Levene's test indicated that equal variances were assumed, $t(176) = -3.38$, $p < .01$, with students knowing that riding with passengers was illegal after the presentation ($M = 5.30$, $SD = 1.68$) than prior to the presentation ($M = 4.44$, $SD = 1.70$). There were no significant differences in their intent to be safe, attitudes toward safety, perceived control, norms after seeing the safety presentation, and the remaining knowledge items which addressed helmet laws, teaching others about safety, and driving ATVs on streets. A closer

TABLE 14.3 Phase One Student ATV Riding Behaviors

Behavior	M	SD
Riding on ATV trails	5.55	1.88
Practicing safe behaviors	5.47	1.81
Wearing a helmet	4.74	2.37
Using an appropriately sized ATV	3.84	2.45
Riding with passengers	3.55	1.94
Talking to others about safety	5.47	1.81

examination of the Phase One knowledge revealed there was little room for improvement at Phase Two, as students already reported high knowledge means about helmet laws ($M = 6.07$, $SD = 1.35$), teaching others about safety ($M = 5.90$, $SD = 1.11$), and driving ATVs on streets ($M = 5.14$, $SD = 1.37$).

A multiple regression with Phase One knowledge, attitudes, norms, control, and intent entered as the independent variables, and Phase Two behaviors entered as the dependent variable indicated that the model significantly predicted behaviors ($F(9,138) = 21.26$, $p < .001$), and accounted for 58% of the variance. The only significant predictor of safe riding behaviors was time one intentions ($\beta = .69$, $p < .01$). To assess whether multicollinearity existed, the tolerance statistics and variance inflation (VIF) statistics were examined. The lowest tolerance statistic was .52 and the highest VIF statistic was 1.92; thus, multicollinearity did not exist between the predictor variables.

For the purposes of Phase Two, seven items were created to assess student learning from the ATV safety presentation (e.g., I learned more about safety than I already knew, I learned something today). Exploratory factor analysis confirmed a unidimensional student learning scale (Eigenvalue 4.58) which accounted for approximately 65% of the variance. The learning items were also reliable ($\alpha = .90$). Students reported a high level of learning ($M = 5.67$, $SD = 1.11$), which is significantly higher than the scale mid-point $t(86) = 18.17$, $p < .01$.

To summarize, the students reported learning a great deal from the safety presentation. Although some of the knowledge gains were not statistically significant, the students perceived learning a lot from the presentation. Specifically, they demonstrated significant changes in their knowledge about machine size and riding with passengers. Knowledge, however, was not a significant predictor of actual behaviors; only intent to engage in safe behaviors had a significant influence on riding behaviors, $F(9,138) = 21.26$, $p < .001$, $\beta = .69$, $p < .01$. The students did not report a change in their intent to engage in safer behaviors, however, behavioral change cannot be assessed with only the first two phases of data collected. Although the educational component (i.e., increasing knowledge) of the safety intervention was effective, future campaigns should work toward targeting the intentions of high-risk populations, which appears to be influential in behavior change. The third phase of data collection should illuminate whether the knowledge gained, intentions, norms, control, and attitudes predict the students' subsequent riding behaviors.[1]

Until We Ride Again

It was evident that ATV riders believed safety is important. Despite their recognition of the importance of safety, many riders were not motivated by that attitude to ride ATVs in safe ways. This campaign made an educational effort to elicit behavioral change, but there is still room to improve safety messages to motivate actual behavioral change in ATV riders such as the ATV rider who admitted, "I do think safety in general is important too, but I guess I'm just lazy."

As this case study closes, it is important to note that this health campaign will continue to undergo evaluation to assess long-term behavioral change in the middle school students. This data collection will be paramount to understanding the impact of the campaign on adolescent ATV riders' behaviors who are returning from their summer break and the primary riding season, in which they may have opportunities to practice the safe behaviors and share their new ATV knowledge with others. Additionally, this long-term assessment contributes to the development of TPB (Ajzen, 1985) as a useful theoretical framework in this context. Finally, this assessment is also helpful in understanding the final stages of the experiential learning process, determining if the graduate student dissemination was effective, and assessing whether the middle school students also experienced Steinaker and Bell's (1979) process. Thus far, the middle school students experienced exposure and participation during the presentation. The results of Phase Three should help determine if the middle school students also identified, internalized, and disseminated the safety information to friends and family.

It is important to note that this study was not without limitations. Despite multiple attempts to recruit participants, a relatively small number of students self-selected to participate in the program. Moreover, because parents needed to first provide consent for their child to participate, it could be that the parents who gave their child permission have an attitude about safety that is different from those who elected not to allow their children to participate. This project also encountered some measurement issues. Norms and control achieved low reliabilities, and should be improved in future studies. Lastly, no data has been collected about the middle school students' experiences of the experiential learning stages or on the graduate students' progression through the stages, and we can only speculate about experiences in these stages. Collecting data about their experiences in these stages would add further information about the extent to which students fully experienced the intervention.

NOTE

1   The third phase of data collection is scheduled for September, four months after the intervention, at the start of a new school year and the conclusion of peak riding season.

Discussion Questions

1. What were the strengths and weaknesses in the application of the underlying theory to this particular health campaign?

2. What are the skills and tangible products that students can acquire from this experiential learning process?

3. What were the most and least surprising findings from each of the phases of data collection? Be able to support your reasoning.

4. What other health communication theories could be useful for designing this health campaign or others? What might those frameworks help investigators focus on?

5. What are the potential benefits and/or limitations to using multiple theoretical frameworks to guide this health campaign and others?

6. Considering the results for Phase One and Phase Two, what findings are likely to be derived in Phase Three?

References

Aitken, M. E., Graham, C. J., Killingsworth, J. B., Mullins, S. H., Parnell, D. N., & Dick, R. M. (2004). All-terrain vehicle injury in children: Strategies for prevention. *Injury Prevention, 10*, 303–307.

Ajzen, I. (1985). From intentions to actions: A theory of planned behavior. In J. Kuhl & J. Beckmann (Eds.), *Action control: From cognition to behavior* (pp. 11–39). Heidelberg: Springer.

Ajzen, I. (2006, January). *Constructing a TpB questionnaire: Conceptual and methodological considerations.* Retrieved from http://people.umass.edu/aizen/pdf/tpb.measurement.pdf

ATV Safety Institute. (n.d.). *Industry background.* Retrieved from http://www.atvsafety.org/

Baxter, L. (1991). Content analysis. In D. M. Montgomery & S. Duck (Eds.), *Discourse: Studying interpersonal interaction* (pp. 239–252). New York, NY: Guilford.

Burgus, S. K., Madsen, M. D., Sanderson, W. T., & Rautiainen, R. H. (2009). Youths operating all-terrain vehicles: Implications for safety education. *Journal of Agromedicine, 14*, 97–104.

Charmaz, K. (2002). Qualitative interviewing and grounded theory analysis. In J. F. Gubrium & J. A. Holstein (Eds.), *Handbook of interview research. Context & method* (pp. 675–694). Thousand Oaks, CA: Sage.

Consumer Federation of America. (2003). *ATV safety crisis. America's children still at risk.* Retrieved from http://www.consumerfed.org/pdfs/atv-safety-crisis-2003-final-all.pdf

Criminal Justice Statistical Analysis Center, West Virginia Division of Criminal Justice Services, & West Virginia Bureau for Public Health. (2008). *All-terrain vehicle (ATV) deaths and injuries in West Virginia: A summary of surveillance and data sources.*

Francis, J. J., Eccles, M. P., Johnston, M., Walker, A., Grimshaw, J., Foy, R., et al. (2004). Constructing questionnaires based on the theory of planned behaviour. *A manual for health services researchers.* United Kingdom: Centre for Health Services Research.

Helmkamp, J. (2009). *Stricter legislation could decrease ATV death rate.* Retrieved from http://www.herald-dispatch.com/opinions/x1495356150/Stricter-legislation-could-decrease-ATV-death-rate

Helmkamp, J., Bixler, D., Kaplan, J., & Hall, A. (2008). All-terrain vehicle fatalities–West Virginia, 1999–2006. *Morbidity and Mortality Weekly Report, 57*, 312–315.

Kolb, A. Y., & Kolb, D. A. (2005). Learning styles and learning spaces: Enhancing experiential learning in higher education. *Academy of Management Learning and Education, 4*, 193–212.

Kotler, P., & Lee, N. R. (2008). *Social marketing. Influencing behaviors for good* (3rd ed.). Los Angeles, CA: Sage.

Ross, R. T., Stuart, L. K., & Davis, F. E. (1999). All-terrain vehicle injuries in children: Industry-regulated failure. *The American Surgeon, 65*, 870–873.

Schultz, J. L., & Higbee, J. L. (2007). Reasons for attending college: The student point of view. *Research and Teaching in Developmental Education, 23*, 69–76.

Steinaker, N., & Bell, M. (1979). *The experiential learning taxonomy: A new approach to teaching and learning.* New York, NY: Academic Press.

Strauss, A., & Corbin, J. (1998). *Basics of qualitative research* (2nd ed.). Thousand Oaks, CA: Sage.

U.S. Consumer Product Safety Commission. (2008). *2007 annual report of ATV-related deaths and injuries*. Retrieved from http://www.cpsc.gov/LIBRARY/atv2007.pdf

Wang, X. (2009). Integrating the Theory of Planned Behavior and attitude functions: Implications for health campaign design. *Health Communication, 24*, 426–434.

Witte, K., Meyer, G., & Martell, D. (2001). *Effective health risk messages: A step-by-step guide.* Thousand Oaks, CA: Sage Publications.

CHAPTER 15

Using Formative Research to Inform Health Campaign Design
Promoting Organ Donation

Ashley E. Anker and Thomas Hugh Feeley

KEY TERMS

Organ donation

Campaign design

Formative research

Summative research

Abstract

The use of organ transplantation as a life-saving treatment option is restricted by the limited number of organs donated each year. To increase the pool of organs available for transplant, health campaigns are developed to provide donation education and to promote donor registration. This chapter reviews two donation campaigns implemented in New York State. Readers are provided with an in-depth look at the campaign planning process with a focus on the roles of formative research, theory, and summative research in campaign development. Critical to the success of both campaigns covered, self-efficacy (i.e., one's perceived ability to overcome barriers and engage in a health behavior) is presented as a central component in message design.

Imagine that you are walking through the Student Union on your college campus. You notice a table draped in a banner proclaiming, "Donate Life." Two of your fellow students are seated behind this table and approach you, asking if you would be willing to register as an organ donor. Is this an effective way of promoting organ donation? Would you be likely to sign an organ donor card as a result of viewing this campaign? How will the students conducting this campaign know if it was effective?

The paragraph above describes an actual donation campaign that was implemented on college campuses across New York State. In the following chapter, readers are introduced to two distinct campaigns to promote organ donation. The first is a college campaign, aimed at encouraging students to become registered organ donors. The second is an educational campaign, aimed at teaching transplant candidates about living liver donation. By reviewing the steps involved in planning, designing, and evaluating these two campaigns, it is anticipated that readers will be more likely to grasp and appreciate the basics of campaign development. Specifically, readers should develop a basic understanding of the transplantation system, understand how formative research contributes to campaign planning, and recognize the importance of summative research in campaign evaluation.

An Overview of Organ Donation

To design an effective health campaign, it is first necessary to have an adequate understanding of the behavior one wishes to promote. To create appropriate messages about organ donation, campaign planners might consider how organ transplants are facilitated, why donation is important, and the methods of becoming an organ donor. To help readers understand the choices made in designing this chapter's campaigns, a brief background on organ donation is provided.

Organ transplantation is generally considered to be a life-saving treatment option. Transplants were first utilized in the 1950s and are relatively common practice today. In 2009, for example, 28,464 transplants were completed in the United States (Organ Procurement and Transplantation Network [OPTN], 2010). Impressively, the procedure has relatively high success rates, with five-year survival rates of transplant recipients reaching up to 82% (OPTN, 2010). Despite the promise and life-saving capabilities of organ transplantation, use of the procedure is severely limited by a lack of organ donors (OPTN, 2010).

There are two methods of becoming an organ donor. Deceased organ donation, or cadaveric donation, occurs when an individual's organs are used for transplant following death. To be eligible for this form of donation, an individual must die in a specific manner, leaving organs healthy for transplant. It is expected that less than 1% of Americans will ever become eligible for cadaveric donation (see Howard & Byrne, 2009). Cadaveric organ donors generally die of brain death, which occurs when the potential donor's brain is no longer capable of carrying out life-sustaining activities (e.g., breathing) and ventilation systems must be used to keep blood and oxygen flowing through organs. It is important to note that a potential donor will not recover from brain death. He or she may become an organ donor, but his or her own life cannot be saved.

After a potential cadaveric donor is declared dead and consent to organ donation is obtained, a team of surgeons removes any healthy organs for transplantation. A single individual can potentially donate eight organs: two kidneys, two lungs, heart, liver, pancreas, and intestine. Organs are then provided to those individuals at the top of the national transplant waiting list, with organs allotted based on factors such as organ size, blood type, medical need, and proximity of the donor to the recipient(s).

An alternative method of becoming an organ donor is to provide a donation (e.g., kidney, partial liver/lung) (Donate Life America, 2010) to another individual while still alive. Living donors can lead a healthy life, while the donated organ potentially saves the life of a transplant recipient. Living donation provides an additional option to those on the transplant waiting list and most often occurs between a transplant candidate and a family member who volunteers as a donor. It is imperative to note that living donation is not without risks. Donors require a recovery time of 2 to 6 weeks (Donate Life America, 2010) and may endure side effects, such as pain at the surgical site or depression/anxiety (see DeLair et al., 2009). Despite these and other risks, success rates of living donation are high (OPTN, 2010), and the surgery is recommended when the benefit to the recipient outweighs the risks to the donor (Barr et al., 2006).

Given the differences between cadaveric and living donation, health campaigns to promote these behaviors often serve two separate purposes. Generally, campaigns focusing on cadaveric organ donation suggest that members of the general public indicate their willingness to become an organ donor, so that their preferences are known in the event of an eligible death. Typical cadaveric organ donation campaigns encourage individuals to: (a) formally register donation intentions (i.e., by signing a donor card, registering with the Department of Motor Vehicles, or registering online)[1] and (b) tell family members of wishes to become a donor. In contrast, living donation campaigns are often aimed at providing education about living donation. As there are risks to becoming a living donor, campaigns of this nature tend to ensure that: (a) transplant candidates are aware of living donation and (b) candidates feel capable and somewhat comfortable speaking with others about living donation options.

Formative Research and Campaign Planning

While background information about a health behavior can provide a context for campaign development, campaign planners should also engage in additional research to address questions associated with the goals of a specific campaign. Ideally, formative research is used to learn more about the characteristics of a campaign's target audience. Formative research is designed to "answer key questions prior to the design of a behavior change intervention" (Schmidt, Wloch, Biran, Curtis, & Mangtani, 2009, p. 391). During the formative research process, campaign planners often aim to examine the knowledge, attitudes, beliefs, or behaviors of a target audience (see Witte, Meyer, & Martell, 2001).

With respect to this chapter's campaigns, the campaigns' authors used the formative research process to explore a commonly recognized problem in organ donation: Why do so many people report positive attitudes toward organ donation, and yet, U.S. donation rates remain so low? To elaborate on this problem, consider that behaviors are often thought to be a reflection of one's attitudes. For example, if one feels positively toward a political candidate, he or she would likely be expected to cast a vote for that candidate in an upcoming election. In organ donation, however, behaviors are not always consistent with the public's reported attitudes. While most individuals report feeling positively toward donation (Feeley & Servoss, 2005), only approximately 52% of the public are registered donors (Gallup Organization, 2005). Thus, organ donation behaviors (e.g., signing a donor card to become a registered donor) have not been consistent with the public's expressed attitudes.

To address this problem of attitude-behavior inconsistency in donation, a group of scholars conducted formative research to determine if alternative factors, aside from attitudes, may explain why individuals do or do not choose to become organ donors. Anker, Feeley, and Kim (2010) explored the concept of *self-efficacy* in organ donation. Self-efficacy is defined as an individual's belief in his or her abilities to overcome barriers and engage in a recommended behavior (Bandura, 1977; Baranowski, Perry, & Parcell, 2002). For example, an individual with high self-efficacy in cadaveric donation perceives he or she can overcome anticipated barriers to donation, in the form of fears or concerns, in order to sign a donor card. Alternatively, a transplant candidate with low self-efficacy in discussing living donation might have concerns about donor safety (see Malago et al., 2003), and thus, may feel incapable of discussing the option of living donation with loved ones.

Anker et al. (2010) elected to explore self-efficacy in organ donation using a sample of predominantly White, second- and third-year college students ($N = 107$; 61 females).[2] College students are often noted as an ideal audience for donation campaigns due to their generally good health and propensity to engage in risky behaviors (e.g., unsafe driving) that could result in one becoming an eligible donor (see Feeley & Servoss, 2005). Anker et al.'s (2010) formative research found that attitudes toward organ donation indirectly predicted donor status (i.e., whether one had signed the state donor registry). Specifically, self-efficacy served as a link between attitudes and donor status. Greater attitudes lead to greater self-efficacy which, in turn, lead to greater likelihood of becoming a registered donor. Once self-efficacy was taken into account, audience members' attitudes toward donation did not directly influence donor status. Moreover, individuals with higher self-efficacy in donation were almost 8 times more likely to become registered organ donors. Hence, individuals who felt able to overcome barriers (e.g., fear) were more likely to become registered organ donors. The preceding findings were derived using a multivariate research design.[3]

The results of Anker et al.'s (2010) formative research suggest that organ donation campaigns may be improved by strengthening audience perceptions of self-efficacy, rather than promoting the development of positive attitudes toward donation. Although Anker et al.'s (2010) work indicates that self-efficacy is essential, it does not outline how self-efficacy can be increased with campaign messages. To effectively shape campaign messages, campaign planners often examine the results of formative research in the context of relevant theories. Thus, the authors turned to Bandura's (1977) Social Cognitive Theory (SCT) for guidance in message development.

Social Cognitive Theory

SCT (see Baranowski et al., 2002 for a review) suggests that behaviors are the result of interactions between individuals and their environment. Within SCT, individuals are limited in their abilities to complete a recommended health action by the existence of perceived barriers to that behavior. Personal barriers are factors internal to an individual and might include lack of knowledge, fears, or emotions related to the targeted behavior. In contrast, environmental barriers are external factors to an individual and might include costs or access to health services.

Organ donation is easily framed within the context of SCT. For example, environmental barriers to cadaveric donation might include a lack of opportunity to register as a donor (Feeley & Servoss, 2005), while personal barriers might include lack of knowledge

(Feeley, 2007), or endorsement of myths, such as beliefs that donation is disfiguring or against religious beliefs (Morgan, Harrison, Afifi, Long, & Stephenson, 2008). It is critical to note that although such donation myths are false, they are worthy of inclusion in donation campaigns, more so because they represent concerns of the target audience. Similarly, environmental barriers to discussing living donation might include lack of a potential donor (i.e., family member) with whom to have the discussion, while personal barriers might include lack of knowledge about living donation (DeLair et al., 2009) or concerns about health risks to the potential donor (Malago et al., 2003).

Self-efficacy is a central component of SCT, as individuals have efficacy beliefs related to their abilities to overcome personal and environmental barriers to behavior (Bandura, 2004). SCT suggests that audience perceptions of self-efficacy can be enhanced through use of verbal persuasion or vicarious experience (Bandura, 1977). Verbal persuasion includes arguments for participation in a behavior, while vicarious experience involves modeling, or demonstrating, a health behavior for audience members. For example, a health campaign to promote the flu vaccination might use verbal persuasion by having a credible spokesperson inform audience members that the flu shot is safe and effective. In contrast, a health campaign relying on vicarious experience might visually show an individual who successfully receives the flu shot. Of the two strategies, vicarious experience is generally found to increase self-efficacy (e.g., Anderson, 2009).

Applying Formative Research and Theory to Campaign Design

To review, formative research on the current chapter's campaigns identified self-efficacy as a key factor in predicting donation behavior (see Anker et al., 2010). By considering formative research in the context of SCT, two strategies—vicarious experience and verbal persuasion—were identified for shaping campaign messages to promote audience perceptions of self-efficacy in organ donation. Next, readers are introduced to two campaigns on cadaveric and living donation. In reviewing these campaigns, emphasis is placed on describing how messages were designed to foster the development of self-efficacy in donation contexts.

Campaign #1: College Campaign to Promote Donor Registration

To promote cadaveric donation, a research team (Feeley et al., 2009) developed a college campaign aimed at encouraging students to register as organ donors. This campaign was implemented in the New York City (NYC) metropolitan area. NYC represents the ideal setting for a campaign to promote donor registration, as only approximately 51% of eligible deaths in NYC result in organ donation, as compared to a national average of about 68% (Scientific Registry on Transplant Recipients [SRTR], 2010).

Recognizing the need for improved donation rates in NYC, Feeley et al. (2009) developed a peer-to-peer campaign to promote donor registration. This campaign was implemented in two stages. First, students who were enrolled in select classes at participating colleges received in-class education about organ donation. Such educational efforts included guest presentations by former donor families, transplant recipients, and healthcare professionals. Subsequent to learning about donation, students who had participated in these courses (i.e., "student campaigners") were challenged to create on-campus campaigns to educate their peers about organ donation and promote donor registration. Student campaigners worked in small groups and developed creative methods of promoting donation, including Facebook groups, posters and brochures, and interactive games, as well as tabling events, in which tables are set up in campus common areas to promote organ donation.

Based on SCT and results of formative research, each stage of the college campaign focused on enhancing perceptions of self-efficacy. The first stage of the college campaign relied on verbal persuasion to enhance student campaigners' own perceptions of self-efficacy in donation. Scholars studying organ donation (e.g., Morgan, 2009) have noted that interpersonal communication can be an effective method of changing perceptions about donation. Thus, during the educational process, student campaigners were allowed to interact with guest lecturers (e.g., donor families, healthcare professionals), who provided accurate information about donation and aimed to resolve students' concerns about donation myths (i.e., addressing personal barriers to donation). Once student campaigners' own perceptions of self-efficacy were enhanced through these in-class communication efforts, they were ready to engage in on-campus campaigning to promote donation to their peers.

Student campaigners were given the freedom to create their own on-campus donation promotion efforts, but they were also encouraged to use tactics that would enhance their peers' self-efficacy in donation. For example, one group, referred to as the "Lifesavers" team, elected to set up tables in campus common areas to promote donation. As college students approached these tables, student campaigners from the "Lifesavers" group provided accurate information about donation and provided the students with free give-aways in the form of donation paraphernalia and Lifesavers® candies. In addition, student campaigners encouraged their peers to sign organ donor registration cards. Those students who registered were also asked to sign their name on a Lifesaver-shaped sticker, indicating their new donor status. Such stickers were displayed on a banner behind the student campaigners' table and ultimately demonstrated the commitment of more than 100 college students to organ donation. The "Lifesavers" group effectively enhanced their peers' self-efficacy in two ways: (a) verbally persuading their peers to become donors by dispelling donation myths in a face-to-face environment and (b) providing their peers with a vicarious experience, as college students watched other students becoming registered donors (i.e., through both the registration process and Lifesaver sticker display).

As an alternative example, another group of student campaigners elected to focus their promotional efforts on encouraging peers to discuss organ donation with family members. This group created an impressive poster display that compared discussing organ donation to other conversations one may have with parents. For example, one poster, showing a picture of a tattoo, read: "My new tattoo rocks and I just donated my organs." The campaign's sub-text read, "If you can tell your family about inking your body, it should be easy to share your decision to donate your organs." Although this campaign takes a markedly different approach from the "Lifesavers" group, it again focuses on enhancing self-efficacy. Verbal persuasion is used to convince audience members that discussing donation can be manageable and perhaps somewhat less stressful than other conversations a student encounters in his or her day-to-day interactions. In total, the college campaign benefited by tailoring messages to address barriers to donation and by providing on-campus modeling, or demonstration, of donation behaviors.

Campaign #2: Educating Transplant Candidates about Living Donation

This chapter's second campaign focuses on living organ donation. As reviewed earlier, living donation campaigns tend to focus on educating transplant candidates about the option of living donation to encourage discussion of the topic with loved ones. Again, self-efficacy can be an integral component of such campaigns, as transplant candidates may perceive barriers to discussing living donation in the form of concerns about the risks, costs, and recovery that may await those who become living donors.

New York State (NYS) provided a unique setting in which to implement a donation campaign. In NYS, transplant centers are required to implement routine annual surveys of former living donors to inquire about their health and quality of life following donation. A research team (DeLair et al., 2009) utilized results from this survey to create a campaign titled, "In their own words: The experiences of living liver donors." This campaign included a brochure, DVD, and website that documented prior living liver donors' experiences with surgery, recovery, costs of donation, employment, and life after donation. The DVD and brochure were then provided to transplant candidates at five NYS transplant centers.

A review of excerpts from prior living liver donors' experiences included in the "In their own words" campaign indicated that campaign materials may enhance perceptions of self-efficacy by addressing perceived barriers to donation. For example, information on donor health was addressed by noting that 93% of surveyed donors ($N = 44$) considered their health "very good" or "excellent." Similarly, in commenting on the surgical process, the campaign's materials indicated that 70% of prior donors were satisfied with the quality of hospital care received. In addition, a realistic view of the donation process was provided, as the materials noted that incision and muscle pain were common following donation (see www.nyclt.org/living_donor/index.php for campaign materials).

Aside from statistical information, the campaign also included quotes from prior living liver donors offering their advice on the process. For example, one donor noted, "Be informed. Ask questions, even if they seem like stupid questions." Such quotes may have prompted self-efficacy, by encouraging transplant candidates and potential living donors to fully explore the donation process.

The prior living liver donors featured in the "In their own words" campaign did not directly engage in verbal persuasion by asking others to become living donors. However, the donors in the campaign offered their accurate, and generally positive, summaries of the donation experience, while simultaneously commenting on perceived barriers to donation (e.g., surgery, employment, recovery). The self-efficacy of transplant candidates was thought to benefit from receipt of these materials, as candidates received accurate information about donation from the perspective of those individuals who they potentially fear communicating with the most (i.e., potential living donors). Thus, the "In their own words" campaign likely benefited from vicarious experience, in that potential living donors and transplant candidates learned about barriers to living donation from the perspective of those who had already donated.

Evaluating Donation Campaigns: The Use of Summative Research

Thus far, this chapter provided readers with an in-depth look at the planning, development, and implementation of two campaigns designed to strengthen self-efficacy in donation. After the research teams implemented these campaigns, they were left with the final responsibility of evaluating the relative outcomes of their efforts (i.e., in terms of confirming, mixed, or non-confirming results; see Frey, Botan, and Kreps, 2000 for detailed discussion of hypothesis testing). For this purpose, the campaigns' authors turned to the process of summative research.

Summative research occurs after the implementation of a campaign for the purpose of evaluating its outcomes. Summative research may use any number of methods (e.g., surveys, focus groups) to determine the effects of a campaign. Results can be useful to determine which aspects of a campaign (e.g., particular messages, specific use of media) were most successful, ambiguous, and least successful, to improve future campaign efforts, and to provide funding agencies with information on project outcomes. Ideally, researchers utilize summative research to evaluate aspects of a campaign that align with initial campaign goals. As both organ donation campaigns aimed to increase self-efficacy, summative research evaluated changes in self-efficacy following campaign exposure.

Evaluation: College Campaign to Promote Donor Registration

As reviewed earlier, the college campaign focused on educating two groups: (a) student campaigners and (b) student campaigners' peers or other college students. Summative research also evaluated the effects of the college campaign on these two groups. To evaluate student campaigners, a pre-/post-test survey was utilized. Student campaigners were given a survey prior, and subsequent to, implementing their on-campus promotional efforts. The survey aimed to determine how self-efficacy and donor registration rates changed following course participation. At pre- and post-test, student campaigners responded to five Likert-type items (e.g., "I am able to overcome any negative feelings I might have about organ donation in order to sign the NYS Organ Donor Registry") designed to measure self-efficacy and indicated their donor status.

At pre-test ($N = 95$), students reported an average self-efficacy rating of 2.71 ($SD = 0.87$) on a four-point scale. By post-test ($N = 60$), their self-efficacy had increased by approximately 17%, with a rating of 3.18 ($SD = 0.78$) and this outcome occurred at $p < 0.01$.[4] In addition, student campaigners' donor registration rates increased from 30% at pre-test to approximately 70% by post-test. Thus, improvements following the course were noted in student campaigners' self-efficacy and donor registration rates. It is important to note, however, that this form of evaluation does not imply causation. That is, although student campaigners' self-efficacy increased, and donor registrations increased, we do not know that self-efficacy alone caused increased donor registrations.

To evaluate the outcomes related to other college students, student campaigners were asked to distribute donor registration cards produced specifically for the college campaign. By counting the signed and collected cards, researchers were able to determine how many new donors were registered from the campaign's efforts (see Feeley et al., 2009 for detail). In total, 1,019 new donor registrations were obtained, indicating that student campaigners were successful in recruiting their peers as new donors.

Evaluation: Educating Transplant Candidates about Living Donation

To evaluate the living liver donation campaign, the research team relied on a post-test only evaluation. Under this research design, the self-efficacy and communication behavior of transplant candidates who viewed the "In their own words" campaign were compared to the behaviors of transplant candidates who did not view the campaign. Self-efficacy was measured using seven Likert-type items (e.g., "I am comfortable discussing the option of living donation with close friends and family"), while one question asked about transplant candidates' discussion of living liver donation with others (i.e., "Have you ever talked about living donation with family or friends?").

In total, 338 participants completed the post-test evaluation. Of this group, 93 individuals (approximately 28%) reported campaign exposure. The remaining 196 participants (approximately 58%) had not viewed the "In their own words" campaign. Of these groups, 77 of 93 individuals with campaign exposure completed the self-efficacy and discussion items. Similarly, 165 of 196 individuals without campaign exposure completed the self-efficacy and discussion items. Of the preceding 77 participants, 78% ($N = 60$) reported discussing donation "a few times" or "many times" with family or friends. Of the subset of 165 individuals, 61% ($N = 101$) had discussed donation "a few times" or "many times" with family or friends. The observed difference between the groups was statistically significant, with $p < 0.001$. Of those who had completed the relevant discussion measure, the group with exposure to the campaign was more likely to discuss living donation with others (see Table 15.1).

Finally, data from NYS transplant centers were tracked to determine how many individuals approached the centers to inquire about becoming a living donor. After the campaign, a 74% increase was observed in the number of individuals who requested an evaluation to potentially act as a living liver donor, from 159 to 276 annual evaluations.

TABLE 15.1 "In Their Own Words:" Campaign Exposure and Discussion of Donation with Family and Friends

POST-TEST COMPLETION ($N = 338$)	
Campaign Exposure ($N = 93/338$; 27.5%)	No Campaign Exposure ($N = 196/338$; 57.9%)
Campaign Exposure completing Discussion Item ($N = 77/93$; 82.8%)	No Campaign Exposure completing Discussion Item ($N = 165/196$; 84.1%)
Campaign Exposure who Discussed Donation ($N = 60/77$; 77.9%)	No Campaign Exposure who Discussed Donation ($N = 101/165$; 61.2%)

Note: Documents the number of participants who discussed donation "a few times" or "many times" with family or friends.

Summary

This chapter demonstrated the many steps involved in campaign planning. Readers are encouraged to rely on formative research and theory when shaping campaign messages. Results of the current case demonstrate how effective planning can be utilized to shape messages designed to reach specific goals (i.e., improvements in self-efficacy). In addition, by matching campaign goals to the questions underlying summative research, campaign success can be accurately assessed.

NOTES

1   Depending on state regulations, an individual can join a donor registry in multiple ways. One may sign a donor card, sign up with a state registry online, or register his or her donation intentions through the Department of Motor Vehicles/driver's license center. Each method ultimately results in the formal placement of one's name on a state donor registry as an intended donor. These registries are examined when an eligible death occurs and help to facilitate the donation process by making family members aware of the deceased individual's intentions to donate.

2   Anker, Feeley, and Kim (2010) only collected demographic information on participant sex. Based on university characteristics, the sample was likely composed of predominantly White college students with an average age of 19.

3   The authors used regression analyses (see Baron & Kenny, 1986) to test self-efficacy as a mediator of the attitude-behavior relationship. Mediating variables serve to explain the relationship between an independent and dependent variable. Essentially, a relationship between an independent variable (i.e., attitudes) and a dependent variable (i.e., donor status) is accounted for, or explained by, a third variable (i.e., self-efficacy). The reader is directed to Frey, Botan, and Kreps (2000) for a more detailed explanation of this method.

4   The social science outcome for standard hypothesis testing is $p < 0.05$. Hence, when p is below 0.05, the result occurred more than chance predicted (see Frey et al., 2000).

Discussion Questions

1. Why might organ donation be a unique or difficult health behavior to promote? What similarities/differences do you see between organ donation and other health behaviors that are more commonly promoted in the mass media?

2. Why do you think self-efficacy plays such an important role in the promotion of organ donation? How would you feel about your ability to complete the donor registration process? What would you consider to be personal or environmental barriers to organ donation? What would motivate you to sign an organ donor card, if you have not already?

3. How did the on-campus organ donation campaign and living liver donation campaigns influence self-efficacy through campaign design? Can you think of alternative methods of enhancing self-efficacy through message design or intervention planning?

4. Both of the campaigns reviewed focused on using peers (i.e., college students, former living liver donors) to promote organ donation. Why do you think similar peers were utilized in promotion efforts? Do you think the use of similar peers contributed to campaign success? What might be some barriers to using peers to promote organ donation?

References

Anderson, R. (2009). Comparison of indirect sources of efficacy information in pretesting messages for campaigns to prevent drunken driving. *Journal of Public Relations Research, 21*, 428–454.

Anker, A. E., Feeley, T. H., & Kim, H. (2010). Examining the attitude-behavior relationship in prosocial donation domains. *Journal of Applied Social Psychology, 40*, 1293–1324.

Bandura, A. (1977). Self-efficacy: Toward a unifying theory of behavioral change. *Psychological Review, 84*, 191–215.

Bandura, A. (2004). Health promotion by social cognitive means. *Health Education & Behavior, 31*, 143–164.

Baranowski, T., Perry, C. L., & Parcel, G. S. (2002). How individuals, environments, and health behavior interact. In K. Glanz, F. M. Lewis, & B. K. Rimer (Eds.), *Health Behavior and Health Education: Theory, Research, and Practice* (pp. 165–184). San Francisco, CA: Jossey-Bass.

Baron, R. M., & Kenny, D. A. (1986). The moderator-mediator variable distinction in social psychological research: Conceptual, strategic, and statistical considerations. *Journal of Personality and Social Psychology, 51*, 1173–1182.

Barr, M. L., Belghiti, J., Villamil, F. G., Pomfret, E. A., Sutherland, D. S., Gruessner, R. W., et al. (2006). A report of the Vancouver Forum on the care of the liver organ donor: Lung, liver, pancreas, and intestine data and medical guidelines. *Transplantation, 81*, 1373–1385.

DeLair, S., Feeley, T. H., Kim, H., del Rio Martin, J., Kim-Schluger, L., Rudow, D. L., et al. (2009). A peer-based intervention to educate liver transplant candidates about living donor liver transplantation. *Liver Transplantation, 16*, 42–48.

Donate Life America. (2010). *Understanding donation: Living donation.* Retrieved from http://www.donatelife.net/UnderstandingDonation/LivingDonation.php

Feeley, T. H. (2007). College students' knowledge, attitudes, and behaviors regarding organ donation: An integrated review of the literature. *Journal of Applied Social Psychology, 37*, 243–271.

Feeley, T. H., Anker, A. E., Watkins, B., Rivera, J., Tag, N., & Volpe, L. (2009). A peer-to-peer campaign to promote organ donation among minority college students. *Journal of the National Medical Association, 101*, 1154–1162.

Feeley, T. H., & Servoss, T. J. (2005). Examining college students' intentions to become organ donors. *Journal of Health Communication, 10*, 237–249.

Frey, L. R., Botan, C. H., & Kreps, G. L. (2000). *Investigating communication: An introduction to research methods* (2nd ed.). Needham Heights, MA: Allyn & Bacon.

Gallup Organization. (2005). *National survey of organ & tissue donation attitudes and behaviors.* Washington D. C. Retrieved from http://www.organdonor.gov/survey2005/

Howard, D. H., & Byrne, M. M. (2007). Should we promote organ donor registries when so few registrants will end up being donors? *Medical Decision Making, 27*, 243–249.

Malago, M., Testa, G., Marcos, A., Fung, J. J., Siegler, M., Cronin, D. C., et al. (2003). Ethical considerations and rationale of adult-to-adult living donor liver transplantation. *Liver Transplantation, 7*, 921–927.

Morgan, S. E. (2009). The intersection of conversation, cognitions, and campaigns: The social representation of organ donation. *Communication Theory, 19*, 29–48.

Morgan, S. E., Harrison, T. R., Afifi, W. A., Long, S. D., & Stephenson, M. T. (2008). In their own words: The reasons why people will (not) sign an organ donor card. *Health Communication, 23*, 23–33.

Organ Procurement and Transplantation Network. (2010). *National data* [database on the Internet]. Retrieved from http://optn.transplant.hrsa.gov/latestData/step2.asp

Schmidt, W., Wloch, C., Biran, A., Curtis, V., & Mangtani, P. (2009). Formative research on the feasibility of hygiene interventions for influenza control in UK primary schools. *BMC Public Health, 9*, 390–397.

Scientific Registry on Transplant Recipients. (2010). *Transplant and OPO Specific Reports* [database on the Internet]. Retrieved from http://www.ustransplant.org/csr/current/csrDefault.aspx

Witte, K., Meyer, G., & Martell, D. (2001). *Effective health risk messages: A step-by-step guide*. Thousand Oaks, CA: Sage Publications.

SECTION VI

Utilizing Innovative Strategies and Partnerships for Meeting Health Needs

Bridging the Health and Digital Divide in a Low-Income Latino/a Immigrant Community

Using Community-Based Participatory Research to Advance Communities' Well-Being[1]

Tamar Ginossar

KEY TERMS

Community-based participatory research

Health Information

Health Disparities

Low-income Latino/as

Abstract

Latino/as are the most digitally underserved ethnic group in the United States (e.g., Fox & Livingston, 2007) and have limited access to online health information. Because health information is essential in making health-related decisions, this disparity is recognized as a public health problem. This case study describes the efforts of a unique community organization to promote access to health information and technology in a low-income Latino/a immigrant community. This chapter is grounded in literature related to community-based participatory research and community media, consumers' health information, as well as technology and health disparities. Diffusion of innovations theory (Rogers, 2003) and social cognitive theory (Bandura, 1986) provide theoretical frameworks that explain the rationale and potential impact of these endeavors. Data collection for this case study included participant observations of group meetings and community presentations, documents and local media coverage, as well as retrospective interviews with the group director and members. The approach delineated in this case study can aid other scholars and community groups in creating their own models of community-based health communication initiatives.

Health disparity is a situation in which health outcomes are unequal and the divide can be made by factors such as race, socioeconomic status, or location (Carter-Pokras & Baquet, 2004). Latino/as are now the largest minority group in the United States, making up about 14% of the total U.S. population (U.S. Census Bureau, 2007). Similar to other immigrants, Latino/a immigrants are vulnerable to serious health disparities, including disparities in access to health information (Kreps, Neuhauser, Sparks, & Villagran, 2008).

Minorities are also less likely than non-Hispanic Whites to receive health services, including clinically necessary procedures, even when controlling for patients' insurance status, income, and access to health care (Smedley, Stith, & Nelson, 2003). When minorities attempt to receive care and health information, they face structural and cultural barriers that interact in complex ways (American Cancer Society, 2006). The Institute of Medicine (Smedley et al., 2003) found evidence that stereotyping, biases, and uncertainty on the part of health care providers can contribute to unequal treatment of Latino/as. A potential way to decrease disparities is to empower health consumers through knowledge and education. The digital divide, however, increases the disparities of underserved health consumers, as most of the digitally underserved also lack access to health care (Chang et al., 2004).

Spanish-speaking Latino/as are less likely than Whites to have access and to use the Internet (Fox & Livingston, 2007). In addition, Latino/a Internet users utilize the Internet less frequently than non-Hispanic Whites (Fox & Livingston, 2007; Lorence, Park, & Fox, 2006). Fewer Latino/a individuals seek health information online, and those who do experience more difficulties in searching for information and feel less confident in their ability to obtain information compared to non-Hispanic Whites (Vanderpool, Kornfeld, Rutten, & Squiers, 2009). Health information is essential in guiding strategic health behaviors, treatments, and decisions (Kreps, 2005). Clearly, online information presents challenges to most consumers, perhaps most notably due to its credibility (Brann & Anderson, 2002). However, in view of the positive effects that health information seeking on the Internet has to consumers' decision making and sense of empowerment (Napoli, 2001), lack of access to the Internet is recognized as contributing to health disparities (Kreps, 2005).

Considering the specific cultural and linguistic needs that characterize Hispanic/Latinos (Marin & Marin, 1991), it is essential to design interventions that address these needs, including access to adequate information at low-literacy levels in both English and Spanish. The current absence of government initiatives to reduce this disparity (Chang et al., 2004) increases the importance of non-governmental organizations (NGOs) in creating and disseminating online health information to Latino/as.

The Community Group La Comunidad Habla

This case study describes the work of a grassroots, community-based initiative to increase low-income Latina's empowerment by providing them with training and access to technology and health information. The group's name, *La Comunidad Habla* (LCH), means "the community speaks." LCH's stated goal is "to support women as leaders in technology and health communication in order to create economic opportunities and advance health equity" (Ginossar & Nelson, 2010a, p. 329). This community group resides in the Southeast Albuquerque neighborhoods of La Mesa and Trumbull Village, one of the city's most disadvantaged areas. The community has many strengths, including other dedicated community organizations and coalitions; however, it also faces many challenges. The community has a high proportion of low-income residents that cope with a plethora of social and economic stressors (Morrison, 2000). Members face one of the city's highest crime rates (Morrison, 2000), which contributes to the stressors they experience. This community also faces multiple barriers to health care and well-being. These barriers include lack of adequate medical insurance, paucity of clinics and providers, and limited English proficiency (LEP) of many community members (Morrison, 2000). LEP influences persons' ability to communicate with health care providers and to receive health information from different sources (Doty, 2003).

LCH's director and founder is a community activist who works and lives in the community. Working in a university-hospital community-based pediatric clinic as a community liaison, she identified the need of women to learn computing skills. She offered an introductory-level computer class for women. This free class was taught in Spanish in a facility provided by a local church. The church also provided child care for participants. Following the success of this class, the activist decided that further outreach was needed. She formed LCH in 2006 with the goal of providing training and advocacy to increase access to health and technology.

LCH collaborated with different community organizations and was funded by a variety of local foundations and state agencies. In 2008, I collaborated with LCH on a community-based participatory research project (Ginossar & Nelson, 2010a, 2010b). This case study is based on data that she collected in the following two years. Methods included participant observations of group meetings and community presentations, analysis of documents that the community group provided as well as Internet and newspaper searches, and retrospective interviews with the group director and members conducted in 2010. In addition, previous scholarly work was reviewed to highlight the approach delineated in this case study. In particular, previous community-based efforts and relevant theoretical underpinnings are reviewed to explain the potential impact of LCH's work and provide a model for other scholars and community organizations.

Theoretical Underpinnings

Diffusion of Innovations Theory

According to diffusion of innovations theory (Rogers, 2003), *diffusion* is the process by which an innovation is communicated through certain channels during a period of time among the members of a social system (Rogers, 2003). In innovations that are successfully diffused, different types of adopters exist, which include: (1) those who invent the innovation, (2) those who are first to adopt it, (3) the early majority, who are followed by (4) the late majority. The last to adopt an innovation, or those who fail to adopt it, are (5) the "laggards." In view of current Internet adoption rates, non-users are at risk of becoming laggards. This is particularly true for individuals and groups with lower income and education levels.

Communication is crucial in diffusion of innovations. People receive information from different channels, including mass media and interpersonal contacts. This information impacts beliefs about the innovations as well of their adoption. Interpersonal communication is most influential on the decision to adopt (Rogers, 2003). Persons' social networks thus influence rates of diffusion. Laggards are often from networks that are comprised of similar individuals and do not have opinion leaders in their social network that would promote diffusion. Nurturing opinion leaders in late adopters' social networks is therefore an important strategy in promoting diffusion (Rogers, 2003). Due to the typical low levels of income of laggards, it is also important to provide incentives for this population (Rogers, 2003).

Social Cognitive Theory

While diffusion of innovation theory provides an explanation of the social environment in which innovations are diffused, *social cognitive theory* (SCT; Bandura, 1986) explains it on the individual level (Bandura, 1986). Therefore, the two theories are compatible in explaining technology adoption (Bandura, 2006). Bandura (1986, 2006) argued that economic resources, socioeconomic status, educational level, family structure, and other factors impact human behavior indirectly, by influencing individuals' motivation, self-efficacy beliefs, personal standards, emotional states, and other self-regulatory influences. According to the theory, *self-efficacy* is the degree to which people believe that they are capable of performing certain actions (Bandura, 1986). These perceptions are created through (a) experiencing the outcomes of one's behavior, (b) observing the outcomes of others' behavior; (c) being persuaded by other individuals, and (d) experiencing different emotional states (Bandura, 1986). Therefore, to increase adoption of Internet use for health information seeking, it is imperative to influence individuals' self-efficacy perceptions regarding Internet use and health information seeking (Rains, 2008).

Strategies for Reaching Underserved Populations

LCH's strategies to reduce the digital and health divide drew on four previous approaches and models, which included use of promotoras (community health lay workers), entertainment-education, community media, and community-based participatory research.

Promotoras de Salud

Promotoras de Salud are Latino/a community health educators who are members of the communities they serve and participate in health promotion programs as recruiters and educators (Larkey, 2006). As community members, their messages are culturally sensitive, they are knowledgeable about community resources, and they are seen as credible within their own communities (Larkey, Gonzalez, Mar, & Glantz, 2008). Therefore, consistent with diffusion of innovations theory (Rogers, 2003), their positioning in their communities' networks allows them to reach isolated, underserved individuals and to promote innovative ideas regarding behavior change in ways that fit cultural needs and expectations (Larkey et al., 2008). In addition, consistent with social cognitive theory (Bandura, 1986), they provide role models to other community members and can positively affect self-efficacy beliefs of underserved individuals. In view of promotoras' demonstrated effectiveness in health promotion, it is expected that this strategy can be implemented in other social-change processes, including technology use even though previously reported efforts to increase use of the Internet in underserved communities have not involved training community members as leaders in technology (Kreps, 2005).

Entertainment-Education

Entertainment-education (E-E) is a mediated strategy used to disseminate ideas to promote behavioral and social change (Singhal & Rogers, 2002; Slater & Rouner, 2002). This approach is used world-wide, typically in radio and television programs (Singhal & Rogers, 2002). The inception of the E-E approach to television programs occurred in production of E-E *telenovelas* (i.e., Latin American Soap operas) (Singhal & Rogers, 2002). The producer, Miguel Sabido, followed Bandura's social learning theory, later renamed social cognitive theory (Bandura, 1986; Singhal & Rogers, 2002). E-E efforts typically aim at increasing self-efficacy beliefs as they relate to the targeted behavior (Smith, Downs, & Witte, 2007; Sood, Menard, & Witte, 2004). These persuasive processes are facilitated by narratives and characters with whom the audience can identify (Singhal & Rogers, 2002; Slater & Rouner, 2002). This identification leads to audiences' learning by observing the characters and adopting the targeted behavior to varying degrees.

Community Media

LCH's director utilized *community media* strategies as a framework. These strategies focus on creation of media content by lay persons (Mody, 1991). Community media strategies attempt to change the current media practices in which only big corporations and development agencies with formal power control the media and create media content (Mody, 1991). The community media approach has been previously used extensively in radio, newspapers, and television production (Mody, 1991). In contrast to the content in these previous mass media, lay persons have the ability to create Internet content (Hargittai & Walejko, 2008). Therefore, this new medium lends itself to be used by media community activists. However, only a few Internet-based health communication interventions have incorporated underserved community members as content creators, and no previous interventions have attempted to integrate low-income Latino/as in content creation. Therefore, there is a need for interventions that will bridge what scholars have referred to as "the participation divide" (Hargittai & Walejko, 2008; see Kreps, 2005 for a discussion of NCI projects to reduce another important divide—the digital divide).

Community-Based Participatory Research

Community-based participatory research (CBPR) is closely aligned with a community media perspective. It is defined as a partnership approach to research that equitably involves community members, organization representatives, and researchers in all aspects of the research process (Israel, Schulz, Parker, & Becker, 2001). Its effectiveness in advancing social justice and long-term changes toward reduction of health disparities has been recognized by the World

Health Organization (WHO; Wallerstein, 2006). In the field of health communication, CBPR is gaining increasing interest as an approach that can promote social justice (Frey & Carragee, 2007; Harter, Dutta, & Cole, 2009). The processes of community-based participatory health communication research include community members first conceptualizing community's needs and detecting possible resources, and then activating them to create sustainable health outcomes (Basu & Dutta, 2008).

LCH's Efforts to Reduce Health and Digital Disparities

Promotoras' Background

To understand the work of LCH, it is important to consider the background of the women who participate in this community group as community leaders/promotoras. The group consists of six to seven Latina immigrants. When one member leaves, a new community member is recruited. The majority of past and present group members are from Mexico, with a few past participants from Central American and Caribbean countries. LCH's director reported that when she joined the group, participants had 7 to 12 years of schooling in their native countries. They were either unemployed or worked at low income/low skill jobs, such as janitors. The group leader reflected on their situation, saying, "These women are marginalized on so many levels. They have low education and limited English proficiency, and they are trapped in low skills jobs that, although pay more than in their birth countries, are keeping them under the poverty line." She proceeded to note that as recent immigrants who lost their social networks in their countries of origin, they further suffered from social isolation. Despite these difficulties, LCH members expressed strong commitment to serving their community.

Promotoras' Training

The group met in weekly sessions lasting two to four hours. These sessions centered on ongoing learning of technical, advocacy, and organizational skills. Technical skills included utilizing web and graphic design software, setting up network connections, as well as creating professional invoices for contract work. Advocacy skills were related to understanding and describing health barriers and disparities, developing educational comics,[2] as well as using the Internet for advocacy. Organizational skills included utilizing time management skills, creating agendas for workshops, as well as establishing and maintaining community networks. Additionally, each member held a managing role in a key project area, such as recruiting, marketing, or maintaining the database. As managers, they had to assure their peers were following deadlines and completing tasks in each area. At the beginning of the weekly sessions, each member provided brief reports on the status of her work and how she was planning to accomplish the project's goals. Since 2006, LCH has recruited and trained 11 promotoras. Three of the current promotoras have been involved in the project since its inception. Their training has been ongoing to keep up with technological changes and skills related to new projects, while continuing the flow of work. One member, commenting on this process, indicated that this was one of the difficulties she encountered: "it was hard to learn to do work on projects while learning how to do these things."

Content Creation

Following community media principles (Mody, 1991), group members actively participated by creating the content of the information communicated to the community. As previously mentioned, they created an interactive website that provided information about health care resources in the community (www.mycommunitynm.org). This included a directory of health care clinics, with a focus on underinsured and uninsured health consumers, and information about the services they provided, (My Community NM, 2010). In addition, they elected to address major barriers to access of health care in the community by incorporating E-E strategies. To this end, they created *fotonovelas*, or illustrated stories that they published on the website and circulated in a print version. The first stage of creating this E-E content included community needs identification, a strategy consistent with community media (Mody, 1991) as well as CBPR principles (Wallerstein, 2006). LCH members discussed the barriers to health care access in their community. They agreed on three major barriers that blocked community members from seeking medical care. One obstacle was paucity of medical clinics in the community and members' difficulties in securing transportation to remote clinics. Due to the poverty-level income of many community residents, many women and men in the community do not own a car. They often resist from using public transportation since they do not know how to use it or how to find their way. The group wrote a story in which a woman learns how to use public transportation called "Lost in the Big City: Overcoming Transportation Barriers." This illustrated story provided practical information about how to find information for using the public bus system.

An additional barrier they identified related to gatekeepers in clinics and other agencies who intimidated recent immigrants by asking for documents such as social security cards and passports. Many community activists believe that these gatekeepers are operating either out of a desire to limit the number of individuals they have to serve, or due to lack of knowledge. These requests result in intimidation of community members. In particular, LCH members noted that these experiences have prevented some Latino/a immigrants from seeking care for their children. The fotonovela, "They Almost Asked For My Dog's Social Security Card!: What to Do When Asked for Unnecessary Documentation," addressed this issue depicting a mother who is trying to access care to Carlito, her sick son, but is intimidated by a case manager. The case manager requires the mother to disclose how she entered the country and to submit her passport and the social security cards of everyone living with her. Carlito's mother later learns from other community members that these requests are unnecessary. She also learns how to defend her rights when encountering such demands from an official person who is not an immigration officer.

The third, and related, barrier to recent immigrants accessing clinics was often being mistreated by clinics' staff. Community members who are underinsured or uninsured turn to medical clinics that provide free or reduced price health care. These medical clinics are typically overcrowded and do not always provide care in a respectful manner (Ginossar, De-Vargas, Sanchez, & Oetzel, 2010). Based on a specific personal story that was deemed typical by the women, they wrote the story "Super Maria & the Complaint: How to File a Complaint in the Health System." It revolved around a woman who learned how to file a complaint in the system after she was wronged and humiliated by a receptionist in a clinic.

When they finished writing the narratives as described above, LCH hired a community artist to draw black-and-white pictures, which they then colored using software. The fotonovelas had English and Spanish versions. In addition to posting the fotonovelas to the website, they printed them and distributed them in the community, including in the pediatric clinic. There was a sufficient budget for a few hundred copies for community members. The stories are now available only online at www.mycommunitynm.org.

Community Outreach and Recruitment

LCH's model for working in the community included creating the interactive website and other materials, as well as training community members in using technology and in health-related advocacy. In a community that is often described as "hard to reach," their recruitment process resulted in having approximately 200 workshops with 1,129 participants in two years, with more than 70% of them being community members. Other participants included service providers and community leaders. The goals of the community-based workshops for local consumers were to facilitate participants' learning of basic computer and Internet skills, consider larger systemic health issues which create inequalities, reflect on their experiences in the health care system, learn self-advocacy skill, and share their experiences and knowledge with others in their community. Community members who participated in these workshops were offered incentives, including provision of onsite childcare, monetary compensation for participation, access to free computer and Internet training, as well as information and support. This provision of incentives is essential in reaching underserved communities, according to diffusion of innovation theory (Rogers, 2003).

The Content of the Workshops

The two-hour training sessions were led by one or more promotoras and included one hour of basic, intermediate, or advanced computer training, and one hour of health resource and advocacy training. Participants used "role play" and acted out the stories. They also discussed their implications, including other scenarios related to healthcare barriers. Observations of these workshops revealed that community members identified with the characters in the fotonovelas and reacted emotionally to the narratives. According to E-E approach, this emotional involvement, also referred to as *parasocial interaction*," is a key to the persuasiveness of E-E messages (Singhal & Rogers, 2002; Slater & Rouner, 2002). This identification with the narratives provides participants with the opportunity to learn by observation. Identifying with the positive outcomes of the stories' characters can enable them to form positive perceptions of their own self-efficacy (Bandura, 1977, 1986). In addition, consistent with social cognitive theory (Bandura, 1977, 1986, 2006), the potential to influence participants' self-efficacy beliefs was created by the provision of successful experiences through the training sessions and access to culturally appropriate, low literacy level, bilingual information about accessing the health care system. Further, the promotoras demonstrated to participants how laypersons from the same low-income Latino/a community can become leaders in technology and health advocacy.

Summary

At a time in U.S. history when the majority of the population benefits from unprecedented access to health information, those who are left behind are likely to suffer from increased marginalization and its associated burden on health outcomes. The approach delineated in this case study offers an innovative model for health communication efforts to help reduce this health disparity. LCH's success in reaching a large number of underserved community members and in training low-income Latinas to become community leaders in health advocacy and technology reveals the potential of underserved individuals to lead changes in their communities. Additionally, this group's work demonstrates low-income Latinas' motivation to access the Internet and health information.

This case study is also important in highlighting some of the difficulties in reaching low-income Latino/as and the particular strategies that are necessary to help meet their needs. As a community-based organization, LCH identified barriers blocking members from accessing health care and Internet use, and worked toward addressing these obstacles. Although their process of needs' identification did not follow scholarly procedures and was based on the promotoras' personal experiences, these identified barriers are consistent with barriers conceptualized in large-scale, national studies (Flores, Abreu, Olivar, & Kastner, 1998). To reach community members, LCH's members utilized a variety of strategies that were consistent with scholarly theories and approaches, including diffusion of innovations theory, social cognitive theory, E-E, and community media/CBPR approaches. They elected to use strategies that they believed were particularly appropriate for use in their community, such as focusing on classes for women and provision of onsite child care.

LCH's grassroots efforts are quite unique. This small community group set forth to achieve a goal that even large, federally funded organizations seldom aspire to tackle. Indeed, the task of decreasing the digital divide in communities that already face a plethora of other pressing stressors is a formidable one. This organization's achievements, training a cadre of formerly marginalized Latinas as community leaders as well as recruiting and training a large number of community members, are impressive. The challenges to maintain these achievements and to increase their reach, however, should also be considered. It is important to secure a long-term improvement of the community's digital and health care access. Clearly, LCH's efforts should be expanded within the specific community they serve and to other communities. To achieve this goal of reducing these health disparities, larger investments of resources should be directed toward efforts to eliminate health and digital divides. Communication scholars and practitioners have a pivotal role in such endeavors as they have the potential to provide much needed skills of message design and content creation. It is thus through collaborations with community organizations and low-income community members that health communication specialists and students can make a long-lasting impact toward social change and social justice.

NOTES

1   The term "Latino/a" is derived from "Latin American." It is considered to best reflect both the diverse national origins and the nearly unitary treatment of Latino/as in the U.S. It is operationalized to include all persons of Latin American origin or descent, irrespective of language, race, or culture, and it specifically excludes individuals of Spanish national origin outside the Western Hemisphere (Hayes-Bautista & Chapa, 1987). "Latino" is a male of Latin American descent, and "Latina" is a female of Latin American descent. In contrast, the term "Hispanic" is operationalized as: "A person of Mexican, Puerto Rican, Cuban, Central or South America or other Spanish culture or origin, regardless of race" (Hayes-Bautista & Chapa, 1987, p. 64). Both terms are recommended for use in the Office of Management and Budget's (OMB's) review of the statistical standards used throughout the federal government to collect and publish data on race and ethnicity (Amaro & Zambrana, 2000).

2   Educational comics, also known as *educational fotonovelas*, have varied uses in health promotion efforts in Latin America as well as in educational efforts in the U.S. targeting Latino/as (Cabrera, Morisky, & Chin, 2002; Valle, Yamada, & Matiella, 2006).

References

Amaro, H., & Zambrana, R. (2000). Criollo, mestizo, mulato, LatiNegro, indigena, white, or black? The US Hispanic/Latino population and multiple responses in the 2000 census. *American Journal of Public Health, 90*, 1724–1727.

American Cancer Society. (2006). Cancer facts & figures for Hispanic/Latinos: 2006–2008. http://www.cancer.org/Research/CancerFactsFigures/index.

Bandura, A. (1977). *Social learning theory.* New York, NY: General Learning Press.

Bandura, A. (1986). *Social foundations of thought and action: A social cognitive theory.* Englewood Cliffs, NJ: Prentice-Hall.

Bandura, A. (2006). On integrating social cognitive and social diffusion theories. In A. Singhal & J. Dearing (Eds.), *Communication of innovations: A journey with Ev Rogers* (pp. 111–135). Beverly Hills, CA: Sage.

Basu, A., & Dutta, M. (2008). The relationship between health information seeking and community participation: The roles of health information orientation and efficacy. *Health Communication, 23*, 70–79.

Brann, M., & Anderson, J. G. (2002). E-medicine and health care consumers: Recognizing current problems and possible resolutions for a safer environment. *Health Care Analysis, 10*, 403–415.

Cabrera, D. M., Morisky, D. E., & Chin, S. (2002). Development of a tuberculosis education booklet for Latino immigrant patients. *Patient Education and Counseling, 46*, 117–124.

Carter-Pokras, O., & Baquet, C. (2004). What is a health disparity? *Public Health Reports, 117*, 426–434.

Chang, B. L., Bakken, S., Brown, S. S., Houston, T. K., Kreps, G. L., Kukafka, R., et al. (2004). Bridging the digital divide: Reaching vulnerable populations. *Journal of the American Medical Informatics Association, 11*, 448–457.

Doty, M. M. (2003). *Hispanic patients' doubleburden: Lack of health insurance and limited English.* New York, NY: The Commonwealth Fund.

Flores, G., Abreu, M., Olivar, M. A., & Kastner, B. (1998). Access barriers to health care for Latino children. *Archives of Pediatrics and Adolescent Medicine, 152*, 1119–1125.

Fox, S., & Livingston, G. (2007). Latinos online. Retrieved from http://www.pewinternet.org/Reports/2007/Latinos-Online.aspx

Frey, L. R., & Carragee, K. M. (Eds.). (2007). *Communication activism: Volume 1. Communication for social change.* Cresskill, NJ: Hampton Press.

Ginossar, T., De-Vargas, F., Sanchez, C., & Oetzel, J. G. (2010). "That word, cancer:" Breast care behavior of Hispanic women in New Mexico. *Health Care for Women International 31*, 68–87.

Ginossar, T., & Nelson, S. A. (2010a). La comunidad habla: Using internet community-based information interventions to increase empowerment and access to health care of low-income Latino/a immigrants. *Communication Education, 59*, 328–343.

Ginossar, T., & Nelson, S. A. (2010b). Using community-based e-health intervention to reduce the health and digital divides with marginalized Hispanic women: The case of la comunidad habla. *Journal of Computer Mediated Communication, 15*, 530–551.

Hargittai, E., & Walejko, G. (2008). The participation divide: Content creation and sharing in the digital age. *Information, Communication and Society, 11*, 239–256.

Harter, L. M., Dutta, M. J., & Cole, C. (Eds.). (2009). *Communicating for social impact: Engaging communication theory, research, and practice.* Cresskill NJ: Hampton Press.

Hayes-Bautista, D. E., & Chapa, J. (1987). Latino terminology: Conceptual bases for standardized terminology. *American Journal of Public Health, 77*, 61–68.

Israel, B. A., Schulz, A. J., Parker, E. A., & Becker, A. B. (2001). Community-based participatory research: Policy recommendations for promoting a partnership approach in health research. *Education for Health, 14*, 182–197.

Kreps, G. L. (2005). Disseminating relevant health information to underserved audiences: Implications of the Digital Divide Pilot Projects. *Journal of Medical Library Assocation, 93*, S68–S73.

Kreps, G. L., Neuhauser, L., Sparks, L., & Villagran, M. M. (2008). The power of community-based health communication interventions to promote cancer prevention and control for at-risk populations. *Patient Education and Counseling, 71*, 315–318.

Larkey, L. K. (2006). Las mujeres saludables: Reaching Latinas for breast, cervical, and colorectal cancer prevention and screening. *Journal of Community Health, 31*, 69–77.

Larkey, L. K., Gonzalez, J., Mar, L., & Glantz, N. (2008). Latina recruitment for cancer prevention education via community based participatory research strategies. *Contemporary Clinical Trials, 30*, 47–54.

Lorence, D. P., Park, H., & Fox, S. (2006). Assessing health consumerism on the Web: A demographic profile of information-seeking behaviors. *Jounral of medical systems, 30*, 251–258.

Marin, G., & Marin, B. V. (1991). *Research with Hispanic populations.* Newbury Park, CA: Sage.

Mody, B. (1991). *Designing messages for development communication: An audience participation-based approach.* New Delhi: Sage.

Morrison, S. (2000). *Evaluation of Albuquerque weed and seed sites: Trumbull and La Mesa neighborhoods:* University of New Mexico Institute for Social Research Statistical Analysis Center.

My Community NM. (2010). Community health and social resources in New Mexico. Retrieved from www.mycommunitynm.org

Napoli, P. M. (2001). Consumer use of medical information from electronic and paper media: A literature review. In R. E. Rice & J. E. Katz (Eds.), *The Internet and health communication: Experiences and expectations* (pp. 79–98). Thousand Oaks, CA: Sage.

Rains, S. A. (2008). Seeking health information in the information age: The role of Internet self-efficacy. *Western Journal of Communication, 17*, 1–18.

Rogers, E. M. (2003). *Diffusion of innovations* (5th ed.). New York, NY: Free Press.

Singhal, A., & Rogers, E. M. (2002). A theoretical agenda for entertainment-education. *Communication Theory, 12*, 117–135.

Slater, M. D., & Rouner, D. (2002). Entertainment-education and elaboration likelihood: Understanding the processing of narrative persuasion. *Communication Theory, 12*, 173–191.

Smedley, B. D., Stith, A. Y., & Nelson, A. R. (Eds.). (2003). *Unequal treatment: Confronting racial and ethnic disparities in healthcare.* Washington, DC: National Academies Press.

Smith, R. A., Downs, E., & Witte, K. (2007). Drama theory and entertainment education: Exploring the effects of a radio drama on behavioral intentions to limit HIV transmission in Ethiopia. *Communication Monographs, 74*, 133–153.

Sood, S., Menard, T., & Witte, K. (2004). The theory behind entertainment-education. In A. Singhal, M. J. Cody, E. M. Rogers & M. Sabido (Eds.), *Entertainment-education and social change: History, research, and practice* (pp. 117–149). Mahwah, NJ: Erlbaum.

U.S. Census Bureau. (2007). *Table 4: Annual estimates of the Hispanic or Latino population by age and sex for the U.S.: April 1, 2000 to July 1, 2006.*

Valle, R., Yamada, A., & Matiella, A. C. (2006). Fotonovelas: A health literacy tool for educating Latino older adults about dementia. *Clinical Gerontologist, 30*, 71–88.

Vanderpool, R. C., Kornfeld, J., Rutten, L. F., & Squiers, L. (2009). Cancer information-seeking experiences: The implications of Hispanic ethnicity and Spanish language. *Journal of Cancer Education 24*, 141–147.

Wallerstein, N. (2006). *What is the evidence on effectiveness of empowerment to improve health?* Copenhagen: World Health Organization (WHO), Regional Office for Europe, Health Evidence Network.

CHAPTER 17

Facilitating Diabetes Management Among Native Americans

The Potential of Online Social Support

James D. Robinson, Jeanine Warisse Turner, Betty A. Levine, and Yan Tian

KEY TERMS

Online diabetes management

Email social support

Native Americans

Health outcomes

Abstract

Physicians and other health care providers (HCP)[1] recognize that effective diabetes management requires close attention to patient lifestyles (Brashers, Neidig, & Goldsmith, 2004; Street et al., 1993; van Dam, 2003). To help HCP more closely monitor patient health, researchers developed the MyCareTeam® system. MyCareTeam® is a web-based diabetes management application that allows patients to upload their blood glucose readings to their physician, access information about diabetes, and interact with their provider via secure email. MyCareTeam® is a subscription program for HCP and not available to the public on an individual patient basis. The data and narrative evidence presented in this chapter are drawn from research involving 109 Native Americans with poorly controlled diabetes.[2] A total of 945 personal messages sent by nurses and physicians to their Native American patients participating in this investigation were content analyzed and found to contain messages of social support (Robinson, Turner, Levine, & Tian, in press). In addition to identifying the nine types of messages sent by HCP, this chapter examines the efficacy of web-based health monitoring systems, the impact of email on patient usage of the MyCareTeam® system, and the impact of email on patient health behaviors. Through the recounted experiences of patients and a health care provider, Donna,[3] insight into web-based health monitoring and the benefits of email interaction may be gained.

Learning about Donna, Her Patients, and the Clinical Context

It is 6:30 p.m., time to go home. Donna is a 43-year-old Hispanic-American nurse who works with Native Americans at the Azule Street Diabetes clinic. Donna is fluent in English and

Spanish and works four 10-hour shifts every week. She has worked with diabetes patients[4] for nine years and is quick to inform new acquaintances that diabetes is an epidemic in the United States. Diabetes affects approximately 24 million Americans, is one of the top five most common chronic medical conditions, and is the seventh leading cause of death in the U.S. (Centers of Disease Control and Prevention (CDC, 2007). Complications resulting from diabetes include nephropathy, neuropathy, retinopathy, high blood pressure, heart disease, depression, stroke, and increased risk of infections (CDC, 2007).

While not required to maintain her licensure, she takes continuing education courses to keep current. She also monitors health statistics on the Centers for Disease Control and Prevention website (www.cdc.gov), so she knows that illnesses/diseases do not treat all ethnic and racial cohorts equally. Native Americans, for example, are at increased risk for heart disease and several types of cancer (e.g., liver, kidney/renal, stomach, and colon) (CDC, n.d.). Native Americans are also more likely to have a stroke, smoke, be obese, and suffer from high blood pressure than their non-Hispanic white adult counterparts (CDC, n.d.). Native American adults are also more likely to die from unintentional injuries or accidents, suffer from mental illness, and commit suicide (CDC, 2003). Some of these health issues can be attributed to factors such as cultural barriers, geographic isolation, inadequate sewage disposal, low income, dramatic levels of alcoholism, and genetics (CDC, 2003).

While interested in the demography of illness/disease, Donna focuses most of her efforts on diabetes patient education. Working at a clinic in the Southwest, Donna realizes Native Americans are more than twice as likely to be diagnosed with diabetes as non-Hispanic white adults of similar age (CDC, 2007). Donna's patients often think of diabetes as being a single disease when it is a constellation of diseases that arise from the body's inability to produce or properly respond to insulin (American Diabetes Association, 2002; CDC, 2007). The hormone insulin is used by the body to regulate the amount of sugar in the bloodstream and convert that sugar into glycogen. This inability to convert glucose to glycogen results in the starving of the body, dehydration, and an accumulation of sugar in the body's tissues and organs which causes irreversible injury over time (American Diabetes Association, 2002).

Two Types of Diabetes

Type I diabetes used to be called juvenile diabetes because it was commonly found in young people. Type I diabetes is now called insulin-dependent diabetes because patients with type I must inject themselves with insulin and can affect people of all ages. Type I diabetics are dependent on these insulin injections because their pancreas cannot make enough insulin to maintain their blood glucose levels. Type I diabetes is relatively rare, accounting for fewer than 10% of all cases of diabetes in the United States. Individuals with type I diabetes are often white and within the "normal" range for weight or thinner (American Diabetes Association, 2002; CDC, 2007).

Type II diabetes is far more common and accounts for more than 90% of all cases of diabetes in the United States (American Diabetes Association, 2002; CDC, 2007). Patients with type II diabetes can typically produce insulin; however, their bodies do not utilize the insulin efficiently and glucose builds up within the bloodstream. While some individuals with type II diabetes must inject insulin, most adults can control their blood sugar through a combination of a healthy diet, moderate exercise, and close monitoring of their blood glucose levels. In addition, many patients use prescription drugs to stimulate the pancreas to produce more insulin, decrease glucose production, and increase insulin sensitivity (American Diabetes Association, 2002; CDC, 2007). Regardless of the type, patients with diabetes are unable to convert glucose into glycogen.

A Typical Day and Key Challenges

Donna spends a few minutes with each of her patients, trying to help them understand the value of a healthy lifestyle. For some patients, the time is spent extolling the virtues of exercise, and for others, it is a discussion of daily dietary requirements. Donna explains to her patients that the management of diabetes is predicated on maintaining near-normal blood glucose levels through healthy dietary practices, moderate exercise, and careful monitoring of blood glucose levels.

Unfortunately, some of Donna's Native American patients are limited to the food they grow in their garden or the processed foods they can obtain at a local convenience store. Her patients often say things like: "I monitor my blood, exercise, and try to eat healthy. I really do. Then, I eat a piece of chocolate cake, and I am sick as a dog. Everyone else is eating the cake and they all think that eating one little piece of cake won't hurt me, but it does." As Donna reports, "it can be frustrating to have a patient say 'I didn't know that' when you know you have told them the same thing four or five times. You feel like a broken record. But it feels pretty good when they do finally catch on."

The Web-Based Health Monitoring System

Donna's clinic was selected to be part of a research project funded by a grant from the U.S. Army Medical Research and Material Command to determine the effectiveness of a web-based diabetes management monitoring system. The diabetes management application is called MyCareTeam®. The website was developed by researchers at Georgetown University and is designed to provide health information about diabetes, and to track patient treatment regimens, exercise, and dietary practices. The content, language level, and graphics available on the website were adapted to be culturally appropriate for the Native American target audience recruited to join the program. The patients monitor their blood glucose readings and then submit those readings via the internet to the HCP working with them at the clinic. Nurses and physicians read the email and examine the blood glucose scores to ensure the treatment regimen is appropriate and effective. The email and all patient health information are stored on secure servers in Washington, DC and under the control of the researchers at Georgetown University.

Blood Glucose Monitoring and the System

At first, Donna was skeptical about MyCareTeam®. Initially, she did not think her patients would use the system. Many of her patients did not have access to a computer. She also worried that those with access would be unwilling to talk about their illness in an email environment. Additionally, she could not imagine emailing her patients and asking what they ate for breakfast that day. While the system sounded "good in theory," she was not sure, initially, that it would allow her to make decisions about the patients' health in real time.

Soon, however, Donna realized her concern that patients would not use the system was unfounded. While some patients were hesitant at the outset, most patients ultimately used the system. Once patients realized they could track their progress, they became enthusiastic about the system. For example, one of her patients, Waskawane, was ecstatic when she told Donna:

> I was very surprised by the ease of use since I don't have very much computer knowledge (only at work). I wish I had more time to explore the website. But it has motivated me to check my blood sugar. I like seeing the logbook with green numbers. And if I have a question, I can look it up or email my doctor.

Donna was growing more aware that the MyCareTeam® system benefits her patients. After the long day, she is ready to go home, but she wants to jot down a few notes about her experiences with MyCareTeam® before leaving. In her meeting with the researchers from Georgetown University, Donna will be asked to file a system efficacy report. In this report, Donna is expected to identify the advantages and disadvantages of the system. Donna wants to be sure she notifies the researchers about Matoaka. Matoaka had been recently diagnosed with type II diabetes and her physician was having trouble adjusting her insulin dose. The ability to closely monitor Matoaka's blood glucose readings and discuss them with her doctor made finding the appropriate dose much easier for Donna. Matoaka also felt much better and did not have to keep returning to the clinic for dosage adjustments. Donna recalled how happy she was that day when she re-read Matoaka's email. Matoaka wrote, "Thanks Donna for all of your help. I am feeling much better and I think we should keep the insulin at this level for now. Let me know what you and Dr. Welby think I should do." Donna looked at Matoaka's blood glucose readings so she could rattle them off in the interview and smiled. She had replied to Matoaka in her email, "Great job Matoaka. I know the past few days have been frustrating, but I think we are figuring things out. You and John have a good night."

Patient Provider Interaction and Email

In addition to monitoring blood glucose scores, MyCareTeam® also allows patients to interact with their doctor and/or a nurse. The majority of adults with internet access would like to be able to communicate with their own physician via email (Liederman, Zimmerman, Athanasoulis, & Young, 2004). Donna has found some patients want as much contact as possible with their HCP, and she believed email could be used to disseminate medical information to patients. A growing body of research has explored the viability of email between patients and HCP, and the findings support Donna's beliefs (Bergmo & Wangberg, 2007; Delbanco & Sands, 2004; Patt, Houston, Sands, & Ford, 2003; Roter, Larson, Sands, Ford, & Houston, 2008). These studies further suggest that email provides an opportunity to augment the communication received through face-to-face encounters. Generally, these studies employ small non-randomized groups[5] of physicians who are willing to participate in such a research project. For example, Patt et al. (2003) drew a national convenience sample[6] ($n = 45$) of physicians[7] who volunteered, were internet savvy, and interacted with at least one patient daily via email.

Despite the pervasiveness and relative advantages, many HCP have been slow to adopt provider-patient email (Bergmo & Wangberg, 2007; Patt et al., 2003). Typically, physicians are concerned with the time associated with responding to patient concerns by email, and they are concerned about not being reimbursed for that time by insurance companies. Bergmo and Wangberg (2007) explored patients' willingness to pay for email communication with their physician. The researchers separated the sample ($n = 199$) into two groups and conducted a randomized controlled trial (RCT)[8] where one group had email access to their general practitioner for one year and the other group did not. Those who had email access to their physician were significantly less likely to be willing to pay for it (Bergmo & Wangberg, 2007).

Bergmo and Wangberg (2007) further suggest that the participants may have realized fewer benefits than expected, or perhaps preferred face-to-face encounters. It may also be that these patients were in relatively good health with few reasons to interact with their physician. The patients that would most value the need for increased opportunities to interact with their HCP would likely be those patients facing the most uncertainty about their health situation. Therefore, use of email communication within chronically ill populations may provide that opportunity. The Native American patients that were using the MyCareTeam® system definitely fit the characteristics of a chronically ill population.

Some scholars have cautioned that the lack of cues available through email could inhibit or diminish the relational dimensions of the encounter (Baur, 2000). Other researchers have explored the extent to which email mimics the communication within traditional patient-physician interactions and found email messages contained task and relational components (Roter et al., 2008). Although the number of participants in the study was small ($n = 8$ physicians and 8 patients)[9] and the sample of email messages was limited to the last five messages sent by the patient and the provider ($n = 74$), the authors concluded that email supported the patient-physician relationship providing an avenue for patients to communicate worries and for physicians to provide a patient-centered response (Roter et al., 2008).

Email and Social Support

While Roter et al. (2008) suggest that email messages may be used to augment face-to-face interactions, Car and Sheikh (2004) have called for research to determine how clinicians can be patient-centered in their email messages. Donna knew that the researchers from Georgetown University believed patients would benefit from socially supportive messages. And she knew the investigators believed that one way email could be patient-centered was by the inclusion of social support. Socially supportive messages are "verbal and nonverbal behaviors that influence how providers and recipients view themselves, their situations, the other, and their relationship and is the principal process through which individuals coordinate their actions in support-seeking and support-giving encounters" (Albrecht, Burleson, & Goldsmith, 1994, p. 421).

Seeking evidence of social support in the email messages is important due primarily to the empirical links that have been found between patient health and social support (for seminal reviews of the literature see Cassell, 1976; Cobb, 1976). More recently, research has linked social support to improved resistance to infections and diseases, increased longevity, a reduction in patient mortality, increased feelings of self-efficacy, enhanced psychological adjustment to health, and social functioning (Albrecht & Adelman, 1987; Blazer, 1982; Brashers et al., 2004; Burleson, 2003; Burleson & MacGeorge, 2002; Dimond, 1979; Hanson & Sauer, 1985; House, Robbins, & Metzner, 1982; Kaplan et al., 1988; Litwak & Messeri, 1989; Orth-Gomer & Johnson, 1987; Seeman et al., 1993).

Donna's Talking Points

Donna had never counted the different types of messages she was sending to her patients, but she was aware that she tried to be friendly, positive and encouraging, as well as informative and helpful in her email messages. And because she believed the MyCareTeam® system was beneficial for her and her patients, she wanted to make a list of talking points before she went home. For each talking point, she also wanted to have a story that supported her position on using web-based monitoring and email with patients. For her first main point, she wrote down "System Effectiveness." Next to the heading, she jotted some notes about how the system had improved the quality of life for some of her patients. One patient, Cheis, had emailed her last week and asked if he could continue using the MyCareTeam® system after the research project had concluded. The patients knew the MyCareTeam® project was ending, and in his email, Cheis reiterated what he had told her previously on the phone. He wrote, "The best part about the system is the direct, timely feedback I get. I hope we get the chance to use it once the program is over. It probably saved my life."

The second talking point on her list was "Patient & Cultural Sensitivity." Next to this bullet point, she wrote about receiving an email from a patient stating, "Sorry I missed my appointment. I had to take my father to the emergency room and I have to ride my bike to the library to use the computer." Before writing in her notes, Donna thought for a moment about how it is "easy" to forget that many patients have problems that make compliance more difficult.

Her third and final talking point was "Relationships." Donna realized the patients she had developed "good" working relationships with were more likely to control their diabetes than the patients she did not know very well. These high-quality relationships were characterized by a deepening understanding of each other, mutual respect earned over time, and an interdependence to attain mutual goals. These relationships can enable the HCP to provide patients encouragement to maintain a healthy lifestyle and some level of regular accountability. As Donna shares, "A good relationship with a patient means they don't want to disappoint you. They will still eat things they shouldn't and they will forget to measure their blood glucose. But they are less likely to just give up when they know they will eventually have to tell you what they have done and they like you enough to care what you think." Donna believes that it is imperative for patients and HCP to form a partnership for treatment to be successful, and her professional judgment has received empirical support (Kahana & Kahana, 2007).

Since chronic illness management and living with diabetes are ongoing problems, many patients report benefits from a sustained relationship with their HCP (Kahana & Kahana, 2007). Thus, the development of remote illness management systems provide a means by which the patient and provider can stay connected. Remote monitoring systems, coupled with online support opportunities, have been found to reduce caregiver stress (Mahoney, Mutschler, Tarlow, & Liss, 2008), improve healthcare (McMahon et al., 2005), and provide a more economic approach to patient assessment and monitoring of rural patients (Santamore et al., 2008). As wireless technology continues to advance, the possibilities for remote monitoring to provide medical information to the HCP grows as well (Turner, 2003; Yu, Ray, & Motoc, 2008).

Some Other Considerations

With her list of talking points now complete, Donna locked the doors to the clinic. She then walked to her car, wondering what the administrators of her clinic will decide. The researchers from Georgetown University had given the clinic the choice of keeping the computers and continuing to use the system, or discontinuing the service once the research project was completed. Donna believed the system was effective and was going to recommend its continuation within the clinic.

Donna was aware that there were going to be costs and difficulties that would arise from continued use of the system. Once the research project was complete, for example, the technical assistance provided by Georgetown University would stop, and they would need to find a local source of technical support. Some of the clinic's physicians were also unwilling to become involved with the system. These doctors perceived the technology to be more trouble than it was worth. Although Donna knew that reading and responding to the email messages only took a minute or two, some of the doctors believed it took all day. Other doctors felt that the time spent interacting with patients was not billable and, thus, a poor option for maintaining their practice. Still other doctors and administrators were concerned about legal complications that could arise. Patients would have a paper trail, or at the very least an electronic trail, outlining only part of what they had been told by their physicians, nurses, and other HCP. In the event that there were charges of malpractice, attorneys could then use email in their efforts to discredit the HCP in court. Finally, patient involvement with the system had been promoted through incentives. Once the research program was complete, these "perks" would also cease. Clinic administrators would then need to either budget for program incentives or find a new benefactor to furnish the running shoes, water bottles, and t-shirts to the patients.

As Donna started her car and began her drive home, she wondered what it would be like to make medical decisions without all of the legal and financial constraints. She decided it would be much easier to make the decisions without all of the political, legal, and financial concerns. As she mulled over these ideas, she began to wonder if the money it would take to continue using the system would be better spent providing free or reduced rate test strips to clinic patients. Many of the patients at the clinic were spending several hundred dollars a year on testing supplies and this outlay was a hardship for those living on a fixed income.

NOTES

1 HCP is an abbreviation commonly used to refer to all types of health care providers. This includes nurses, physicians, technicians, pharmacists, and a host of other medical professionals.

2 All of the studies that came from the MyCareTeam® data received approval from the Institutional Review Board (IRB) at Georgetown University Medical Center (Washington, DC), the local Indian Health Service IRB, and the U.S. Army Human Research Protections Office (HRPO). For discussion and explanation of the IRB process, see Kramer & Dougherty (2005).

3 All of the patients, physicians, and nurses signed informed consent forms before entering into the MyCareTeam® project. To protect the identity of patients and HCP, pseudonyms are used throughout this chapter.

4 In this clinical context, "diabetes patients" is more likely to be used than "individuals living with diabetes." See chapter 10 (this volume) for the latter phrasing.

5 Researchers prefer to use random samples because there is a higher likelihood that the sample will closely resemble the population. In medical studies, however, researchers often use non-randomized samples because it is not possible or feasible to draw truly random samples. In experiments, random assignment is often more important than random selection because the treatment is expected to change the experimental group, and as long as the two groups are equivalent, the fact that they are not truly random does not destroy the validity of the study findings.

6 Investigators often draw samples, small yet ideally representative subsets of larger populations, to conduct most investigations. There are many types of samples ranging from non-randomized or purposive (i.e., the participants are members of some ongoing group [like a support group], meet inclusion criteria [such as being Native American and having diabetes]; and are not selected randomly to participate). A convenience sample is comprised of participants who happen to be available for a study and who do not have to meet detailed inclusion criteria, such as travelers waiting to board a plane. The nature of the sample drawn has implications for how well the results will generalize to others in the population. Please see Davis, Gallardo, and Lachlan (2010) and Frey, Botan, and Kreps (2000) for detailed discussions.

7 The physician areas of specialization were not identified within the investigation.

8 A RCT refers to one type of experimental design frequently employed in tests of the efficacy of medical treatments. In an RCT, the levels of the independent variable (e.g., aspirin or placebo) are assigned to the subjects randomly in an effort to reduce selection bias.

9 Other demographic information about the physicians and patients, such as their ages, medical specializations, diseases, education, race, or sex was not provided.

Discussion Questions

1. What do you think Donna should do? Should Donna recommend the continued use of the MyCareTeam® System? Why?

2. Do you think the MyCareTeam® System makes a meaningful difference to patients? How?

3. Would the patients be better off with free testing supplies? Why?

4. Would the patients receive better care if they merely had more office visits or phone calls from their HCP? Why?

References

Albrecht, T. L., & Adelman, M. B. (1987). *Communicating social support*. Newbury Park, CA: Sage.

Albrecht, T., Burleson, B., & Goldsmith, D. (1994). Supportive communication. In M. Knapp, & G. Miller (Eds.), *Handbook of interpersonal communication* (pp. 419–459). Thousand Oaks, CA: Sage.

American Diabetes Association. (2002). Implications of the United Kingdom Prospective Diabetes Study. *Diabetes Care, 25*, S28–S32.

Baur, C. (2000). Limiting factors on the transformative powers of email in patient-physician relationships: A critical analysis. *Heath Communication, 12*, 239–259.

Bergmo, T. S., & Wangberg, S. C. (2007). Patients' willingness to pay for electronic communication with their general practitioner. *European Journal of Health Economics, 8*, 105–110.

Blazer, D. (1982). Social support and mortality in an elderly community population. *American Journal of Epidemiology, 115*, 684–694.

Brashers, D. E., Neidig, J. L., & Goldsmith, D. J. (2004). Social support and the management of uncertainty for people living with HIV or AIDS. *Health Communication, 16*, 305–331.

Burleson, B. R. (2003). The experience and effects of emotional support: What the study of cultural and gender differences can tell us about close relationships, emotion and interpersonal communication. *Personal Relationships, 10*, 1–23.

Burleson, B. R., & MacGeorge, E. L. (2002). Supportive communication. In M. L. Knapp, & J. A. Daly (Eds.), *Handbook of interpersonal communication* (3rd ed., pp. 374–424). Thousand Oaks, CA: Sage.

Car, J., & Sheikh, J. (2004). Email consultations in healthcare: Scope and effectiveness. *British Medical Journal, 329*, 435–438.

Cassel, J. (1976). The contribution of social environment in host resistance. *American Journal of Epidemiology, 104*, 107–123.

Centers for Disease Control and Prevention. (2007). National diabetes fact sheet: General information and national estimates on diabetes in the United States, 2007. Retrieved from http://www.cdc.gov/diabetes/pubs/pdf/ndfs_2007.pdf

Centers for Disease Control and Prevention. (n.d.). Fact sheet: Trends in diabetes prevalence among American Indian and Alaska Native children, adolescents, and young adults—1990–1998. Retrieved from http://www.cdc.gov/diabetes/pubs/factsheets/aian.htm

Centers for Disease Control and Prevention. (2003). Injuries among Native Americans: Fact sheet, 2003. Retrieved http://www.cdc.gov/ncipc/factsheets/nativeamericans.htm

Cobb, S. (1976). Social support as a moderator of life stress. *Psychosomatic Medicine, 38*, 300–314.

Davis, C. S., Gallardo, H. L., & Lachlan, K. A. (2010). *Straight talk about communication research methods*. Dubuque, IA: Kendall-Hunt.

Delbanco, T. L., & Sands, D. (2004). Electrons in flight - email between doctors and patients. *New England Journal of Medicine, 350*, 1705–1707.

Dimond, M. (1979). Social support and adaptation to chronic illness: The case of maintenance hemodialysis. *Research in Nursing and Health, 2*, 101–108.

Frey, L. R., Botan, C. H., & Kreps, G. L. (2000). *Investigating communication: An introduction to research methods* (2nd ed.). Boston: Allyn & Bacon.

Hanson, S. M., & Sauer, W. J. (1985). Children and their elderly parents. In W. J. Sauer, & R. T. Coward (Eds.), *Social support networks and the care of the elderly* (pp. 41–66). New York: Springer.

House, J. S., Robbins, C., & Metzner, H. L. (1982). The association of social relationships and activities with mortality: Prospective evidence from the Tecumseh community health study. *American Journal of Epidemiology, 116*, 123–140.

Kahana, E., & Kahana, B. (2007). Health care partnership model of doctor-patient communication in cancer prevention and care among the aged. In H. D. O'Hair, G. L. Kreps, & L. Sparks (Eds.), *The handbook of communication and cancer care* (pp. 37–54). Cresskill, NJ: Hampton Press.

Kaplan, J. R., Salonen, J. T., Cohen, R. D., Brand, R. J., Syme, S. L., & Puska, P. (1988). Social connections and mortality from all causes and cardiovascular disease: Prospective evidence from Eastern Finland. *American Journal of Epidemiology, 128*, 370–380.

Kramer, M. W., & Dougherty, D. S. (Eds.). (2005). Communication research and institutional review boards [Special issue]. *Journal of Applied Communication Research, 33*(3).

Liederman, E., Zimmerman, E., Athanasoulis, M., & Young, M. (2004). Systemwide rollout of doctor-patient secure web messaging. In P. Whitten, & D. Cook (Eds.), *Understanding health communication technologies* (pp. 244–250). San Francisco, CA: Jossey-Bass.

Litwak, E., & Messeri, P. (1989). Organizational theory, social supports, and mortality rates: A theoretical convergence. *American Sociological Review, 54*, 49–66.

Mahoney, D., Mutschler, P., Tarlow, B., & Liss, E. (2008). Real world implementation lessons and outcomes from the Worker Interactive Networking (WIN) Project: Workplace-based online caregiver support and remote monitoring of elders at home. *Telemedicine and e-Health, 14*, 224–234.

McMahon, G., Gomes, H., Hohne, S., Ming-Jye Hu, T., Levine, B., & Conlin, P. (2005). Web-based care management in patients with poorly controlled diabetes. *Diabetes Care, 28*, 1624–1629.

Orth-Gomer, K., & Johnson, J. V. (1987). Social network interaction and mortality: A six year follow-up study of a random sample of the Swedish population. *Journal of Chronic Disease, 40*, 949–957.

Patt, R. M., Houston, T., Sands, D., & Ford, D. (2003). Doctors who are using email with their patients: A qualitative exploration. *Journal of Medical Internet Research, 5*, article e9. Retrieved from http://www.jmir.org/2003/2/e9/

Robinson, J. D., Turner, J. W., Levine, B. A., & Tian, Y. (in press). Expanding the walls of the healthcare encounter: Support and outcomes for patients online. *Health Communication*.

Roter, D., Larson, S., Sands, D., Ford, D., & Houston, T. (2008). Can e-mail messages between patients and physicians be patient-centered? *Health Communication, 23*, 80–86.

Santamore, W. P., Homka, C., Kashem, A., McConnell, T., Menapace, F., & Bove, A. (2008). Accuracy of blood pressure measurements transmitted through telemedicine in underserved populations. *Telemedicine and e-Health, 14,* 333–338.

Seeman, T. A., Berkman, Kahout, F., Lacroix, A., Glynn, R., & Blazer, D. (1993). Intercommunity variations in the association between social ties and mortality in the elderly: A comparative analysis of three communities. *Annals of Epidemiology, 3,* 325–335.

Smith, K. E., Levine, B. A., Clement, S. C., Ming-Jye Hu, T., Alaoui, A., & Mun, S. K. (2004). Impact of MyCareTeam® for poorly controlled diabetes mellitus. *Diabetes Technology & Therapeutics, 6,* 828–835.

Street, R., Piziak, V., Carpentier, W., Herzog, J., Hejl, J., Skinner, G., & McLellan, L. (1993). Provider-patient communication and metabolic control. *Diabetes Care, 16,* 714–721.

Turner, J. W. (2003). Telemedicine: Expanding health care into virtual environments. In T. Thompson, M. Dorsey, K. Miller, & R. Parrott (Eds.), *Handbook of Health Communication* (pp. 515–535). Mahwah, NJ: Lawrence Erlbaum Associates.

Van Dam, R. M. (2003). The epidemiology of lifestyle and risk for type 2 diabetes. *European Journal of Epidemiology, 8,* 1115–1125.

Yu, W., Ray, P., & Motoc, T. (2008). WISH: A wireless mobile multimedia information system in healthcare using RFID. *Telemedicine and e-Health, 14,* 362–369.

CHAPTER 18

The Breast Cancer and Environment Research Centers: A Transdisciplinary Model

Kami J. Silk, Lindsay B. Neuberger, Samantha A. Nazione, and Janet Osuch

KEY TERMS

Transdisciplinary

Breast cancer

Group formation

Research centers

Abstract

Breast cancer, a potentially devastating disease that affects hundreds of thousands of women each year, requires comprehensive research approaches to lessen its prevalence and severity. Transdisciplinary centers, such as the Breast Cancer and Environment Research Centers (BCERC), are among the most innovative research models investigating major public health issues. The BCERC involve multiple team members from different areas of expertise (i.e., biology, epidemiology, communication, advocacy) to investigate and disseminate information related to environmental causes of breast cancer. This case study introduces and explains the transdisciplinary research approach through the eyes of Anna, a new graduate student joining the BCERC research team. The case study reveals connections with organizational communication and group development, as well as provides observations related to structure, stakeholder involvement, and collaborative relationships within the BCERC. Finally, the case study illustrates the transdisciplinary model of the BCERC as challenging in its application, yet beneficial in facilitating meaningful research outcomes.

Breast Cancer Background

Although great strides have been made in detecting and treating breast cancer, 192,370 women were diagnosed with breast cancer in the United States in 2009 alone, and 40,170 women died from the disease that same year (American Cancer Society, 2009). Breast cancer is the fifth leading cause of death for women in high-income countries (World Health Organization, 2009).

Breast cancer has not always been a primary research focus for scientists. In fact, breast cancer was once considered an unspeakable disease that received little scientific or media attention. Starting early in the twentieth century, a select group of highly motivated and privileged women used their connections with physicians and advertising executives to bring mainstream attention to breast cancer and to fuel research in the area (Osuch et al., under review). Later, female celebrities and United States First Lady Betty Ford spoke openly of their battles with breast cancer in an attempt to promote changes in the radical methods used to treat the disease.

The visibility of these movements led thousands of women to take charge of their health and fueled women's motivation to advocate tirelessly for research on a range of potential risk factors associated with breast cancer (Osuch et al., under review). Research into the causes of breast cancer is now a priority in the United States, garnering millions of dollars of research funds each year from the National Cancer Institute, National Institute for Environmental Health Sciences, and other government and private entities, including $35,000,000 over seven years (2003–2010) for The Breast Cancer and Environment Research Centers (BCERC).

The BCERC evolved out of the need for more comprehensive research models that would bring together a wide range of expertise to study and address large societal health problems. Some research has shown that certain chemicals found in the environment (e.g., BPA, PFOA)[1] and lifestyle factors during early childhood (e.g., eating a balanced diet to maintain a healthy weight) can impact later breast cancer risk (BCERC, 2009). The BCERC focuses research efforts to further understand such environmental antecedents to breast cancer and disseminate those findings to the public. This type of collaborative research is uniquely able to speed the dissemination of information to the public (Emmons, Viswanath, & Colditz, 2008). The centers' ultimate goal is to help effectively combat breast cancer across the lifespan by increasing participation in early steps designed to reduce harmful exposures and maintain healthy lifestyles.

The goal of this case study is to introduce the BCERC as an exemplar of transdisciplinary research. The case emphasizes links with organizational communication and group development, as well as provides observations related to structure, stakeholder involvement, and collaborative relationships within the BCERC. The case weaves the experience of Anna, a new graduate student in health communication who joins the BCERC as a research assistant, into its explication of the transdisciplinary model.

Transdisciplinarity Defined

Although much research and scholarship has been situated in strict disciplinary contexts (e.g., biology, psychology, communication), models to improve the quality and efficiency of scientific research have moved from disciplinary to interdisciplinary to multidisciplinary and now transdisciplinary research orientations. Disciplinary research approaches a problem using a specific paradigm primarily situated in one discipline, while interdisciplinary and multidisciplinary research draw from two or more disciplines, respectively. Alternatively, the transdisciplinary model merges varied disciplinary perspectives to construct a synthesis of concepts and methods in a completely new approach (Kreps & Maibach, 2008). Transdisciplinary research projects "transcend individual departments or specialized knowledge bases because they are intended to solve ... research questions that are, by definition, beyond the purview of the individual disciplines" (Gebbie, Rosenstock, & Hernandez, 2003, pp. 117–118). The transdisciplinary approach is perhaps the most novel model with its emphasis on the translation of research findings into plain language, thereby increasing the likelihood of a practical impact on the daily lives of lay individuals.

The assumptions behind the transdisciplinary research model are different than more traditional paradigms, requiring researchers and stakeholders (e.g., advocates, funding agencies) to broaden their purview regarding the participatory nature of research (Hall, Feng, Moser, Stokols, & Taylor, 2008). The BCERC may challenge researchers' mental models of how research should be conducted due primarily to its unique structure of teams, collaborations, and centers that are inclusive of advocates and social scientists (Senge, 2006). For the BCERC to succeed, stakeholders must maintain an open mind and constantly ask questions to foster the creativity and productivity associated with the transdisciplinary model (Senge, 2006).

Case Study

The Transdisciplinary BCERC Team

Anna is excited to join the BCERC research team at her university because breast cancer has impacted her life already. Anna's mother, a breast cancer survivor who has undergone surgery, chemotherapy, and radiation, has been cancer free for almost a year now. Elaine Harris, Ph.D., a communication professor and one of the principal investigators for the BCERC, has selected Anna as a research assistant because her undergraduate background in biology pairs nicely with Dr. Harris' need to translate scientific findings from animal and human studies to more easily understandable messages. Dr. Harris is confident that Anna will be able to adapt to the diverse composition of the BCERC's transdisciplinary focus with her biology background and communication research interests.

Prior to her first research team meeting with BCERC stakeholders, Anna wants to learn more about the BCERC and its structure so she looks at the project's national website. She finds that the project is funded by the National Institute of Environmental Health Sciences (NIEHS) and the National Cancer Institute (NCI). The BCERC is located across four research centers in the U.S. and includes collaborations among universities, cancer centers, and advocacy groups. She notes that advocates, biologists, epidemiologists, and communication researchers are organized across three "cores" at most of the centers: biology, epidemiology, and community outreach and translation cores (COTC). The three cores work together on a unique set of scientific questions focused on chemical, physical, biological, and social factors that work with genetic factors to possibly cause breast cancer. Anna notes that while each core has a definitive function, it is also the case that each BCERC core includes members from each of the other two cores to ensure that different stakeholder orientations contribute to the research, translation, and dissemination efforts of the BCERC. It seems that the BCERC is quite an extensive project with its blend of biologists who conduct research on mice and rats to examine the influence of certain chemicals, epidemiologists who study risk factors among cohorts of young girls, and COTC members who focus on translation and dissemination of breast cancer risk reduction messages. Anna is thus impressed.

Anna's Initial BCERC Meeting

As they walk across campus to the first BCERC meeting of the semester, Anna is focused on Dr. Harris as she describes the BCERC and its objectives. Dr. Harris explains that the BCERC was funded three years ago and that several different researchers across campus and even advocates would be at this meeting of the group. Anna feels a little nervous about working with the BCERC as her previous research experience has been in animal laboratories with one lead researcher to whom she reported; the BCERC model seems markedly different with the collection of epidemiologists, biologists, social scientists, and advocates sitting around the conference table. She figures she has a lot to learn. As the meeting progresses, she is surprised at the lively conversation that develops due to the conflicting perspectives represented by the stakeholders at the conference room table.

As Anna observes the group's communication patterns, she is reminded of something from a classic reading on group development which suggests that groups go through a predictable progression: forming, storming, norming, performing, and adjourning (Tuckman, 1965). According to Tuckman's model, after the initial formation of a group, members often undergo a period of uncertainty and sometimes even antagonism referred to as storming. Clearly, the BCERC members were doing a bit of storming as they asserted their differing views about when to communicate results from the ongoing research projects. After groups "storm," they establish common goals or norms that allow them to perform as a group, and ultimately adjourn or end after the group's goals are met. Anna believes the group will reach some agreement that will help them meet the primary objective of investigating environmental influences on breast cancer. She also realizes that perhaps direct and assertive conversations are necessary to promote the best action plans for the BCERC. It seems to Anna that everyone's viewpoint has added value for investigating and communicating about breast cancer.

Although she came with Dr. Harris, a member of the communication core, Anna finds it easy to take on the view of multiple stakeholders at the table. Due to her academic and personal experiences, she has much in common with the biologists, communication scientists, and advocates. Anna can discern the reasons behind the multiple viewpoints of everyone, and she notices that key differences in opinion revolve around stakeholder orientations as well as collaboration processes for translation and dissemination. It becomes very clear to Anna that reasons for participating in the BCERC vary widely across group members, and the reasons are based on the members' orientations to breast cancer as a personal, public health, and/or research problem. She can tell that all of the BCERC stakeholders care deeply about solving the breast cancer problem, and every stakeholder understands that environmental exposure is a potential culprit for an increased risk of breast cancer. The stakeholders seem to differ considerably, however, in how they enact these beliefs and values.

For example, Anna sees that the biology and epidemiology researchers are primarily focused on systematic and longitudinal research studies with human and animal subjects. They are interested in conducting research in their areas of expertise so they can contribute to our scientific understanding of breast cancer. Breast cancer advocates, in contrast, are focused on educating and communicating to the public about environmental risks to help lower potentially harmful exposures and behaviors, thus reducing breast cancer occurrence. Communication researchers, like Dr. Harris, are interested in conducting translational research so that messages can be readily understood and internalized by high-risk lay audiences. Anna wonders if all of these differing orientations are necessary for the BCERC to be effective in addressing their research questions.

Anna's Assessment of the BCERC's Transdisciplinary Model

Anna's first BCERC meeting wraps up after a little more than an hour and she has a number of questions written down in her notebook. Dr. Harris knows the BCERC model is quite different from Anna's previous research experiences and concludes she and Anna should debrief about the meeting.

"A lot to take in, isn't it?" Dr. Harris comments.

"Transdisciplinary research sounds like such an ideal model. I guess I thought it would be easier." Anna looks at Dr. Harris with a sense of resignation as they enter the elevator and head back to her office.

Dr. Harris, however, is optimistic about the process. "It *is* a good model, Anna, but just like anything else in the world there are both pros and cons to it, aren't there?" Dr. Harris grabs two bottles of water out of her mini fridge, hands one to Anna and invites her to sit across from her. "What did you notice?"

"Well, you've got a whole bunch of really smart people in one tiny conference room. I kind of felt out of place with only a bachelor's degree."

Dr. Harris laughs. "That is actually one of the key strengths of this model. We have a vast range of knowledge, skills, and abilities, which allows us to accomplish more as a team than individually—some might call it synergistic. It enriches the ideas we generate and how we problem solve. In the BCERC, we all depend on each other. The scientists carry out experiments on potential risk factors, the social scientists conduct message design research, and the advocates participate in translation and dissemination efforts." Anna knows the process is more complicated than that, but she appreciates Dr. Harris's attempt to distill it for her.

"It still seems like it might be really difficult to get things done with so many different perspectives competing with each other." If they can't make quick decisions, Anna ponders, how in the world would they ever get to the performing stage of Tuckman's model?

"The transdiciplinary approach probably does take longer at times, particularly when it comes to big decisions about research directions, but this model has actually facilitated the speed of the research process at times because of the communication mechanisms we have established." Dr. Harris pauses to take a sip of her water. "For example, each core has monthly telephone conferences, we have subcommittees that meet regularly, and we have an annual conference in the fall and an annual integration meeting in the spring. All of these things help us to communicate frequently and in depth, which allows us to move forward more quickly with new ideas. Often times, researchers do not know about others' work because it sometimes takes years for them to publish their findings."

"Years?" Anna repeats. She had no idea. She thought research findings would move faster in the digital communication age.

Dr. Harris nods. "Instead of waiting for studies to grind through the publication process, BCERC researchers are able to discuss their most recent findings so they can make more informed decisions about their work and its direction. The annual conferences in particular really allow everyone to share findings with each other in a timely manner. Did you know that biomedical research is infrequently translated and disseminated to the public? Rosenberg (2003) calls this deficit a national crisis! I don't know about that, but I can tell you from my experience with other grants that the COTC has been able to disseminate more information to communities on this project than on any other project I've ever worked on. Of course, the advocates have had a large hand in that."

"I thought it was really great that you let the advocates sit in on the research team meetings." Anna had made a mental note to tell her mother about the advocate presence. Maybe her mother would want to be involved in the future.

"Actually, I think it's great that *they* let *us* sit in on those meetings." Dr. Harris nods with sincerity. "The BCERC wouldn't exist if these women hadn't lobbied for years to get funding to study environmental exposures. Besides providing input from a perspective of someone who has been touched by the disease, they've helped shape the BCERC research agenda and been critical in the recruitment and retention of research participants, which is crucial for the longitudinal epidemiology studies. Most of the advocates are experts in their own right and know more than I do about the science of breast cancer. They are amazing resources."

"It seemed like certain people weren't in favor of some of the decisions being made though." Although Anna did not catch every comment made in the meeting, it was evident that everyone was not always completely content with the progression of the discussion and subsequent decisions.

"Well, we're all here to fight breast cancer from an environmental perspective, but we often differ on the best way to meet that common goal. Are you familiar with the precautionary principle?" Anna shakes her head. She'd heard the term used several times in the meeting but didn't want to ask what it meant.

Dr. Harris jumps into lecture mode. "In general, BCERC advocates support the precautionary principle, which according to Raffensperger and Tickner (1999) calls for protective actions toward the environment, even when the evidence of harm remains uncertain. This is why advocates promote communicating potential risks as soon as possible, which contradicts the scientific norms of researchers who wait for conclusive evidence to be revealed over time."

Anna nods her head thoughtfully.

Dr. Harris continues, "Overall, biologists and epidemiologists are generally more conservative regarding public dissemination of scientific findings, particularly those findings that are not yet published in scientific journals. The tension about *when* to communicate research findings is not uncommon in contexts of emerging science as researchers struggle to fit their findings into the larger puzzle of related research and advocates attempt to warn the public about potential dangers. These two goals often conflict with the advocates consistently supporting the precautionary principle to communicate research results earlier rather than later if any evidence of potential harm is possible."

"That's a difficult decision." Anna could clearly imagine the arguments for both sides. "I guess I would want to know if there was something that *might* help my mother remain cancer free, but I also wouldn't want her to get excited about possibilities that scientists couldn't agree upon—that would be confusing." Anna's mother is constantly seeking out new information that could improve her chances of remaining cancer free and her family's chances of prevention; however, if that information is incorrect, it wouldn't help anyone.

"Well, as Baralt (2009) noted, the different perspectives are coming from different backgrounds. Unfortunately, this can lead to mistrust, perceptions of disrespect, and general frustration for the BCERC members. Our BCERC team has different interests, training, and goals in many ways. The advocates' desire to eradicate breast cancer is an intense and personal one, whereas researchers are more focused on a longitudinal scientific approach because of their training and need for continued research funding." Dr. Harris rolled back in her chair and pulled a book out from a low hanging shelf. She placed it in front of Anna. "Have you read Peter Senge's work on the *Fifth Discipline*?"

Anna shakes her head to indicate her lack of familiarity with Senge's work.

"He talks about the structure of organizations and one component is personal mastery, which is about learning how to obtain your vision given reality. I think this was a big challenge for everyone in the BCERC, but Senge encourages us not to temper our vision because of reality, and instead recommends we learn to work around any barriers to create real results."

"Sounds like that's probably easier said than done." During the meeting, Anna had felt frustrated at times listening to what she perceived as great ideas and then hearing another member of the group explain all the reasons they could not do them. "And there are just so many people to please in order to get a consensus."

Dr. Harris knows the structure of the BCERC is challenging with its multi-center and transdisciplinary approach, but she also wants Anna to understand the value of the process.

"I think it's easy for each of us to get caught up in our own way of thinking and our own discipline's work. Senge would tell us we struggle with team learning. It's difficult for all of us to put the needs of the BCERC as a whole before our personal or departmental needs. We started with a shared goal, but that isn't enough to help us bond in order to create the most effective outcomes. I'm sure you've learned from projects during your undergraduate experience how difficult group work can be."

"Definitely." Anna smiles. "I've dealt with slackers, bossy team members, know-it-alls, jokers, and some really focused and conscientious group members too."

"Working with the BCERC can be similar. We're all invested in this project, but that doesn't guarantee we'll all agree or even be able to get all of our schedules to line up for a meeting. Anna, I want you to know that many great outcomes have already emerged from this project. We have developed public health messages that provide risk reduction recommendations for young girls and women who are at high risk for breast cancer. This was a deliberative decision-making process that narrowed the BCERC research findings to specific chemicals that should be avoided. The biologists worked with advocates and communication researchers to make this happen, and we were able to obtain supplemental grant funding to empirically test the messages with our target audience of mothers. We are proud of these accomplishments but also know that the BCERC model is a work in progress and in its early stages of development. We are building the model as we go."

Anna feels thankful for a few minutes of Dr. Harris's time but knows she has to rush to make it to class on time.

"Now don't forget to take a look over those messages and make revisions based on the advocate feedback we got today." Dr. Harris reminds Anna. "We have another meeting in a few weeks and we want to make sure these messages are ready for dissemination soon."

Anna assures Dr. Harris she will work on them over the weekend as she grabs her bag and heads for class. She walks down the hallway content with her new research assignment and thankful to have a better understanding of the research team and how she can fit in. She also feels like the transdisciplinary model of the BCERC has room for improvement and hopes to be a part of these improvements as the project's newest team member.

This chapter was made possible by the Breast Cancer and the Environment Research Centers grant number U01-ES12800 from the National Institute of Environmental Health Sciences (NIEHS), and the National Cancer Institute (NCI), NIH, DHHS. Its contents are solely the responsibility of the authors and do not necessarily represent the official views of the NIEHS or NCI, NIH.

NOTE

1   Perfluoroctanoic Acid (PFOA) and Bisphenol A (BPA) are man-made chemical compounds used in many consumer products that contain plastic or rubber. Research on mice and rats indicates these chemicals as potential risk factors for cancer. The BCERC is currently studying these chemicals to understand how they function as a risk factor in human models. Fact sheets about these chemicals are available at www.bcerc.org.

Discussion Questions

1. How did Anna's background prepare her for working with the BCERC team? How would your background prepare you for working with the BCERC team?

2. Identify strengths and weaknesses of the transdisciplinary model. How could weaknesses be built into strengths?

3. What roles should advocates, biologists, epidemiologists, and communication researchers play in the transdisciplinary model? How much should their roles intersect with each other?

4. When do you think researchers should share scientific findings with the lay public? What role do ethics play in making this decision?

5. What other societal problems merit the use of a transdisciplinary research approach? Why? What stakeholders would be essential for the transdisciplinary team? Why?

References

American Cancer Society, Inc. (2009). *How many women get breast cancer?* Retrieved from www.cancer .org/docroot/CRI/content/CRI_2_2_1X_How_many_people_get_breast_cancer_5.asp?sitearea

Baralt, L. (2009, August). Lay-expert collaboration in federal environmental breast cancer research: A progress report. Presented at the annual American Sociological Association meeting in San Francisco, CA. Retrieved from http://www.allacademic.com//meta/p_mla_apa_research_ citation/3/0/5/9/3/pages305935/p305935-1.php

Breast Cancer and the Environment Research Centers (BCERC). (2010). Retrieved from http://www .bcerc.org

Emmons, K. M., Viswanath, K., & Colditz, G. A. (2008). The role of transdisciplinary collaboration in translating and disseminating health research, lessons learned, and exemplars of success. *The American Journal of Preventative Medicine, 35*, S204–S210.

Gebbie, K., Rosenstock, L., & Hernandez, L. M. (Eds.). (2003). *Who will keep the public healthy: Educating health professionals for the 21st century.* Institute of Medicine. Washington, DC: The National Academies Press.

Hall, K. L., Feng, A. X., Moser, R. P., Stokols, D., & Taylor, B. K. (2008). Moving the science of team science forward, collaboration and creativity. *The American Journal of Preventative Medicine, 35*, S243–S249.

Kreps, G. L., & Maibach, E. W. (2008). Transdisciplinary science: The nexus between communication and public health. *Journal of Communication, 58*, 732–748.

Osuch, J. R., Price, C., Barlow, J., Miller, K., Hernick, A., & Fonfa, A. (under review). An historical perspective on breast cancer activism in the United States: From education and support to partnership in scientific research. *Journal of Women's Health.*

Raffensperger, C., & Tickner, J. (Eds.) (1999). *Protecting public health and the environment: Implementing the precautionary principle.* Washington, DC: Island Press.

Rosenberg, R. N. (2003). Translating biomedical research to the bedside: A national crisis and call to action. *Journal of the American Medical Association, 289*, 1305–1306.

Senge, P. M. (2006). *The fifth discipline: The art and practice of learning the organization.* New York: Random House.

Tuckman, B. (1965). Development sequence in small groups. *Psychological Bulletin, 63*, 384–399.

World Health Organization. (2009). *Women's health.* Retrieved from http://www.who.int/mediacentre/ factsheets/fs334/en/

SECTION VII

Framing Public Health Initiatives

CHAPTER 19

The HPV Mandatory Vaccination Controversy
Creating a Frame of Perspective for Public Health Initiatives

Jennifer A. Malkowski, Valerie R. Renegar, and George N. Dionisopoulos

KEY TERMS

Vaccination

Public health rhetoric

HPV

Frames of perspective

Abstract

In June 2006, the vaccine GARDASIL® was approved by the U.S. Food and Drug Administration (FDA) as a way to prevent infection from four strains of the Human Papillomavirus (HPV) responsible for cervical cancer and genital warts. Less than one year after FDA approval, Texas Governor Rick Perry issued an Executive Order requiring HPV vaccination for girls entering sixth grade as of September 2008. A debate soon emerged regarding state government's obligation to safeguard the health of its people and the rights of individuals to make their own decisions about matters affecting their health and their children's health. Two prominent sides emerged and competed to classify HPV and its causes to support or counter mandatory vaccination. To understand the dynamics of discussions about vaccination policy, this chapter applies frame analysis to the central rhetorical texts (Goffman, 1974) shaping the mandatory vaccination debate. In doing so, this chapter examines the implications of political framing as a communicative strategy used to legitimize, or delegitimize, particular policy actions to illuminate the types of factors policymakers consider when promoting particular policy actions.

Issues of public health and personal responsibility are becoming increasingly visible in modern American culture. In recent years, public discussions about vaccination technologies have highlighted an ongoing tension between public health and personal responsibility. Although vaccination technologies have successfully worked to eradicate easily communicable diseases, more than $1 billion is awarded annually to vaccine causalities under the National Childhood Vaccine Injury Act of 1986 (Fisher, 2007). This discrepancy has created a polarized understanding of how vaccines should serve the general public. Individuals who oppose vaccination technologies contend that vaccinations can contribute to health risks of conditions other than the disease the vaccine is meant to prevent (Fisher, 2007). These individuals also suggest that those risks associated with vaccines can be higher for some people because of genetic and other biological differences, and that policy officials do not take these differences into consideration when making decisions regarding public health (Fisher, 2007; Whalen, 2006). However, pro-vaccination advocates argue that when an individual exercises his/her so-called right to refuse vaccination, they are placing others at risk and attribute a general rise in public health risks preventable through vaccination, such as tuberculosis and measles, to individuals refusing to vaccinate themselves and their children (Steinhauer & Harris, 2008). Because the climate surrounding vaccination technologies has largely been defined by these two competing positions, health professionals charged with promoting new health advances seeking to eradicate certain communicable diseases inevitably face arduous challenges when introducing vaccines to the general public.

In June 2006, a vaccine that blocks women from infection from four strains of the human papillomavirus (HPV), the world's most common sexually transmitted disease (STD),[1] was approved by the U.S. Food and Drug Administration (FDA). More than 100 strains of HPV have been identified as transmittable via genital contact (Kaiser Family Foundation, 2010). The majority of those strains are asymptomatic and will resolve on their own. However, 30 HPV strains have been linked to genital warts, cervical cancer, and other less common forms of genital and oral cancers (Gardner, 2007; Kaiser Family Foundation, 2010). At the time of its arrival to market, GARDASIL® was introduced as the only way to prevent infection from two strains of HPV thought to be responsible for 70% of all cases of cervical cancer and two other strains of HPV responsible for about 90% of all cases of genital warts (Centers for Disease Control and Prevention [CDC], 2010). Although GARDASIL® could not protect against all strains of HPV, the deputy secretary of the Department of Health and Human Services called the HPV vaccine, "a major step forward in public health protection" (Rubin, 2006, ¶ 4) and insisted that due to GARDASIL®, the United States could "now include the worst types of HPV and most cervical cancer among the diseases that no one need suffer and die from" (Gellene, 2006, p. A4). To facilitate this prospect, therefore, the question of how, and to whom, this vaccine should be administered became a topic of debate.

According to the American Cancer Society, across the United States, in 2004, 28,720 women were estimated to have died of genital system cancers (i.e., uterine cervix, uterine corpus, ovary, vulva, vagina, and other genital) (Jemal et al., 2004, Table 1). Among residents of Texas alone, an estimated 3,400 cases of uterine cervix and uterine corpus cancer were detected in 2004 (Jemal et al., 2004, Table 4). Therefore, while national awareness campaigns and public policy officials introduced and actively promoted the GARDASIL® vaccine (CDC, 2010; Dooren, 2006), Texas Governor Rick Perry pursued a more aggressive approach and issued a state mandate to vaccinate sixth grade girls in Texas (Associated Press, 2007). In the ensuing discussion, he and parental rights advocates publicly debated how the HPV vaccination should best be distributed to the public. This debate illuminates the tension between state "government's obligation to safeguard the health of its people and the rights of individuals to make their own decisions about matters affecting their health and their children" (Hendricks, 2007, p. F1).

This particular debate presents students, scholars, health professionals, and politicians with an opportunity to analyze ways that public and private health agendas are promoted in the public sphere and the resonance of each with the general public.

This chapter begins by tracing the history of U.S. vaccination policy and then discusses details of the 2007 HPV vaccination case. Following an introduction of frame analysis, two competing mandatory HPV vaccination frames of perspective are compared. This comparison encourages the key stakeholders above to rethink strategies for framing public health issues to maintain control in debates concerning mandatory health behaviors.

U.S. Vaccination Policy

Two historical events are pivotal to the initial acceptance of mandatory vaccines in the United States: World War I with the introduction of the influenza vaccine and World War II with the introduction of the polio vaccine (Oshinsky, 2007). The influenza vaccination was initially mandated within the military where its success abroad encouraged compliance at home. Shortly thereafter, a vaccine against polio "led to the largest public health experiment in American history" by recruiting two million volunteers (Oshinsky, 2007, ¶ 7). Dr. Leroy Burney, the Surgeon General of the Public Health Service at the time, attributed the success of the vaccine to the fact "that many people [were] beginning to heed the advice of physicians and public health officials" (Zwirn, 2007, ¶ 1). However, the United States has experienced a shift in medical research from physicians and public health officials on behalf of the public to a venture of pharmaceutical companies motivated by profit (Conrad, 2007). This shift has led to a general distrust in the motives behind government vaccination mandates and poses an inherent challenge to those politicians framing messages to address public health concerns (Oshinsky, 2007).

The 2007 HPV Vaccination Controversy

More than a decade ago, the prevalence of STDs in American society was deemed a hidden epidemic (Eng & Butler, 1997) and little has changed since then. Recent studies show that STDs and sexually transmitted infections (STIs) have achieved epidemic status (Brown, 2007; "STDs," 2008). Although government agencies, public health organizations, non-governmental agencies (NGOs), students, scholars, and media outlets continue to deliberate publicly about STDs, only half of the people who test positive for HPV intend to disclose that information to intimate partners (Kahn et al., 2005). In line with conclusions offered about disclosure patterns for people who are HIV positive (see Greene, Derlega, Yep, & Petronio, 2003), these findings suggest that individual privacy concerns currently trump concerns for the greater good. Further evidence of this shift away from a public health agenda was witnessed in public deliberation about the best method for distributing the HPV vaccination.

When Texas Governor Rick Perry issued an Executive Order that would require the HPV vaccination of all girls entering sixth grade in Texas as of September 2008 (Associated

Press, 2007), he met opposition from parental rights advocates and pro-abstinence groups who voiced medical and ethical concerns regarding mandatory vaccinations. This analysis of the text of Governor Perry's State-of-the-State Address given on February 6, 2007, and the discourse of Perry's opposition presented in February 2007 articles from the top circulating U.S. newspapers[2] reveal why the private family decision frame of perspective succeeded over a public health agenda. The opportunity to eliminate the threat of cervical cancer, a disease that continues to kill women worldwide, would seem to be a unified call to action; however, this case suggests that how HPV, its causes, and vaccination policy were framed contributed to an ongoing public-versus-private interests debate.

Frames of Perspective

According to Goffman (1974), we actively organize and interpret our life experiences to make sense of them. Goffman used the term "frames" to define the "principles of organization that govern events—at least social ones—and our subjective involvement in them" (pp. 10–11). The act of framing involves the selection of some aspects of a perceived reality that are made more salient in a communicating text to promote a particular "problem definition, causal interpretation, moral evaluation, and/or treatment recommendation" (Entman, 1993, p. 52). Frames, thus, define the world in terms of benefits and costs and are, therefore, as important to social interaction and progress as language (Edelman, 1993; Entman, 1993).

Traditionally "principles of organization that govern events" have been discussed according to how a frame establishes the parameters of political positions (Goffman, 1974, pp. 10–11). A frame of perspective differs from the way frames have been commonly understood in communication literature in that a frame functions as the limits of a particular view of reality whereas a frame of perspective functions as a template to understand reality. Any given frame of perspective creates a narrative about the particular issue it depicts, and how well a frame of perspective resonates with larger cultural narratives determines the success level of that particular frame. Moreover, narratives that successfully resonate with the general public as a whole reveal certain cultural tendencies that lend an understanding and predictability toward specific frames of perspective. To better understand the nuances of frames of perspectives as they relate to larger cultural narratives, let's briefly discuss how Americans have come to understand end-of-life decision-making. With regard to frames of perspectives, it can be argued that within the United States, end-of-life discourse is characterized by the belief that Americans have a right to die a "dignified" death (Hyde & McSpiritt, 2007, p. 152). We suggest that over time, frames of perspective have worked to actively distinguish death as a symbol of life to embed end-of-life discourse within a larger narrative that defines what it means to live an American life. In other words, across American culture, the right to die a dignified death is often understood as a matter of freewill, autonomy, and/or "quality of life" (Hyde & McSpiritt, 2007, p. 163). Therefore, when there is evidence to suggest that an American audience embraces certain frames of perspective, those frames of perspective lend insight into a larger narrative that defines what it means to be American (i.e., free, autonomous, and virtuous). We suggest that a similar framing process characterizes HPV vaccination discourse. Therefore, defining which frames of perspectives are present, and which subsequent narrative is most successful, can help us to understand the larger narratives framing the public HPV debate.

Perry's Frame of Perspective

Political officials work to create and influence public beliefs about the causes of particular outcomes to justify some actions and to build opposition to others (Edelman, 1993). One method to achieve this end is to place information in a unique context so that certain elements of an issue receive more attention from the general public (Kahneman & Tversky, 1984). It is important to note that a frame of perspective operates to actively influence an audience's judgment of a situation. That is, although frames of perspective may appear to emerge from an organic, audience-centered process, ultimately a frame of perspective is created by, and for, the goals of the speaker. Within the HPV mandatory vaccination debate, Perry's frame of perspective works to establish the role of government as that of a moral guardian with the responsibility of making decisions to save lives. This analysis reveals that Perry's frame of perspective is defined by the images of cancer as an impending enemy, the vaccine recipient as a victim, and the solution as morally good. Using these images, Perry aligns his argument with a larger narrative of moral obligation.

Impending Enemy

In 2007, cervical cancer was predicted to strike about 11,500 women in the United States and claim an estimated 3,670 lives (Hendricks, 2007). The overarching problem that the virus and cancer represent centers on chronic health conditions facing society; however, the specific cause of cancer-related deaths remains contested: blame the virus that causes abnormal cervical cells, or blame cancer once it has been found in the tissues of the cervix?[3] The ambiguity surrounding causal attribution results in a discursive opening from which oppositional frames of perspective can emerge (Mukherjee, 2000). Perry chose to align his definition of cancer with the assumption that cancer is a villain that a leader needs to eliminate.

Frames that contain emotionally charged words such as "evil" or "cancer" are likely to evoke similar reactions across audiences and are often persuasive (Entman, 2003). The section of Perry's (2007) address concerning healthcare began with a narrative describing a young girl's "fight for [her] life against a deadly disease," a fight that the child, Marin, ultimately lost at the age of four (¶ 41). Perry declared "for all the little Marin's of this world, we must do everything in our power to defeat cancer" (¶ 43). The age of the girl (four) and the type of cancer (brain cancer) did not directly illustrate the typical experience associated with cervical cancer; however, it did help to distinguish the enemy as one that preyed on small children. Perry used the technique of problem-as-cancer to help define the consequences of HPV as one that involved the safety of children whose well-being was society's responsibility.

Perry stated, "It is a tragedy whenever we lose someone to a deadly disease, and it breaks my heart when people die prematurely from conditions that are completely preventable," thus prefacing the importance and promised effectiveness of his initiative (¶ 57). He then framed the HPV vaccine as the "hope of ultimate victory against this disease" and introduced his Executive Order (¶ 45). Perry's frame of perspective highlighted the need to protect the public against a deadly, impending enemy, more specifically, the need to protect young girls against cervical cancer.

Girls as Victims

Protecting children against enemies is something that core American values seek to ensure. In this way, the term "child" evokes emotion across audiences. Such symbols (i.e., "enemies" and "children") invoke emotion and capitalize on already established cultural and social ideologies (Zahariadis, 2003). In June 2006, the FDA approved GARDASIL® for use in "girls and women ages 9 through 26" (Rubin, 2006, ¶ 8). This large age range presents a broad spectrum for how the image of the vaccine recipient might be constructed. For instance, while a 26-year-old woman may be regarded as an autonomous individual within American culture, a 9-year-old child is often regarded as vulnerable. Perry's choice to define the vaccine recipients as young girls justifies the state acting on their behalf and in, what Perry has decided is, their best interest. Elaborating further, children are cast as vulnerable and, thus, in need of protection and guidance.

Governor Perry (2007) devoted a portion of his State-of-the-State Address to "the human side of the healthcare issue" and proceeded to depict the face, life, and needs of that human side throughout his speech (¶ 39). Perry reminded the audience that "cancer does not discriminate based on age," and that "it [could] strike . . . the smallest of children" (¶ 41). Throughout his speech, Perry reiterated terms like "smallest" (¶ 41), "young" (¶ 47), "youngest" (¶ 58), "too young" (¶ 52), "little" (¶ 43), "precious" (¶ 42), and "prematurely" (¶ 57) to portray the victim of disease as a young, helpless child with her long life ahead of her. Uncertainty surrounding how HPV is understood among the general population presented Perry with an opportunity to define vaccine recipients as young and helpless, thereby necessitating government intervention as a moral obligation aimed at protecting life.

Morally Good

Perry's frame of perspective aligns with a popular media trend that tends to "frequently endorse the self-transcendence values of universalism and benevolence" with regard to cancer treatment and prevention (Hoffman & Slater, 2007, p. 69). Therefore, Perry taps into two related narratives that correspond with higher level principles of universalism and benevolence: religious faith and American cultural ideologies. In accordance with these characteristics, Perry (2007) introduced the section of his State-of-the-State Address with the following claim: "A man of faith once told me that the statistics of death are one out of one;" that is, everyone will ultimately meet death. This quotation served to define Perry as a man aligned with religious affiliation (¶ 40). In his concluding remarks, Perry (2007) spoke directly to his opposition: "There will be critics of what we attempt. Some will fight for the status quo, even when change is needed for the greater good" (¶ 133). Taken together, these two statements help Perry bring together the concepts of fighting for that which is good and that which emerges from a faith-based calling as a way to redefine the situation in terms of moral obligation, a moral obligation that resonates both with being a person of faith and with being American. Therefore, Perry strategically incorporated terms associated with his nationality and faith-based ideology—"good," "high road," "greater good," and "the good fight"—to align with the moral obligations of his audience. Furthermore, Perry acknowledged that "our task is not easy, but none of us were sent here to do what is easy, but to do what is right" (¶ 133). This statement reinforced faith-based ideologies by claiming that we were "sent here" to do "what is right," implying purpose associated with humanity and morals associated with action. This method likely resonated with members of his audience who share a similar conviction that pursuing the "greater good" is a moral obligation.

Parental Rights' Frame of Perspective

Those who opposed Perry's Executive Order share a frame of perspective that understands HPV as a consequence of the "conscious will." Subsequently, the moral concerns of parents are represented through a redefinition of the problem as an STD, not cancer, and a redefinition of the recipient as a young woman, not a helpless child. This analysis reveals that the parental rights' frame of perspective is defined by the images of government mandates as infringing on private rights and responsibilities associated with their children's moral guidance and safety. Using these images, the parental rights aligns their argument with a larger narrative of responsible parenting.

Moral Guidance

Within the United States, the ethical principles of public health have encouraged individuals to vaccinate themselves and their children against easily communicable diseases (Hendricks, 2007). HPV is not necessarily easily communicable, however, because the infection is transmitted by sexual contact. One parental advocate commented that "to require little innocent girls to have a vaccine against a disease that is linked to sexual immorality is an outrage" (Talley, 2007, p. B8). HPV and cancer prevention are reframed in terms of a "lifestyle choice" (Uribarri, 2007, p. B3) by those who interpret the disease more in terms of how it is spread rather than its consequences. One U.S. Senator articulated that "HPV is not caught by sitting next to someone in class but by sexual contact, which often is a lifestyle choice," and that "using school laws … to mandate vaccination against a sexually transmitted infection, is to use the ends to justify the means" (Hendricks, 2007, p. F1). Through a redefinition of the problem, parental rights advocates thus reframed the mandate as superfluous and offensive to parents who make health decisions on behalf of their daughters.

One parent explained, "I'm insulted by [the government] trying to tell me what's right for my children." The parent continued, "I'm a good parent. I tell [my child] what's right and wrong" (Uribarri, 2007, p. B3). This perspective frames the potential vaccination recipient as a young woman who was familiar with her sexuality, or who soon would be, and the problem as dependent on parenting and the recipient's ability to choose between "right and wrong." This perspective also frames the solution of HPV in terms of abstinence. As of 2010, Texas is an abstinence-only sex education state that designates issues regarding pre-marital sexual activity as a private, not governmental, responsibility. A conservative parent commented, "If the state can mandate the HPV vaccine, then why not mandate the distribution of condoms to protect our children against other STDs? This is not the state's business" (Trawick, 2007, p. B6). By reframing Perry's position as contradictory to core conservative Texan values, many parents worked to redefine their role as active and responsible parents.

Safety

The safety concerns of the conservative parents dismantled Perry's "solution" by emphasizing its scientific uncertainty surrounding the vaccine. They also stressed that they believe government is incapable of making the healthiest choice for each child. One concerned mother illustrated the complexities of the HPV infection and vaccination when she said, "I am generally a big supporter of vaccines. However, mandatory vaccines are for infectious diseases—such as polio. Cancer is not infectious" (Thomas, 2007, p. B8). Additionally, "this drug [the HPV vaccine] has no track record" (Delaney, 2007, p. B6). Carreyrou (2007) concurs, reporting that of the more than 25,000 patients who participated in clinical trials of GARDASIL®, only 1,184 were preteen girls, which can be seen as a "thin base of testing upon which to make a vaccine mandatory" (p. D1). The scientific uncertainty accompanying the short timeframe between FDA approval and Perry's Executive Order yielded an adversarial reframing of Perry's mandate as an abuse of governmental jurisdiction and an irresponsible decision threatening the health of children.

A general distrust in new scientific advances is articulated by parents who comment that "This vaccine is new! What guarantees do we have that we won't see these females or their offspring giving birth to babies with 'unexplained' defects or chromosomal abnormalities?" (Talley, 2007, ¶ 3), and that "they say no serious side effects have appeared. That's not a guarantee they won't appear down the road. Nor is the FDA's approval any assurance. Remember Celebrex? Vioxx? Prempro? Thalidomide?" (Delaney, 2007, p. B6). These individuals illustrate a general distrust of political intrusion in private matters by highlighting the uncertain outcomes linked to this vaccine and past governmental agency failures. One parent articulated the cost of government interference by claiming that "[a government mandate] replaces the parents with the state. You're not only turning parents' rights upside down, but you're also subjecting children to an experimental vaccine" (Hoppe, 2007, ¶ 20). Crucial also is high uncertainty concerning whether the initial vaccination will offer lifetime protection, or if another strain of HPV will develop if the strains that are currently most prevalent are eliminated (Carreyrou, 2007).

Parental rights advocates also emphasized their role as guardians of their children's health. One parent commented, "Give us the facts, let us work with our doctors to make our own decisions about whether the known (and unknown) risks are worth it, and keep the governor and state out of this decision" (Talley, 2007, p. B8). These opinions were also voiced within the political sphere. Republican Lt. Governor David Dewhurst commented "that while the HPV vaccine can play a very important role in preventing cervical cancer, I don't think government should ever presume to know better than the parents" (MacLaggan, 2007, p. A1). These parental rights advocates opposed Perry's mandate as a violation of private citizen rights concerning the health and well-being of their children. As audience members, then, parental rights advocates redefined Perry's "solution" to cervical cancer risk as one that disregarded their ability to become educated about scientific advances, make responsible decisions regarding the health of their daughters, and become positive change agents.

NOTES

1   More than 25% of U.S. women ages 14 to 59 are infected with HPV, which is believed to cause most cases of cervical cancer (Mundell, 2007). According to the Centers for Disease Control and Prevention (CDC), at least half of men and women will carry the virus at some point in their lives (CDC, 2010).

2   This study analyzed arguments found in the following national newspapers: *USA Today, The Wall Street Journal, The New York Times, Los Angeles Times*, and *The Washington Post*, which were the top five circulating papers in the United States as of May 8, 2006 (Associated Press, 2006), and the following Texas newspapers: *The Fort Worth Star, The Houston Chronicle, The Austin American-Statesman, The Dallas Morning News*, and *The San Antonio Express*.

3   According to the National Cancer Institute (2010), stages are used to describe the progression of cervical cancer in order to classify patients and prescribe treatment options. When abnormal cells are first detected in the innermost lining of a patient's cervix, that patient is said to be experiencing Stage 0 cervical cancer. Abnormal cells may lead to cancer. A patient is diagnosed with Stage I cervical cancer when cancer forms in the cervix. Stage II-IV diagnoses classify a patient according to which areas of the body cancer has spread to outside of the cervix.

Discussion Questions

1. The case suggests that issues like mandatory vaccination pit those concerned about public health against those who hold strict views regarding individual privacy. To what extent are these concerns mutually exclusive? Consider how a single frame of perspective might incorporate both public and private concerns at the same time. What might an integrated frame look like?

2. Can you identify other narratives within the field of public health? What do these other narratives suggest concerning the predictable nature of cultural tendencies in the United States? How might they be applied to this issue?

3. This chapter suggests that there was a definitional ambiguity in the way cervical cancer was discussed in this public health debate. What was the nature of the ambiguity and what other public health issues evidence a similar definitional ambiguity that can help account for differing perspectives concerning how the issue should be addressed?

4. In his State-of-the-State Address, Governor Rick Perry used martial metaphors such as "the good fight on the front lines," or that his critics would "fight for the status quo." How might these metaphors have had a role in provoking the sharp response to his plan for mandatory HPV vaccinations? What other types of metaphors might he have used to explain the reasoning behind this plan?

5. At what point do private decisions concerning health care become public issues? Are there lessons from this case study that can help us to map how future, similar discussions should proceed to ensure that most stakeholders can be satisfied with the decision?

References

Associated Press. (2006, May 8). Circulation at the top 20 newspapers. *Editor & Publisher*. Retrieved from http://www.editorandpublisher.com

Associated Press. (2007, February 5). Texas governor urged against cancer order. *New York Times*. Retrieved from http://www.newyorktimes.com

Brown, D. (2007, February 28). Millions in U.S. infected with HPV: Study finds virus strikes a third of women by age 24. *Washington Post*, p. A1.

Carreyrou, J. (2007, February 7). Moves to vaccinate girls for cervical cancer draw fire as Merck lobbies states to require shots, some fret over side effects, morals. *Wall Street Journal*, p. D1.

Centers for Disease Control and Prevention. (2010, July). *HPV information for young women*. Retrieved from http://www.cdc.gov/std/hpv/STDFact-HPV-vaccine-young-women.htm

Conrad, P. (2007). *The medicalization of society: On the transformation of human conditions into treatable disorders*. Baltimore, MD: John Hopkins University Press.

Delaney, K. (2007, February 7). Many questions remain. *San Antonio Express*, p. B6.

Dooren, J. C. (2006, June 9). Merck cervical-cancer vaccine is approved for use in women; Gardasil could sharply cut key viruses behind disease; CDC to set forth guidelines. *Wall Street Journal*, p. A16.

Edelman, M. (1993). Contestable categories and public opinion. *Political Communication, 10*, 231–242.

Eng, T. R., & Butler, W. T. (Eds.). (1997). The hidden epidemic: Confronting sexually transmitted diseases. *Committee on Prevention and Control of Sexually Transmitted Diseases. Institute of Medicine*. Washington, DC: National Academy Press.

Entman, R. M. (1993). Framing: Toward clarification of a fractured paradigm. *Journal of Communication, 43*, 51–58.

Entman, R. M. (2003). Cascading activation: Contesting the White House's frame after 9/11. *Political Communication, 20*, 415–432.

Fisher, B. L. (2007, February 1). Risk, racism, and the HPV vaccine [Letter to the editor]. *Washington Post*, p. A14.

Gardner, A. (2007, February 11). Drugmaker assists in pushing for mandate for HPV vaccination. *Washington Post*, C5.

Gellene, D. (2006, June 9). Cervical cancer vaccine approved: The FDA OKs a drug that could prevent a leading killer of women worldwide. But some fear the cost of the shots will be a deterrent. *Los Angeles Times*, p. A4.

Goffman, E. (1974). *Frame analysis: An essay on the organization of experience*. Cambridge, MA: Harvard University Press.

Greene, K., Derlega, V., Yep, G., & Petronio, S. (2003). *Privacy and disclosure of HIV in interpersonal relationships: A sourcebook for researchers and practitioners*. Mahwah, NJ: Lawrence Erlbaum Associates.

Hendricks, M. (2007, February 5). HPV vaccine: Who chooses?; Because immunization can prevent cervical cancer, bills seek to mandate shots. Some say such measures are ethically suspect. *Los Angeles Times*, p. F1.

Hoffman, L. H., & Slater, M. D. (2007). Evaluating public discourse in newspaper opinion articles: Values-framing and integrative complexity in substance and health policy issues. *Journalism & Mass Communication Quarterly, 84*, 58–74.

Hoppe, C. (2007, February 3). Perry orders HPV vaccine. *Dallas Morning News*. Retrieved May 7, 2007 from LexisNexis database.

Hyde, M. J., & McSpiritt, S. (2007). Coming to terms with perfection: The case of Terri Schiavo. *Quarterly Journal of Speech, 93*, 150–178.

Jemal, A., Tiwari, R. C., Murray, T., Ghafoor, A., Samuels, A., Ward, E., Feuer, E. J., & Thun, M. J. (2004). Cancer statistics, 2004. *CA: A Cancer Journal for Clinicians, 54*, 8–29.

Kahn, J. A., Slap, G. B., Bernstein, D. I., Kollar, L. M., Tissot, A. M., & Hillard, P. A., (2005). Psychological, behavioral, and interpersonal impact of human papillomavirus and Pap test results. *Journal of Women's Health, 14*, 650–659.

Kahneman, D., & Tversky, A. (1984). Choice, values, and frames. *Political Communication, 10*, 55–76.

Kaiser Family Foundation. (2010, February). *HPV vaccines and cancer in the U.S.* Retrieved from www.kaiseredu.org

MacLaggan, C. (2007, February 6). Perry's HPV vaccine order draws backlash from GOP. *Austin American-Statesman*, p. A1.

Mukherjee, R. (2000). "Now you see it, now you don't:" Naming privacy, framing policy. *Critical Studies in Media Communication, 17*, 469–492.

Mundell, E. J. (2007, February 27) 1 in 4 U.S. women carries cervical cancer virus. *Washington Post*, Retrieved February 16, 2007 from the Proquest database.

National Cancer Institute. (2010, April). *Stages of cervical cancer*. Retrieved from www.cancer.gov

Oshinsky, D. (2007, February 4). Preventive medicine. *New York Times*. Retrieved December 13, 2010 from http://www.nytimes.com

Perry, R. (2007, February 6). *State-of-the-state address*. Speech presented in Austin, TX. Retrieved from http://governor.state.tx.us

Rubin, R. (2006, June 8). First-ever cancer vaccine approved. *USA Today*. Retrieved from http://www.usatoday.com

STDs rife among US teenage girls: One in four teenage girls in the United States has a sexually-transmitted disease, a study has indicated. (2008, March 11). *BBC News*. Retrieved March 11, 2008 from http://newsvote.bbc.co.uk

Steinhauer, J., & Harris, G. (2008, March 21). Rising public health risk seen as more parents reject vaccines. *New York Times*. Retrieved from www.nytimes.com

Talley, L. (2007, February 8). Requirement an outrage [Editorial]. *San Antonio Express*, p. B8.

Thomas, K. (2007, February 7). Vaccine raises questions [Editorial]. *San Antonio Express*, p. B8.

Trawick, J. D. (2007, February 12). Perry's mandate wrong. *San Antonio Express*, p. B6.

Uribarri, A. G. (2007, February 12). Proposal to require HPV vaccine stirs concerns: Some believe making California schoolgirls get inoculated against the sexually transmitted virus would violate parental rights. *Los Angeles Times*, p. B3.

Whalen, J. (2006, August 23). Armed with new vaccines, drug makers target teenagers. *Wall Street Journal*, p. B1.

Zahariadis, I. (2003). *Ambiguity & choice in public policy: Political decision making in modern democracies*. Washington, DC: Georgetown University Press.

Zwirn, E. (2007, March 5). 50 years ago 100 years ago. *ICIS Chemical Business America*. Retrieved April 28, 2008 from LexisNexis database.

CHAPTER 20

Ensuring Individuals Have the Opportunity to Live to Their *Full Potential*

Reframing Injury and Violence Prevention and Response

Lucinda Austin, Jane Mitchko, Wendy Holmes, and Carol Freeman

KEY TERMS

Injury and violence prevention and response

Framing theory

Diffusion of innovations theory

Coordinated communication

Abstract

The Centers for Disease Control and Prevention's National Center for Injury Prevention and Control (NCIPC) recognized a need to increase awareness concerning the prevalence and preventability of injury and violence, and move audiences to take action. As a result, in January 2007, NCIPC began a collaborative initiative with partner organizations (e.g., state health departments and national organizations focused on injury and violence issues) to identify a new approach to communicating about injury. NCIPC then convened with these partner organizations, in addition to conducting public focus groups and interviews with injury and violence prevention and response professionals, to identify a new frame for communicating about injury. Drawing from this research, the frame of living to one's "full potential" received the most support as a strong cultural value statement for communicating about injury. The Framing Guide, *Adding Power to Our Voices,* subsequently was developed to help injury professionals apply the new frame and coordinate communication. NCIPC conducted additional focus groups and in-depth policymaker interviews to test the frame and coordinated messaging recommendations. NCIPC then launched a comprehensive framing initiative to educate staff and partners about the new frame and coordinated messaging. Initial framing efforts were evaluated using a multi-tier research approach incorporating quantitative and qualitative methods. The results indicated that significantly more partners and staff were using the frame and coordinated messaging after the launch of the framing initiative.

The case of the National Center for Injury Prevention and Control's (NCIPC's) coordinated framing initiative is an exemplar for developing a theoretically driven health communication campaign, conducting formative research, implementing a strategic approach, and beginning the evaluation process. This national initiative should provide insight into health communication challenges faced by government organizations and health communicators seeking to coordinate messaging on a large scale. This case addresses a public health challenge, highlights a theory-based approach, expands framing theory through original research, and identifies key lessons learned for students and health professionals.

The Problem: Individuals' Role in Injury and Violence Prevention and Response

Injury surveillance data show that injury and violence is a formidable threat to Americans of all ages and a leading cause of morbidity for the young and old (U.S. Department of Health and Human Services [DHHS], 2010a). Injuries can be unintentional, such as those resulting from impaired driving, older adult falls, or household fires, or intentional, such as those resulting from violence or suicide. The Centers for Disease Control and Prevention (CDC) mortality data show that injuries are the leading cause of death in the United States for individuals ages 1 through 44 (U.S. DHHS, 2010a). In 2006, individuals of all ages sustained close to 30 million reported injuries, resulting in more than 179,000 deaths (U.S. DHHS, 2010a). In 2000, these injuries cost $80 billion in medical care costs and an additional $326 billion in lost productivity (Finkelstein, Corso, & Miller, 2006). In 2007, the estimated costs of violence in the U.S. exceeded $70 billion in a single year (U.S. DHHS, 2008a).

By any count, injury and violence is a pressing public health problem in the U.S.; however, most people discern only a small slice of the problem—a neighbor who falls, a local teen killed in an automobile crash, or a TV report about a victim of violence. From these seemingly random and individual occurrences, a broader context of injury as an important and preventable public health threat is not easy for individuals to comprehend. Statistics about injury and violence do not make a sufficiently convincing argument to change behavior or focus the resources necessary to have a measurable impact. Yet research has repeatedly shown that injuries can be prevented, lives can be saved, and the pain, suffering, and medical expenses caused by injury can be significantly lowered (U.S. DHHS, 2008a). NCIPC, and other organizations in the injury and violence prevention and response field, have developed evidence-based programs to help prevent injuries and mitigate the impact of injuries when they occur. Although these programs have demonstrated some positive impacts, they have addressed only a fraction of the larger injury and violence problem (U.S. DHHS, 2008a).

In October 2006, NCIPC first convened partner organization meetings on injury and violence prevention and response issues, messages, and audiences. Partners agreed that a communication strategy intersecting all areas of injury and violence was needed to overcome shared communication challenges and objectives for the field of injury prevention.[1] Barriers to successful communication about injury and violence as a public health problem were identified at this meeting. Among the common challenges facing injury and violence prevention are:

- Low levels of personal relevance or connections to injury;
- Enduring beliefs of injury and violence as unpredictable and unpreventable;

- Lack of knowledge of existing solutions to reduce the impact of injury and violence;
- Lack of individuals' sense of control over their risk environment (e.g., homes, workplaces, and schools);
- Lack of understanding of the definition of injury and scope of the injury problem;
- Stigma associated with several types of injury, such as sexual violence and suicide, hampering open discussion;
- Confusion about whose responsibility injury and violence prevention is, leading to the fracturing of the search for solutions;
- Lack of understanding of injury and violence as a public health issue;
- Subpar funding for injury programs compared with the magnitude of the problem;
- Media coverage focusing on individual events rather than the broader injury context; and
- Lack of understanding that the consequences of violence extend beyond physical injury.

Thus, there is a great need for organizations working in the injury and violence prevention and response field to become aware of these challenges and collaborate to overcome them. Subsequently, in January 2007, NCIPC moved forward to identify a new approach to communicating about injury and to overcome these barriers. The objectives were to (a) develop an overarching injury and violence prevention message for use in communication, positioning injury as an important public health problem and (b) reframe the public's understanding of injury and violence to foster political and social will to lessen the burden of injury, which would include raising awareness as well as influencing attitudes and behaviors among key publics and decision makers.

Key Partners and Audiences

A socioecological perspective stresses the importance of influence at multiple levels including individual, interpersonal, institutional, community, and society levels (McLeroy, Bibeau, Steckler, & Glanz, 1988; Sallis & Owen, 2004; see also chapter 8 of this volume). These multiple levels of influence are interdependent and affect one another. It is not sufficient for one level of the socioecological model to be affected, such as individual behavior; a sound communication approach also seeks to affect policies and organizations that can support these initiatives. NCIPC is thus working with various partner organizations to communicate to various stakeholders. Key partners to ensuring a national coordinated communication approach include:

- NCIPC divisions and staff;
- Partner non-governmental organizations (NGOs) and individual professionals across the spectrum of injury at local, state, and national levels; and
- State public health offices working in injury and violence prevention and response.

A coordinated communication strategy would support these partners in communicating with their primary audiences: policymakers; the American public, including populations affected by specific injury and violence issues; employers; grant-making institutions; and media.

The Solution: A Coordinated Communication and Framing Approach

At present, many Americans do not value injury and violence prevention as highly as other public health issues (Dodge, 2008; Goss, 2006; Sleet & Moffett, 2009). According to framing theory (Entman, 1993; Scheufele & Tewksbury, 2007), this lack of recognition may be occurring because large segments of the public do not realize how addressing injury reflects their closely held values or why it should be a top priority. Framing theory suggests that to connect the problem of injury to individuals in a salient way, a common frame and coordinated and consistent messaging about injury is needed with which members of the general public and injury professionals alike can identify. As message framing affects how individuals make associations to a particular issue, creating new, consistent, repetitive communication can allow individuals to connect to an injury or violence prevention issue from a new perspective. Utilizing a coordinated communication approach (i.e., the use of a common frame and messaging strategies as described later in the chapter) can begin to change the way that individuals think about injury and violence. Coordinated communication can start to address some of the preceding challenges, helping the public to better understand and value the importance of injury and violence prevention and response.

Application of Framing Theory

Framing theory highlights how health information can be portrayed in a way that may influence publics' perceptions of that information and their perceptions of an organization or issue (Entman, 2003; Hallahan, 1999; Scheufele & Tewksbury, 2007; Tankard, 2001). Entman (1993) defined framing through selection and salience: "To frame is to select some aspects of a perceived reality and make them more salient in a communicating text, in such a way as to promote a particular problem definition, causal interpretation, moral evaluation, and/or treatment recommendation for the item described" (1993, p. 52). Framing theory (Entman 2003; Scheufele, 1999) acknowledges that certain issues or problems can be framed in such a way that they influence receivers' perceptions of the issues; however, receivers also develop their own frames and are situated in a culture that contains frames.

Dominant frames are value frames that are held by most individuals in a society or culture. As Entman described (1993; 2003), dominant frames are those which have "the highest probability of being noticed, processed, and accepted by the most people" (Entman, 1993, p. 56). Entman (1993) suggested that dominant frames are those with which a majority of individuals can identify and connect, and are reflected in the larger society of the audience members. According to Entman (1993), as these frames are heavily rooted in individuals' beliefs, communication should not go directly against dominant frames in most cases.

Communicators can use dominant frames, however, by linking information to related cultural values highlighting connections that individuals may fail to perceive. Schwartz (2007) defined cultural values as beliefs tied to affect, "goals that motivate action," and criteria that guide decision-making and evaluation (p. 39). Schwartz noted that the importance of cultural values guides subsequent action. For example, if a value is only mildly important to an individual compared to other values, the individual would be less likely to take an action requiring concerted effort. Messages should have greater impact when they are presented in a way that reflects and relates to broad and deeply held societal values. While the majority of individuals in a given society may connect with dominant frames, not all societal members will share these values, however. Additionally, long-standing dominant frames may be shifted over time (Aronowitz, 2008).

Framing studies have revealed that intentional framing in press releases and organizational communication affects media coverage (Danowski, 2008; Darmon, Fitzpatrick, & Bronstein, 2008; Liu, 2009). For example, Liu (2009) studied government and media frames of disaster coverage, and they found that most of the news media frames matched those used by state emergency managers in their press releases. Danowski (2008) studied framing effects of a university public relations campaign and found that use of the campaign frame in media increased by more than 400% during the course of the campaign. In a similar manner, Darmon et al. (2008) studied how Kraft™ intentionally framed messages regarding obesity in their press releases and how these messages were reflected in media coverage about Kraft™; findings revealed that Kraft™'s obesity prevention frames were displayed in related media coverage.

Although this research is somewhat limited, findings suggest that changing the way an organization communicates about an issue can affect related media coverage. Some research findings also suggest that the framing of messages, particularly for behaviors perceived to have high risks (i.e., high potential loss), has a statistically significant and consistent impact on audiences (Kühberger, 1998; Meyerowitz & Chaiken, 1987; Rothman, Salovey, Antone, Keough, & Martin, 1993).

Identifying a Frame

NCIPC used framing theory to develop messages that were anticipated to have greater impact on the public's perceptions by presenting injury in a way that reflects deeply held societal values and links to dominant frames. Together with partner organizations, NCIPC identified three distinct message sets matching U.S. cultural values as identified by representative national surveys of "American" cultural values (Schwartz, 2007).[2] These are to enjoy life unencumbered, have basic needs such as safety and health met, and live ambitiously and independently. While these dominant U.S. frames have been identified through national survey research, not all individuals in the U.S. will necessarily identify with these frames, particularly individuals within specific localized subcultures. In combination with coordinated messaging and framing, NCIPC also recognized the need to tailor communication to specific localized audiences as appropriate.

The message sets matching dominant frames were tested through in-depth interviews with injury and violence professionals (*n* = 18) and through nine focus groups (*n* = 42 with 4 to 5 participants in each) with the general public on specific injury and violence issues (Austin, Mitchko, Freeman, Kirby, & Milne, 2009). From this initial research, the message frame "We want a society where people can live to their full potential" received the most support as a strong cultural value statement. Overall, the most participants identified with the idea of living to their "full potential" and helping others to do the same. This value stood out as one that could speak to those with an existing interest in injury and violence prevention and response, as well as those with little previous exposure to the topic. The frame of "living to one's full potential," however, may at times actually conflict with violence if not worded with care, implying that victims of violence could be to blame for not preventing the act of violence. The findings also revealed that unintentional injury and acts of violence are perceived differently due in part to factors of blame. Additionally, extra steps would need to be taken for individuals to perceive violence as part of the larger injury problem. Most participants understood that injury and violence prevention and response were important elements of ensuring that people could live life to its fullest potential. Phrasing regarding prevention was understood as long as it was not suggesting trying to live in an injury- or violence-free world, which was considered to be unrealistic.

A Coordinated Communication Approach

As a result of this research, NCIPC developed *Adding Power to Our Voices*—a framing guide to help injury professionals apply the new frame and coordinate communication across the injury field (U.S. DHHS, 2010b). The guide provided specific recommendations for incorporating the frame into messages to aid communication among constituents, members, and supporters. The framing guide offered templates and samples on how to develop messages using the "full potential" frame and, based upon the present research, emphasized messaging points for a coordinated communication approach. These considerations include to:

- Frame preventive and response actions as giving people more freedom to live up to their full potential and being able to pursue their goals;
- Make a strong and dramatic statement about the injury problem;
- List a wide range of injuries that can help frame the injury field as one;
- Use positive, action-oriented statements to present solutions early in messages;
- Link to specific injury issues and programs to customize messages to injury areas;
- Highlight the value of personal responsibility and community action— characterize organizations as partners;
- Reinforce the science of injury and violence prevention stressing preventability of most injuries;

- Ensure that messages include a call to action;

- Find ways to reinforce the value message;

- Ensure that messages do not have the unintended consequence of implying that victims of violence are to blame—violence prevention requires greater focus on individual responsibility for refraining from violence and on community-level change;

- Avoid exhaustive lists of the statistics of the injury problem, as many individuals want to know about potential solutions, how they will be accomplished, and what they will cost; and

- Consider using social math (i.e., figures presented in a way that are easy for audiences to understand) to emphasize the issue and make points relevant.

Evaluating Coordinated Communication Recommendations

A second phase of this study assessed the injury frame and coordinated messaging recommendations outlined in the framing guide through message testing of three injury areas identified as priority injury areas for NCIPC through prior research and morbidity and mortality data (U.S. DHHS, 2010a): child maltreatment, older adult fall prevention, and Traumatic Brain Injury (TBI). Twelve focus groups ($n = 66$ with 5 to 7 participants each) were conducted with parents of youth and older adults due in part to their connection to the priority injury areas. State and local policymakers ($n = 7$) were also interviewed to gain insight into their communication preferences, more so since policymakers are a key audience for NCIPC and are fundamental in changing the political and social will around injury prevention and response. Findings from the research supported the recommendations in the framing guide. Participants preferred:

- Strong and dramatic statements about the injury problem;

- Concise and action-oriented messages with a clear call to action;

- Positive messages that described tangible benefits to them;

- Specific injury information customized to one injury area;

- A focus on community action and reinforcement about the responsibility for injury and violence prevention and response;

- Science-driven information (particularly desired by policymakers); and

- Social math examples with which they strongly identified, such as those relating to their geographic area or a specific topic with which they were familiar.

Implementing a Coordinated Initiative with Staff and Partners

Incorporating findings from the message testing phase, a framing training session was conducted in May 2009 with NCIPC staff and partner organizations. The training introduced the framing guide to staff and partners and educated them about using the "full potential" frame and coordinated message strategies around injury and violence prevention and response. Additional activities were undertaken to support the implementation of the frame including partner calls and additional Web and in-person trainings with partners and state offices, as well as a collaborative online workspace for partners and staff. NCIPC also offers ongoing technical assistance to staff and partner organizations.

Evaluating Adoption of a Coordinated Approach

To evaluate how NCIPC staff and partner organizations have been using the "full potential" frame and the guide's recommendations, NCIPC used a multi-tiered research approach incorporating quantitative and qualitative methods. Diffusion of innovations theory (Rogers, 2003) served as a guiding theoretical framework to evaluate staff and partners' stages of change and perceived attributes about the framing guide and the new frame. The initial training was evaluated through: (a) quantitative baseline and follow-up assessments ($n = 100$) completed by staff and partners prior to and eight months after the training, (b) in-depth interviews ($n = 24$) with staff and partners eight months post training, and (c) baseline and follow-up content analyses of NCIPC and partner organizations' websites ($n = 952$ Web pages).

Diffusion of innovations theory helps to explain how innovations are communicated over time within social systems (Baker & Rogers, 1998; Berwick, 2003; Rogers, 2003). Stages in the innovation-decision process include knowledge, persuasion, decision, implementation, or confirmation. These stages affect organizations' movement along a continuum of innovation adoption ranging from knowledge to confirmation. In this evaluation, organizational stages of change were assessed formally through the questionnaire and expanded upon during the interviews.

Additionally, individuals' perceptions of characteristics about the framing guide and the concept frame were assessed through questionnaires and interview guides. As diffusion of innovations theory (Rogers, 2003) posits, innovation characteristics affect the adoption of innovations; in particular, individuals that perceive these characteristics to be present are predicted to adopt the innovation more quickly. These innovation characteristics follow: (a) *relative advantage* refers to the perceived benefits of this innovation over other similar approaches, (b) *compatibility* refers to the fit of the innovation with how individuals think, (c) *observability* explains the visibility of others' success with the innovation, (d) *complexity* describes the ease of incorporation into existing efforts, and (e) *trialability* refers to the ability to try the innovation with little risk.

Evaluation results revealed that participants perceived the frame and coordinated communication positively, and significantly more individuals in the post-training analysis were in the implementation, $t(90) = -3.70$, $p < .001$, and confirmation, $t(98) = -2.38$, $p = .019$, stages of change of using the frame and coordinated message strategies. Diffusion of innovations attributes were significantly related to innovation adoption and accounted for nearly 40% of the variance in the use of the guide, $R^2 = .39$, $F(6, 92) = 9.84$, $p < .01$.[3] Interview findings also revealed additional structural and societal factors that affected adoption of the guide such as internal, political organizational factors and lack of resources, as well as lack of communication and strategic coordination.

Developing a Long-term National Strategic Implementation Plan

Framing theory posits that changing how individuals frame concepts such as injury can affect their perceived importance of the problem and actual behavior change; however, changing individuals' association is time intensive and requires extensive repetition as such changes are likely to be gradual. In order for the "full potential" frame and coordinated messaging to become more pervasive, a long-term strategy was also needed to guide this initiative in future years. As a result, a 10-year national strategy was developed to ensure continuity of program objectives and to continue to encourage use of the frame by additional partner organizations and staff, as well as state injury and violence prevention offices. The goal of this strategic plan is to encourage national adoption of the "full potential" frame and the coordinated communication principles for communicating about injury. An evaluation at the end of this initiative's conclusion would help to determine whether the key publics' and decision makers' perceptions of injury and violence had changed over time and to examine changes in the political and social will to help prevent injuries and violence.

Lessons Learned

NCIPC's coordinated communication initiative highlighted research at multiple stages of the process. Multiple rounds of research are needed to develop message concepts, test developed concepts, and monitor adoption of this initiative. This type of initiative is resource intensive and may not show results in behavior change (e.g., preventive health actions) immediately, although it should show greater attitude influence during the long term if partners and key influencers participate in the initiative. Framing is not an immediate process; to change public perception of an issue through changing value-based frames, much time and resources are needed, including partner support.

This initiative also revealed that the same language may not apply for every audience or topic when trying to coordinate messaging; however, the same overarching concept frame (e.g., living to one's full potential and enjoying quality of life) can still apply. When possible, language incorporating the concept frame should be tailored to meet the needs of specific audiences.

Additionally, it can be difficult when working with scientists and others who do not perceive themselves as communication specialists to introduce the idea of framing messages and thinking through concept frames for each specific injury and audience. Individuals who are not trained communicators generally prefer messages and materials to be developed for them by communication staff. In this initiative, partners were willing to coordinate communication, but generally only if it was easy for them to do so or if it seemed to make sense for their specific audiences. Individuals' perceptions of the diffusion of innovations (Rogers, 2003) attributes generally served as an indicator for their use of the coordinated communication efforts.

NOTES

1   CDC NCIPC began with a macro-level approach to collaboration. NCIPC believed that this would be an ambitious, yet realistic, goal as partners encouraged and supported the initiative.

2   This study was part of a larger global study of cultural values constituting 80 different representative samples from 67 nations and 70 different cultural groups. A specific *n* value is not noted for the U.S. study.

3   Findings reflect multiple linear regression analysis; this statistical test enables investigators to ascertain the extent to which predictor or independent variables influence an outcome (i.e., dependent variables). Independent variables were diffusion of innovations attributes: relative advantage, compatibility, observability, complexity, and trialability. Individuals' reported regular use of the guide and frame (i.e., confirmation stage of diffusion of innovations) was assessed as the dependent variable. Social science standards for significance are $p < .05$; as $p < .01$ here, this finding was statistically significant and not due to chance (Frey, Botan, & Kreps, 2000; Leech, Barrett, & Morgan, 2008). Multicollinearity (i.e., when two or more independent variables in a regression model are strongly correlated) was not a strong factor, as variables were not highly correlated. Tolerance values were between .328 and .568 and VIF values were 1.76 to 3.05. Please see Leech et al. (2008) for detailed discussion.

Discussion Questions

1. In this specific case, what strategies might NCIPC have used other than framing to overcome the challenges injury and violence prevention faced?

2. How would you evaluate the outcomes of a framing initiative?

3. What ethical implications, if any, must be considered when undertaking a framing initiative?

4. What examples of "framing" health topics have you seen around you in advertisements or health communication campaigns?

5. Is framing theory appropriate for any health communication initiative? Why or why not?

6. How could framing theory be applied to other health topics? Describe specific examples.

References

Aronowitz, R. (2008). Framing disease: An underappreciated mechanism for the social patterning of health. *Social Science and Medicine, 67*, 1–9.

Austin, L., Mitchko, J., Freeman, C., Kirby, S., & Milne, J. (2009). Using framing theory to unite the field of injury and violence prevention and response: "Adding Power to Our Voices." *Social Marketing Quarterly, 15*(S1), 35–54.

Baker, T. E., & Rogers, E. M. (1998). Diffusion of innovations theory and work-site AIDS programs. *Journal of Health Communication, 3*, 17–28.

Berwick, D. M. (2003). Disseminating innovations in health care. *Journal of the American Medical Association, 289*, 1969–1975.

Danowski, J. A. (2008). Short-term and long-term effects of a public relations campaign on semantic networks of newspaper content: Priming or framing? *Public Relations Review, 34*, 288–290.

Darmon, K., Fitzpatrick, K., & Bronstein, C. (2008). Krafting the obesity message: A case study in framing and issues management. *Public Relations Review, 34*, 373–379.

Dodge, K. A. (2008). Framing public policy and prevention of chronic violence in American youths. *American Psychologist, 53*, 573–590.

Entman, R. M. (1993). Framing: Clarification of a fractured paradigm. *Journal of Communication, 43*, 51–58.

Entman, R. M. (2003). Cascading activism: Contesting the White House's frame after 9/11. *Political Communication, 20*, 415–432.

Finkelstein, E. A., Corso, P. S., & Miller, T. R. (2006). *Incidence and economic burden of injuries in the United States*. New York, NY: Oxford University Press.

Frey, L. R., Botan C. H., & Kreps, G. L. (2000). *Investigating communication: An introduction to research methods* (2nd ed.). Needham Heights, MA: Allyn & Bacon.

Goss, K. A. (2006). *Disarmed: The missing movement for gun control in America*. Princeton, NJ: Princeton University Press.

Hallahan, K. (1999). Seven models of framing: Implications for public relations. *Journal of Public Relations Research, 11*, 205–242.

Kühberger, A. (1998). The influence of framing on risky decisions: A meta-analysis. *Organizational Behavior and Human Decision Processes, 75*, 23–55.

Leech, N. L., Barrett, K. C., & Morgan, G. A. (2008). *SPSS for intermediate statistics: Use and interpretation* (3rd ed.). Mahwah, NJ: Lawrence Erlbaum and Associates.

Liu, B. F. (2009). An analysis of U.S. government and media disaster frames. *Journal of Communication Management, 13*, 268–283.

McLeroy, K. R., Bibeau, D., Steckler, A., & Glanz, K. (1988). An ecological perspective on health promotion programs. *Health Education Quarterly, 15*, 351–377.

Meyerowitz, B. E., & Chaiken, S. (1987). The effect of message framing on breast self-examination attitudes, intentions and behaviors. *Journal of Personality and Social Psychology, 52*, 500–510.

Rogers, E. M. (2003). *Diffusion of innovations* (5th ed.). New York, NY: The Free Press.

Rothman, A. J., Salovey, P., Antone, C., Keough, K., & Martin, C. D. (1993). The influence of message framing on intentions to perform health behaviors. *Journal of Experimental Social Psychology, 29*, 408–433.

Sallis, J. F., & Owen, N. (2004). Ecological models of health behavior. In K. Glanz, B. K. Rimer, & F. M. Lewis (Eds.), *Health behavior and health education: Theory, research, and practice* (pp. 462–484). San Francisco, CA: Jossey-Bass.

Scheufele, D. A., (1999). Framing as a theory of media effects. *Journal of Communication, 49*, 103–122.

Scheufele, D. A., & Tewksbury, D. (2007). Framing, agenda setting, and priming: The evolution of three media effects models. *Journal of Communication, 57*, 9–20.

Schwartz, S. H. (2007). A theory of cultural value orientations: Explication and applications. In Y. Emser, & T. Pettersson (Eds.), *Measuring and mapping cultures: 25 years of comparative value surveys* (pp. 31–78). Boston, MA: Brill.

Sleet, D., & Moffett, D. (2009). Framing the problem: Injuries and public health. *Family & Community Health: The Journal of Health Promotion & Maintenance, 32*, 88–97.

Tankard, J. W. (2001). The empirical approach to the study of media framing. In S. D. Reese, O. H. Gandy, & A. E. Grant (Eds.), *Framing public life: Perspectives on media and our understanding of the social world* (pp. 95–106). Mahwah, NJ: Lawrence Erlbaum.

U.S. Department of Health and Human Services. Centers for Disease Control and Prevention. National Center for Injury Prevention and Control. (2008a). *The history of violence as a public health issue*. Retrieved from http://www.cdc.gov/violenceprevention/pdf/history_violence-a.pdf

U.S. Department of Health and Human Services. Centers for Disease Control and Prevention. National Center for Injury Prevention and Control. (2008b). *Public health injury surveillance and prevention: A program that works*. Retrieved from http://www.cdc.gov/ncipc/dir/07_112887%20 PHISP%20Booklet%20final.pdf

U.S. Department of Health and Human Services. Centers for Disease Control and Prevention. National Center for Injury Prevention and Control. (2010a). *Web-based injury statistics query and reporting system* (WISQARS). Retrieved from http://www.cdc.gov/injury/wisqars

U.S. Department of Health and Human Services. Centers for Disease Control and Prevention. National Center for Injury Prevention and Control. (2010b). *Adding power to our voices: A framing guide for communicating about injury* (2nd ed.). Atlanta, GA: CDC.

INDEX

Subjective norm, 138–139
Summative research, 221–223
Support group, 62, 68
    interaction, case
        study, 63–68
Surveys, designing, 203
Systematic formative
    research, 152
System efficacy report, 248

T
Tangible aid social support, 62
Technical skills, 236
Theory of Planned Behavior.
    See Planned behavior theory
Theory of Reasoned Action
    (TRA), 169
Title VI of the 1964 Civil
    Rights Act, 51

Transdisciplinarity, defined,
    259–260
Transdisciplinary research
    model, BCERC
    assessment of, 262–265
    meeting, 261–262
    research team, 260–261
    stakeholders, 260–261
Transtheoretical model, 153,
    155–158
Tuckman's model, 261, 262
Type I diabetes, 246
Type II diabetes, 247

U
Uncertainty management, 120
University of Kentucky Health
    Communication Conference
    (KCHC), 3

U.S. Department of Health
    and Human Services
    (DHHS), 106
U.S. vaccination policy, 273

V
Vaccination
    policy, 273
    technologies, 271–272
Verbal behavior, 250

W
Web-based health monitoring
    system, 247–248
Western States Communication
    Association (WSCA), 3
WHO, 87, 235–236